The Sapient Mind

The Sapient Mind:
Archaeology meets neuroscience

Edited by

Colin Renfrew
McDonald Institute for Archaeological Research
University of Cambridge
Cambridge, UK

Chris Frith
Niels Bohr Interacting Minds Project
Aarhus University Hospital
Aarhus, Denmark

Emeritus Professor of Neuropsychology
University College London
London, UK

Lambros Malafouris
McDonald Institute for Archaeological Research
University of Cambridge
Cambridge, UK

PHILOSOPHICAL TRANSACTIONS —OF— THE ROYAL SOCIETY **B** BIOLOGICAL SCIENCES

Originating from a Theme Issue first published in Philosophical
Transactions of the Royal Society B: Biological Sciences
http://publishing.royalsociety.org/philtransb

The preparation for this volume was undertaken with the support of
The International Balzan Prize Foundation (based at Milan and Zurich)
http://www.balzan.it/default.aspx?lang=en

OXFORD
UNIVERSITY PRESS

OXFORD

UNIVERSITY PRESS

Great Clarendon Street, Oxford ox2 6DP

Oxford University Press is a department of the University of Oxford.
It furthers the University's objective of excellence in research, scholarship,
and education by publishing worldwide in

Oxford New York

Auckland Cape Town Dar es Salaam Hong Kong Karachi
Kuala Lumpur Madrid Melbourne Mexico City Nairobi
New Delhi Shanghai Taipei Toronto

With offices in

Argentina Austria Brazil Chile Czech Republic France Greece
Guatemala Hungary Italy Japan Poland Portugal Singapore
South Korea Switzerland Thailand Turkey Ukraine Vietnam

Oxford is a registered trade mark of Oxford University Press
in the UK and in certain other countries

Published in the United States
by Oxford University Press Inc., New York

British Library Cataloguing in Publication Data
Data available

Library of Congress Cataloging in Publication Data
Data available

Typeset by Cepha Imaging Private Ltd, Bangalore, India

Printed on acid-free paper by
the MPG Books Group in the UK

ISBN 978-0-19-956199-5

1 3 5 7 9 10 8 6 4 2

Contents

List of Contributors

Maurice Bloch Department of Anthropology, London School of Economics, London WC2A 2AE, UK (m.e.bloch@lse.ac.uk)

Thierry Chaminade Functional Imaging Lab, Institute of Neurology, University College London, 12 Queen Square, London WC1N 3BG, UK

Fiona Coward British Academy Centenary Project, Department of Geography, University of London, Royal Holloway, Egham TW20 0EX, UK (fiona.coward@rhul.ac.uk).

Scott H. Frey Lewis Center for Neuroimaging, University of Oregon, Eugene, OR 97403-5288, USA Department of Psychology, University of Oregon, Eugene, OR 97403-1227, USA (shfrey@uoregon.edu)

Chris D. Frith Wellcome Trust Centre for Neuroimaging, University College London, 12 Queen Square, London WC1N 3BG, UK; Center for Functionally Integrative Neuroscience, University of Åarhus, 8000 Åarhus C, Denmark. Address for correspondence: Niels Bohr Interacting Minds Project, Åarhus University Hospital–Århus Sygehus, Nørrebrogade 44, Building 30, 8000 Århus C, Denmark (cfrith@fil.ion.ucl.ac.uk).

Clive Gamble British Academy Centenary Project, Department of Geography, University of London, Royal Holloway, Egham TW20 0EX, UK

Chris Gosden School of Archaeology, University of Oxford, 36 Beaumont Street, Oxford OX1 2PG, UK (chris.gosden@arch.ox.ac.uk)

Edwin Hutchins Department of Cognitive Science, University of California San Diego, 9500 Gilman Drive, La Jolla, CA 92093-0515, USA (ehutchins@ucsd.edu)

J. Scott Jordan Department of Psychology, Campus Box 4620, Illinois State University, Normal, IL 61790-4620, USA (jsjorda@ilstu.edu)

Günther Knoblich Radboud University Nijmegen, Donders Institute for Brain, Cognition, and Behavior, Centre for Cognition, P.O. Box 9104, 6500 HE Nijmegen, The Netherlands (g.knoblich@donders.ru.nl)

Sander van der Leeuw School of Human Evolution and Social Change, Arizona State University, PO Box 872404, Tempe, AZ 85287-2402, USA

Lambros Malafouris McDonald Institute for Archaeological Research, University of Cambridge, Cambridge CB2 3ER, UK (lm243@cam.ac.uk)

Dwight Read Department of Anthropology, UCLA, Los Angeles, CA 90095, USA (dread@anthro.ucla.edu)

Colin Renfrew McDonald Institute for Archaeological Research, Downing Street, Cambridge CB2 3ER, UK (acr10@cam.ac.uk)

Andreas Roepstorff Department of Social Anthropology and Centre for Functionally Integrative Neuroscience, University of Åarhus, 8000 Åarhus, Denmark (andreas@pet.au.dk)

Kathy Schick Department of Anthropology and Cognitive Science Program, Indiana University, Student Building 130, 701 East Kirkwood Avenue, Bloomington, IN 47405-7100, USA

Natalie Sebanz School of Psychology, University of Birmingham, Edgbaston, Birmingham B15 2TT, UK

Dietrich Stout Institute of Archaeology, University College London, 31–34 Gordon Square, London WC1H 0PY, UK (dietrich.stout@ucl.ac.uk)

Nicholas Toth Stone Age Institute, 1392 West Dittemore Road, Gosport, IN 47433, USA

Introduction. The Sapient Mind: Archaeology meets neuroscience

The turn of the twenty-first century has seen a new era in the cognitive and brain sciences that allows us to address the age-old question of what it means to be human from a whole new range of different perspectives. Our knowledge of the workings of the human brain increases day by day and so does our understanding of the extended, distributed, embodied and culturally mediated character of the human mind. The problem is that these major ways of thinking about human cognition and the threads of evidence that they carry with them often seem to diverge, rather than confront one another.

What is presently missing, and urgently needed, is a systematic attempt to bridge the analytic gap between those defining trends in the study of mind. This was the principal challenge for 'The sapient mind' meeting that took place in the McDonald Institute for Archaeological Research, Cambridge between 14 and 16 September 2007 and which forms the basis of this special issue. Our aim was to channel the huge emerging analytic potential of current neuroscientific research in the direction of a common integrated research programme targeting the big picture of human cognitive evolution, both before and most importantly after the so-called speciation phase, i.e. the period when biological and cultural coevolution worked together to develop the genetic basis of the human species, as we know it (Renfrew 2008).

Following that, a good way for the reader to approach and conceptualize the contributions that make up this volume is to view them as the component parts of a broader cross-disciplinary experiment. The aim of this experiment is to enable archaeology, anthropology and neuroscience to bring together, under the same general working hypothesis, the neural, behavioural and material correlates of human cognitive becoming. There are many factors that indicate or contribute to a good experimental design but a key feature probably lies in the central question. The question that lies at the heart of this volume is rather straightforward, i.e. *the sapient mind*: what makes the human mind unique? What is the sapient mind made of? What is less simple and straightforward, however, is how precisely should this central question be approached or understood.

Up to now, working in isolation, both archaeology and neuroscience have made a number of important contributions to the study of human intelligence. Archaeology, for instance, can now give us a good idea about *where*, and an approximate idea about *when*, *Homo sapiens* appeared. The place is Africa and the time somewhere between 100 000 and 200 000 years ago. Recent DNA studies can now confirm the out-of-Africa human dispersal hypothesis of approximately 60 000 years ago, whereas new archaeological discoveries, like the findings from the Blombos Cave in Africa, have changed our understanding of when and where the emergence of most behavioural features usually associated with modern human intelligence first appeared (Renfrew 2008). Neuroscience, on the other hand, based on a quite different scale of spatial and temporal resolution can also give us a good indication about where in the human brain these modern human capacities (e.g. language, symbolic capacity, representational ability, theory of mind (ToM), causal belief, learning by teaching, 'we' intentionality, sense of selfhood) can be identified and the possible neural networks and cognitive mechanisms that support them.

The challenge facing us then is how do we put all these different facets and threads of evidence about the human condition back together again? Naturally, the attempted cooperation and cross-fertilization is not an easy task given the different kinds of information, procedures and analytic scales that define the ways the human mind is approached and understood from different disciplinary perspectives. However, if our attempted cross-disciplinary experiment is to add something new and important to our current knowledge then it needs to move beyond the logic of the 'localizer' and tell us something about the *why* and *how* rather than simply the *where* and *when* of human cognitive becoming. Knowing when and where things are happening in cognitive evolution is important and interesting but does not explain much. Focusing on the interface between brain and culture, the papers that comprise this special Theme Issue struggle to define, reframe and identify some crucial aspects of the human condition, which we think could facilitate this attempted partnership between archaeology and neuroscience.

Consider for instance what Renfrew calls the 'sapient paradox' (2008): if the biological basis of our species has been established perhaps for as much as 200 000 years, then why have the novel behavioural aspects of our 'sapient' status taken so long to emerge? Why is it that all major evidence in the archaeological record indicating important changes in human intelligent behaviour came long after the appearance of modern anatomy? An interesting observation that archaeology allows us to make, and which also poses a great challenge to the neuroscientist, is that many of the crucial and enduring aspects of the human condition (symbols, value, religion, literacy, etc.) appear relatively recently in the archaeological record and can certainly be seen as the emergent products of various cultural developmental trajectories, rather than innate biological capacities. Could it be then that brain anatomy and the biological endowment of our species *H. sapiens* as this emerged between 200 000 and 100 000 years ago is only part of the story? Moreover, would it be more productive, especially from a long-term perspective, to explore the assumption that human intelligence 'spreads out' across the body–world boundary, thus extending beyond skin and skull into culture and the material world?

Many contributions in this volume argue precisely that (Gosden 2008; Hutchins 2008; Jordan 2008; Malafouris 2008; Renfrew 2008; Roepstorff 2008) although they may differ on how precisely they conceptualize this extended anatomy of the human mind. However, despite these differences in perspective and theoretical presuppositions, a common thread that unites all papers in this issue is their agreement about the special roles that materiality, cultural practices and social interaction play in the shaping of the human mind throughout its long evolutionary and developmental trajectories. Two major consequences follow from that. On the one hand that an effective cooperation between archaeology and neuroscience must aim to provide a better understanding of the role of this constitutive intertwining of brains, bodies, things and cultural practices in the shaping and evolution of human cognitive capacities. On the other hand, that the hallmark of human cognitive evolution may not be based on the ever-increasing sophistication or specialization of a modular mind, but upon an ever-increasing representational flexibility that allows for environmentally and culturally derived plastic changes in the structure and functional architecture of the human brain.

Take for instance tool manufacture and use, a topic that has been the centre of archaeological discussion and debate for some decades now. Human brains and technology, in the form of intentionally modified stone tools, have been coevolving for at least the past 2.6 Myr, yet the relationship between them remains controversial and poorly understood. Thus, understanding the bases in the brain of complex tool use and toolmaking emerges as a key issue in human cognitive evolution. Tool-use abilities also constitute one of the most easily identifiable points at which neuroscience and archaeology meet, given that it is now possible using the new brain imaging methods to explore their neurological foundation in the modern human brain. In this context, Stout *et al.* (2008) present important new results from a PET study during experimental stone toolmaking, which support a coevolutionary hypothesis linking the emergence of language and toolmaking. In particular, their imaging data show that neural circuits supporting stone toolmaking partially overlap with language circuits, which suggests that these behaviours share a foundation in more general human capacities for complex, goal-directed action and are likely to have evolved in a mutually reinforcing way. This important link between complex tool use and language is also discussed in the contribution by Frey (2008). His paper presents new data from brain-injured patients and functional neuroimaging studies that indicate a possible brain network participating in the representation of both familiar tool-use skills and communicative gestures. Although from an evolutionary perspective these correlations cannot demonstrate the direction of cause and effect, they constitute a significant development in the long-standing issue of the possible relations between language and tool use in human evolution. More importantly, they suggest new and important interactions between brain and culture, which may help us understand why it is that only humans have developed such an extensive and universal material culture.

Closely related to this issue concerning the difference that enabled human beings to develop complex technologies, is also the question as to why it took humans so long to 'invent' and accelerate innovation. Read & van der Leeuw (2008) identify two major phases in the coevolutionary spiral between brain and culture relevant to the human capacity for technological innovation. In the first phase it is biology, and in particular limited working memory capacity, which constrains technological change. In the second phase however, characterized by the 'innovative explosion' in the evolution of artefact technologies that we observe in the last 25 000 years or so, a very different dynamic is occurring between humans and the material world. The biological constraint seems to have been lifted. Technological change is no longer constrained by the capacities of working memory, thus enabling an acceleration in the pace of change in technology. It thus appears that to understand the coevolutionary spiral between brain, body and culture it is not sufficient to discern the possible causal correlations that the changes observed in one of them might effect upon the others. It lies also in discerning the possible ways that the actual nature of the relation between them might have changed in the course of human evolution.

Indeed, although separating biology from culture sometimes makes good analytic sense, relevant to some problems in human cognitive evolution, it should not obscure the more interesting issue of how they are combined. Integrating different analytic units and scales of time, the papers that comprise this Theme Issue seek to understand how different types of data, and the questions upon which those data are being brought to bear, are enmeshed and related as different aspects of a common phenomenon that we call 'the sapient mind'.

To illustrate this central point let us use the example of Dauya discussed in the paper by Hutchins (2008). Dauya comes from the Wawela village on Boyowa Island in the

Trobriand Islands of Papua New Guinea. Dauya is a preliterate magician/astronomer responsible for fixing the agricultural calendar of the village to a seasonal calendar. This is a difficult task, given that the weather patterns in the Solomon Sea vary from year to year, but also a very important task, since the correct timing of the preparations of the gardens relevant to changes in the weather is crucial for the crop production of the village. Dauya accomplishes his task by examining the sky searching for Kibi (what we call the Pleiades) among the stars that are visible just before dawn. When Kibi is visible in the pre-dawn glow, then it is time to begin preparing the gardens. This might look like a trivial task to the analytically preoccupied modern western thinker but it is also a task that clearly involves some of the most crucial elements that make up a sapient mind.

The question to ask then is what makes possible this unique cognitive accomplishment of Dauya's mind, namely, determining the seasons with great precision? Is it his brain size or the small differences in the DNA that separates him from our closest living relatives, the chimpanzees? Dauya's brain and body is an evolutionary product and thus different in important ways from the brains of any other present or past primates. However, although his biological endowment is certainly a crucial constraining or enabling factor it is not sufficient to generate an understanding of how Dauya identifies Kibi in the sky. To answer that question we need to situate Dauya in his social and cultural context. First we need to understand Dauya as a social animal. It is only then that Dauya's cognitive capacities can be fully appreciated and together help us to understand the uniquely human ways he looks at the sky and constructs his agricultural calendar.

However, what does human sociality really consist of? From the perspective of neuroscience one way to answer that is to look for the basic ingredients of social interaction. For instance, Knoblich & Sebanz (2008) argue in their contribution that the distinctive feature of joint action in humans is to be found in the way we are able to process other humans' intentions and to keep them apart from our own. They build their case around four different scenarios aimed at specifying the possible basic interpersonal mechanisms that support the type of intentionality required to engage in joint action, cultural learning and communication. From the perspective of archaeology, however, social interactions are dependent not only on face-to-face interactions between individuals but also on the active incorporation of material culture. Social and symbolic constructions with a clear material basis, like for instance the notions of value and property, constitute the very basis of social interaction (Renfrew 2008). It is this increasing engagement with material culture that enabled face-to-face interactions among humans to be scaled up in the course of human becoming (Coward & Gamble 2008). Human social life cannot be understood apart from its material entailments and that is why, according to Gosden (2008), we need to develop a kind of 'social ontology' that will enable us to look at the way human capabilities of mind and body are brought about through an interaction with the material world without attributing a causally determinant position to any one.

Meanwhile Bloch (2008) adds, from the standpoint of anthropology, a further dimension of human sociality. He proposes that in contrast to what we see in other social animals, human sociality is double in that it has both transactional *and* transcendental elements. What this means, more simply, is that the social position of Dauya as an astronomer in Trobriand society *transcends* the predictable achievements of the individual. The transcendental social element requires the ability to identify and interact with each other not in terms of how people appear to the senses at any particular moment but as if they were something else: astronomers, magicians, priests or transcendental beings. According to

Bloch, it is in those transcendental roles where the fundamental difference between human and, for instance, chimpanzee sociability lies. Moreover, the fundamental operation that underpins and makes possible this transcendental element of human sociality and by extension the phenomenon of religion is the capacity for imagination. Thus, it is only through understanding the neurological evidence for the development of this capacity and of its social implications that we will account for religious-like phenomena.

But where does the previous consideration leave our initial question about Dauya's cognitive accomplishments? The key point that seems to emerge out of most contributions in this Theme Issue lies in the recognition that Dauya's calendar is as much a cultural accomplishment as a cognitive accomplishment. It is an accomplishment orchestrated by a set of ways of seeing the sky and a way of being in the social and material world. The role of Dauya's brain is crucial but his unique ability to fix the agricultural calendar does not reside either in brain, body or culture. It resides instead where brain, body and culture conflate (Malafouris 2008), i.e. in the embodied processes by which Dauya as a social creature has been encultured into the practices of Trobriand astronomy (Hutchins 2008).

Thus the crucial question we need to ask here concerns precisely these embodied processes that allow cultural practices to build upon the human biological endowment in order to produce cognitive accomplishments. This leads us to the theme that underlies in one way or another all the papers in this issue and constitutes also a possible conceptual bridge between archaeology and neuroscience, i.e. *learning*. If we are to identify a single process or capacity as the key behind the accomplishments of Dauya's mind then the place to look would be at the way sapient minds 'learn to learn'. Indeed, according to Frith (2008), there is something special in Dauya's ability to benefit from cultural learning and the accumulated knowledge of Trobriand astronomy. That special something which seems to be unique to the human race is Dauya's ability to recognize and learn from instruction rather than from mere observation. Without this ability to learn by instruction and deliberately to share knowledge, Dauya could never have seen the sky as a meaningful sign in the complex system of Trobriand astronomy. Dauya's task to read the sky and construct his calendar would have been extremely difficult, if not impossible, to fulfill by mere observation, imitation and 'affordance learning'. Prolonged apprenticeship and formal instruction into Trobriand astronomy as a cultural practice is the key.

Approaching these issues we should not forget, however, that much of the social signalling that enables us to learn about the world is not restricted to the dyadic engagement between humans but includes also various processes of material engagement. Inanimate objects, material arrangements and symbols can also be used as powerful deliberate social signals thus playing a crucial role in the extraordinary achievements of the human race during the last few thousand years. Thus, to approach the problems of learning and cultural transmission effectively a partnership between neuroscientists and archaeologists working on different aspects and time scales of these processes is required. What is needed to make this partnership most productive is a series of ideas that allow us to think about brains, bodies and material things in combination and thus to understand the possible links between brain and cultural plasticity. We hope that this special Theme Issue will help clarify the ground and stimulate further research to this end.

The papers printed here were first published as a special Theme Issue in the 'Philosophical Transactions of the Royal Society Series B'.

The papers that comprise this special Theme Issue derive from a symposium, 'The sapient mind: archaeology meets neuroscience', that took place in the McDonald Institute for Archaeological Research, Cambridge between 14 and 16 September 2007. We want to thank the British Academy and the Guarantors of Brain for sponsoring this meeting. We want to thank all the participants of this meeting; Tim Ingold and Robin Dunbar for chairing the sessions, our discussants Daniel Wolpert, Paul Mellars, Nicholas Humphrey and Richard Gregory, and especially our speakers for their excellent contributions. Finally, we thank James Joseph at the *Phil. Trans. R. Soc. B* editorial office for his patience in putting this special issue together. The work of Lambros Malafouris at the McDonald Institute for Archaeological Research is funded by the Balzan Foundation.

Colin Renfrew[1],*
Chris Frith[2,3]
Lambros Malafouris[1],*

References

Bloch, M. 2008 Why religion is nothing special but is central. *Phil. Trans. R. Soc. B* **363**, 2055–2061. (doi:10.1098/rstb.2008.0007)

Coward, F. & Gamble, C. 2008 Big brains, small worlds: material culture and the evolution of the mind. *Phil. Trans. R. Soc. B* **363**, 1969–1979. (doi:10.1098/rstb.2008.0004)

Frey, S. H. 2008 Tool use, communicative gesture, and cerebral asymmetries in the modern human brain. *Phil. Trans. R. Soc. B* **363**, 1951–1958. (doi:10.1098/rstb.2008.0008)

Frith, C. D. 2008 Social cognition. *Phil. Trans. R. Soc. B* **363**, 2033–2039. (doi:10.1098/rstb.2008.0005)

Gosden, C. 2008 Social ontologies. *Phil. Trans. R. Soc. B* **363**, 2003–2010. (doi:10.1098/rstb.2008.0013)

Hutchins, E. 2008 The role of cultural practices in the emergence of modern human intelligence. *Phil. Trans. R. Soc. B* **363**, 2011–2019. (doi:10.1098/rstb.2008.0003)

Jordan, J. S. 2008 Wild agency: nested intentionalities in cognitive neuroscience and archaeology. *Phil. Trans. R. Soc. B* **363**, 1981–1991. (doi:10.1098/rstb.2008.0009)

Knoblich, G. & Sebanz, N. 2008 Evolving intentions for social interaction: from entrainment to joint action. *Phil. Trans. R. Soc. B* **363**, 2021–2031. (doi:10.1098/rstb.2008. 0006)

Malafouris, L. 2008 Between brains, bodies and things: *tectonoetic* awareness and the extended self. *Phil. Trans. R. Soc. B* **363**, 1993–2002. (doi:10.1098/rstb.2008.0014)

Read, D. & van der Leeuw, S. 2008 Biology is only part of the story. *Phil. Trans. R. Soc. B* **363**, 1959–1968. (doi:10.1098/rstb.2008.0002)

Renfrew, C. 2008 Neuroscience, evolution and the sapient paradox: the factuality of value and of the sacred. *Phil. Trans. R. Soc. B* **363**, 2041–2047. (doi:10.1098/rstb.2008.0010)

Roepstorff, A. 2008 Things to think with: words and objects as material symbols. *Phil. Trans. R. Soc. B* **363**, 2049–2054. (doi:10.1098/rstb.2008.0015)

Stout, D., Toth, N., Schick, K. & Chaminade, T. 2008 Neural correlates of Early Stone Age tool-making: technology, language and cognition in human evolution. *Phil. Trans. R. Soc. B* **363**, 1939–1949. (doi:10.1098/rstb.2008.0001)

[1]The McDonald Institute for Archaeological Research, University of Cambridge, Cambridge CB2 3ER, UK E-mail address: mcdrenf@hermes.cam.ac.uk; lm243@cam.ac.uk
[2]Wellcome Centre for Neuroimaging, UCL, London WC1N 3BG, UK
[3]Center for Functional Integrative Neuroscience, Åarhus University Hospital, Nørrebrogade 44, Building 30, 8000 Åarhus C, Denmark

1

Neural correlates of Early Stone Age toolmaking: technology, language and cognition in human evolution

Dietrich Stout, Nicholas Toth, Kathy Schick and Thierry Chaminade

Archaeological and palaeontological evidence from the Early Stone Age (ESA) documents parallel trends of brain expansion and technological elaboration in human evolution over a period of more than 2 Myr. However, the relationship between these defining trends remains controversial and poorly understood. Here, we present results from a positron emission tomography study of functional brain activation during experimental ESA (Oldowan and Acheulean) toolmaking by expert subjects. Together with a previous study of Oldowan toolmaking by novices, these results document increased demands for effective visuomotor coordination and hierarchical action organization in more advanced toolmaking. This includes an increased activation of ventral premotor and inferior parietal elements of the parietofrontal praxis circuits in both the hemispheres and of the right hemisphere homologue of Broca's area. The observed patterns of activation and of overlap with language circuits suggest that toolmaking and language share a basis in more general human capacities for complex, goal-directed action. The results are consistent with coevolutionary hypotheses linking the emergence of language, toolmaking, population-level functional lateralization and association cortex expansion in human evolution.

Keywords: brain; tool; positron emission tomography; Oldowan; Acheulean; Broca's area

1.1. Introduction

Human brains and technology have been coevolving for at least the past 2.6 Myr since the appearance of the first intentionally modified stone tools (Semaw *et al.* 1997). Roughly 90% of this time span, from 2.6 to 0.25 Myr ago, is encompassed by the Early Stone Age (ESA; generally known outside Africa as the Lower Palaeolithic). This period witnessed a technological progression from simple 'Oldowan' stone chips to skilfully shaped 'Acheulean' cutting tools, as well as a nearly threefold increase in hominin brain size (figure 1.1). These parallel trends of brain expansion and technological elaboration are defining features of human evolution, yet the relationship between them remains controversial and poorly understood (Gibson & Ingold 1993; Ambrose 2001; Wynn 2002; Stout 2006). This is largely due to a lack of information regarding the cognitive and neural foundations of technological behaviour. From this evolutionary perspective, understanding the brain bases of complex tool-use and toolmaking emerges as a key issue for cognitive neuroscience (Johnson-Frey 2003; Iriki 2005).

Ongoing research with macaques (Maravita & Iriki 2004) and humans (Frey *et al.* 2005; Johnson-Frey *et al.* 2005) has identified putatively homologous parietofrontal prehension

Electronic supplementary material is available at http://dx.doi.org/10.1098/rstb.2008.0001 or via http://journals.royalsociety.org.

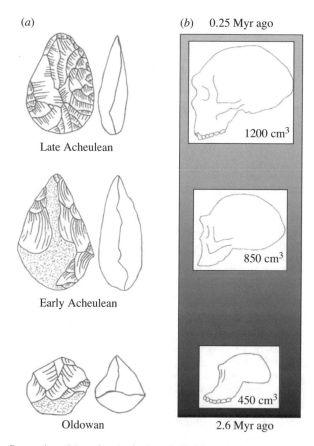

(a)

(b)   0.25 Myr ago

Late Acheulean

1200 cm³

Early Acheulean

850 cm³

Oldowan

450 cm³

2.6 Myr ago

Figure 1.1. Early Stone Age (*a*) technological and (*b*) biological change. Elements drawn after Klein (1999).

circuits supporting simple, unimanual tool use in both the species. Building on this work, a recent fluorodeoxyglucose positron emission tomography (FDG-PET) study of Oldowan toolmaking in technologically naive modern humans (Stout & Chaminade 2007) documented reliance on one such anterior parietal–ventral premotor grasp system as well as additional sensorimotor and posterior parietal activations related to the distinctive demands of this uniquely hominin skill. Of particular interest was the bilateral recruitment of human visual specializations (Orban *et al.* 2006) in the dorsal intraparietal sulcus (IPS). In contrast, there was no observed activation of prefrontal cortex (PFC).

These results suggest that evolved parietofrontal circuits enhancing sensorimotor adaptation, rather than higher level prefrontal action planning systems, were central to early ESA technological evolution. This is consistent with the fossil evidence of expanded posterior parietal lobes but relatively primitive prefrontal lobes in hominins leading up to the appearance of the first stone tools (Holloway *et al.* 2004). However, this study of novice toolmakers did not address expert performance. Subjects learned to detach sharp-edged stone flakes in a least-effort fashion, but did not replicate the well-controlled, systematic and productive flaking seen at many Oldowan sites (e.g. Semaw 2000; Delagnes & Roche 2005).

Such skilled Oldowan flaking might hypothetically involve strategic elements and neural substrates not implicated in novice toolmaking. This is even more probable with respect to the more complex Acheulean toolmaking techniques that began to develop after *ca* 1.7 Myr ago.

Oldowan toolmaking involves the production of sharp-edged flakes by striking one stone (the core) with another (the hammerstone). Effective flake detachment minimally requires visuomotor coordination and evaluation of core morphology (e.g. angles, surfaces) so that forceful blows may reliably be directed to appropriate targets. Skilled flake production, in which many flakes are removed from a single core, potentially adds a strategic element because successive flake removals leave 'scars' which may be used to prospectively create and/or maintain favourable flaking surfaces. If such strategizing is important to skilled Oldowan toolmaking, one might expect an increased recruitment of prefrontal action planning and execution systems (Passingham & Sakai 2004; Ridderinkhof *et al.* 2004; Petrides 2005), including anterior cingulate cortex (ACC) and dorsolateral prefrontal cortex (dlPFC), in which activity is modulated by the complexity of motor planning tasks (Dagher *et al.* 1999). Expert familiarity with objects and actions involved in the toolmaking task might also be reflected in the activation of the left inferior parietal lobe (IPL), a region commonly activated in tasks involving familiar tools (Lewis 2006), including pantomime, action planning and action evaluation. The left posterior IPL in particular may be associated with the representation of stored motor programmes for familiar tool-use skills (Johnson-Frey *et al.* 2005). The activation of left posterior temporal cortex, commonly associated with semantic knowledge of tools and tool-use (Johnson-Frey *et al.* 2005; Lewis 2006), might be expected for similar reasons.

Putatively strategic task elements are greatly expanded in Acheulean toolmaking, which requires the intentional shaping of the core to achieve a predetermined form (figure 1.2). The prototypical Acheulean artefact is the so-called 'hand axe', a more-or-less symmetrical, teardrop-shaped tool well suited for butchery and other heavy duty cutting tasks (Schick & Toth 1993). Although initially quite crude, by the later ESA (less than 0.5 Myr ago) these tools achieved a level of refinement indicative of advanced toolmaking skills (Edwards 2001) and perhaps even of aesthetic concerns beyond the purely utilitarian. Such later Acheulean forms were the focus of the current study, providing maximum contrast with the Oldowan toolmaking task.

One common Acheulean toolmaking method known from prehistory (Toth 2001) is the production of hand axes on large (greater than 20 cm) flake 'blanks' struck from boulder cores. Subsequent shaping of the tool involves three overlapping stages of flaking, as described in Stout *et al.* (2006). First, a relatively large, dense hammerstone is used to create a regular edge around the perimeter of the blank, centred between the two faces. This 'roughing out' stage serves to create viable angles and surfaces for the subsequent removal of large thinning flakes. 'Primary thinning and shaping' then aims to reduce the overall thickness of the piece and to begin imposing the desired symmetrical shape. Thinning flakes must be relatively thin and long, travelling at least halfway across the piece in order to reduce thickness in the centre. Prior to each thinning flake removal, intensive, light flaking is done along the perimeter with a smaller hammerstone to steepen, regularize and strengthen the edge. Thinning flakes are then struck using either the hammerstone or a baton of antler, bone or wood, which acts as a 'soft' hammer facilitating the removal of thin flakes. The baton is most extensively used in the final stage,

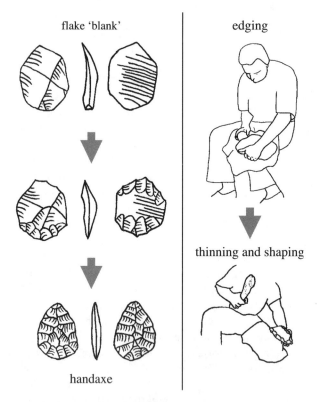

flake 'blank'

edging

thinning and shaping

handaxe

Figure 1.2. Acheulean toolmaking. Elements drawn after Inizan *et al.* (1999).

'secondary thinning and shaping', which involves more intensive edge preparation through flaking and abrasion/grinding in order to ensure highly controlled flake removals that establish a thin, symmetrical tool with straight and regular edges.

From a toolmaker's perspective, later Acheulean hand axe making seems much more demanding than Oldowan flaking, requiring (i) greater motor skill and practical under-standing of stone fracture (i.e. influence of angles, edges and surfaces), (ii) more elabo-rate planning including the subordination of immediate goals to long-term objectives (figure 1.3), and (iii) an increased number of special purpose knapping tools and techni-cal operations. In comparison with Oldowan flaking, later Acheulean toolmaking might thus be expected to produce increased activity in (i) parietofrontal prehension circuits involved in manual perceptual–motor coordination (Rizzolatti *et al.* 1998; Maravita & Iriki 2004; Frey *et al.* 2005), (ii) prefrontal action planning systems potentially including ACC and dlPFC (Dagher *et al.* 1999; Passingham & Sakai 2004; Petrides 2005), and (iii) left posterior parietal and temporal cortices associated with semantic representations for the use of familiar tools (Johnson-Frey *et al.* 2005).

In order to test these predictions, we conducted a second FDG-PET study of ESA toolmaking by expert subjects. Unfortunately, stone toolmaking is not a common skill in the modern world, and hence recruitment of expert subjects presents a unique challenge. The current study included three professional archaeologists, each with more than 10 years toolmaking experience. Despite this limited sample size, the FDG-PET procedure

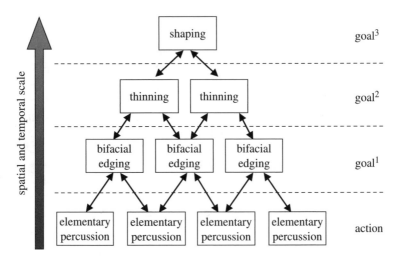

Figure 1.3. Multi-level organization of Acheulean toolmaking.

yielded a large signal to noise ratio sufficient for statistical analysis. Following the methods established in the previous study, brain activation data were collected for two toolmaking tasks: Oldowan flake production and Acheulean hand axe making. As in the previous study, toolmaking tasks were contrasted with a control task consisting of bimanual percussion without flake production. Results from the current study were also contrasted with novice (post-practice) data from the previous study.

1.2. Material and methods

(a) Experimental subjects

Three healthy, right-handed subjects (one female) between 30 and 55 years of age participated in the study. The subjects were professional archaeologists with more than 10 years stone toolmaking experience and already familiar with Oldowan and Late Acheulean technologies. All subjects gave informed written consent. The study was performed in accordance with the guidelines from the declaration of Helsinki and was approved by the Human Subjects Committee at Indiana University, Bloomington.

(b) Experimental tasks

Each subject performed three experimental tasks.

(i) *Control.* Subjects were instructed to forcefully strike together cobbles without attempting to produce flakes. They were given no specific instructions as to the manner in which to strike the stones together. This control was designed to match gross visuo-motor elements of the experimental task without involving the elements of percussive accuracy, core rotation and support distinctive to stone toolmaking.

(ii) *Oldowan toolmaking*. On a subsequent day, the subjects were instructed to produce 'Oldowan-style' flakes from the cobbles from the cart. They were instructed to focus on the production of flakes that would be 'useful for cutting', rather than on the shape of the residual cores. No further instructions regarding toolmaking methods were given.

(iii) *Acheulean toolmaking*. On a third day, the subjects were instructed to make one or more 'typical Late Acheulean' hand axes, as time permitted. Obsidian flake blanks were provided on the cart. The relatively large blanks were supported on the left thigh rather than held in the hand (figure 1.2). Nevertheless, the left hand played a key role in manipulating, orienting and stabilizing the blank. Stone working tools are highly personal items to which individuals become accustomed, and subjects were allowed to use their own tools, including hammerstones, antler batons and protective pads for the thigh. Tools were standardized in the sense that each subject used those they were familiar with, rather than each using the same (unfamiliar) tools.

The subjects performed all tasks comfortably seated on a chair with an array of stone raw materials available within easy reach on a cart to their left. The selection of materials from those provided was a component of all tasks. Cobbles were collected at a gravel quarry in Martinsville, IN, and included a range of sizes, shapes and materials, primarily limestone, quartzite and variously metamorphosed basalt (e.g. greenstone). Obsidian blanks had previously been struck from a discoidal boulder core, but were otherwise unmodified.

(c) Functional imaging

The use of the relatively slowly decaying radiological tracer ^{18}fluoro-2-deoxyglucose ([^{18}F] FDG) allowed for naturalistic task performance outside the confines of the scanner. A venous catheter to administer the tracer was inserted in a vein of the foot. Thirty seconds after the condition started, a 10-mCi bolus of [^{18}F]FDG, produced on-site, was injected. Each task was performed for 40 min, well past the tracer uptake period, and was followed by a 45 min PET scanning session.

Whole brain FDG-PET imaging was performed using an ECAT 951/31 PET scanner (Siemens Medical Systems, Inc., Hoffman Estates, IL) at the Indiana University School of Medicine, Department of Radiology. Sixty-three continuous 128×128 transaxial images with a slice thickness of 2.43 mm and an in-plane axial resolution of 2.06 mm (field of view: $263.68 \times 263.68 \times 153.09$ mm^3) were acquired simultaneously with colli-mating septa retracted operating in a three-dimensional mode. The correction for attenu-ation was made using a transmission scan collected at the end of each session.

(d) Image analysis

Images were reconstructed and analysed using standard SPM2 procedures. For each sub-ject, images were realigned to the control condition scan, normalized into the Montreal Neurological Institute (MNI) stereotaxic space and smoothed using a 6 mm full-width at half-maximum Gaussian filter convolution. A population main effect model with three conditions (control condition, Oldowan toolmaking and Acheulean toolmaking) from the three subjects was selected, leaving 4 d.f. from nine images. Linear contrasts assessing differences between toolmaking conditions and the control condition were used to create statistical parametric maps. Coordinates are expressed in terms of the MNI template.

In a previous experiment, naive subjects practiced Oldowan toolmaking but did not reach an expert level of performance (details in Stout & Chaminade 2007). A second analysis was performed to investigate the interaction between expertise and toolmaking. A 2×2 factorial design was used, with two within-subject conditions (Oldowan toolmaking and control) and two populations (experts, $n = 3$ and novices from the previous experiment, $n = 6$), leaving 15 d.f. from 18 images. In addition to linear contrasts assessing differences between toolmaking conditions and the control condition in both the populations, we focused on the interaction between the two factors. The interaction contrast ((experts, Oldowan–experts, control)–(novices, Oldowan–novices, control)) revealed areas significantly increased in experts during Oldowan toolmaking compared to control but not in novices during Oldowan toolmaking compared to control. Inclusive masking with the contrast experts, Oldowan–experts, control ($p < 0.01$) was used to ensure directionality of the interaction. The reverse interaction, masked with novices, Oldowan–novices, control was used to reveal areas significantly increased in novices doing Oldowan tools compared to control but not in experts doing Oldowan tools compared to control. All contrasts were thresholded at $p < 0.001$ uncorrected and extent $k > 5$. Reported contrast estimates were recorded at the statistically most significant voxel of the clusters.

(e) Artefact analysis

All artefacts produced during recording sessions were collected. Oldowan artefacts (flakes, cores and fragments) were analysed with respect to typological classification, frequency, technological characteristics, mass, linear dimensions and morphology. Hand axes were analysed with respect to typological classification (i.e. shape), mass and linear dimensions. Statistical analyses were conducted using SPSS.

1.3. Results

(a) Toolmaking performance

All subjects succeeded in producing characteristic Oldowan and Late Acheulean artefacts. As in actual archaeological assemblages, performance was evaluated on physical characteristics of the artefacts produced. Expert Oldowan toolmaking differed from that of novices (Stout & Chaminade 2007) in the greater number of cores ($t' = -5.55$; d.f. $= 4.11$; $p = 0.062$) modified during the given time, the greater number of flakes and fragments produced ($t' = -4.55$; d.f. $= 2.68$; $p = 0.025$), and the greater absolute length ($p < 0.05$) and relative elongation ($p < 0.05$) of flakes produced. Experts were also much more likely to use scars left by previous flakes as a striking surface for further flake removals, as evidenced by the distribution of original, weathered cobble surface ('cortex') on flakes (Pearson's $\chi_5^2 = 42.13$, $p < 0.001$). As a result of these differences, the core types (e.g. 'chopper', 'discoid', 'polyhedron'; Leakey 1971) produced by experts were more similar to those found at actual Oldowan sites than was the case with novices.

Hand axes produced were also typical of those that might be found in the Late Acheulean, less than 500 kyr ago. Subjects each produced from 1 to 3 hand axes, as shown

Table 1.1. Experimental hand axe attributes.

Subject	Hand axes produced	Mass (g)	Length (mm)	Breadth (mm)	Thickness (mm)	Breadth/ thickness
1	1	1960	250	140	56	2.50
2	1	1174	223	133	45	2.96
3	3	549	160	106	35	3.03
		482	147	112	33	3.39
		792	192	137	39	3.51

in table 1.1. The uniformly high breadth/thickness ratios obtained reflect a high level of refinement.

(b) PET results

Table 1.2 gives results for the two contrasts of interest: Oldowan toolmaking versus control, and Acheulean toolmaking versus control. Bilateral parietal clusters, in the superior and inferior lobules and in the IPS, overlapped in the two contrasts, as did most of the early visual activities in the posterior occipital cortices (Brodmann areas (BA) 17 and 18). In contrast, differences were found in the higher order visual areas of the occipital (BA 19) and temporal cortices and in the frontal cortex. A large right inferior temporal gyrus activation was found for Oldowan toolmaking. Only in the left hemisphere (LH) lateral and ventral precentral gyrii (BA 6) did the activity for the two toolmaking tasks overlap. Oldowan toolmaking was additionally associated with activity in the orbitofrontal cortex, while Acheulean toolmaking yielded a number of additional clusters in the dorsal precentral (BA 6) gyrus bilaterally, particularly strong in the right hemisphere (RH), as well as in the RH ventral precentral (BA 6) and inferior prefrontal (BA 45) cortices. Contrast estimates for the two toolmaking tasks in the RH supramarginal, ventral precentral and inferior prefrontal gyrii are illustrated in figure 1.4.

The second analysis compared the brain activity during Oldowan toolmaking and the control conditions in the experts scanned here to the brain activity in the same tasks scanned in toolmaking novices after they received some training (Stout & Chaminade 2007). The experiments with experts and with novices contained the same conditions, allowing their inclusion in a single multi-group analysis. Trained novices and experts differed in the expertise in toolmaking, but both had prior exposure to Oldowan toolmaking, ruling out a response to novelty and surprise in novices. A network of occipital, parietal and frontal areas was found in the contrasts between Oldowan toolmaking and control for the two populations, listed in the electronic supplementary material, table 1.1. Most occipital activations overlapped, with the exceptions of some ventral clusters (right fusiform and left lingual gyrii) and the rightparietooccipital sulcus. In the frontal cortex, there were more activated clusters in novices than in experts, though the left ventral precentral gyrus cluster was reported in table 1 for Oldowan toolmaking. There was a posterior shift in one of the superior parietal clusters (from $x, y, z = 24, -46, 60$ in novices to $24, -72, 58$ in experts) as well as a bilateral supramarginal gyrus (SMG) activity for experts only (BA 40).

An interaction contrast was used to report areas involved in Oldowan toolmaking in experts only (table 1.3), revealing activity in the RH occipital cortex and superior parietal lobule and in the SMG bilaterally. These later inferior parietal clusters of activity are

Table 1.2. Location of activated clusters found in contrasts between Oldowan toolmaking and control and between Acheulean toolmaking and control by expert tool knappers. ($p < 0.001$ uncorrected, $k > 5$, $n = 3$. Clusters are organized by cortical regions and ordered by decreasing z-coordinate within each region. Blank spaces indicate a lack of significant activation. Coordinates are relative to the Montreal Neurological Institute standard template brain. BA, Brodmann area.)

location		BA	Oldowan-control				Acheulean-control			
			x	y	z	t-score	x	y	z	t-score
frontal cortex										
right	dorsal precentral gyrus	6					34	58	58	46.33
left	dorsal precentral gyrus	6					−24	58	58	17.27
left	lateral precentral gyrus	4/6	−46	−16	44	14.16	−44	−14	46	17.16
left	ventral precentral gyrus	6	−52	6	28	9.72	−52	6	28	12.24
right	ventral precentral gyrus	6					60	2	26	19.68
right	inferior prefrontal gyrus	45					48	34	10	17.08
left	orbital gyrus	11	−24	32	−22	15.1				
parietal cortex										
left	superior parietal lobule	5	−14	−54	70	14.46	−14	−54	70	12.59
right	superior parietal lobule	7	24	−60	66	11.74	22	−62	68	13.42
right	intraparietal sulcus	7/40	34	−52	60	15.34	34	−52	60	12.32
left	intraparietal sulcus	7/40	−28	−48	52	12.37	−28	−48	52	13.81
left	supramarginal gyrus	40	−48	−32	40	8.67	−48	−32	42	10.40
right	supramarginal gyrus	40	58	−30	36	14.98	58	−30	36	19.57
temporal cortex										
right	inferior temporal gyrus	20/21/37	52	−50	−10	30.49				
occipital cortex										
left	parieto-occipital sulcus	19/7	30	−88	44	12.07	−22	−62	58	9.62
left	parieto-occipital sulcus	19/7	−16	−86	38	34.22				
left	superior occipital gyrus	19	32	−66	32	10.9	−16	−86	38	62.34
right	middle occipital gyrus	19	22	−88	28	10.54	20	−88	30	9.21
right	middle occipital gyrus	18	4	−86	24	21.59	4	−86	24	19.42
left	cuneus	18	18	−96	2	28.65	18	−96	2	18.09
right	calcarine sulcus	17	−12	−84	−6	24.98	−12	−84	−6	44.93
left	lingual gyrus	17	30	−68	−10	31.65				
right	lingual gyrus	19	30	−76	−16	26.18				
right	fusiform gyrus	18					30	−76	−16	14.15

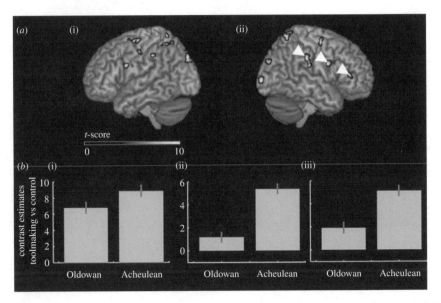

Figure 1.4. Main effects of expert toolmaking. (*a*) Lateral renders of brain activation ((i) left and (ii) right) during expert Acheulean toolmaking (see table 2). (*b*) Estimates for the contrasts Oldowan versus control and Acheulean versus control at the peak of the (i) supramarginal, (ii) ventral precentral, and (iii) inferior frontal clusters in the right hemisphere (white arrows on the right hemisphere render).

shown in figure 1.5, with contrast estimates showing a significant increase in activity during Oldowan toolmaking compared to control in experts, but not in novices. No clusters survived in the reverse interaction, indicating that there were no brain regions more active in Oldowan toolmaking versus control in novices but not in experts.

1.4. Discussion

Functional imaging research with modern humans cannot directly reveal the cognitive capacities or neural organization of extinct hominin species, but can clarify the relative demands of specific, evolutionarily significant behaviours. Used in conjunction with archaeological (Ambrose 2001; Wynn 2002), fossil (Holloway *et al.* 2004) and comparative (Passingham 1998; Rilling 2006) evidence, such information helps to constrain hypotheses about human cognitive and brain evolution. The results of the current study provide evidence of increased sensorimotor and cognitive demands related to the changing nature of expert performance (cf. Kelly & Garavan 2005) and to the complexity of toolmaking methods, and suggest important relationships between ESA technological change and evolving hominin brain size, functional lateralization and language capacities.

(a) Expert Oldowan toolmaking

As expected, expertise was associated with increased IPL activation during Oldowan toolmaking. However, contrary to expectation, this activation was strongly bilateral.

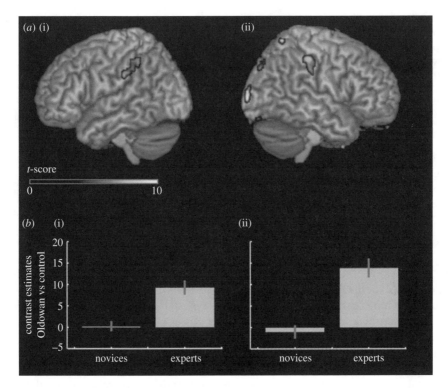

Figure 1.5. Interaction between expertise and toolmaking. (*a*) Lateral renders of brain activation ((i) left and (ii) right) during expert Oldowan toolmaking (see table 1.3). (*b*) Estimates for the contrast Oldowan versus control in novice and expert toolmakers at the peak of the (i) left and (ii) right supramarginal clusters.

This was surprising given the substantial imaging evidence of LH dominance for tasks involving familiar tools, regardless of the hand involved (Lewis 2006), as well as the strong association of ideomotor apraxia with lesions of the LH (Johnson-Frey 2004). Indeed, the left IPL activation is commonly reported for tasks involving manipulable objects and fine finger movements (Grezes & Decety 2001; Lewis 2006), and is thought to reflect a role in the visuospatial coding of moving limbs (i.e. the 'body schema'; Chaminade *et al.* 2005) and/or storage of internal models for planning object-related movements (i.e. 'action schemas'; Buxbaum *et al.* 2005).

Stored tool-use action schemas could engage the posterior regions of IPL (Johnson-Frey *et al.* 2005), whereas an anterior part would respond to action possibilities relative to tools (Kellenbach *et al.* 2003). Increased left IPL recruitment during expert Oldowan toolmaking is located in this more anterior region. This activation clearly relates to greater task familiarity in experts, and may reflect reliance on visuospatial body schemas that incorporate (Maravita & Iriki 2004) the handheld core and hammerstone. It would also be consistent with the hypothesis that regions adjoining human anterior IPS are involved in the storage of visuospatial properties associated with tool manipulation (Johnson-Frey *et al.* 2005). Combined with the observed right superior parietal lobule

Table 1.3. Location of activated clusters in the interaction between toolmaking and expertise. (The interaction contrast (experts, Oldowan–experts, control)–(novices, Oldowan–novices, control), $p < 0.001$ uncorrected, $k > 5$, was inclusively masked with the contrast experts, Oldowan–experts, control ($p < 0.01$) to ensure directionality. Coordinates are relative to the Montreal Neurological Institute standard template brain. BA, Brodmann area.)

location		BA	x	y	z	t-score
parietal cortex						
right	superior parietal lobule	7	28	−60	68	11.45
right	supramarginal gyrus	40	56	−30	48	9.18
left	supramarginal gyrus	40	−56	−28	30	7.90
occipital cortex						
right	calcarine sulcus	17	14	−100	6	16.25
right	middle occipital gyrus	19	28	−84	38	8.37
right	lingual gyrus	18	16	−80	−12	8.64

activity and a lack of any significant increase in the temporal cortex activity, these results indicate that expert Oldowan toolmaking performance depends more upon enhanced sensorimotor representations of the tool + body system than upon stored action semantics of the kind recruited by normal subjects planning the use of everyday tools (Johnson-Frey *et al.* 2005).

The right SMG activation in expert Oldowan toolmaking, although unexpected, most probably relates to the naturalistic task design. LH dominance is generally less pronounced during actual tool-use action execution than during more 'conceptual' imagery or planning tasks (Lewis 2006), and this has been reported for SMG specifically (Johnson-Frey *et al.* 2005). Bilateral SMG activation in the current study is thus consistent with the conclusion that expert performance is supported by an enhanced knowledge of the action properties of the tool + body system, rather than semantic knowledge about appropriate patterns of tool use. Bilateral activation is also likely to reflect a manual laterality effect similar to that seen in primary motor and sensory cortices, with right SMG contributing to the important action of the left hand supporting and orienting the core. This initially appears contrary to the well-documented phenomenon of motor equivalence seen in studies of handwriting (Rijntjes *et al.* 1999; Wing 2000) in which secondary sensorimotor cortices for the dominant hand are activated regardless of the effector used (e.g. toe, non-dominant hand). However, the role of the non-dominant hand in Oldowan toolmaking is not simply to execute gestures more typically done with the dominant hand but rather to properly position and support the core to receive the action of the dominant hand. The task is inherently bimanual, with distinct but complementary roles for the two hands.

A similar bimanual organization may be seen in many naturalistic human tool-using actions, such as sweeping, shovelling, threading a needle, striking a match or cutting paper with scissors, in which the non-dominant hand provides a steady spatial 'frame' for the higher frequency action of the dominant hand (MacNeilage *et al.* 1984; Guiard 1987). This characteristic division of labour probably reflects hemispheric specializations, with the stable support role of the left hand mapping onto well-known RH specializations for visuospatial processing, particularly at larger spatiotemporal scales (Gazzaniga 2000), and specifically including the activation of right SMG in visuospatial decision making (Stephan *et al.* 2003).

That bilateral SMG activation emerges in expert compared to novice toolmakers suggests that proper bimanual coordination, and particularly the left-hand support role, develops only after substantial practice. Novices instead appear focused on the more rapid percussive movements of the right hand, supported by LH parietofrontal prehension circuits. This different approach to the task probably explains major differences in the performance of novices and experts. In comparison to novices, expert toolmakers were able to remove more and larger flakes from cores, and thus to generate heavily worked artefacts similar to those found at actual Oldowan sites. Larger, longer flakes travel further across core surfaces and leave relatively flat scars and acute angles on the core rather than the rounded edges typical of novice performance (Stout & Chaminade 2007). Consistent success in large flake detachment thus tends to produce advantageous morphology for further flake removals without the need for explicit and detailed planning by the toolmaker.

It had been hypothesized that such action sequences might involve a strategic element similar to that assessed by neuropsychological tests of motor planning (Dagher *et al.* 1999), and supported by similar prefrontal action planning and execution systems. This does not appear to be the case (table 1.3; electronic supplementary material, table 1.1). The current results instead support the idea that expert Oldowan toolmaking is enabled by greater sensorimotor control for effective flake detachment, supported by enhanced representations of the body+tool system and particularly of the larger scale spatio-temporal 'frame' provided by the RH–left-hand system. This is consistent with ethno-graphic accounts emphasizing the perceptual–motor foundations of many strategic regularities in stone toolmaking action organization (Stout 2002; Roux & David 2005).

(b) Late Acheulean toolmaking

The most striking result of the comparison between expert Oldowan and Late Acheulean toolmaking was an increase in the RH activity, including both SMG and new clusters in the right ventral premotor cortex (PMv, BA 6) and the inferior prefrontal gyrus (BA 45) (table 1.2, figure 1.5). This probably reflects an increasingly critical role for the RH–left-hand system in hand axe production as well as the involvement of more complex and protracted technical action sequences (cf. Hartmann *et al.* 2005). The increased right SMG activation extends the trend seen in expert Oldowan knapping and is best interpreted as reflecting further increases in the importance of visuospatial representations of the tool + body system in this task. Similarly, the novel activation of the right PMv may be attributed to increased motor demands relating to the manipulation, support and precise orientation of the larger Acheulean hand axe. Precise and forceful left-hand grips become increasingly critical as the piece is thinned in order to absorb shock and prevent accidental breakage, a concern that is much less salient in Oldowan knapping.

The activation of right inferior PFC (BA 45) during Acheulean toolmaking is of particular interest because PFC lies at the top of the brain's sensory and motor hierarchies (Passingham *et al.* 2000) and plays a central role in coordinating flexible, goal-directed behaviour (Ridderinkhof *et al.* 2004). Thus, PFC activation during hand axe production probably reflects greater demands for complex action regulation in this task. Ventrolateral PFC (vlPFC) in particular (including BA 45) seems to be involved in associating perceptual cues with the actions or choices they specify (Passingham *et al.* 2000), particularly when these actions are subordinate elements within ongoing, hierarchically structured action sequences (Koechlin & Jubault 2006). This underlying function may help explain the apparent overlap of language and praxis circuits in the inferior prefrontal gyrus. It is also consistent with the distinctive technical requirements of hand axe making, which include the skilful coordination of perception and action in pursuit of higher order goals (figure 3). In contrast, hypothesized dorsolateral PFC and ACC 'action planning circuit' activation was not observed. Dorsolateral PFC has been associated with the prospective (Passingham & Sakai 2004) monitoring and manipulation of information within working memory, and is commonly activated in tasks that separate planning from execution (e.g. Dagher *et al.* 1999; Johnson-Frey *et al.* 2005). The activation of ventrolateral, but not dorsolateral, PFC indicates that Acheulean toolmaking is distinguished by cognitive demands for the coordination of ongoing, hierarchically organized action sequences rather than the internal rehearsal and evaluation of action plans.

The localization of vlPFC activation to RH probably reflects demands for such action coordination that are particular to the left-hand core support and manipulation aspect of the task. This is consistent with the general task structure of stone knapping in which the RH/left-hand system provides goal-directed contextual 'frames' modulating the functionality of relatively rapid, and repetitive percussive actions by the LH–right-hand system. Parietofrontal (inferior parietal–ventral premotor) praxis circuits are activated bilaterally; however, increased requirements for cognitive control in the RH–left-hand system specifically may explain the exclusive activation of right vlPFC. Such localization of cognitive control to the same hemisphere as task execution has previously been reported in a visuospatial decision task (Stephan *et al.* 2003).

As in Oldowan knapping, lateralized patterns of brain activation and manual task organization probably relate to hemispheric specializations. For example, the right vlPFC is thought to play a dominant role in response inhibition and task-set switching (Aron *et al.* 2004). These abilities are critical to successful hand axe production, which involves frequent and highly flexible shifts between different technical operations and goals (e.g. platform preparation, bifacial edging, thinning) as well as the continual rejection of immediately attractive opportunities in favour of actions serving longer term objectives. Perhaps for similar reasons, lesion studies indicate an important RH contribution to the successful completion of multistep mechanical problems (Hartmann *et al.* 2005). The increasingly anterior and RH-dominant frontal activation during Late Acheulean toolmaking reflects the more complex, multi-level structure of the task (figure 1.3), which includes the flexible iteration of multi-step processes in the context of larger scale technical goals. This characterization further invites comparison with the hierarchy of phonological-, syntactic-, semantic- and discourse-level processing that is characteristic of human linguistic behaviour (Hagoort 2005; Rose 2006).

(c) Tools, language and laterality in human evolution

Hypotheses linking language and tool-use have typically focused on the LH and its contributions to rapid, sequential and hierarchically organized behaviour (e.g. Greenfield 1991; Corballis 2003). This reflects a widespread perception of LH dominance for both language and praxis. However, it is well known that the RH plays an important role in language processing, particularly with respect to larger scale phenomena such as metaphor, figurative language, connotative meaning, prosody and discourse comprehension (Bookheimer 2002). Similarly, it is becoming apparent that the RH contributes substantially to elements of perception and action on larger spatio-temporal scales, including perceptual grouping (Gazzaniga 2000), task-set switching and inhibition (Aron *et al.* 2004), decision making in ambiguous situations (Goel *et al.* 2007), and naturalistic tasks involving multiple steps and objects (Hartmann *et al.* 2005). Bilateral activations observed during ESA toolmaking reflect multiple levels of overlap with cortical language circuits and suggest potential evolutionary interactions.

The anterior premotor cortex shares important functional and connectional characteristics with posterior PFC (Petrides 2005) and appears to play a role in phonological processing (Bookheimer 2002; Hagoort 2005). The activation of left anterior PMv during novice (Stout & Chaminade 2007) and expert Oldowan knapping corroborates the existing evidence of overlap between manual praxis and language processing (Hamzei *et al.* 2003; Rizzolatti & Craighero 2004), and may reflect an underlying role for this region in sensorimotor unification (Hagoort 2005) and conditional response selection (Petrides 2005)across modalities. Overlapping phonological and manual control in PMv is consistent with motor hypotheses of language origins linking manual coordination with evolving capacities for speech production (Kimura 1979; MacNeilage *et al.* 1984; Lieberman 2002). The specific recruitment of this region during Oldowan knapping provides a direct connection with evidence of hominin toolmaking skills going back 2.6 Myr. This suggests an alternative or addition to the emphasis placed on intransitive gestures and manual protolanguage in many recent evolutionary scenarios (e.g. Rizzolatti & Arbib 1998; Corballis 2003), insofar as selection on toolmaking ability could also have indirectly contributed to the enhanced articulatory control so central to human language evolution (Studdert-Kennedy & Goldstein 2003).

Brain activation during hand axe making further indicates reliance on increasingly anterior and right lateralized PFC in a region also associated with discourse-level prosodic and contextual language processing (Bookheimer 2002). It is likely that the common denominator in these technical and linguistic tasks is their requirement for the coordination of behavioural elements into hierarchically structured sequences (Greenfield 1991; Koechlin & Jubault 2006) on the basis of contextual information integrated over relatively long time spans (cf. Bookheimer 2002). Archaeological evidence of ESA technological change thus traces a trajectory of ever more skill-intensive, bimanual toolmaking methods that overlap functionally and anatomically with important elements of the human faculty for language. This trend further coincides with the emergence of population-level manual lateralization (Steele & Uomini 2005) and the dramatic expansion of prefrontal and parieto-temporal association cortices (Holloway *et al.* 2004; Rilling 2006). Such correlations cannot demonstrate the direction of evolutionary cause and effect, but do suggest important interactions.

(d) Conclusions

Results presented here provide further evidence of the value of the archaeological record of technological change in understanding human cognitive evolution (Wynn 2002). More specifically, they document a trend of increasingly sophisticated hominin engagement with materials in ESA toolmaking, supported by neurally based capacities for effective visuomotor coordination and hierarchical action organization. Neural circuits supporting ESA toolmaking partially overlap with language circuits, strongly suggesting that these behaviours share a foundation in more general human capacities for complex, goal-directed action and are likely to have evolved in a mutually reinforcing way. These trends and relationships are consistent with archaeological, palaeontological and comparative evidence of emerging population-level functional lateralization and association cortex expansion in human evolution.

We gratefully thank Colin Renfrew, Chris Frith and Lambros Malfouris for organizing the Sapient Mind conference, and all the participants for their lively and helpful discussion. We are particularly grateful to Scott Frey for his comments on a draft of this paper (although all remaining errors are ours alone) and to Kevin Perry and Susan Geiger of the Indiana University PET Imaging Center. Funding was provided by the Stone Age Institute.

References

Ambrose, S. 2001 Paleolithic technology and human evolution. *Science* **291**, 1748–1753. (doi:10.1126/ science.1059487)

Aron, A. A., Robbins, T. W. & Poldrack, R. A. 2004 Inhibition and the right inferior frontal cortex. *Trends Cogn. Sci.* **8**, 170–177. (doi:10.1016/j.tics.2004.02.010)

Bookheimer, S. 2002 Functional MRI of language: new approaches to understanding the cortical organization of semantic processing. *Annu. Rev. Neurosci.* **25**, 151–188. (doi:10.1146/annurev. neuro.25.112701.142946)

Buxbaum, L. J., Johnson-Frey, S. H. & Bartlett-Williams, M. 2005 Deficient internal models for planning hand–object interactions in apraxia. *Neuropsychologica* **43**, 917–929. (doi:10.1016/j. neuropsychologia.2004.09.006)

Chaminade, T., Meltzoff, A. & Decety, J. 2005 An fMRI study of imitation: action representation and body schema. *Neuropsychologica* **43**, 115–127. (doi:10.1016/j.neuropsychologia.2004. 04.026)

Corballis, M. C. 2003 From mouth to hand: gesture, speech, and the evolution of right handedness. *Behav. Brain. Sci.* **26**, 199–260. (doi:10.1017/S0140525X03000062)

Dagher, A., Owen, A. M., Boecker, H. & Brooks, D. J. 1999 Mapping the network for planning: a correlational PET activation study with the Tower of London task. *Brain* **122**, 1973–1987. (doi:10.1093/brain/122.10.1973)

Delagnes, A. & Roche, H. 2005 Late Pliocene hominid knapping skills: the case of Lokalalei 2C, West Turkana, Kenya. *J. Hum. Evol.* **48**, 435–472. (doi:10.1016/j.jhevol. 2004.12.005)

Edwards, S. W. 2001 A modern knapper's assessment of the technical skills of the Late Acheulean biface workers at Kalambo Falls. In *Kalambo Falls prehistoric site* (ed. J. D. Clark). The earlier cultures: Middle and Earlier Stone Age, pp. 605–611. Cambridge, UK: Cambridge University Press.

Frey, S. H., Vinton, D., Norlund, R. & Grafton, S. T. 2005 Cortical topography of human anterior intraparietal cortex active during visually guided grasping. *Cogn. Brain Res.* **23**, 397–405. (doi:10.1016/j.cogbrainres. 2004.11.010)

Gazzaniga, M. S. 2000 Cerebral specialization and interhemispheric communication: does the corpus callosum enable the human condition? *Brain* **123**, 1293–1326. (doi:10.1093/brain/ 123.7.1293)

Gibson, K. R. & Ingold, T. 1993 *Tools, language and cognition in human evolution.* Cambridge, UK: Cambridge University Press.

Goel, V., Tierney, M., Sheesley, L., Bartolo, A., Vartanian, O. & Grafman, J. 2007 Hemispheric specialization in human prefrontal cortex for resolving certain and uncertain inferences. *Cereb. Cortex* **17**, 2245–2250. (doi:10.1093/ cercor/bhl132)

Greenfield, P. M. 1991 Language, tools, and brain: the development and evolution of hierarchically organized sequential behavior. *Behav. Brain Sci.* **14**, 531–595.

Grezes, J. & Decety, J. 2001 Functional anatomy of execution, mental simulation, observation, and verb generation of action: a meta-analysis. *Hum. Brain Mapp.* **12**, 1–19. (doi:10.1002/1097-0193(200101)12:1 <1::AID-HBM10>3.0.CO;2-V)

Guiard, Y. 1987 Asymmetric division of labor in human skilled bimanual action: the kinematic chain as a model. *J. Motor Behav.* **19**, 486–517.

Hagoort, P. 2005 On Broca, brain, and binding: a new framework. *Trends Cogn. Sci.* **9**, 416–423. (doi:10.1016/ j.tics.2005.07.004)

Hamzei, F., Rijntjes, M., Dettmers, C., Glauche, V., Weiller, C. & Buchel, C. 2003 The human action recognition system and its relationship to Broca's area: an fMRI study. *Neuroimage* **19**, 637–644. (doi:10.1016/S10538119(03)00087-9)

Hartmann, K., Goldenberg, G., Daumuller, M. & Hermsdorfer, J. 2005 It takes the whole brain to make a cup of coffee: the neuropsychology of naturalistic actions involving technical devices. *Neuropsychologia* **43**, 625–637. (doi:10.1016/j.neuropsychologia.2004.07.015)

Holloway, R., Broadfield, D. & Yuan, M. 2004 *The human fossil record. Brain endocasts—the paleo-neurological evidence*, vol. 3. Hoboken, NJ: Wiley-Liss.

Inizan, M.-L., Reduron-Ballinger, M., Roche, H. & Tixier, J. 1999 *Technology and terminology of knapped stone*. Nanterre, France: C.R.E.P.

Iriki, A. 2005 A prototype of *Homo faber*: a silent precursor of human intelligence in the tool-using monkey brain. In *From monkey brain to human brain: a Fyssen foundation symposium* (eds S. Dehaene, J.-R. Duhamel, M. D. Hauser & G. Rizzolatti), pp. 253–271. Cambridge, MA: MIT Press.

Johnson-Frey, S. H. 2003 What's so special about human tool use? *Neuron* **39**, 201–204. (doi:10.1016/ S0896-6273(03) 00424-0)

Johnson-Frey, S. H. 2004 The neural bases of complex tool use in humans. *Trends Cogn. Sci.* **8**, 71–78. (doi:10.1016/ j.tics.2003.12.002)

Johnson-Frey, S. H., Newman-Norlund, R. & Grafton, S. T. 2005 A distributed left hemisphere network active during planning of everyday tool use skills. *Cereb. Cortex* **15**, 681–695. (doi:10.1093/cercor/bhh169)

Kellenbach, M. L., Brett, M. & Patterson, K. 2003 Actions speak louder than functions: the importance of manipulability and action in tool representation. *J. Cogn. Neurosci.* **15**, 30–45. (doi: 10.1162/089892903321107800)

Kelly, A. M. & Garavan, H. 2005 Human functional neuroimaging of brain changes associated with practice. *Cereb. Cortex* **15**, 1089–1102. (doi:10.1093/cercor/ bhi005)

Kimura, D. 1979 Neuromotor mechanisms in the evolution of human communication. In *Neurobiology of social communication in primates* (eds L. H. D. Steklis & M. J. Raleigh), pp. 179–219. New York, NY: Academic Press.

Klein, R. G. 1999 *The human career*. Chicago, IL: University of Chicago Press.

Koechlin, E. & Jubault, T. 2006 Broca's Area and the hierarchical organization of human behavior. *Neuron* **50**, 963–974. (doi:10.1016/j.neuron.2006.05.017)

Leakey, M. D. 1971 *Olduvai Gorge. Excavations in Beds I and II, 1960–1963*, vol. 3. New York, NY: Cambridge University Press.

Lewis, J. W. 2006 Cortical networks related to human use of tools. *Neuroscientist* **12**, 211–231. (doi:10.1177/1073858 406288327)

Lieberman, P. 2002 On the nature and evolution of the neural bases of human language. *Am. J. Phys. Anthropol.* **45**, 36–62. (doi:10.1002/ajpa.10171)

MacNeilage, P. F., Studdert-Kennedy, M. G. & Lindblom, B. 1984 Functional precursors to language and its lateralization. *Am. J. Physiol. Regul. Integr. Comp. Physiol.* **246**, R912–R914.

Maravita, A. & Iriki, A. 2004 Tools for the body (schema). *Trends Cogn. Sci.* **8**, 79–86. (doi: 10.1016/j.tics.2003.12. 008)

Orban, G. A., Claeys, K., Nelissen, K., Smans, R., Sunaert, S., Todd, J. T., Wardak, C., Durand, J.-B. & Vanduffel, W. 2006 Mapping the parietal cortex of human and nonhuman primates. *Neuropsychologia* **44**, 2647–2667. (doi:10. 1016/j.neuropsychologia.2005.11.001)

Passingham, R. E. 1998 The specializations of the human neocortex. In *Comparative neuropsychology* (ed. A. D. Milner), pp. 271–298. New York, NY: Oxford University Press.

Passingham, R. E. & Sakai, K. 2004 The prefrontal cortex and working memory: physiology and brain imaging. *Curr. Opin. Neurobiol.* **14**, 163–168. (doi:10.1016/j.conb.2004. 03.003)

Passingham, R. E., Toni, I. & Rushworth, M. F. S. 2000 Specialisation within the prefrontal cortex: the ventral prefrontal cortex and associative learning. *Exp. Brain Res.* **133**, 103–113. (doi:10.1007/ s002210000405)

Petrides, M. 2005 The rostral-caudal axis of cognitive control within lateral frontal cortex. In *From monkey brain to human brain: a Fyssen Foundation symposium* (eds S. Dehaene, J.-R. Duhamel, M. D. Hauser & G. Rizzolatti), pp. 293–314. Cambridge, MA: MIT Press.

Ridderinkhof, K. R., van den Wildenberg, W. P. M., Segalowitz, S. J. & Carter, C. S. 2004 Neurocognitive mechanisms of cognitive control: the role of prefrontal cortex in action selection, response inhibition, performance monitoring, and reward based learning. *Brain Cogn.* **56**, 129–140. (doi:10.1016/j.bandc.2004.09.016)

Rijntjes, M., Dettmers, C., Buchel, C., Kiebel, S., Frackowiak, R. S. J. & Weiller, C. 1999 A blueprint for movement: functional and anatomical representations in the human motor system. *J. Neurosci.* **19**, 8043–8048.

Rilling, J. K. 2006 Human and nonhuman primate brains: are they allometrically scaled versions of the same design. *Evol. Anthropol.* **15**, 65–77. (doi:10.1002/evan.20095)

Rizzolatti, G. & Arbib, M. A. 1998 Language within our grasp. *Trends Cogn. Sci.* **21**, 188–194.

Rizzolatti, G. & Craighero, L. 2004 The mirror–neuron system. *Annu. Rev. Neurosci.* **27**, 169–192. (doi:10.1146/ annurev.neuro.27.070203.144230)

Rizzolatti, G., Luppino, G. & Matelli, M. 1998 The organization of the cortical motor system: new concepts. *Electroencephalogr. Clin. Neurophysiol.* **106**, 283–296. (doi:10.1016/S0013-4694(98)00022-4)

Rose, D. 2006 A systematic functional approach to language evolution. *Camb. Archaeol. J.* **16**, 73–96. (doi:10.1017/ S0959774306000059)

Roux, V. & David, E. 2005 Planning abilities as a dynamic perceptual–motor skill: an actualistic study of different levels of expertise involved in stone knapping. In *Stone knapping: the necessary conditions for a uniquely hominin behaviour* (eds V. Roux & B. Bril), pp. 91–108. Cambridge, UK: McDonald Institute for Archaeological Research.

Schick, K. D. & Toth, N. 1993 *Making silent stones speak: human evolution and the dawn of technology*. New York, NY: Simon & Schuster.

Semaw, S. 2000 The world's oldest stone artefacts from Gona, Ethiopia: their implications for understanding stone technology and patterns of human evolution 2.6–1.5 million years ago. *J. Archaeol. Sci.* **27**, 1197–1214. (doi:10.1006/jasc.1999.0592)

Semaw, S., Renne, P., Harris, J. W. K., Feibel, C. S., Bernor, R. L., Fesseha, N. & Mowbray, K. 1997 2.5-million-yearold stone tools from Gona, Ethiopia. *Nature* **385**, 333–336. (doi:10.1038/ 385333a0)

Steele, J. & Uomini, N. 2005 Humans, tools and handedness. In *Stone knapping: the necessary conditions for a uniquely hominin behaviour* (eds V. Roux & B. Bril), pp. 217–239. Cambridge, UK: McDonald Institute for Archaeological Research.

Stephan, K. E., Marshall, J. C., Friston, K. J., Rowe, J. B., Ritzl, A., Zilles, K. & Fink, G. R. 2003 Lateralized cognitive processes and lateralized task control in the human brain. *Science* **301**, 384–386. (doi:10.1126/science. 1086025)

Stout, D. 2002 Skill and cognition in stone tool production: an ethnographic case study from Irian Jaya. *Curr. Anthropol.* **45**, 693–722. (doi:10.1086/342638)

Stout, D. 2006 Oldowan toolmaking and hominin brain evolution: theory and research using positron emission tomography (PET). In *The Oldowan: case studies into the earliest Stone Age* (eds N. Toth & K. Schick), pp. 267–305. Gosport, IN: Stone Age Institute Press.

Stout, D. & Chaminade, T. 2007 The evolutionary neuroscience of tool making. *Neuropsychologia* **45**, 1091–1100. (doi:10.1016/j.neuropsychologia.2006.09.014)

Stout, D., Toth, N. & Schick, K. 2006 Acheulean toolmaking and hominin brain evolution: a pilot study using positron emission tomography. In *The Oldowan: case studies into the earliest Stone Age* (eds N. Toth & K. Schick), pp. 321–331. Gosport, IN: Stone Age Institute Press.

Studdert-Kennedy, M. & Goldstein, L. 2003 Launching language: the gestural origins of discrete infinity. In *Language evolution* (eds M. H. Christiansen & S. Kirby), pp. 235–254. Oxford, UK: Oxford University Press.

Toth, N. 2001 Experiments in quarrying large flake blanks at Kalambo Falls. In *Kalambo Falls prehistoric site* (ed. J. D. Clark). The earlier cultures: Middle and Earlier Stone Age, pp. 600–604. Cambridge, UK: Cambridge University Press.

Wing, A. M. 2000 Motor control: mechanisms of motor equivalence in handwriting. *Curr. Biol.* **10**, R245–R248. (doi:10.1016/S0960-9822(00)00375-4)

Wynn, T. 2002 Archaeology and cognitive evolution. *Behav. Brain. Sci.* **25**, 389–438. (doi:10.1017/S0140525X025 30120)

2

Tool use, communicative gesture and cerebral asymmetries in the modern human brain

Scott H. Frey

Determining the brain adaptations that underlie complex tool-use skills is an important component in understanding the physiological bases of human material culture. It is argued here that the ways in which humans skilfully use tools and other manipulable artefacts is possible owing to adaptations that integrate sensory–motor and cognitive processes. Data from brain-injured patients and functional neuroimaging studies suggest that the left cerebral hemisphere, particularly the left parietal cortex, of modern humans is specialized for this purpose. This brain area integrates dynamically representations that are computed in a distributed network of regions, several of which are also left-lateralized. Depending on the nature of the task, these may include conceptual knowledge about objects and their functions, the actor's goals and intentions, and interpretations of task demands. The result is the formation of a praxis representation that is appropriate for the prevailing task context. Recent evidence is presented that this network is organized similarly in the right- and left-handed individuals, and participates in the representation of both familiar tool-use skills and communicative gestures. This shared brain mechanism may reflect common origins of the human specializations for complex tool use and language.

Keywords: praxis; tool use; gesture; apraxia; neuroimaging; hand dominance

2.1. Introduction

The Palaeolithic record indicates that our ancestors began modifying rocks for pounding at least 2.5 Myr ago (Ambrose 2001). Subsequently, rocks were attached to sticks to create compound tools that were capable of generating higher impact forces. These hammers, as well as many other manipulable artefacts, have been refined into their various modern forms through a process of cumulative cultural evolution (Basalla 1988; Tomasello 1999). Though difficult to trace in the fossil record, advancing technology was accompanied by the evolution of specific manual skills involved in the use of these implements. Given that all primates possess the ability to dexterously reach, grasp and manipulate objects with their hands, why is it that only humans have developed such an extensive and universal material culture?

One possibility is that modifications to the neural circuits of the primate brain involved in the sensory–motor control of manual prehension underlie these human specializations. Training macaques to use simple tools that extend their normal manual abilities (e.g. reaching with a stick (Iriki *et al.* 1996) or grasping with a set of tongs (Umiltà *et al.* 2008)) induces experience-dependent modifications in sensory–motor representations. Likewise, while the gross functional organization of areas involved in the manual prehension may be conserved (Rizzolatti & Craighero 2004; Grefkes & Fink 2005), there are regional differences between monkey and human brains (Preuss *et al.* 1996; Orban *et al.* 2004).

Yet, can human tool-use skills really be understood strictly in terms of sensory–motor adaptations? Consider the use of the modern claw hammer. The most stable way to grasp this, or any other object, is at its centre of mass (Blake *et al*. 1992), and this location can be rapidly and often very accurately estimated on the basis of an object's perceived shape (Goodale *et al*. 1994; Johnson-Frey 2005b). If the actor's goal is pounding a nail, however, grasping the hammer by its head may not be ideal. Instead, an actor possessing knowledge about the functionality of the hammer would probably select a less stable grip, but one that is better suited for pounding. By grasping the handle at different distances from the centre of mass, the skilled carpenter can further optimize the trade-off between force and precision in accordance with the prevailing task demands. If bent by an errant blow, it might even become necessary to reverse the grip in order to remove the compromised nail with the hammer's claw. Or, the actor may decide to pass the hammer to a colleague in which case grasping the hammer by its head might actually be preferred.

As this example makes clear, the ways in which we skilfully interact with tools and other artefacts are highly context dependent, and aspects of this context are not specified by the physical properties of the task or actor's body. Though certainly necessary, sensory–motor processes alone are therefore insufficient to account for this flexibility. These skills are also influenced by conceptual knowledge about objects and their functions, the actor's intended goals and interpretations of prevailing task demands. These various sources of sensory–motor and cognitive information are somehow integrated to form internal representations that constrain and guide manual praxis, engendering a flexibility that is absent even in the tool-using behaviours of our nearest living relatives (Povinelli 2000; Johnson-Frey 2003). Determining the neural mechanisms that make this possible is elemental to understanding the origins of human material culture.

2.2. The left cerebral hemisphere and praxis

It has been known for more than a century that damage, especially to the left cerebral hemisphere of humans, can lead to apraxia—an impairment in the representation of acquired skills that cannot be attributed to difficulties in linguistic, sensory or lower level motor functions such as weakness or paralysis (Geschwind & Kaplan 1962; Heilman & Rothi 1997; Leiguarda & Marsden 2000). The difficulties experienced by these patients are not primarily with the sensory–motor control, as they often perform well when allowed to actually use objects. Instead, their impairments come to the fore when faced with tasks such as pantomime or imitation that require accessing stored action representations under circumstances that provide minimal contextual support. The fact that their problems occur when using either upper limb indicates that the affected internal representations are at a level of abstraction that is independent of the limb involved in producing the movements.

The ability to pantomime familiar tool or object use skills in response to a verbal command has long been considered a critical test for diagnosing apraxia because it isolates the retrieval of stored praxis representations in response to minimally informative stimuli. Several investigations have used functional neuroimaging to examine the neural mechanisms underlying the performance of this task (for reviews see Johnson-Frey 2004 and Lewis 2006). Consistent with lesion loci in apraxia (Haaland *et al*. 2000), retrieval and planning of these actions is consistently associated with increased activity in a distributed network of areas in the left cerebral hemisphere that includes a combination of areas within parietal, premotor, prefrontal and posterior temporal cortices (Moll *et al.* 2000; Choi *et al.* 2001; Ohgami *et al.* 2004; Rumiati *et al.* 2004; Johnson-Frey *et al.* 2005c; Fridman *et al.* 2006). This left cerebral asymmetry is observed regardless of whether the forthcoming actions involve the use of the left or right hands (Moll *et al.* 2000; Choi *et al.* 2001; Ohgami *et al.* 2004; Johnson-Frey *et al.* 2005c). By contrast, sensory–motor functions involved in actually pantomiming these skills are represented in a largely symmetrical system. Both hemispheres show increased activity in parietal and premotor areas when executing these actions, with pronounced engagement of the primary sensory–motor cortex contralateral to the involved limb (Johnson-Frey *et al.* 2005c).

2.3. The praxis representation network

Together, the patient and neuroimaging data converge on the hypothesis that functions involved in representing manual praxis skills are asymmetrically organized in the modern human brain. Retrieval and planning of these actions reliably activates a distributed network in the left cerebral hemisphere and damage in these areas frequently results in apraxia. Though several proposals have been offered on the basis of neuropsychological data (Rothi *et al.* 1991; Cubelli *et al.* 2000; Buxbaum 2001), a complete understanding of the processes taking place within this architecture is lacking.

An alternative approach is to consider what modifications to the sensory–motor control of prehension in primates might be necessary to accommodate human tool-use skills. A useful starting point is a computational model developed to explain how objects' visual affordances constrain the selection of grasping actions (Fagg & Arbib 1998). The foundation of the Fagg, Arbib, Rizzolatti and Sakata (FARS) model is anatomical and physiological data indicate that grasping actions are represented in a network consisting of interconnected areas of the macaque inferior parietal lobule and ventral premotor cortex (Rizzolatti & Matelli 2003). Parietal cortex is viewed as playing a critical role in selecting manual actions through the integration of multiple sources of information received from other regions distributed throughout the cerebral cortex. For instance, in addition to sensory information about objects' spatial attributes (e.g. form, size, orientation) and the properties of the hand and the arm, parietal cortex also receives input about the objects' identities from the inferotemporal cortex. Likewise, areas of the prefrontal cortex provide information on the prevailing task demands. These inputs bias the selection of an appropriate grasp representation in the parietal cortex, and this choice then determines which motor prototypes in the ventral premotor cortex are activated and passed to the primary motor cortex for execution.

Aspects of this framework can be extended to accommodate human praxis where the selection of actions is heavily influenced by cognition. This view is a departure from traditional conceptualizations of the left parietal cortex as a repository for stored praxis representations (for a history, see Leiguarda & Marsden 2000 and Goldenberg 2003). Instead, this region is cast in the role of dynamically assembling praxis representations to satisfy constraints that are provided by computations undertaken in a multitude of other brain regions. The exact computations, and thus the other brain areas involved, will be highly dependent on the particular demands of the task (i.e. context dependent) that, as illustrated earlier for the use of a hammer, often evolve through time. Tool-use pantomime, for instance, requires access to conceptual knowledge of manipulable objects and their functions, and the left posterior temporal cortex appears to play a role in representing this information (Damasio *et al.* 2001; Mahon *et al.* 2007; Martin 2007). Likewise, the relationship between a verbally cued object and any associated movements is arbitrary, and the dorsal premotor cortex is involved in representing these conditional stimulus–response associations (Grafton *et al.* 1998; Picard & Strick 2001). The middle frontal gyrus may likewise contribute information pertaining to the actor's prospective goals (Duncan & Owen 2000; Rowe *et al.* 2000; Buccino *et al.* 2004). If visual objects were provided as cues, then areas of the fusiform gyrus in the temporal cortex involved in coding object's visual properties would be engaged (Chao *et al.* 1999), and so forth. If this system is really so flexible, then it might be expected to also participate in constructing representations even of those meaningful praxis skills that do not involve using artefacts.

2.4. Tool use and communicative gestures

It is believed that advanced tool use preceded and may have played a role in the evolution of gestural communication (Bradshaw & Nettleton 1982; Gibson 1993). If so, then one might expect to find common neurological substrates involved in representing both types of praxis skills. Yet, the prevailing wisdom in neuropsychology is that acquired tool-use skills and communicative gestures involve two distinct representational systems (Rothi *et al.* 1991; Cubelli *et al.* 2000; Buxbaum 2001). This view is based on observations that apraxic patients who falter at tool-use pantomime are often less impaired (Roy *et al.* 1991; Foundas *et al.* 1999), or completely unaffected (Rapcsak *et al.* 1993; Dumont *et al.* 1999), when performing communicative gestures (e.g. waving hello). To date, only a single neuroimaging study has attempted to identify areas involved in representing these skills (Fridman *et al.* 2006). Given the data from brain-lesioned patients, it is surprising that no differences were detected in the parietal cortex. Instead, only the left ventral premotor cortex responded more when planning tool-use actions versus communicative gestures. The interpretation of these findings is challenging due to the fact that only the right hand was tested. The difference in the left ventral premotor cortex could be specific to the use of the contralateral right hand, for example.

Recently, we revisited this issue (Kroliczak & Frey 2007). The brain activity of 12 healthy right-handed adults was monitored by functional magnetic resonance imaging (fMRI) while they retrieved stored praxis representations in response to randomly ordered verbs denoting familiar tool-use actions (e.g. 'cutting') or communicative gestures (e.g. 'beckoning'). In conditions designed to control for linguistic stimulus processing, participants were presented with verbs denoting familiar mental actions (e.g. 'believing'). On each trial, they were instructed to read the stimulus word and, in the case of verbs denoting physical actions, prepare to undertake the associated movements using either their right (experiment 1) or left (experiment 2) hands. After a variable length delay interval, they were cued to reproduce the planned actions gently, taking care not to destabilize their heads. As in the previous studies introduced above, we found that retrieving and planning transitive actions for subsequent production with either hand increased activity in the left parietal, dorsal premotor, middle frontal and posterior temporal cortices (figure 2.1). Importantly, these very same areas showed increased activity when retrieving and planning intransitive gestures for subsequent production with either limb. In fact, no brain areas showed significantly greater activity when planning either behaviour relative to the other. That apraxic patients are sometimes less affected when performing communicative gestures may indicate that tool-use pantomime is simply a task that places more demands on this system, perhaps because it requires participants to represent both the absent objects (a key piece of contextual information) and the associated actions.

These findings are also important in that they provide neurological evidence consistent with hypothesized links between the origins of tool use and language (Greenfield 1991), including the suggestion that tool use may have played a causal role in the evolution of gestural communication (Bradshaw & Nettleton 1982; Gibson 1993). The acquisition of these behaviours, particularly through imitation (Buccino *et al.* 2004) and/or observational (Frey & Gerry 2006) learning, may involve Broca's area. Yet, contrary to what might be expected on the basis of previous models (Greenfield 1991), we find no evidence to suggest that Broca's area is a critical substrate for representing these skills once established, at least not in the adult modern human brain (figure 2.1). Instead, the neural overlap between tool use and communicative gestures is actually much more extensive and distributed. As for why this might be, an interesting possibility to consider hinges on the fact that both classes of behaviour can be viewed as goal-directed, manipulative acts. Rather than affecting inanimate objects through direct application of force, communicative gestures often target individuals in whom we hope to evoke a certain behavioural response. Gallagher & Frith (2004) found that observing such instrumental gestures activated many of these same left-lateralized areas, while observing gestures that expressed the actor's internal emotional state engaged a distinct network in regions of temporal and para-cingulate cortices implicated in mentalizing tasks. Though our lack of cues for expressive gestures in the present experiments precludes us from addressing this issue, whether or not such a dissociation is observed when retrieving representations for subsequent production is an interesting question for future work.

All of the studies discussed thus far have exclusively involved right-handed (i.e. left-hemisphere motor dominant) individuals. Whether or not a similar pattern of left cerebral asymmetry is present in lefthanders is a question whose answer could shed additional light on the origins and nature of the praxis system.

2.5. Hand dominance and praxis

Other primates do show hand preferences under certain circumstances (Hopkins & Pearson 2000; Hopkins & Russell 2004). Yet, none are known to display the population-level bias evident in humans where approximately 90% of individuals consistently favour their right hand for fine motor tasks (Coren & Porac 1977; Annett 2006). Evidence from the fossil and archaeological records suggests that this right-hand (i.e. left-hemisphere) bias for manual control existed very early in our lineage (Steele 2006). Our understanding of the relationship between hand dominance and acquired praxis skills at the neurological level is, however, incomplete.

One possibility is that our right-hand dominance is a reflection of the left-lateralized system for representing manual praxis (Geschwind & Galaburda 1985; Heilman 1997). It could also be true that hand dominance and praxis rely on separable mechanisms, but that there is an advantage to having them co-located in the same cerebral hemisphere. This arrangement would, for example, eliminate the need for interhemispheric transfer by

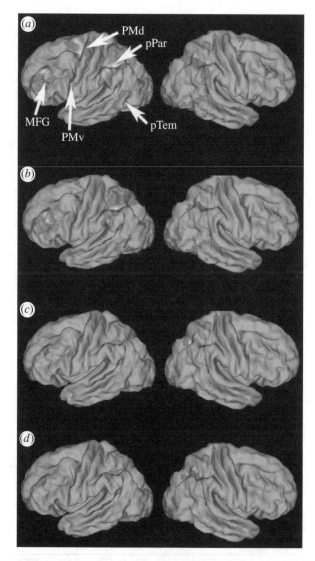

Figure 2.1. Brain areas in healthy right-handed adults which show increased activity relative to resting baseline when planning familiar tool-use pantomimes or communicative gestures. To facilitate visualization, activation maps are displayed on a partially unfolded template brain. (*a*) Planning tool-use pantomimes for production with the right hand is associated with greater activity in the left posterior parietal (pPar), dorsal (PMd) and ventral (PMv) premotor cortices, middle frontal gyrus (MFG) and frontal and posterior temporal (pTem) cortices. Effects are smaller in the homologous regions of the right cerebral hemisphere. (*b*) A similar network is engaged when planning communicative gestures for production with the right hand. Though less pronounced, these same areas also show increased activity when planning (*c*) tool-use pantomimes or (*d*) communicative gestures for production with the left hand. Please see colour plate section for a colour version of this figure.

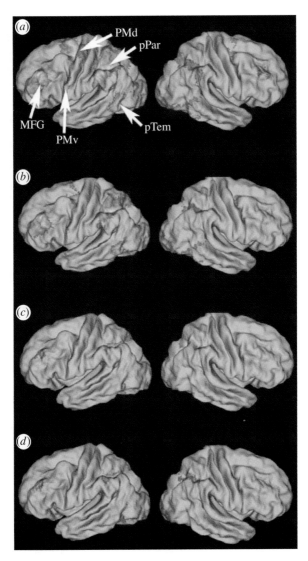

Figure 2.1. Brain areas in healthy right-handed adults which show increased activity relative to resting baseline when planning familiar tool-use pantomimes or communicative gestures. To facilitate visualization, activation maps are displayed on a partially unfolded template brain. (*a*) Planning tool-use pantomimes for production with the right hand is associated with greater activity in the left posterior parietal (pPar), dorsal (PMd) and ventral (PMv) premotor cortices, middle frontal gyrus (MFG) and frontal and posterior temporal (pTem) cortices. Effects are smaller in the homologous regions of the right cerebral hemisphere. (*b*) A similar network is engaged when planning communicative gestures for production with the right hand. Though less pronounced, these same areas also show increased activity when planning (*c*) tool-use pantomimes or (*d*) communicative gestures for production with the left hand.

allowing praxis representations to be accessed directly by areas in the left hemisphere which are involved in controlling distal movements of the contralateral right hand. In either case, these hypotheses predict a strong linkage between hand dominance and praxis skills. Accordingly, left-handers should represent acquired manual skills in their motor dominant right hemispheres. Evidence is surprisingly scarce. While it is true that some left-handers do show signs of apraxia following right hemisphere lesions (Poeck & Kerschensteiner 1971; Valenstein & Heilman 1979; Dobato *et al.* 2001), the same can be said for some right-handed patients (Marchetti & Della Sala 1997; Raymer *et al.* 1999). On the neuroimaging side, left-handed participants do show greater recruitment of right parietal, frontal and temporal cortices than right-handers when listening to the sounds made by using handheld tools versus animals, and this might reflect automatic activation of right-lateralized praxis representations (Lewis *et al.* 2006).

Alternatively, it could be that the mechanisms responsible for hand dominance and praxis are relatively independent (Lausberg *et al.* 1999). If so, then most left-handers should also represent praxis skills in their left hemispheres. This view receives support from a large study of adults undergoing unilateral inactivation of the cerebral hemispheres presurgically (i.e. Wada testing). Results indicate that the ability to pantomime actions is more closely associated with the laterality of language functions than hand dominance (Meador *et al.* 1999). Over 90% of right-handers are also left-hemisphere dominant for language (Knecht *et al.* 2000*a*). In left-handers, there is greater variability with approximately 70% showing left-hemisphere dominance and the rest displaying either a bilateral or right-lateralized organization (Kimura 1983; Knecht *et al.* 2000*b*). Additional support for the separation of mechanisms involved in praxis and hand dominance can be found in our earlier investigations of tool-use pantomime in left-and right-handed patients who had undergone complete surgical transections of the corpus callosum to treat medically intractable epilepsy (i.e. 'split brain' surgery; Johnson-Frey 2005*a*). Both individuals in the study are left-hemisphere dominant for language. Despite their handedness differences, both were also found to be most accurate when stimuli were presented to their isolated left hemispheres and pantomimes were produced with their right hands.

We recently completed an fMRI project using the same procedure described above to look at the representation of familiar tool-use actions and communicative gestures in a sample of strongly left-handed individuals. The preliminary results are largely similar to those of the right-handed individuals discussed earlier. Retrieving and planning both types of actions was associated with increased activity within the same left-lateralized regions. Along with our earlier split brain results, these findings suggest that, in modern humans, praxis representations and hand dominance may rely on relatively independent neurological mechanisms.

2.6. Summary

Though difficult to investigate through the fossil record, the manual skills involved in using complex tools and other manipulable artefacts are a key component of human material culture. Determining the brain mechanisms that underlie these human specializations has the potential to yield critical insights into their origins, and the methods of cognitive neuroscience make such inquiry possible in the modern human brain. I have argued that sensory– motor adaptations in systems that control prehension are necessary, but not sufficient to explain the complex and flexible ways in which humans routinely use tools and other manipulable artefacts. These praxis behaviours are influenced as well by cognitive processes that provide contextual information beyond what is available to the senses. Conceptual knowledge about objects and their functions, the actors' goals and interpretations of task demands all influence the selection of these praxis behaviours. Evidence from apraxic patients and functional neuroimaging studies converge on the hypothesis that the human left cerebral hemisphere is asymmetrically involved in the processes that make this possible. Rather than serving as a repository for skill memories, the left parietal cortex is said to assemble praxis representations dynamically in order to fit the multiple constraints provided by a variety of computations distributed throughout the left hemisphere and possibly beyond. The result is the formation of an internal praxis representation that can be used to guide contextually appropriate actions. There are reasons to believe that critical aspects of this system are organized similarly in both right-and left-handed individuals, and therefore these functions may be relatively independent of those responsible for hand dominance. Furthermore, the very same brain areas involved in representing familiar tool-use skills also show increased activity when retrieving and planning communicative gestures. This is consistent with the hypothesis that human specializations for tool use and language have common origins.

This research was conducted with approval from the Institutional Review Board at the University of Oregon.

S.H.F. has also published as 'Scott H. Johnson and Scott H. Johnson-Frey'. This work was supported by a grant (NS053962) from the NIH/NINDS. The author thanks Gregory Kroliczak for his assistance with figure preparation.

References

Ambrose, S. H. 2001 Paleolithic technology and human evolution. *Science* **291**, 1748–1753. (doi:10.1126/science.1059487)

Annett, M. 2006 The distribution of handedness in chimpanzees: estimating right shift in Hopkins' sample. *Laterality* **11**, 101–109.

Basalla, G. 1988 *The evolution of technology*. New York, NY: Cambridge University Press.

Blake, A., Brady, J. M. & Blake, A. 1992 Computational modeling of hand eye coordination. *Phil. Trans. R. Soc. B* **337**, 351–360. (doi:10.1098/rstb.1992.0113)

Bradshaw, J. L. & Nettleton, N. C. 1982 Language lateralization to the dominant hemisphere: tool use, gesture and language in hominid evolution. *Curr. Psychol. Rev.* **2**, 171–192. (doi:10.1007/BF02684498)

Buccino, G., Vogt, S., Ritzl, A., Fink, G. R., Zilles, K., Freund, H. J. & Rizzolatti, G. 2004 Neural circuits underlying imitation learning of hand actions: an event-related fMRI study. *Neuron* **42**, 323–334. (doi:10.1016/S0896-6273(04)00181-3)

Buxbaum, L. J. 2001 Ideomotor apraxia: a call to action. *Neurocase* **7**, 445–458. (doi:10.1093/neucas/7.6.445)

Chao, L. L., Haxby, J. V. & Martin, A. 1999 Attribute-based neural substrates in temporal cortex for perceiving and knowing about objects. *Nat. Neurosci.* **2**, 913–919. (doi:10.1038/13217)

Choi, S. H., Na, D. L., Kang, E., Lee, K. M., Lee, S. W. & Na, D. G. 2001 Functional magnetic resonance imaging during pantomiming tool-use gestures. *Exp. Brain Res.* **139**, 311–317. (doi:10.1007/s002210100777)

Coren, S. & Porac, C. 1977 Fifty centuries of right-handedness: the historical record. *Science* **198**, 631–632. (doi:10.1126/science.335510)

Cubelli, R., Marchetti, C., Boscolo, G. & Della Sala, S. 2000 Cognition in action: testing a model of limb apraxia. *Brain Cogn.* **44**, 144–165. (doi:10.1006/brcg.2000.1226)

Damasio, H., Grabowski, T. J., Tranel, D., Ponto, L. L., Hichwa, R. D. & Damasio, A. R. 2001 Neural correlates of naming actions and of naming spatial relations. *Neuroimage* **13**, 1053–1064. (doi:10.1006/nimg.2001. 0775)

Dobato, J. L., Baron, M., Barriga, F. J., Pareja, J. A., Vela, L. & Sanchez Del Rio, M. 2001 Apraxia cruzada secundaria a infarto parietal derecho. *Rev. Neurol.* **33**, 725–728.

Dumont, C., Ska, B. & Schiavetto, A. 1999 Selective impairment of transitive gestures: an unusual case of apraxia. *Neurocase* **5**, 447–458.

Duncan, J. & Owen, A. M. 2000 Common regions of the human frontal lobe recruited by diverse cognitive demands. *Trends Neurosci.* **23**, 475–483. (doi:10.1016/ S0166-2236(00)01633-7)

Fagg, A. H. & Arbib, M. A. 1998 Modeling parietal– premotor interactions in primate control of grasping. *Neural Netw.* **11**, 1277–1303. (doi:10.1016/S0893-6080 (98)00047-1)

Foundas, A. L., Macauley, B. L., Raymer, A. M., Maher, L. M., Rothi, L. J. & Heilman, K. M. 1999 Ideomotor apraxia in Alzheimer disease and left hemisphere stroke: limb transitive and intransitive movements. *Neuropsychiatry Neuropsychol. Behav. Neurol.* **12**, 161–166.

Frey, S. H. & Gerry, V. E. 2006 Modulation of neural activity during observational learning of actions and their sequential orders. *J. Neurosci.* **26**, 13 194–13 201. (doi:10.1523/JNEUROSCI. 3914-06.2006)

Fridman, E. A., Immisch, I., Hanakawa, T., Bohlhalter, S., Waldvogel, D., Kansaku, K., Wheaton, L., Wu, T. & Hallett, M. 2006 The role of the dorsal stream for gesture production. *Neuroimage* **29**, 417–428. (doi:10.1016/ j.neuroimage.2005.07.026)

Gallagher, H. L. & Frith, C. D. 2004 Dissociable neural pathways for the perception and recognition of expressive and instrumental gestures. *Neuropsychologia* **42**, 1725–1736. (doi:10.1016/ j.neuropsychologia.2004.05.006)

Geschwind, N. & Galaburda, A. M. 1985 Cerebral lateralization. Biological mechanisms, associations, and pathology: I. A hypothesis and a program for research. *Arch. Neurol.* **42**, 428–459.

Geschwind, N. & Kaplan, E. A. 1962 Human cerebral disconnection syndromes. *Neurology* **12**, 675–685.

Gibson, K. R. 1993 The evolution of lateral asymmetries, language, tool-use, and intellect (eds J. Bradshaw & L. Rogers). *Am. J. Phys. Anthropol.* **92**, 123–124.

Goldenberg, G. 2003 Apraxia and beyond: life and work of Hugo Liepmann. *Cortex* **39**, 509–524.

Goodale, M. A., Meenan, J. P., Bulthoff, H. H., Nicolle, D. A., Murphy, K. J. & Racicot, C. I. 1994 Separate neural pathways for the visual analysis of object shape in perception and prehension. *Curr. Biol.* **4**, 604–610. (doi:10.1016/S0960-9822(00)00132-9)

Grafton, S. T., Fagg, A. H. & Arbib, M. A. 1998 Dorsal premotor cortex and conditional movement selection: a PET functional mapping study. *J. Neurophysiol.* **79**, 1092–1097.

Greenfield, P. M. 1991 Language, tools, and brain—the ontogeny and phylogeny of hierarchically organized sequential behaviour. *Behav. Brain Sci.* **14**, 531–550.

Grefkes, C. & Fink, G. R. 2005 The functional organization of the intraparietal sulcus in humans and monkeys. *J. Anat.* **207**, 3–17. (doi:10.1111/j.1469-7580.2005. 00426.x)

Haaland, K. Y., Harrington, D. L. & Knight, R. T. 2000 Neural representations of skilled movement. *Brain* **123**, 2306–2313. (doi:10.1093/brain/123.11.2306)

Heilman, K. M. 1997 Handedness. In *Apraxia: the neuropsychology of action* (eds L. J. G. Rothi & K. M. Heilman), pp. 19–28. Hove, UK: Psychology Press.

Heilman, K. M. & Rothi, L. J. G. 1997 Limb apraxia: a look back. In *Apraxia: the neuropsychology of action* (eds L. J. G. Rothi & K. M. Heilman), pp. 7–18. Hove, UK: Psychology Press.

Hopkins, W. D. & Pearson, K. 2000 Chimpanzee (*Pan troglodytes*) handedness: variability across multiple measures of hand use. *J. Comp. Psychol.* **114**, 126–135. (doi:10.1037/0735-7036.114.2.126)

Hopkins, W. D. & Russell, J. L. 2004 Further evidence of a right hand advantage in motor skill by chimpanzees (*Pan troglodytes*). *Neuropsychologia* **42**, 990–996. (doi:10.1016/ j.neuropsychologia.2003.11.017)

Iriki, A., Tanaka, M. & Iwamura, Y. 1996 Coding of modified body schema during tool use by macaque postcentral neurones. *Neuroreport* **7**, 2325–2330.

Johnson-Frey, S. H. 2003 What's so special about human tool use? *Neuron* **39**, 201–204. (doi:10.1016/S0896-6273(03)00424-0)

Johnson-Frey, S. H. 2004 The neural bases of complex tool use in humans. *Trends Cogn. Sci.* **8**, 71–78. (doi:10.1016/j.tics.2003.12.002)

Johnson-Frey, S. H., Funnell, M. G., Gerry, V. E. & Gazzaniga, M. S. 2005*a* A dissociation between tool use skills and hand dominance: insights from left and right-handed callosotomy patients. *J. Cogn. Neurosci.* **17**, 262–272. (doi:10.1162/0898929053124974)

Johnson-Frey, S. H., Vinton, D., Norlund, R. N. & Grafton, S. G. 2005*b* Cortical topography of the human anterior intraparietal area. *Cogn. Brain Res.* **23**, 397–405. (doi:10.1016/j.cogbrainres.2004.11.010)

Johnson-Frey, S. H., Newman-Norlund, R. & Grafton, S. T. 2005*c* A distributed left hemisphere network active during planning of everyday tool use skills. *Cereb. Cortex* **15**, 681–695. (doi:10.1093/cercor/bhh169)

Kimura, D. 1983 Speech representation in an unbiased sample of left-handers. *Hum. Neurobiol.* **2**, 147–154.

Knecht, S., Deppe, M., Drager, B., Bobe, L., Lohmann, H., Ringelstein, E. & Henningsen, H. 2000*a* Language lateralization in healthy right-handers. *Brain* **123**, 74–81. (doi:10.1093/brain/123.1.74)

Knecht, S., Drager, B., Deppe, M., Bobe, L., Lohmann, H., Floel, A., Ringelstein, E. B. & Henningsen, H. 2000*b* Handedness and hemispheric language dominance in healthy humans. *Brain* **123**, 2512–2518. (doi:10.1093/brain/123.12.2512)

Kroliczak, G. & Frey, S. H. 2007 Role of left parietal cortex in representation of familiar transitive and intransitive manual actions. In *Thirteenth Annual Meeting of the Organization for Human Brain Mapping, Chicago*.

Lausberg, H., Gottert, R., Munssinger, U., Boegner, F. & Marx, P. 1999 Callosal disconnection syndrome in a left-handed patient due to infarction of the total length of the corpus callosum. *Neuropsychologia* **37**, 253–265. (doi:10.1016/S0028-3932(98)00079-7)

Leiguarda, R. C. & Marsden, C. D. 2000 Limb apraxias: higher-order disorders of sensorimotor integration. *Brain* **123**, 860–879. (doi:10.1093/brain/123.5.860)

Lewis, J. W. 2006 Cortical networks related to human use of tools. *Neuroscientist* **12**, 211–231. (doi:10.1177/1073858406288327)

Lewis, J. W., Phinney, R. E., Brefczynski-Lewis, J. A. & DeYoe, E. A. 2006 Lefties get it "right" when hearing tool sounds. *J. Cogn. Neurosci.* **18**, 1314–1330. (doi:10.1162/jocn.2006.18.8.1314)

Mahon, B. Z., Milleville, S. C., Negri, G. A., Rumiati, R. I., Caramazza, A. & Martin, A. 2007 Action-related properties shape object representations in the ventral stream. *Neuron* **55**, 507–520. (doi:10.1016/j.neuron.2007.07.011)

Marchetti, C. & Della Sala, S. 1997 On crossed apraxia. Description of a right-handed apraxic patient with right supplementary motor area damage. *Cortex* **33**, 341–354.

Martin, A. 2007 The representation of object concepts in the brain. *Annu. Rev. Psychol.* **58**, 25–45. (doi:10.1146/annurev.psych.57.102904.190143)

Meador, K. J., Loring, D. W., Lee, K., Hughes, M., Lee, G., Nichols, M. & Heilman, K. M. 1999 Cerebral lateralization: relationship of language and ideomotor praxis. *Neurology* **53**, 2028–2031.

Moll, J., de Oliveira-Souza, R., Passman, L. J., Cunha, F. C., Souza-Lima, F. & Andreiuolo, P. A. 2000 Functional MRI correlates of real and imagined tool-use pantomimes. *Neurology* **54**, 1331–1336.

Ohgami, Y., Matsuo, K., Uchida, N. & Nakai, T. 2004 An fMRI study of tool-use gestures: body part as object and pantomime. *Neuroreport* **15**, 1903–1906. (doi:10.1097/00001756-200408260-00014)

Orban, G. A., Van Essen, D. & Vanduffel, W. 2004 Comparative mapping of higher visual areas in monkeys and humans. *Trends Cogn. Sci.* **8**, 315–324. (doi:10.1016/j.tics.2004.05.009)

Picard, N. & Strick, P. L. 2001 Imaging the premotor areas. *Curr. Opin. Neurobiol.* **11**, 663–672. (doi:10.1016/S0959-4388(01)00266-5)

Poeck, K. & Kerschensteiner, M. 1971 Ideomotor apraxia following right-sided cerebral lesion in a left-handed subject. *Neuropsychologia* **9**, 359–361. (doi:10.1016/0028-3932(71)90032-7)

Povinelli, D. J. 2000 *Folk physics for apes: the chimpanzee's theory of how the world works*. New York, NY: Oxford University Press.

Preuss, T. M., Stepniewska, I. & Kaas, J. H. 1996 Movement representation in the dorsal and ventral premotor areas of owl monkeys: a microstimulation study. *J. Comp. Neurol.* **371**, 649–676. (doi:10.1002/(SICI)1096-9861 (19960805) 371:4<649::AID-CNE12>3.0.CO;2-E)

Rapcsak, S. Z., Ochipa, C., Beeson, P. M. & Rubens, A. B. 1993 Praxis and the right hemisphere. *Brain Cogn.* **23**, 181–202. (doi:10.1006/brcg.1993.1054)

Raymer, A. M., Merians, A. S., Adair, J. C., Schwartz, R. L., Williamson, D. J., Rothi, L. J., Poizner, H. & Heilman, K. M. 1999 Crossed apraxia: implications for handedness. *Cortex* **35**, 183–199.

Rizzolatti, G. & Craighero, L. 2004 The mirror-neuron system. *Annu. Rev. Neurosci.* **27**, 169–192. (doi:10.1146/ annurev.neuro.27.070203.144230)

Rizzolatti, G. & Matelli, M. 2003 Two different streams form the dorsal visual system: anatomy and functions. *Exp. Brain Res.* **153**, 146–157. (doi:10.1007/s00221-0031588-0)

Rothi, L. J., Ochipa, C. & Heilman, K. M. 1991 A cognitive neuropsychological model of limb praxis. *Cogn. Neuropsychol.* **8**, 443–458. (doi:10.1080/02643299108253382)

Rowe, J. B., Toni, I., Josephs, O., Frackowiak, R. S. & Passingham, R. E. 2000 The prefrontal cortex: response selection or maintenance within working memory? *Science* **288**, 1656–1660. (doi:10.1126/science.288. 5471.1656)

Roy, E. A., Square-Storer, P., Hogg, S. & Adams, S. 1991 Analysis of task demands in apraxia. *Int. J. Neurosci.* **56**, 177–186. (doi:10.3109/00207459108985414)

Rumiati, R. I., Weiss, P. H., Shallice, T., Ottoboni, G., Noth, J., Zilles, K. & Fink, G. R. 2004 Neural basis of pantomiming the use of visually presented objects. *Neuroimage* **21**, 1224–1231. (doi:10.1016/j.neuroimage.2003. 11.017)

Steele, J. U. N. 2006 Humans, tools and handedness. In *Stone knapping: the necessray conditions for a uniquely hominin behaviour* (eds V. Roux & B. Bril), pp. 217–239. Cambridge, UK: MacDonald Institute.

Tomasello, M. 1999 The human adaptation for culture. *Annu. Rev. Anthropol.* **28**, 509–529. (doi:10.1146/annurev. anthro.28.1.509)

Umiltà, M. A., Escola, L., Intskirveli, I., Grammont, F., Rochat, M., Caruana, F., Jezzini, A., Gallese, V. & Rizzolatti, G. 2008 When pliers become fingers in the monkey motor system. *Proc. Natl Acad. Sci. USA* **105**, 2209–2213. (doi:10.1073/pnas.0705985105)

Valenstein, E. & Heilman, K. M. 1979 Apraxic agraphia with neglect-induced paragraphia. *Arch. Neurol.* **36**, 506–508.

3

Biology is only part of the story

Dwight Read and Sander van der Leeuw

The origins and development of human cognition constitute one of the most interesting questions to which archaeology can contribute today. In this paper, we do so by presenting an overview of the evolution of artefact technology from the maker's point of view, and linking that development to some hypotheses on the evolution of human cognitive capacity. Our main hypothesis is that these data indicate that, in the first part of the trajectory, biological limits to cognitive capacity were a major constraint that limited technology, whereas, in the second part, this biological constraint seems to have been lifted and others have come in its place. But these are modifiable by means of conceptual frameworks that facilitate concept innovation and therefore enable learning, thereby permitting acceleration in the pace of change in technology. In the last part of the paper, we elaborate on some of the consequences of that acceleration.

Keywords: cognition; artefact technology; innovation; evolution; cognitive constraints

3.1. Introduction

In this paper, we are interested in extrapolating from what we know about the development of prehistoric technologies to the evolution of human cognition. Our interest is driven by the following (unsolved) questions concerning the history of human technology:

(i) Given that primates, for millions of years, have made and used simple tools, but have not developed any complex technologies, what is different about human beings that enabled them to develop the latter?
(ii) Are the enabling factors biological, are they social/cultural or are they a bit of both?
(iii) When was that capacity acquired? Was that the result of a sudden change, an incremental one or a more complex process that combined both?
(iv) Why did it take so long to 'invent' and accelerate innovation?
(v) Why did the rate of innovation increase so rapidly, once that point was reached?

3.2. Part one: from primates to modern humans

Numerous authors (e.g. Stout *et al.* 2000 and references therein) have argued that changes in the technology of artefact production and in artefact form, variety and diversity relate to cognitive changes, but what constitutes those cognitive changes has remained unclear due to our as yet imprecise understanding of how the brain functions. Some suggestions have been made, which are as follows: Ambrose (2001, p. 1751), for example, argues that the composite tools which appear *ca* 300 kyr BP may relate to language development since

Electronic supplementary material is available at http://dx.doi.org/10.1098/rstb.2008.0002 or via http://journals.royalsociety.org

'explaining how to make one is the equivalent of a recipe or short story' (see also electronic supplementary material, section1).

Others (Coolidge & Wynn 2005) have pointed to the role of working memory (Baddeley & Hitch 1974; Baddeley 1986) for understanding the development of complex artefacts.[1] Working memory integrates (episodic, conscious) short-term memory with (declarative and procedural, preconscious and non-conscious) long-term memory through a central executive (intentionality) that involves 'the ability to maintain memory representations in a highly-active (conscious) state ... [that] consist of plans of action, short- or long-term goals, or task-relevant stimuli' (cf. Engle *et al.*1999*a*; Kane & Engle 2000, 2002; Coolidge & Wynn 2005, p. 8).

Neurologically, it is located in the prefrontal and parietal cortices and in areas of the sensory cortex (Miller 2000; Fuster 2001, 2002; Pasternak & Green-lee 2005). The prefrontal cortex is relatively much larger in humans than in non-human primates (Semendeferi *et al.* 2001) and changes in skull morphology towards a high forehead and non-prognathic face enables the expansion of the prefrontal cortex (Lieberman *et al.* 2002). Hence, the expansion of the relevant brain areas leading to increased working memory is consistent with evolutionary changes in hominid morphology. Moreover, Fuster (2001) argues that the prefrontal cortex is the area of the brain that links memory of the past to perception of the present and anticipation of the future, and that it is therefore the area where 'choice' resides.

Coolidge & Wynn (2005) have addressed recent expansion in the capacity of working memory for modern *Homo sapiens* by suggesting that genetic mutation expanded less-developed working memory into 'enhanced working memory (EWM)'—comparable to the working memory of modern-day humans—certainly by 13 kyr BP, most probably by 30 kyr BP and possibly as far back as 80 kyr BP. Coolidge & Wynn consider four kinds of evidence for EWM: (i) contingency planning, (ii) innovative plans of action, (iii) temporally remote action, and (iv) the use of cultural algorithms (p. 16). But they address only the genetic event for the appearance of EWM rather than the evolutionary sequence from an ancestral hominid with working memory comparable to that of chimpanzees to the vastly larger working memory of modern *H. sapiens*. We therefore compare the overall pattern of change in working memory, measured through the increase in the short-term working memory (STWM), with the pattern of change in the design of artefacts over the same time horizon.

(a) Working memory in chimpanzees (Pan paniscus)

We estimate the STWM in chimpanzees in two ways: directly based on performance of tasks and indirectly by examining individual development trajectories for working memory in modern *H. sapiens* from birth to puberty.

(i) Direct evidence

The data on nut cracking by chimpanzees are particularly informative. Nut cracking requires manipulation of three objects: an anvil; the nut; and a hammerstone (see also electronic supplementary material, section 2). Although chimpanzees observe each other cracking nuts, about one-quarter of them never learn to carry out the sequence involving the three objects, suggesting an STWM of size 2. Other data on token combinations, object manipulation, gesture combinations, as well as a study of number recall by a chimpanzee (taught to link number symbols with quantities) all suggest that their STWM is of the order of 2 ± 1 (see the review in Read 2006). This contrasts with an STWM of 7 ± 2 associated with modern humans.

(ii) Indirect evidence

Figure 3.1 shows the growth trajectory for working memory in modern *H. sapiens* based on a meta-analysis of several datasets and with STWM used for the units of the vertical axis (see also electronic supplementary material, section 3). The figure shows that, assuming that working memory develops at essentially the same rate in *Pan* as in *Homo*, the data on *Homo* imply that STWM = 2 is achieved at approximately 3–4 years of age, precisely the age period for which nut-cracking behaviour begins to appear (when it appears!) in *Pan*. Thus, the indirect evidence on STWM for *Pan* is consistent with assigning STWM = 2 to *Pan*.

The difference in the time needed for the development of working memory accounts for the difference in STWM between *Pan* and *Homo*. In *Pan*, STWM increases only to approximately 2 at the age of puberty (approx. 3–4 years of age for *Pan* females; males reach puberty approx. 2–3 years later), whereas, for *Homo*, STWM increases to 7 at approximately 12 years of age. This difference between adult *Pan* and *Homo* individuals

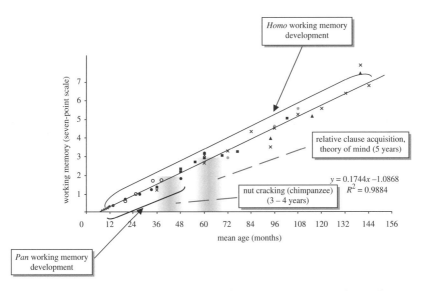

Figure 3.1. Trend line projected from the regression of time delay response (Diamond & Doar 1989) regressed on infant age. Data rescaled for each dataset to make the trend line pass through the mean of that dataset. Working memory scaled to STWM = 7 at 144 months. 'Fuzzy' vertical bars compare the age of nut cracking among chimpanzees with the age for relative clause acquisition and theory of mind conceptualization in humans. •, Imitation (Alp 1994); +, time delay (Diamond & Doar 1989); ×, number recall (Siegel & Ryan 1989); ×, total language score (Johnson *et al.* 1989); ×, relative clauses (Corrêa 1995); ■, count label, span (Carlson *et al.* 2002); ○, 6 month retest (Alp 1989); ▲, world recall (Siegel & Ryan 1989); ■, spatial recall (Kemps *et al.* 2000); ◦, relative clauses (Kidd & Bavin 2002); -, spatial working memory (Luciana & Nelson 1998); —, linear (time delay; Diamond & Doar 1989).

allows for conceptualizations by *Homo* which do not occur in *Pan*. 'Theory of mind',[2] for example, does not develop in *Homo* individuals until approximately 4–5 years of age when STWM = 3, and the same is true of relative clause acquisition. Theory of mind has been controversial as to whether it is (Hare *et al*. 2000, 2001; Premack & Premack 2000) or is not (Povinelli & Eddy 1996; Heyes 1998) present in *Pan*. STWM = 2 ± 1 would imply that it is not found in *Pan*.

Both theory of mind and relative clause acquisition require that a third concept must be active in working memory while the relationship between (at least) two concepts is being considered. To project an action onto another individual associated with one's own behaviour, for example, requires that one cognizes oneself doing the behaviour as well as another person as a possible actor for that behaviour. This would not be possible with STWM = 2. A similar comment applies to relative clause acquisition since it depends on recursive reasoning, and recursive reasoning is impossible with STWM = 2 (Read 2006).

These data imply that we can assume a STWM = 2 ± 1 for the beginning of artefact formation by either *Pan* or pre-*Homo*. A simple striking of one cobble with another as a way to fracture one of the cobbles could be done with STWM = 2. However, flaking requires a consistent striking angle of less than 90°, and therefore it requires that one does not only conceptualize how the two objects are to be manipulated, but also that one keeps the angle of percussion active in working memory. Moreover, part of the working memory load for nut cracking is 'scaffolded' by having the objects in the visual field and by observing other individuals cracking nuts, but the task of keeping the striking angle less than 90° cannot be scaffolded. One must therefore conclude that even though nut cracking is achievable by *Pan*, flaking is not.

(b) Changes in cognitive capacity reflected in artefacts

Systematic artefact production requires control, if not conceptualization, by the (human or non-human primate) knapper of the actions that constitute artefact production. For artefact production, we make a distinction between an (abstract) concept and the instantiation of that concept in a material form, in which the conceptual level reflects what must be cognized in order for the artefact to be instantiated. Instantiation—the process linking concept with material object—need not account for all possible features or attributes of the material object (Read 2007), as some properties are inherent to whatever technology is involved. Stone knapping, for example, will leave scars on the object from which flakes are removed through knapping even if the ensemble of flake scars is mechanical and not intentional.

(i) Geometric and topological categories of artefacts

The simplest representation of a concrete object combines its geometry and topology, as abstracted from the artefact as object. From the geometry, we can 'reverse engineer' the concept–instantiation–object sequence to infer what minimal concept would be necessary to account for the production of an object that instantiates that concept. We will follow Pigeot's (1991) argument that a combination of topological and simple geometric properties constitutes the conceptual system that has been instantiated. For example, Pigeot argues that an Oldowan chopper has the underlying geometry of a line with instantiation as the cutting edge of the chopper. The deviation of the actual edge from a line is due to iteratively removing flakes to induce an edge on an 'edge-less' cobble.

(ii) Time sequence for categories of artefacts
Since the size of STWM relates directly to the complexity of a sequence of actions that can be conceptualized and used to direct actions, we view the size of STWM as a cognitive constraint on the complexity of the artefacts that can be conceived and instantiated by the knapper until STWM = 7 had been reached during hominid evolution.[3] We suggest that the following time sequence for the appearance of categories of artefacts also reflects increased demand on STWM.

Stage i. Dimensionality: none (pre-hominid divergence)
(a) *Concept: object attribute; action: repeated.* This category includes artefacts of which the functional attributes for the task at hand are already present on the object in its natural state. The object may be modified in order to enhance the attributes of interest prior to use. Modification may be repetitive. A chimpanzee's preparation of a small branch to be used for obtaining termites by removing its leaves and small side branches is a prototypical example (see also electronic supplementary material, section 4).
(b) *Concept: relationship between objects.* This category includes examples such as the use of anvil and hammerstone in nut cracking. The functionality depends on the relationship between the entity being acted upon (e.g. the nut) and the instrument(s) (e.g. the anvil and the hammerstone) used in the action (see also electronic supplementary material, section 5).

Stage ii. Concept: imposed attribute; action: repeated; dimensionality: zero-dimensional (unknown dating, above 2.6 Myr BP)
This category would include instances where the attribute(s) that give(s) the object its functionality is (are) not present in the natural state of the object but is (are) introduced through simple modification of the object. The object may be modified more than once through repetition, but multiple modifications can be performed in any order (see also electronic supplementary material, section 6).

Stage iii. Concept: flaking; action: repetition; dimensionality: zero-dimensional (2.6 Myr BP)
This category includes true flakes (rather than debris from breaking one rock with another). Flaking requires comprehension that the striking table has a substantial effect on the breaking pattern of a stone, and that an incident angle of less than 90° produces a fracture known as conchoidal fracturing that is the basis for stone tool knapping. More than one flake can be removed from the same 'core', especially if the flake is the intended consequence of the action and not the fracture pattern left on the core. No dimensionality is involved, as the only conceptualization required is of the form: incident angle < 90° → flake, and the shape of the flake is happenstance from the viewpoint of the action. The functionality of the flake arises from the fact that the edge of the flake produced in this manner is suitable for cutting or scraping tasks without further modification (see also electronic supplementary material, section 7).

We consider stage iii to place greater demands on STWM than stages i–ii. Beyond all the conceptual requirements of stages i–ii, the knapper also needs to control for the striking angle. Knapping can be repetitive, though there need not be any overall plan or design (see Delagnes & Roche 2005). The fact that the knappers at Lokalalei 1 were primarily producing simple *débitage* implies that the repetitive flaking at Lokalalei 2C was cognitively more demanding than the simple, repeated flaking at Lokalalei 1.

Stage iv. Concept: edge; action: iteration; dimensionality: one-dimensional
(2.0 Myr BP) = mode 1

The Oldowan industry and the Oldowan chopper, in particular, characterize stage iv. Whereas in stage iii, the core was the remnant of a cobble after flakes were removed, in the Oldowan industry, the core is the goal and the flakes removed may be incidental to this goal. This change in object versus remnant implies conceptual shift (van der Leeuw 2000). The core has the property that it 'may be modified by flaking' (van der Leeuw 2000, p. 75), whereas a flake cannot be flaked (it can be retouched, but that involves change in the scale for the flaking). The core conceptually shifts from being the remnant to the goal, and the flaking is aimed at producing functional edge. Rather than being formed by repetitive removal of flakes (as in the case of the Lokalalei 2C 'organized débitage'), in the Oldowan case, the goal is to produce an edge, and so each flake removal is dependent on the previous one: 'It appears that the initial trimming had a tyrannical control on later trimming. The first blow seems to have anchored the rest; concepts of proximity, boundary and order then extended the trimming from this starting point' (Wynn & McGrew 1989, p. 387). The edge is thus formed by conceptually transforming repetitive flaking into iterative flaking aimed at imposing an edge on part of the cobble, and it is this edge that gives the Oldowan chopper its functionality.

According to Wynn & McGrew (1989, p. 387), the flaking of the edge also had a topological consequence as it 'divided the spatial field of the cobble into two realms'. But in our opinion, that is not quite correct. While the edge begins to divide the total surface of the cobble into two, that division is not complete until the edge is self-intersecting. We are therefore observing an ambiguous situation: is the edge merely a 'line drawn on the (complex) surface of the cobble' (i.e. a one-dimensional feature) or is it the beginning of a two-dimensional approach that divides the cobble's surface into two separate surfaces intersected by a line? But such ambiguities are characteristic of all the transitions we are observing, such as the transformation of repetitive into iterative flaking, and that between knapping an intersecting edge that, in passing, encloses a surface and taking large flakes off a surface that then, in passing, produces an intersecting edge (see also electronic supplementary material, section 8).

Stage v. Dimensionality: two-dimensional

(a) *Concept: closed curve; action: iteration; edge as a generative element*

(1.5 Myr BP) = mode 2. The next step fundamentally changes the topology by the simple expedient of continuing the edge until it intersects itself to make a closed curve. What was an irregular 'natural' surface (of a cobble) with a line (the edge) imposed on it is transformed into two surfaces, each having the topology of a surface inside a line closed upon itself. Thus, the surface of the stone (including cortex) is now divided into two surfaces, each inside a closed curve, and whose intersection is the closed curve. This allows for the two surface portions to be modified through flaking, and thus opens the conceptual pathway to bifaces, and to hand axes whose two surfaces are extensively flaked. In effect, by closing the edge on itself, the geometry of the topology is changed from one- to two-dimensional (see also electronic supplementary material, section 9).

(b) *Concept: surface; action: iteration (500 kyr BP) = mode 2*. As noted by Wynn (2002), beginning *ca* a 500 kyr BP, hand axes shift from a focus on edges (where the surface is largely determined by flaking aimed at producing an edge) to a focus on two (top and bottom) surfaces bounded by an edge. The surface is no longer a 'residual category' but its shape and form becomes the intent of the knapping (Graves 1994). The shift is from *débitage* technology in which the flaking has to do with 'l'aménagement final d'un bord et de l'extrémité en outil' ('forming the edge and end of the tool'; Boëda 1991, p. 55) to *façonnage* technology in which the flaking is used to form a desired shape, in this case the shape of the biface: '*façonnage* is predominantly manifest as bifaces, *based around a plane of intersection separating two interdependent surfaces* that may be hierarchical or non-hierarchical, biconvex or plano-convex, depending on the precise operational chain and type of blank used (Boëda *et al.* 1990)', where 'the two surfaces are organized in relation to each other' (White & Ashton 2003, p. 604, emphasis added; see also electronic supplementary material, section 10).

Stage vi. Concept: surface; action: algorithm; dimensionality: two-dimensional (300 kyr BP) = mode 3
We suggest that a major conceptual shift occurs with the introduction of Levallois flaking in the Middle Palaeolithic. The surface as a concept instantiated in hand axes is formed using the same flake technology as occurs in earlier stages. The difference between the earlier approaches and Levallois knapping resides in a shift from viewing flaking as a means to produce an object or to form an edge, to viewing flaking as a means to form a surface through control over the location and angle of the flaking. The surface of the flake is now brought under the control of the knapper.

Moreover, this technique optimized the efficient knapping of surfaces by ensuring that removing one flake is at the same time the preparation for the next removal. Product and object are identified with each other in the knapper's conceptualization. The characterization of the Levallois method given by Boëda (1995) clearly shows the sense in which this method becomes an algorithm for the production of flakes, rather than simply a particular method for the removal of a flake (see figure B of the electronic supplementary material, section 11). It allows for repeated, but not recursive, application of the algorithm to the same core so as to produce a number of flakes whose characteristics are under the control of the knapper (see also electronic supplementary material, section 11).

The technique is, in Pigeot's (1991, pp. 184–186) view, the culmination of the development of control over flaking causing the shape of the original nodule to become less important.

Stage vii. Concept: intersection of planes; action: recursion; dimensionality: three-dimensional (less than 50 kyr BP) = mode 4
Prismatic blade technology replaces Levallois methods wherever it occurs (primarily North Africa, northern and western Asia and Europe; Bar-Yosef & Kuhn 1999), but is not a transformation of the latter. Boëda (1986), in a comparison of Levallois and Upper Palaeolithic nuclei, distinguishes the two technologies by arguing that the Levallois technology is based on two crosscutting surfaces that form a functional hierarchy. This limits productivity because the production of a predetermined flake is at the detriment of one of the two surfaces

(the 'true' Levallois surface), hence it recedes systematically during flake production (see also electronic supplementary material, section 12).

Prismatic blade technology, on the other hand, controls the flaking technique in such a way that the removal of a blade maintains the form of the core from which it is removed, so the next step simply acts on the output (the form of the core volume) of the previous step. Since the location of the next blade detachment is determined by the previous detachment and the previous detachment preserves the form of the core, the blade production process (namely begin with a striking surface at right angles to the exploited surface, then detach a blade of controlled width through percussion) is directly enacted on the core that is the output of the previous instance of blade production

Thus, what seems to be different about prismatic blade production is that it is based upon recursive application—to the core volume—of the algorithm that determines the process by which the blades are obtained: 'Each blade is produced *by the same process* as the one preceding it, a monotonous process. As with other skilled knapping, it also requires rhythm ...' (Clark 1987, p. 268, emphasis added). The Levallois method, in contrast, allows only for repetition since the surface from which a flake is to be detached must be reformed, thus the flake removal process must start anew for the next flake.

We suggest that the recursion of stage vii may be an exaptation of cognitive changes that had already led to neurological capacities of the brain that enabled recursive logic.

(c) Implications of the changes in working memory

(i) The relationship of technological change to change in STWM

Although we do not have any direct evidence on the relationship between encephalization and working memory, we can make the following indirect argument. Encephalization is presumed to relate to the ability to deal with more complex reasoning, among other capacities. There is a strong correlation between general fluid intelligence (reasoning and problem-solving ability) and working memory (Engle *et al.* 1999*b*; Engle 2002), hence we can assume that the STWM component of working memory and encephalization are correlated. Let us make the assumption that the relationship is linear as a first approximation (see also electronic supplementary material, section 13).

We can graph change in the encephalization quotient (EQ) during hominid evolution from a common ancestor with *Pan* and rescale the change in the EQ to a STWM scale, assuming STWM = 2 for *Pan* and STWMZ7 for modern *H. sapiens* (see the left and right vertical axes in figure 3.2). We can then determine the implied STWM for a fossil hominid group based on its estimated encephalization. Finally, we place a vertical 'fuzzy bar' (in order to emphasize measurement imprecision) at the estimated time for the appearance of each of stages iii–vii, based on archaeological and palaeontological data (figure 3.2).

(ii) Implications of change in STWM

We offer the following interpretation of changes in encephalization, STWM and stone tool technology over hominid evolution. Beginning with STWM = 2 for *Pan*, stage iii (control of flaking) occurs when STWM = 3, which is consistent with the fact that stage iii conceptually requires STWM = 3 as discussed previously. Stage iv (control of an edge) occurs after increased encephalization when STWM = 4, again consistent with the increased conceptualization involved in using iterative flaking to form an edge. Stage v

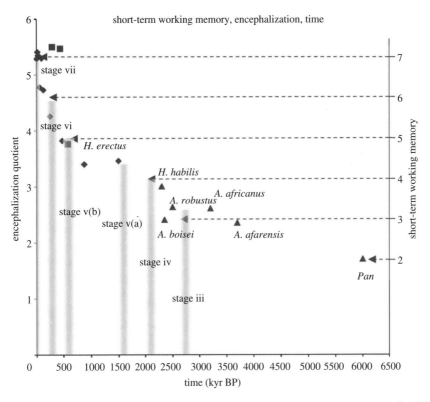

Figure 3.2. Graph of encephalization quotient (EQ) estimates based on hominid fossils and *Pan*. Early hominid fossils have been identified by taxon. Each data point is the mean for hominid fossils at that time period. Height of the 'fuzzy' vertical bars is the hominid EQ corresponding to the date for the appearance of the stage represented by the fuzzy bar. Right vertical axis represents STWM. Data are adapted from as follows: triangles, Epstein (2002); squares, Rightmire (2004); diamonds, Ruff *et al*. (2004). EQ = brain mass/($11.22 \times$ body mass$^{0.76}$) (Martin 1981).

(forming a closed boundary, hence a surface) occurs after a slight increase in encephalization and increase in STWM to STWM = 4.5, which is consistent with the argument we made previously that the change from stage iv to stage v is more of an elaboration on stage v (closure of an edge) rather than the introduction of a qualitatively new concept. Stage v(a) (conceptualization of a surface as a two-dimensional concept) occurs with STWM = 5, but this is only a small change from stage v (STWM ~ 4.5). The change from stage v to stage v(a) is thus conceptually not a major change. This is consistent with the change primarily from making a hand axe using the *débitage* technique to making a hand axe using *façonnage* technique. Stage vi (Levallois method) occurs after a period of rapid encephalization with STWM = 6, consistent with the Levallois method involving a new concept, namely an algorithmic approach to knapping based on the relationship between a solid and a method for flake removal, with producing the flake as the goal of the method. Finally, stage vii (prismatic blade technology, recursion) also occurs after a period of rapid encephalization with change in STWM to STWM = 7; that is, a change in STWM to the value that occurs in modern *H. sapiens*. Prismatic blade technology leads to a florescence of kinds and forms of stone tools, which appears to build off the level of conceptualization possible with working memory the same as it is for humans today. With respect to language, Coolidge & Wynn (2007, p. 709), for example, have postulated that 'enhanced working memory [working memory comparable to that of modern humans], by way of recursion, may have allowed the speaker to 'hold in mind' a much greater number of options, and as such, give the speaker a greater range of behavioural flexibility and even creativity' and suggest the origin of what they call EWM via a 'genetic neural mutation, sometime within the last 100,000 years' (p. 710), a conclusion consistent with the scenario we have postulated for the shift from stage vi to stage vii.

3.3. Part two: modern humans

Once this stage has been reached, there is no reason to impute further evolutions in working memory, but we see an 'innovative explosion' in the evolution of artefact technologies. In effect, if we observe the technologies developed in the last 25 000 years or so, we are quickly convinced that a threshold has been crossed, and that modern humans have entered a different era, in which a very different dynamic is occurring between humans and the material world. In the following sections we describe that transition and the first stages of the new dynamic. The sheer multitude of different kinds of artefacts and logical operations that emerge forces us to change our focus and the language we use. We have to move a level of generalization up and focus on rather broad categories of change, hence losing direct connection between specific sequences of manufacture and the conceptual operations they entail.

The hypothesis that we propose to explain this sudden acceleration in the pace of technological change is the fact that it is no longer constrained by the capacities of working memory. Indeed, even superficial observation of modern technologies, languages and other human achievements indicates that modern humans' current STWM of 7 seems adequate to deal with very complex operations indeed.

But that introduces other questions, such as 'are there other constraints that come into play?', 'what are some of the consequences of this acceleration?', etc. We will try to answer some of them along the way.

(a) New kinds of tools, new materials

(i) The end of the Upper Palaeolithic and Mesolithic (25–10 kyr BP)
During this period, we see numerous important new techniques emerge almost simultaneously.[4] One is the manufacture of 'microliths', small stone tools testifying to the control toolmakers have over finer and finer details in the production process and *extending the range by orders of magnitude for the volume* manipulated by toolmakers. These microliths occur in an increasingly wide range of shapes, which implies that there is a closer match between individual objects and their intended functions. Toolmakers must have acquired an improved capability to analyse the requirements their artefacts should meet in order to be most effective, and a *more versatile spatial topology*.

Although it is unlikely that this time period includes the first use of non-stone materials in tools, one now observes a substantive number of instances of the use of other materials (wood, bone, antler, etc.) alongside stone in making tools. This implies the development of a wide new range of (motor and other) skills and tools to work all of these materials.

A closely related innovation is the introduction of *composite tools*, consisting of a number of microliths hafted together in objects of wood or bone. This implies the *conceptual reversibility of scalar hierarchies*: not only are tools made by reducing a larger piece of stone into one or more small flakes, which are retouched to give them the required shape, but also these small pieces are then assembled into something larger.

(ii) The Neolithic (ca 10 000–7000 yr BP) New artefact making techniques

Beginning in the Neolithic, stone tools are transformed beyond recognition by the introduction of grinding. This development completes the mastery of stone—working scales going from the macro- to the microscopic. Neolithic stone axes and adzes are first roughly flaked out of appropriately fine-grained blocks of stone. Next, they are refined by removing smaller and smaller flakes. And finally, the toolmaker removes microscopically small particles by pecking or grinding. The resulting objects have a completely smooth surface, which can be as flat, rounded or irregular as desired. *Control over the final shape is complete, as is the use of different scales of removal from the initial stone block—from very large flakes to individual grains.*

The making of *containers* was introduced between 12 000 and 9000 yr BP (depending on the material and the world region), made of wood, leather, stone and pottery. In each case, the manufacturing technique is different. Nonetheless, some conceptual innovations are the same:

—The introduction of a different topology—a *surface around a void*. This requires the conceptual separation of the surface of an object from its volume, and making the distinction between the outside and inside surfaces. Neither is conceivable in the absence of a true three-dimensional conception of objects. Natural containers may have served as examples, but recreating them conceptually was nevertheless an important innovation.

—The inversion of the sequence of manufacturing—*beginning with the smallest particles and assembling them into larger objects*. In basketry and weaving, small fibres combine into longer and thicker strands and are then coiled or woven into two- or three-dimensional objects. Pottery making uses naturally coherent small particles, but early techniques combine them into long and thick linear objects (coils), and these into three-dimensional shapes.

—Closely related is the *correction of errors* by undoing work and returning to a point earlier in the manufacturing sequence. This presumes that *control loops link the past with the present and the future*, but also that *actions are conceived of as being reversible*.

—In the case of pottery, metallurgy and other complex techniques, the *separation between different stages of production* is pushed a step further. Resource procurement, paste preparation, shaping, decoration and firing occur sequentially, and the maker has to keep all these stages in mind during the whole process. This involves tracking a large number of embedded control loops in working memory.

A changing relationship with the environment
These and other conceptual advances opened up new realms of problem-solving and invention, including the transformation of subsistence risks—from a daily concern over which people had little control, to a seasonal or pluriannual concern over which they had a little more control. This was achieved

(i) by combining a mobile lifestyle with the breeding and herding of domesticated animals and/or the seasonal cultivation of wild plants, or
(ii) by sedentism and cultivating domesticated plants.

Spatially, this required a *two-dimensional 'map' of the landscape* and, in the case of cultivation, the conceptual distinctions between 'inside' and 'outside' marked by the perimeter of gardens or fields—as well as between 'self' and 'other', which was acquired as part of the conceptualization of kinship systems. *Temporally* speaking, cultivation and herding stretched the temporal sequences and temporally separate parts of a 'manufacturing' sequence much further than is the case in artefact manufacture.

When cultivating and herding, people no longer cull and harvest nature for their subsistence, but *intervene* and *invest* in their natural environment in the expectation that they can change it, even if only locally. This *limits the adaptive flexibility of the people involved*. Whereas gathering and hunting involve intermittent, almost instantaneous (albeit periodic) interactions between the temporalities of the natural environment and the rhythms of human subsistence needs, herding, cultivation and domestication necessarily involve a *longer-term conception of the symbiosis* between humans and their food sources. This in turn involves a change in the relationship between people and their environment from being reactive to the environment to being interactive with it.

Survival continues to depend on the adequacy of subsistence and survival techniques, but is no longer defined by just the capability to find and harvest wild resources. Increasingly, it is defined by the ability to control the environment through means such as

—simplifying the environment, for example by homogenizing it locally, replacing natural vegetation by more homogenous planted vegetation,
—optimizing and narrowing the range of dependencies on the natural environment, for example by focusing on particular crops or particular animals for subsistence, and
—diversifying technical know-how to closely match the resources available in the local and regional environment in which they live.

In this process, the coupling between humans and their environments became much tighter, initiating a true coevolution between the two. The investments made in the environment and in one's social and technological adaptation to it encouraged increased investment in known environments and subsistence strategies. But it thereby also introduced long-term risks inherent in following a single survival strategy, as well as the need to deal with those risks.

Increasing demographic aggregation
Consequently, problem-solving rather than moving to a new location became the key to survival. This set in motion another positive feedback loop in which problems prompted a search for solutions, leading to more problems, etc. This feedback loop explains in our eyes the exponential growth in both innovation and population density over the last 10 000 years,

---

Box 3.1.

Problem-solving structures knowledge → more knowledge increases the information processing capacity → this in turn allows the cognition of new problems → creates new knowledge → knowledge creation involves more and more people in processing information → enables and triggers increases in group size and degree of aggregation → these increases create more problems → augment the need for problem-solving → problem-solving structures more knowledge, etc.

---

which is summarized in box 3.1 (cf. van der Leeuw & McGlade 1997; van der Leeuw & Aschan-Leygonie 2005):

The result is the continued accumulation of knowledge, and thus of information processing capacity, *enabling* a concomitant increase in matter, energy and information flows through the society, the growth in the number of people participating in that society and the subsequent need to reduce the time involved in communication which, in our opinion, led to urbanization (cf. Read & LeBlanc 2003). But that is another story (cf. van der Leeuw 2007).

3.4. Conclusion

Returning to the beginning of this paper with the benefit of hindsight, we can now answer the questions posed there by describing the emergence of the human species as a dominant player on Earth as a bootstrapping process in which we can distinguish two phases.

The first of these is predominantly biological and consists of the growth of human cranial capacity, the development of the frontal lobe and the increase in working memory capacity. These three developments prepared the way for a second phase, in which humans slowly gained an edge over other species and over their physical environment by developing the faculty that distinguishes modern humans from all other species: the capacity to learn and to learn how to learn.[5] This capacity allowed them to categorize, to make abstractions and to hierarchically organize them, and thus to develop the capacity to identify and solve ever more complex problems by inventing suitable conceptual tools. They learned various kinds of (symbolic and other) means to communicate among themselves, and they increased their capacity to transform their natural and material environment in many different ways, and at many spatial and temporal scales.

Hence, from *ca* 12 kyr BP, we observe a drastic acceleration in the speed of invention and innovation. Many new categories of artefacts emerge, new materials are used, new techniques are introduced and new ways to deal with aspects of the material world are 'discovered' in the comparatively short time span of a few thousand years. The acceleration is so overwhelming that the way of life of most humans on Earth changes: rather than live in small non-sedentary groups, people concentrate their activities, invent different subsistence strategies, and in some cases become sedentary.

This 'invention explosion' of the Mesolithic and Neolithic is the result of the fact that human beings have internalized the conceptual apparatus necessary to conceive of space in nested dimensions (zero, one, two and three) across a wide range of spatial scales (from the individual fibre or grain to the landscape), to separate a surface from the volume it encloses, to use different topologies, to distinguish and relate time and space, to distinguish between different sequences of cause and effect, to plan, etc.

From the perspective of the development of working memory, a threshold has clearly been crossed. With a STWM of 7, innovation was no longer an additive process, but became an exponential one because combinatorial possibilities of existing concepts now could be the basis for generating new concepts. Human beings achieved an exponential increase in the dimensionality of the conceptual hyperspace ('possibility space') that governed their relationship with the external world. This afforded them a quantum leap in the number of degrees of freedom of choice they had in dealing with their material and ideational environment.

Once that stage has been reached, working memory (and with it, biological changes in humans' information processing capacity) no longer constrained the introduction of more and more, and more complex, 'tools for thought'. We have reached a critical point, where human-induced generation of new concepts and new relationships (physical, environmental and social)—and thus cultural evolution—takes over from biological evolution in the development of humans' means of adapting to their physical and social environment.

Together, these advances greatly increase the number of ways at people's disposal to tackle the challenges posed by their environment. This allows them to meet more and more complex challenges in shorter and shorter time frames. Hence, it triggers a rapid increase in our species' capability to invent and innovate in many different domains.

But the other side of the coin was that these solutions, by engaging people in the manipulation of a material world that they only partly controlled, ultimately led to new, often unexpected, challenges that required the mobilization of great effort to be overcome in due time. In this process, human societies invested more and more in control over their environment (such as by building infrastructure) and anchored them more and more closely to the territory in which they lived. The symbiosis that emerged between different landscapes and the life-ways invented and constructed by human groups to deal with them eventually narrowed the spectrum of adaptive options open to the individual societies concerned, and thereby drove them to devise new (and more complex) solutions, with increasingly unexpected consequences. Overall, increasing control over the material and natural environment was balanced by increasing societal complexity (Read 2002), which was not always possible to keep under control.

Endnotes

1   The term 'working memory' is a bit of a misnomer as the cognitive function that is involved does not just involve memory but also includes attention (Baddeley 1993). Baddeley was expanding on the earlier notion of short-term memory to include what he referred to as an executive function coupled with a phonological loop and a visuospatial sketchpad (Coolidge & Wynn 2005).

2   Theory of mind refers to 'the ability to attribute mental states—beliefs, intents, desires, pretending, knowledge, etc.—to oneself and others and to understand that others have beliefs, desires and intentions that are different from one's own' (Wikipedia 2007; cf. Premack & Woodruff 1978).

3 This is no different from what has been argued in linguistics. According to Just and Carpenter, for example, while in principle there is no limit to the amount of embedding that can occur with relative clauses, the comprehensibility of sentences with multiply embedded relative clauses is directly related to the size of working memory (Just & Carpenter 1992).

4 In archaeology, it is often very difficult to determine the sequence in which phenomena appear, in part either owing to a lack of dates or because dates have a wide margin of errors, but also because our record is often so fragmentary that it is very easy to miss the first manifestation of a phenomenon.

5 Their capacity to process information is genetically encoded, but the information they process, and the ways in which they do so, is not. It is socio-culturally and self-referentially developed and maintained.

References

Alp, I. E. 1994 Measuring the size of working memory in very young children: the imitation sorting task. *Int. J. Behav. Dev.* **17**, 125–141. (doi:10.1177/016502549401700108)

Ambrose, S. H. 2001 Paleolithic technology and human evolution. *Science* **291**, 1748–1753. (doi:10.1126/science.1059487)

Baddeley, A. 1986 *Working memory*. Oxford, UK: Oxford University Press.

Baddeley, A. 1993 Working memory or working attention? In *Attention: selection, awareness, and control: a tribute to Donald broadbent* (eds A. D. Baddeley & L. Weiskrantz), pp. 152–170. Oxford, UK: Oxford University Press.

Baddeley, A. & Hitch, G. J. 1974 Working memory. In *Recent advances in learning and motivation* (ed. G. A. Bower), pp. 47–90. New York, NY: Academic Press.

Bar-Yosef, O. & Kuhn, S. L. 1999 The big deal about blades: laminar technologies and human evolution. *Am. Anthropol.* **101**, 322–338. (doi:10.1525/aa.1999.101.2.322)

Boëda, E. 1991 Approche de la variabilité des systèmes de production lithique des industries du Paléolithique Inférieur et Moyen: chronique d'une variabilité attendue. *Techniques & Culture* **17-18**, 37–79.

Boëda, E. 1995 Levallois: a volumetric construction, methods, a technique. In *The definition and interpretation of Levallois technology* (eds H. L. Dibble & O. Bar-Yosef), pp. 41–67. Madison, WI: Prehistory Press.

Boëda, E., Geneste, J.-M. & Meignen, L. 1990 Identification de chaînes opératoires lithiques du Paléolithique ancien et moyen. *Paléo* **2**, 43–80.

Carlson, S. M., Moses, L. J. & Breton, C. 2002 How specific is the relation between executive function and theory of mind? Contributions of inhibitory control and working memory. *Infant Child Dev.* **11**, 73–92. (doi:10.1002/icd.298)

Clark, J. E. 1987 Politics, prismatic blades, and Mesoamerican civilization. In *The organization of core technology* (eds J. Johnson & C. Morrow), pp. 259–284. Boulder, CO: Westview Press.

Coolidge, F. L. & Wynn, T. 2005 Working memory, its executive functions, and the emergence of modern thinking. *Camb. Archaeol. J.* **15**, 5–26. (doi:10.1017/ S0959774305000016)

Coolidge, F. L. & Wynn, T. 2007 The working memory account of Neandertal cognition—how phonological storage capacity may be related to recursion and the pragmatics of modern speech. *J. Hum. Evol.* **52**, 707–710. (doi:10.1016/j.jhevol.2007.01.003)

Corrêa, L. M. S. 1995 An alternative assessment of children's comprehension of relative clauses. *J. Psycholinguist. Res.* **24**, 183–203. (doi:10.1007/BF02145355)

Delagnes, A. & Roche, H. 2005 Late Pliocene hominid knapping skills: the case of Lokalalei 2C, West Turkana, Kenya. *J. Hum. Evol.* **48**, 435–472. (doi:10.1016/j.jhevol. 2004.12.005)

Diamond, A. & Doar, B. 1989 The performance of human infants on a measure of frontal cortex function, the delayed-response task. *Dev. Psychobiol.* **22**, 271–294. (doi:10.1002/ dev.420220307)

Engle, R. W. 2002 Working memory capacity as executive attention. *Curr. Dir. Psychol. Sci.* **11**, 19–23. (doi:10.1111/ 1467-8721.00160)

Engle, R. W., Kane, M. J. & Tuholski, S. W. 1999a Individual differences in working memory capacity and what they tell us about controlled attention, general fluid intelligence, and functions of the prefrontal cortex. In *Models of working memory: mechanisms of active maintenance and executive control* (eds A. Miyake & P. Shah), pp. 28–61. Cambridge, UK: Cambridge University Press.

Engle, R. W., Tuholski, S. W., Laughlin, J. E. & Conway, A. R. A. 1999b Working memory, short-term memory, and general fluid intelligence: a latent-variable approach. *J. Exp. Psychol. Gen.* **128**, 309–331. (doi:10.1037/00963445.128.3.309)

Epstein, H. T. 2002 Evolution of the reasoning brain. *Behav. Brain Sci.* **25**, 408–409. (doi:10.1017/ S0140525X02270077)

Fuster, J. M. 2001 The prefrontal cortex—an update: time is of the essence. *Neuron* **30**, 319–333. (doi:10.1016/S0896-6273(01)00285-9)

Fuster, J. M. 2002 Frontal lobe and cognitive development. *J. Neurocytol.* **31**, 373–385. (doi:10.1023/ A:102419 0429920)

Graves, P. 1994 Flakes and ladders: what the archaeological record cannot tell us about origins of language. *World Archaeol.* **26**, 158–171.

Hare, B., Call, J., Agnetta, B. & Tomasello, M. 2000 Chimpanzees know what conspecifics do and do not see. *Anim. Behav.* **59**, 771–785. (doi:10.1006/anbe.1999.1377)

Hare, B., Call, J. & Tomasello, M. 2001 Do chimpanzees know what conspecifics know? *Anim. Behav.* **61**, 139–151. (doi:10.1006/anbe.2000.1518)

Heyes, C. M. 1998 Theory of mind in nonhuman primates. *Behav. Brain Sci.* **21**, 101–114. (doi:10.1017/S0140525X 98000703)

Johnson, J., Fabian, V. & Pascual-Leone, J. 1989 Quantitative hardware stages that constrain language development. *Hum. Dev.* **32**, 245–271.

Just, M. A. & Carpenter, P. A. 1992 A capacity theory of comprehension: individual differences in working memory. *Psychol. Rev.* **99**, 122–149. (doi:10.1037/0033-295X. 99.1.122)

Kane, M. J. & Engle, R. W. 2000 Working memory capacity, proactive interference, and divide attention: limits on long-term memory retrieval. *J. Exp. Psychol. Learn. Mem. Cogn.* **26**, 333–358.

Kane, M. J. & Engle, R. W. 2002 The role of the prefrontal cortex in working memory capacity, executive attention, and general fluid intelligence: an individual-differences perspective. *Psych. Bull. Rev.* **9**, 637–671.

Kemps, E., De Rammelaere, S. & Desmet, T. 2000 The development of working memory: exploring the complementarity of two models. *J. Exp. Psychol.* **77**, 89–109. (doi:10.1006/jecp.2000.2589)

Kidd, E. & Bavin, E. L. 2002 English-speaking children's comprehension of relative clauses: evidence for general–cognitive and language-specific constraints on development. *J. Psycholinguist. Res.* **31**, 599–617. (doi:10.1023/ A:1021265021141)

Lieberman, D. E., McBratnehy, B. M. & Krowitz, G. 2002 The evolution and development of cranial form in *Homo sapiens*. *Proc. Natl Acad. Sci. USA* **99**, 1134–1139. (doi:10. 1073/pnas.022440799)

Luciana, M. & Nelson, C. A. 1998 The functional emergence of prefrontally-guided working memory systems in four- to eight-year old children. *Neuropsychologia* **36**, 273–293. (doi:10.1016/ S0028-3932(97)00109-7)

Martin, R. D. 1981 Relative brain size and basal metabolic rate in terrestrial vertebrates. *Nature* **293**, 57–60. (doi:10. 1038/293057a0)

Miller, E. K. 2000 The prefrontal cortex and cognitive control. *Nat. Rev. Neurosci.* **1**, 59–65. (doi:10.1038/ 35036228)

Pasternak, T. & Greenlee, M. W. 2005 Working memory in primate sensory systems. *Nat. Rev. Neurosci.* **6**, 97–107. (doi:10.1038/nrn1603)

Pigeot, N. 1991 Reflexions sur l'histoire technique de l'homme: de l'évolution cognitive à l'évolution culturelle. *Paléo* 3, 167–200.

Povinelli, D. J. & Eddy, T. J. 1996 *What young chimpanzees know about seeing*. Monographs of the Society for Research on Child Development, vol. 61 (series no. 247).

Premack, D. & Premack, A. 2000 *Original intelligence*. New York, NY: McGraw-Hill.

Premack, D. & Woodruff, G. 1978 Does the chimpanzee have a theory of mind? *Behav. Brain Sci.* **1**, 515–526.

Read, D. 2002 A multitrajectory, competition model of emergent complexity in human social organization. *Proc. Natl Acad. Sci. USA* **99** (suppl. 3), 7251–7256. (doi:10.1073/pnas. 072079999)

Read, D. 2006 Working memory: a cognitive limit to nonhuman primate recursive thinking prior to hominid evolution? In *CogSci 2006 Proceedings*, 2674–2679.

Read, D. 2007 *Artefact classification: a conceptual and methodological approach*. Walnut Creek, CA: Left Coast Press.

Read, D. & LeBlanc, S. 2003 Population growth, carrying capacity, and conflict. *Curr. Anthropol.* **44**, 59–85. (doi:10.1086/344616)

Rightmire, G. P. 2004 Brain size and encephalization in Early to Mid-Pleistocene *Homo. Am. J. Phys. Anthropol.* **124**, 109–123. (doi:10.1002/ajpa.10346)

Ruff, C. B., Trinkhaus, E. & Holliday, T. W. 1997 Body mass and encephalization in Pleistocene *Homo. Nature* **387**, 173–176. (doi:10.1038/387173a0)

Semendeferi, K., Armstrong, E., Schletcher, A., Zilles, K. & Van Hoesen, G. W. 2001 Prefrontal cortex in humans and apes: a comparative study of area. *Am. J. Phys. Anthropol.* **114**, 224–241. (doi:10.1002/1096-8644(200103)114:3< 224::AID-AJPA1022>3.0.CO;2-I)

Siegel, L. S. & Ryan, E. B. 1989 The development of working memory in normally achieving and subtypes of learning disabled children. *Child Dev.* **60**, 973–980. (doi:10.2307/1131037)

Stout, D., Toth, N. & Schick, K. 2000 Stone tool-making and brain activation: positron emission tomography (PET) studies. *J. Archaeol. Sci.* **27**, 1215–1223. (doi:10.1006/jasc.2000.0595)

van der Leeuw, S. E. 2000 Making tools from stone and clay. In *Australian archaeologist: collected papers in honour of Jim Allen* (eds A. Anderson & T. Murray), pp. 69–88. Coombs, Australia: Academic Publishing.

van der Leeuw, S. 2007 Information processing and its role in the rise of the European world system. In *Sustainability or collapse?* (eds R. Costanza, L. J. Graumlich & W. Steffen), pp. 213–241. Cambridge, MA: MIT Press (Dahlem Workshop Reports).

van der Leeuw, S. E. & McGlade, J. 1997 Archaeology and nonlinear dynamics: new approaches to long-term change. In *Archaeology: time, process and structural transformations* (eds S. van der Leeuw & J. McGlade), pp. 1–31. London, UK: Routledge.

van der Leeuw, S. E. & Aschan-Leygonie, C. 2005 A long-term perspective on resilience in socio–natural systems. In *Addressing complex system couplings* (eds U. Svedin & H. Lilienstrom), pp. 227–264. London, UK: World Scientific.

White, M. & Ashton, N. 2003 Lower Palaeolithic core technology and the origins of the Levallois method in north-western Europe. *Curr. Anthropol.* **44**, 598–609. (doi:10.1086/377653)

Wikipedia_contributors 2007 Theory of mind. See http://en. wikipedia.org/w/index.php?title= theory_of_mind&oldidZ153636658.

Wynn, T. 2002 Archaeology and cognitive evolution. *Behav. Brain Sci.* **25**, 389–438. (doi:10.1017/ S0140525X02 530120)

Wynn, T. & McGrew, W. C. 1989 An ape's view of the Oldowan. *Man (n.s.)* **24**, 383–398. (doi:10. 2307/2802697)

Big brains, small worlds: material culture and the evolution of the mind

Fiona Coward and Clive Gamble

New developments in neuroimaging have demonstrated that the basic capacities underpinning human social skills are shared by our closest extant primate relatives. The challenge for archaeologists is to explain how complex human societies evolved from this shared pattern of face-to-face social interaction. We argue that a key process was the gradual incorporation of material culture into social networks over the course of hominin evolution. Here we use three long-term processes in hominin evolution—encephalization, the global human diaspora and sedentism/agriculture—to illustrate how the cultural transmission of material culture allowed the 'scaling up' of face-to-face social interactions to the global societies known today. We conclude that future research by neuroimagers and archaeologists will need to investigate the cognitive mechanisms behind human engagement with material culture as well as other persons.

Keywords: cultural transmission; hominin evolution; social networks; global diaspora; neuroimaging; Palaeolithic archaeology

4.1. Introduction

Understandings of the cognitive basis of face-to-face interaction fundamental to both primate and human societies have recently been revolutionized by new neuroimaging techniques. In particular, studies have provided empirical support for a shared theory of mind where the embodied simulation of others' actions, rather than an abstract representational theory of behaviour, underpins understanding of the actions, sensations and emotions of others (Gallese & Lakoff 2005; Gallese *et al.* 2004). It is this common cognitive basis, with its implications for a deep ancestry, which is proving most provocative for those studying human evolution (Stout *et al.* 2008; Grove & Coward 2008). In this paper we set out to expand these interdisciplinary collaborations by adding an archaeological perspective. This necessarily prioritizes the material aspect of social interaction, highlighting the fact that we currently know very little about the neural capacities for the relationships that humans have with other animate and apparently 'inanimate' entities.

Animals and objects have formed a fundamental element in networks of human agency and sociality throughout our *ca* 5 Myr evolution as an encephalized species. For example, the basic skills underpinning interaction with material culture are present in our primate relatives in both the old and new worlds (McGrew 1992; de Amoura & Lee 2004; Davidson & McGrew 2005), suggesting a long-time depth for the cognitive basis of such engagement. However, the scale of human involvement with material culture by far outstrips anything known from other animal species both quantitatively and qualitatively. Furthermore, this scale has increased dramatically during hominin[1] evolution in the *ca* 2.5 Myr since the oldest known stone technologies (Semaw *et al.* 1997; Gamble 2007).

Collaboration between neuroimagers and archaeologists has the potential to illuminate the process by which hominins developed this uniquely human capacity for engagement with material culture. Both disciplines have recently advanced by emphasizing the fundamentally embodied character of cultural transmission and it is in this area that dialogue promises to be most fruitful. But this exchange of views will only be achieved if archaeologists first address some conceptual issues.

4.2. What needs to change in the study of human evolution

The study of human evolution remains committed to a Cartesian model of cognition and consciousness in which the process of thinking is abstracted from its real-world context. Its practitioners are also largely uninterested in theory, even evolutionary theory (Foley 2001, p. 5), relying instead on sequence and correlation to reveal trends in the data. Archaeologists in particular feel safest with populations (Flannery 1967; Clark 1992) rather than individuals as their unit of study (though see Gamble & Porr 2005), and with a model of rational behaviour based on the economic costs of procuring food. How the food quest was organized leaves tangible traces—camps, tools and residues from foraging and agriculture—and these serve as proxies for variation in reproductive success between species such as Neanderthals and modern humans, and for distinguishing between such problematic economic categories as hunters and farmers.

Similar proxies are used to document the trend in cognitive ability. Here the Cartesian model is most evident through the notion of symbolism and the key role it is thought to play in the human revolution of 50 000 years ago. Chase & Dibble (1987, p. 265) examined the rare 'symbolic' items from Neanderthal archaeology 'with an eye towards assessing the degree to which arbitrary categories and symbols structured behaviours'. They concluded that there was little or no evidence—unsurprising, given that they concentrated on material symbols that can trace an unbroken ancestry from contemporary societies, such as 'figurines' and 'jewellery'. Moreover, when it comes to explaining why such items are commonly encountered after 50 000 years ago and associated with modern humans, the answer is invariably that 'substantial amounts of brainpower' (Henshilwood & Marean 2003; but see McBrearty & Brooks 2000; Zilhao 2007), together with language, were now involved.

In particular, the rational approach, using direct material proxies to identify key behaviours, has failed to deliver much of interest concerning the changing structure of hominin society (Johnson & Earle 1987). By comparison with the extensive literature on ape sociality and cognition (e.g. Barrett & Henzi 2005), a study of hominin social life has barely begun (Mithen 1996; Gamble 1999). The reason is simple; even though hominins had brains two or three times larger than apes, their societies apparently lacked material proxies for social institutions such as markets, assemblies and temples. In the absence of such proxies, it would seem little or nothing can be inferred. Neither does the rational approach have much to say beyond the functional about the history of technology and materials. In this paradigm, artefacts are merely externalized mental constructs.

4.3. Embodied knowledge and imaginary geographies

In emphasizing the embodied character of cultural transmission, we need to avoid falling into the trap of merely promoting from the opposite direction the mind/body dualism we have just criticized. Rather, the notion of 'embodied knowledge' is used here as a corrective to traditional archaeological approaches that tacitly endorsed the notion of abstract decontextualized cognition. We use the term here in reference both to Gibsonian ambulatory perception, which emphasizes the sensory capacities of the body as the primary means of engagement with the world (Gibson 1979), and to 'embodied', 'extended' or 'distributed' approaches within cognitive science (see Anderson (2003) for review, also Hutchins (2008)), linguistics (Lakoff & Johnson 1980, 1999) and neuroscience (e.g. Maravita & Iriki 2004), all of which suggest that cognition is not an abstract symbolizing process but fundamentally structured by the inescapable fact that the biological processes constituting 'mind' are part of a body which is constantly interacting with the world.

The change we advocate, and that opens up the prospect of a more fruitful collaboration with neuroscience, is the adoption of a relational approach to a much wider set of archaeological data. A relational approach (Gamble 1999, 2007) does not seek to separate hominins from their worlds for analytical purposes. Instead, the focus of its investigation shifts to the *connections* that constitute them within those worlds. From a relational perspective, the entities themselves—individuals, objects and animals—have no essential qualities *per se* but rather are effects or outcomes of their connectedness (e.g. Law 1999, p. 3; see also Gosden 2008). As such, a relational perspective is not necessarily opposed to or separate from a 'rational' reading of the data, but complementary to it.

The shift in standpoint will allow us to address such issues as the evolution of intentionality and the emotions. We will be able to ask whether these changes selected for social bonds that also functioned as scaffolds for the imaginary cognitive geographies identified by Gallese & Lakoff (2005, p. 9): 'All human beings entertain the capacity to imagine worlds that they have or have not seen before, to imagine doing things that they have or have not done before'. Without such cognitive ability there would, for example, be no archaeology, no interest in human evolution and indeed no humans as we conceive them.

Here we will argue that the ability to create and people such imaginary geographies constitutes a basic hominin rather than exclusively human ability (Gamble 2007). It is not an evidence of either a lately evolved modern mind or a sapient revolution (Renfrew 2008); later developments were instead the outcome of a general shift towards the increasing use of material culture to supplement face-to-face interactions between individuals. Such relational questions do not necessarily require better identified proxies in order to consider hominin social life and material culture—a shift in our conceptual approaches can reveal many new relationships, hitherto obscured from view in the archaeological data by a purely rational approach.

4.4. What needs addressing in human evolution

Although embodiment has recently become a topic of interest in archaeology (e.g. Hamilakis *et al.* 2002; Sofaer 2006), for the most part archaeologists have yet to follow up the consequences of departing from a Cartesian approach for a perspective in which knowledge is seen as mapped in our sensory–motor system, and therefore embodied (Gallese *et al.* 2004). One such consequence is that emotions are seen as playing a key role, characterizing the human brain (LeDoux 1998) but always also embodied (Niedenthal 2007). For example, Turner (2000) has argued that positive emotions were pressed into service to facilitate the evolution of more complex social behaviour, with hominin evolution demonstrating a trend away from low sociality and individualism towards more group-oriented social structures, which can be investigated by reference to group size and the scale of hominin groups' imaginary geographies. These developments required conceptual changes within the early learning environment of the infant, with the outcome of selection for these positive emotions leading to 'the expansion of the anterior cingulate gyrus, as the centre for playfulness and mother–infant bonding, (and which) may also have been rewired to produce a more generalized source for happiness and propensities for bonding, altruism, and reciprocity beyond the mother–infant dyad (Turner 2000, p. 112).'

While an admittedly speculative account, Turner's emphasis on the emotions is suited to a relational rather than strictly rational account of hominin evolution. The task for archaeologists is to integrate material culture into the early learning environments of children. In this context, material culture and emotions do not exist independently; rather, the latter frame experience while the former embodies the concept on which these developing relationships are based.

4.5. A timetable to hominin evolution

The trend in hominin evolution is illustrated here by Dunbar's social brain model (2003), using increasing group size as a measure of complexity (figure 4.1).

The model is less concerned with the taxonomy of the various fossils and more with the overall trend in encephalization. Brains are expensive metabolically, and strong selection is required to account for the expansion and the consequent costs involved, e.g. the

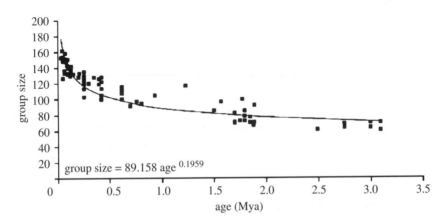

group size = 89.158 age $^{0.1959}$

Figure 4.1. Group sizes predicted for extinct hominins from the strong relationship demonstrated between neocortex ratio and group size among extant primates. Data from Aiello & Dunbar 1993. In fossil hominins, the expansion of the neocortex accounts for the increase in total brain size that can be measured in fossil crania. Mya, million years ago.

increased risk of parturition (Aiello 1998). Adaptations for sociality are put forward as one source of such a selective pressure since larger group size brings evolutionary benefits in defence against predators and foraging opportunities through sharing. However, the model is currently light on the mechanisms behind the increased complexity of social life. What were these social bonds and networks based upon and how were they organized into more complex patterns? In particular, what role did material culture play in this trend to complexity?

The earliest stone artefacts are currently *ca* 2.5 Myr old (Semaw *et al.* 1997), thus dating to very early in the process of encephalization. The subsequent evolution of brains and artefacts reflects an entangled history that needs careful unravelling if we are to avoid trite narratives about progress towards modernity. Here, we will structure our discussion of the archaeological data around three processes occurring over the course of hominin evolution.

(i) A sharp increase in encephalization 500 000 ± 100 000 years ago. This is much earlier than the artefactual changes that began 300 000 years ago in Africa (McBrearty & Brooks 2000) and gathered pace after 100 000 years ago (d'Errico *et al.* 2003; Henshilwood & Marean 2003). The predicted group sizes at 500 kyr ago probably required language to facilitate interaction (Dunbar 1993). Of interest at this time are life-history changes and the evolution of early learning environments of childhood and the extent to which these were critical to cultural transmission.

(ii) The global human diaspora (Gamble 1993; Cavalli-Sforza & Cavalli-Sforza 1995), starting with the first appearance of *Homo erectus* (sensu lato) outside Africa *ca* 1.7 Myr ago and continuing even after the arrival of ocean-going modern humans in Australia *ca* 60 000 years ago (Gamble in press). To what extent does this diaspora depend on the ability to construct imaginative geographies that also supported distributed social networks?

(iii) The widespread appearance of sedentism and then agriculture 15 000–8000 years ago, which changed human experience in ways that some believe was fundamental for the modern mind (Cauvin 2000; Renfrew 2001; Watkins 2004*b*). However, sedentism needs to be understood in the context of the social networks and small-world societies that supported them. A comparative approach must look at both sides of this apparent divide.

These processes are emphatically *not* revolutions (Gamble 2007). Nor do we necessarily consider them to be *the* three 'big events' in hominin evolution; we simply use them here as temporal markers to organize a long-term perspective based on archaeological evidence. Discussing each in turn, we will demonstrate that all are underpinned by changing social relationships between hominins—and, crucially, between hominins and the material world—building on a basic hominid cognitive repertoire expanded during hominin evolution through the spinning of networks of social relationships that link us over increasing distances through space and time.

4.6. Encephalization, childhood and cultural and social transmission

The concepts of children and childhood are a good example of the kinds of crucial information that rational approaches to hominin evolution often overlook. Children are an almost invisible category in archaeology (Derevenski 2000) and particularly so during hominin evolution. We can find their tiny footprints (Roveland 2000), on occasion their skeletons and very rarely their weaning foods (Mason *et al.* 1994), but further proxies such as cradles, carrying slings and pacifiers are absent. The rational approach assumes, quite reasonably, that they were present (they are, after all, themselves a proxy for reproductive success, the ultimate evolutionary goal). However, it regards them as uninvestigatable, much like the study of hominin society before art, monumental architecture and ball courts (Childe 1951, p. 85; Leach 1973; Gamble 1999, pp. 1–7; Wobst 2000, p. 43).

And yet the mother–child dyad, along with adult pair bonding, is one of the principal units in the construction of hominid social life. Social relationships are the medium and mode of cultural transmission, providing the networks along which 'objects' disseminate, and it is in childhood that the bases for these relationships, so crucial to cultural transmission, are established.

New research is beginning to demonstrate how the mirror neuron system informs on the mechanisms of cultural transmission; the information necessary to imitate the acts— and infer the intentions—of others is immediately present in their actions as spectators' mirror neuron systems automatically map the observed actions onto their own motor systems in logically entrained sequences of action (Gallese *et al.* 2004, 2007). One point of interest here is *how* such sequences become entrained. One hypothesis is that it occurs by repeatedly experiencing sequences of actions 'as they are habitually performed or observed in the social environment' (Gallese *et al.* 2007, p. 137).

It follows that, while the neural mechanisms behind imitation and transmission are innate (Gallese *et al.* 2007, p. 145), they are only part of a complex of biological, ethological and social factors that are necessarily related to its evolution. Skeletal and locomotive adaptations such as the size and pelvic orientation of a bipedal hominid mean that increased brain size must be associated with secondary altriciality and delayed maturity, with a concomitant temporal extension of the time available for enculturation and enskillment (see Smith & Tompkins 1995; Grove & Coward 2008), as most cultural transmission occurs vertically, i.e. from parents to children[2] (Shennan & Steele 1999; Hosfield in press). The derived pattern of human life history also includes a substantial period of post-reproductive life, an innovation that makes little sense outside a way of life where the handing down of complex skills learnt over a lifetime is adaptive (Peccei 1995; Hawkes *et al.* 1998; O'Connell *et al.* 1999). Moreover, encephalization is also related to a reduction in the size of the gut and an increase in the proportion of meat in the diet (Aiello & Wheeler 1995). Exploitation of meat, a high-quality patchy food, is associated with larger range sizes and social groups and necessarily more complex skills for its appropriation which must be learned by each new generation (Foley & Lee 1991; Smith & Tompkins 1995). On a less rational note, hunting is also necessarily associated with new forms of social relationships forged through communal hunting strategies and/or division of labour, and the sharing of large 'packets' of meat too substantial for individuals to consume alone.

What lies at the heart of all of these changes is sociality; the relationships between individuals and the mechanisms by which those bonds are initiated and sustained. At the fine scale of individual imitation and transmission, these same relationships also underpin cultural transmission. At a larger scale, innovations and varied forms of material culture are disseminated in a manner analogous to genes (e.g. Boyd & Richerson 1985; Shennan 2002); but again, these practices are part and parcel of the wider social networks that link individuals and communities in space and time, as we will discuss later in relation to agriculture, sedentism and small worlds.

As Fonagy *et al.* (2007, p. 297) propose, 'evolution has left it to the intimate relationships of early childhood to elaborate the capacity for social cognition fully'. They argue that the capacity of the brain to adapt to ever more challenging physical and social environments cannot be fixed by genetics (see also Deacon (1997) and discussion in Grove & Coward (2008)). Instead, such adaptation is facilitated for the infant during a prolonged childhood by a group of trusted adults, many of whom will be kin, what they call attachment figures (see also Frith 2008).

Elsewhere, one of us (Gamble 2007, pp. 225–230) has introduced the concept of the childscape, the environment for growth, which consists not only of attachment figures but also emotionally charged arrays including items of material culture. As Hespos & Spelke's (2004) work with five-month-old babies demonstrates, the significance of these material arrays is that infants think first in material rather than linguistic categories, and establish the relationships between forms[3] in an experiential metaphorical manner (Bloom 2004); a good example of knowledge structured by the embodied nature of experiential learning. A relational approach interested in considering children in an evolutionary context does not therefore need child-like material proxies. Instead, it begins with the proposition that the individual is emotionally connected to materials and carers from the first. Moreover, as neuroscience shows, a rigid distinction between body and brain is counterproductive for an understanding of the evolving structure of this cognitive attachment (Gallese *et al.* 2004, 2007; Rizzolatti & Craighero 2004; Gallese 2006; Fonagy *et al.* 2007). In the same way, a division between objects and persons can also be rejected as both are targets for the emotional association, or agency (Gell 1998; Gosden & Marshall 1999; Dobres & Robb 2000), that drives the connections between them—the object of interest in a relational approach. In a relational approach, objects and people are not distinguished by some prior 'essence' but as a result of the web of relationships each is a part of (e.g. Law 1999); from this perspective, people can be considered as a particular category of 'thing' with their own characteristic properties or affordances (Gibson 1979; Strathern 1998; Jordan 2008).

4.7. Imaginative geographies, global diasporas and distributed networks

Among primates—and so probably also among our ancestors, the australopithecines—the primary mechanism for negotiating these social relationships is grooming. The downside, as Dunbar has pointed out, is that any individual can groom only one other individual at a time. In contrast, auditory resources such as vocal chorusing, laughter, singing and speech can be directed towards several individuals simultaneously, and could therefore have been used to sustain groups the size of those predicted for *H. erectus* on the basis of neocortex ratio (figure 4.1; Dunbar 1993). Dunbar's work further suggests that these auditory resources are likely to have increased in complexity over time: archaic *sapiens* groups, predicted to be larger again, would need more complex forms of social 'language', while *Homo sapiens*' extremely large group sizes need the time-and-energy-efficient resources of metaphorical language to sustain them (Dunbar 1993).

But there has been a shift away from a focus on the semiotic content of speech recently, with researchers emphasizing instead its basis in embodied experience (Lakoff & Johnson 1980; see also Rizzolatti & Craighero 2004; Gallese & Lakoff 2005; Gallese *et al.* 2007; Roepstorff 2008). Not only is it argued that language itself may arise from individuals' common embodied experience, but it has also been recognized that much of the meaning in any instance of conversation is conveyed by fundamentally corporal cues including stance, bodily movement, facial expression, prosody and intonation, which also underpin joint attention, attunement and intentionality (Rizzolatti & Craighero 2004; Mithen 2005; Knoblich & Sebanz 2008).

But of course corporal and auditory resources, if indeed we can separate them out, are not the only social resource that we have to draw on in our social projects. If they were, there would not be much of an archaeological record. We also have *things*: material resources. And while there are spatial and temporal limits beyond which we cannot hear someone trying to talk to us, or see them to judge their conversational stance, material resources persist in both time and space. As one of us has argued (Gamble 1998), this is what allows the extension of social networks beyond the spatial and temporal limitations of individual physical bodies and instances of interaction, and was a key mechanism of the global diaspora of modern humans.

In addition to the long-term temporal trend in vocal and linguistic resources discussed by Dunbar, therefore, there is also a spatial dimension to social relationships: different resources are necessarily associated with very different geographical scales of interaction and relationship. Corporal, embodied strategies such as grooming are practicable only in situations of co-presence, while auditory resources such as speech allow interaction with others within hearing distance. Material resources, however, can travel considerable distances in both space and time.

It is important to emphasize that each new social resource does not replace but adds to those previously used, so that embodied, vocal material and symbolic resources all become interlinked in the practice of everyday life. However, what we so seem to see during hominin evolution is the gradual adoption of material resources to complement our primate heritage of corporal and emotional social strategies.

A good example is provided by Inuit Inuksuit (singular Inuksuk). These waymarking cairns constructed through the Arctic, like such cairns elsewhere across the globe, have multiple 'uses'. They act as markers for human paths and animal migration routes, to signal nearby peoples, special places, caches, etc. These structures are maintained with great care; tellingly, they are often constructed to resemble humans, and the word in fact means something that 'acts in the capacity of a human' (Hallendy 2000; Varney Burch 2007). Some Inuksuit date back generations, and specific examples are mentioned in the Aya-yait (Varney Burch 2007), the travelling songs passed between generations that help the travellers remember the series of directions involved in long trips in the absence of memorable natural waymarks in Arctic environments. The sameness of snow-bound landscapes, the quality of light and the extremes of weather that often result in 'white-outs' where visual cues to direction and movement are virtually non-existent mean that moment-to-moment navigation occurs by almost unconscious reading of the subtle alignments of snow, ice and wind: 'there is no line separating Earth and sky; there is no intermediate distance, no perspective or contour; visibility is limited; and yet there is an extraordinarily fine topology that relies not on points or objects but rather on haeccities, on sets of relations (winds, undulations of snow … the creaking of ice…)' (Deleuze & Guattari 1987 (2004), p. 421).

Children must be enculturated, or enskilled through an 'education of attention' in Ingold's terms (2000), into an understanding of this world through a guiding of their bodily experience of it (the use of corporal, emotional resources) as well as through discursive means such as the rote learning and repetition of the Aya-yait travelling songs (auditory resources) which refer specific Inuksuk (material resources) as nodes in the topology of movement and interaction.

Further examples might include the relational material 'maps' of Australian Aborigines and Polynesian and Micronesian groups. The Aboriginal spear-thrower illustrated by Ingold (2000, p. 368) and the 'wave-and-wind' charts of the Micronesian Marshall Islanders (Turnbull 1991) are material resources that are similarly complemented by and work in tandem with corporal and less material resources: the embodied, enskilled experience of moving through the land-or seascape, and the myths and narratives associated with such journeys—for example, the stories of the dreamtime. These narratives contribute to the transmission of these skills by associating the landscape, its paths, tracks, denizens and the temporality and skills that structure it with known mythical persons, such that knowledge of it becomes *personal*, a question of relationships between individuals. Landscape (and seascape), paths and routes become integrated into social topologies rather than cognitive maps, and the traversing of them is better viewed as the enactment of a narrative than as an exercise in Cartesian geography.

Although these examples are all drawn from modern human groups, they do serve to illustrate how children are enskilled into the use of the different forms of social resource that function together in the negotiation of a variety of landscapes.

However, even this more relational perspective on material resources remains rather Cartesian in its division of subject and object. One of the most striking features of human life is the extent to which we interact with entities other than our fellow humans, and one of the most lively debates in archaeology concerns the status of material culture—as object or as subject, passively imitated, used, traded, etc., or as playing an active, reflexive role in these practices (Kopytoff 1986; Tilley 1996; Gosden & Marshall 1999; Wobst 2000; Ingold 2002; Jones 2002).

The question of whether objects have agency is too broad an issue to address here. We will also leave aside the problem of semiotic meaning: objects may or may not have agency or 'meaning' *per se*, and archaeologists may or may not ever be able to approach that (Tilley 1993; Knappett 2005). But what we can do is to investigate the *effect* of material culture (Conkey 1995; Gosden 2001, p. 164; Coward & Gamble in press). The foregoing are rather practical examples of culturally transmitted skills and material culture that allow geographical and temporal extension, but ethnographical and anthropological literature has long demonstrated how objects become integrated into social relationships. They may be invested with great personal and emotional significance, to the point of being considered intentional, living subjects (Kopytoff 1986; Strathern 1988; Hoskins 1998; Coward & Gamble in press). For example, Inuit retain a strong emotional attachment to those Inuksuit believed to have been constructed by their ancestors (Varney Burch 2007). The wealth of mnemonic, metaphorical and metonymic references that derives from the biographies of items of material culture thus has the effect of connecting people together across the landscape (Gosden & Marshall 1999; Chapman 2000; Coward & Gamble in press). In this light, for example, a necklace such as those found in Upper Palaeolithic graves atAvendes Iboussieres and St-Germain-de-la-Rivière in France becomes a set of metonymic references to the red deer of whose canines it is composed; a mnemonic for the occasions of hunting, trade and/or exchange that brought these together; and metaphorical of the relationships with those people with whom one engaged in these interactions and the places and occasions when these took place (d'Errico & Vanhaeren 2002; Vanhaeren & d'Errico 2005).

For this reason, we would very much like to see neurology investigate not just the physical dimensions of primate and human interaction with items of material culture, but how these relate to the emotional and mnemonic significance of particular objects. Mirror neuron research demonstrates an innate, embodied response to other individuals' motor actions among primates: canonical neurons appear to represent not only goal-directed actions but also the potential for such actions based on the objects to hand (Grèzes & Decety 2002; Grèzes *et al*. 2003). The mirror neuron literature would thus appear to confirm that the 'affordances' of an item of material culture are directly perceived by an observer (Gallese 2000), as Gibson (1979) had previously argued, and therefore that perception is always immediately and preconsciously integrated into embodied, active projects. In this way, the object itself can perhaps be seen as providing affordances for embodied action, a possibility that invites some interesting questions about the ways in which the perception of material objects relates to the cultural transmission of manufacture and use.

4.8. Agriculture, sedentism and small worlds

We have established, then, that social relationships are the *sine qua non* of cultural transmission and, among humans at least, objects of material culture become incorporated in these relationships, enabling their temporal and geographical extension beyond the here-and-now of primate sociality. However, the varying properties of different kinds of material culture both constrain and enable different kinds of activities, inviting some uses and precluding others (Parker-Pearson & Ramilisonina 1998; Tilley 2004). In addition, different individuals will always operate in different contexts with different resources to hand and, as a result, will necessarily construct for themselves very different material networks. But, at the same time, individuals are also always part of groups with shared histories and shared understandings about the appropriateness or otherwise of particular practices and performances. These cross-cutting trends are what result in the varyingly patterned co-associations of different kinds of material resources that are understood archaeologically as 'cultures'.

The nature of the networks of social relationships between individuals and groups is thus a crucial determinant of the archaeological patterning of material culture—indeed, given the arguments for the active role of material culture in the forging and maintenance of these networks, the archaeological record is best seen as *part of*, and not a passive reflection of, those social networks. The links between the nodes, represented by shared items of material culture, may be forged directly by the transport, trade, exchange, etc. of objects; alternatively they may represent imitation or dissemination of the technologies or ideas behind them. Either way, they document a link, a relationship, between nodes. So the various elements of material culture that are held in common between sites become the heterogeneous relationships connecting the individual elements into multiple inter-linked networks. And in this way, a social network perspective can potentially take us from the patterning of things to the structuring of relationships, as called for by Barrett (2000 (1988), p. 28).

One of us (F.C.) is currently using a social network perspective to address the shift to increasingly sedentary ways of life and the gradual adoption of stone-built architecture in the Near East during the Epipalaeolithic and Early Neolithic (*ca* 18 000–*ca* 8000 radiocarbon years BP). Considerable importance has been attached to the first appearance of permanent built structures as implying a relative fixity of social patternings that may persist between generations, acting as an external form of enculturation and 'symbolic storage device' and sparking a new form of cognition among sedentary agriculturalists (e.g. Renfrew 1998; Watkins 2004*a,b*). However, there are no straightforward associations between mobility, unstructured use of space and hunting and gathering on the one hand, and permanent architecture, sedentism and the symbolic or structured use of space on the other hand: there are, for example, mobile agriculturalists, mobile hunter–gatherers who cultivate plants and sedentary hunter–gatherers (e.g. Terrell 2007).

Each of these groups clearly has very different ways of thinking about using and structuring space that vary from the immaterial and ephemeral through to the physical and semi-permanent. Cribb's (1991) study comparing pastoral tent dwellings and village houses in Turkey found that, despite the obvious differences in the building materials used, the tent and the house were virtually identical in their underlying organizational templates. There is nothing necessarily 'unstructured' about the kinds of non-permanent constructions used by mobile peoples: even just the placing of sticks in the ground to represent a 'doorway' acts to structure movement and activity along gender and age lines in temporary !Kung encampments (Whitelaw 1994, p. 217). Nor are the stone-built constructions of the Neolithic necessarily 'permanent' *per se*: sites and houses in the Epipalaeolithic and Early Neolithic demonstrate continuous maintenance, reworking and remodelling, burning, rebuilding, abandonment and reuse. As Prussin (1989, p. 141) reminds us, 'The concept 'temporary' is not synonymous with 'transient'; the concept of 'permanent' is distinct from 'stationary''.

We prefer to view the gradual shift in the forms and materialities of structures as integral to the social relationships of which they were a part—a response to a different social context in which people used alternative resources to approach some new social problems relating to the changing scale of their worlds. Constructed environments—whether primate 'nests' (Groves & Pi 1985; Kolen 1999) or Pre-Pottery Neolithic B (PPNB) houses—have a very obvious effect on the distribution and trajectories of bodies in space that is a fundamental part of the negotiation and practice of social relationships (Hillier & Hanson 1984; Barrett 1994). The layout and construction of houses is often referenced to the body (Carsten & Hugh-Jones 1995), to the extent that they form a material metaphor for the experience of living and being social (Hodder 1990; Tilley 1999).

However, this experience is not the same for everyone, everywhere. As the scale and diversity of the social relationships involved increases—as it did, dramatically, during the global diasporas detailed in the previous section—such experience may diverge widely. While the basic cognitive mechanisms discussed above, supported by material culture, make it possible in theory to establish social relationships with anyone, in practice it may be extremely difficult to find a common denominator from which to commence social interaction.

In mobile groups, the networks of social relationships are diffuse, open and ephemeral, shifting and changing almost constantly as groups and individuals break up and aggregate. But the basic unit is small and structured around groups of very close kin, who all know each other extremely well (Lofland 1973; Wilson 1988; Whitelaw 1991). The individual performances of social interaction are face-to-face, personal. They use corporal resources: bodily movement and expression, and intimate conversational stances (Hillier & Hanson 1984; Wilson 1988).

In less mobile groups, the option of fissioning, of breaking away from the group, becomes less feasible almost by definition. And as the number of individuals in any group increases, there is of course an exponential increase in the inter-individual relationships that are possible. But these social ties take time and energy to maintain, and they are also cognitively demanding in terms of integrating the relevant social information (Dunbar 1992, 1993, 2003; Gamble 1999; Watts 2003). It is simply not possible for everyone to have the kind of strong, complex relationship that characterizes kin relationships with everyone else in the same society. In larger groups, therefore, individual relationships become simplified, reducing the potential 'overload' of information (Lofland 1973), so that the relationships between people have fewer dimensions, being categorized according to a few key characteristics. Thus, knowledge of others whom you meet only in very particular contexts is *categorical* rather than simply biographical (Granovetter 1973, 1983; Lofland 1973; Milgram 1977; Rapoport 1981; Milroy 1987, cited Gamble 1996; cf. Bloch 2008).

Thus, in high-density, strongly linked small-scale groups such as extended families, the behaviours and performances appropriate to particular temporal and spatial contexts are so well known, and activities so highly routinized, that people do not need much in the way of clues from their environment to tell them how to act (Douglas 1973, p. 78; Coser 1975; Rapoport 1990). For example, in many Australian Aboriginal camps,sweeping the ground around the shelter two or three times a day to alter its surface texture is enough to indicate a private domain (Rapoport 1990, p. 16). In larger scale, less-dense societies, however, it becomes necessary to create specialized 'settings' to cue appropriate behaviour, so that contemporary western dwellings may have fences, paths, porches and several doors and gates to achieve the same goal of indicating privacy (Rapoport 1990, p. 16). Increasing social scale is accompanied by increasing redundancy of performative cues through the elaboration of material environments that compensate for weak or 'categorical' knowledge of the people with whom one must interact (Rapoport 1969, p. 30; Granovetter 1973, 1983; Lofland 1973; Bernstein cited Coser 1975; Donley-Reid 1990, p. 115; Kent 1990; Sanders 1990, p. 71; Whitelaw 1991, p. 165, 1994, p. 238).

Such a shift to increasingly well-defined material and social environments has long been considered characteristic of the Epipalaeolithic and Early Neolithic of the Near East (see Renfrew 1998; Watkins 2004*a,b*; Runciman 2005). However, the alternative model suggested here posits that instead of a step change, material resources such as permanent built structures were incorporated gradually into social practices as the scale of social life increased; a social network perspective will allow testing of this hypothesis through quantitative analysis of the near eastern Epipalaeolithic and Early Neolithic.

Clearly, corporal and material resources are not mutually exclusive: even today, we use corporal resources, very intimate body-based forms of interaction, alongside our more formal architectures. Small-and large-scale forms of sociality intersect and interlace, grading into and becoming layered onto one another. Nevertheless, it would seem that as groups and societies increase in scale, material resources become more and more essential to maintain social relationships with others who are becoming increasingly 'distant' in social and physical space.

4.9. Conclusion: The sapient body and the mind of the artefact

The challenge that faces the long-term study of hominin evolution is to understand how 'the mind' is grounded in real-world contexts. A concerted effort by neuroscientists and archaeologists working together may provide fundamental insight into the mechanisms of social life and how this structures our relationships not only with other people but also with material culture.

We have focused here on three trends in hominin evolution: rapid encephalization; a global diaspora; and the built environment. Our argument is that the sapient mind is best approached through the study of local and immediate cultural transmission, which is always necessarily *social* transmission, grounded first and foremost in the social relationships forged between individuals and between groups using the different kinds of resources available to hand.

We have argued that the rapid encephalization seen among early hominins is intimately related to deepening of social relationships between individuals, enacted using the intimate, face-to-face social resources that are our primate inheritance. The changes in hominin life-history and metabolic budgets clearly reflect selection for a way of life in which the construction and maintenance of social bonds through the incorporation of material culture into our social networks is of primary importance.

The extension of these social relationships in time and space built on this increasing engagement with material culture was marked by the commencement of a phase of rapid geographical expansion. Using material objects to forge and maintain imaginary geographies that spanned the globe, hominins could navigate their way across the world as well as among each other—hence, the scale and diversity of material culture of the last 100 000 years (Gamble 2007, ch. 7).

Seen in this light, the gradual development of Neolithic *Homo urbanus* marks not so much a new state of mind as an increasingly fine-tuned ability to manipulate social networks over these great temporal and geographical scales using a variety of resources, but increasingly reliant on material objects and environments in a world where increased geographical distance was accompanied by much greater social distance.

Through neuroimaging studies, we are beginning to understand some of the cognitive mechanisms that underpin the corporal social resources used in face-to-face interactions among hominins as well as among primates and humans. But, the evolutionary question remains: how are such interactions 'scaled up' in time and space to allow, for example, global diasporas and small worlds? We have argued here that these developments are best explained by the adoption and the increasing use of material resources, and to that end our interest is in the neurological mechanisms for emotional and social investment in material culture.

Artefacts do not have minds of their own. But neither do people. Both are caught up from the first in networks of action that are the basis for our ability to people the world, live in settled communities and diversify our material worlds beyond anything known to other species. The selective pressures and the mechanism for doing so came from the social relationships that underpin our imaginary geographies and make our minds so distinctive. However, these relationships are dependent not only on face-to-face interactions between individuals, a basic primate strategy, but also on the active incorporation of a material culture into those relationships.

Our research is supported by grants from the British Academy Centenary Project: *From Lucy to Language: the archaeology of the Social Brain*. We would also like to thank the other participants of the Sapient Mind conference and two anonymous referees for their stimulating comments and discussion.

Endnotes

1   Hominins include ourselves (humans) and all our fossil ancestors, while hominids include humans, hominins and the great apes.
2   Cultural transmission can also be horizontal and oblique (for example, within or between peer groups) or formal or informal a (formal education or apprenticeships versus more or less discursive forms of childhood enskillment; Boyd & Richerson 1985).
3   These were the fit between a ring and a post or a cylinder and a container; examples of instruments and containers (see Gamble (2007) for further discussion).

References

Aiello, L. C. 1998 The 'expensive tissue hypothesis' and the evolution of the human adaptive niche: a study in comparative anatomy. In *Science in archaeology: an agenda for the future* (ed. J. Bayley), pp. 25–36. London, UK: English Heritage.
Aiello, L. C. & Dunbar, R. 1993 Neocortex size, group size and the evolution of language. *Curr. Anthropol.* **34**, 184–193. (doi:10.1086/204160)
Aiello, L. C. & Wheeler, P. 1995 The expensive-tissue hypothesis: the brain and the digestive system in human and primate evolution. *Curr. Anthropol.* **36**, 199–221. (doi:10.1086/204350)
Anderson, M. L. 2003 Embodied cognition: a field guide. *Artif. Intell.* **149**, 91–130. (doi:10.1016/S0004-3702(03) 00054-7)
Barrett, J. C. 1994 Defining domestic space in the Bronze Age of southern Britain. In *Architecture and order: approaches to social space* (eds M. Parker-Pearson & C. Richards), pp. 87–97. London, UK: Routledge.
Barrett, J. C. 2000 [1988] Fields of discourse: reconstituting a social archaeology. In *Interpretive archaeology* (ed. J. Thomas), pp. 23–32. London, UK: Leicester University Press.
Barrett, L. & Henzi, P. 2005 The social nature of primate cognition. *Proc. R. Soc. B* **272**, 1865–1875. (doi:10.1098/ rspb.2005.3200)
Bloch, M. 2008 Why religion is nothing special but is central. *Phil. Trans. R. Soc. B* **363**, 2055–2061. (doi:10.1098/rstb. 2008.0007)
Bloom, P. 2004 Children think before they speak. *Nature* **430**, 410–411. (doi:10.1038/430410a)
Boyd, R. & Richerson, P. J. 1985 *Culture and the evolutionary process*. Chicago, IL: University of Chicago Press.
Carsten, J. & Hugh-Jones, S. (eds) 1995 *About the house: Lévi-Strauss and beyond*. Cambridge, UK: Cambridge University Press.
Cauvin, J. 2000 *The birth of the gods and the origins of agriculture*. Cambridge, UK: Cambridge University Press.
Cavalli-Sforza, L. L. & Cavalli-Sforza, F. 1995 *The great human diasporas: the history of diversity of evolution*. Reading, MA: Perseus Books.
Chapman, J. 2000 *Fragmentation in archaeology: people, places and broken objects in the prehistory of south eastern Europe*. London, UK: Routledge.
Chase, P. G. & Dibble, H. 1987 Middle Palaeolithic symbolism: a review of current evidence and interpretation. *J. Anthropol. Archaeol.* **6**, 263–293. (doi:10.1016/ 0278-4165(87)90003-1)
Childe, V. G. 1951 *Social evolution*. London, UK: Watts.

Clark, G. A. 1992 A comment on Mithen's ecological interpretation of Palaeolithic art. *Proc. Prehist. Soc.* **58**, 107–109.

Conkey, M. W. 1995 Making things meaningful: approaches to the interpretation of the Ice Age imagery of Europe. In *Meaning in the visual arts: views from the outside. A centennial commemoration of Erwin Panofsky* (ed. I. Lavin), pp. 49–64. Princeton, NJ: Institute for Advanced Study, Princeton University Press.

Coser, R. 1975 The complexity of roles as seedbed of individual autonomy. In *The idea of social structure: essays in honor of Robert Merton* (ed. L. Coser), pp. 236–263. New York, NY: Harcourt Brace Jovanovich.

Coward, F. & Gamble, C. In press. Materiality and metaphor in earliest prehistory. In *The cognitive life of things* (eds C. Renfrew & L. Malafouris). Cambridge, UK: McDonald Institute Monographs.

Cribb, R. 1991 *Nomads in archaeology*. Cambridge, UK: Cambridge University Press.

Davidson, I. & McGrew, W. C. 2005 Stone tools and the uniqueness of human culture. *J. R. Anthropol. Inst.* **11**, 793–817. (doi:10.1111/j.1497-9655.2005.00262.x)

Deacon, T. 1997 *The symbolic species: the co-evolution of language and the human brain*. London, UK: Allen Lane.

de Amoura, A. C. & Lee, P. C. 2004 Capuchin stone tool use in Caatinga dry forest. *Science* **306**, 1909. (doi:10.1126/ science.1102558)

Deleuze, G. & Guattari, F. 1987 (2004) *A thousand plateaus: capitalism and schizophrenia*. London, UK: Continuum.

Derevenski, J. S. (ed.) 2000 *Children and material culture*. London: Routledge.

d'Errico, F. & Vanhaeren, M. 2002 Criteria for identifying red deer (Cervus elaphus) age and sex from their canines. Application to the study of Upper Palaeolithic and Mesolithic ornaments. *J. Archaeol. Sci.* **29**, 211–232. (doi:10.1006/jasc.2001.0687)

d'Errico, F. *et al.* 2003 Archaeological evidence for the emergence of language, symbolism, and music: an alternative multidisciplinary perspective. *J. World Prehist.* **17**, 1–70. (doi:10.1023/A: 1023980201043)

Dobres, M.-A. & Robb, J. 2000 *Agency in archaeology*. London, UK: Routledge.

Donley-Reid, L. W. 1990 A structuring structure: the Swahili house. In *Domestic architecture and the use of space: an interdisciplinary cross-cultural study* (ed. S. Kent), pp. 114–127. Cambridge, UK: Cambridge University Press.

Douglas, M. 1973 *Natural symbols*. Harmondsworth, UK: Pelican Books.

Dunbar, R. I. M. 1992 Neocortex size as a constraint on group size in primates. *J. Hum. Evol.* **20**, 469–493. (doi:10.1016/0047-2484(92)90081-J)

Dunbar, R. I. M. 1993 Coevolution of neocortical size, group size and language in humans. *Behav. Brain Sci.* **16**, 681–735.

Dunbar, R. I. M. 2003 The social brain: mind, language and society in evolutionary perspective. *Annu. Rev. Anthropol.* **32**, 163–181. (doi:10.1146/annurev.anthro.32.061002. 093158)

Flannery, K. V. 1967 Culture history versus cultural process: a debate in American archaeology. *Sci. Am.* **217**, 119–122.

Foley, R. A. 2001 In the shadow of the modern synthesis? Alternative perspectives on the last fifty years of palaeoanthropology. *Evol. Anthropol.* **10**, 5–15. (doi:10.1002/15206505(2001)10:1<5:: AID-EVAN1008>3.0.CO;2-Y)

Foley, R. A., Lee, P. C., Widdowson, E. M., Knight, C. D. & Jonxis, J. H. P. 1991 Ecology and energetics of encephalization in hominid evolution. *Phil. Trans. R. Soc.* B **334**, 223–232. (doi:10. 1098/rstb.1991.0111)

Fonagy, P., Gergely, G. & Target, M. 2007 The parent–infant dyad and the construction of the subjective self. *J. Child Psychol. Psychiatr.* **48**, 288–328. (doi:10.1111/j.14697610.2007.01727.x)

Frith, C. D. 2008 Social cognition. *Phil. Trans. R. Soc.* B **363**, 2033–2039. (doi:10.1098/rstb. 2008.0005)

Gallese, V. 2000 Agency and motor representations: new perspectives on intersubjectivity. *Paper presented at the Workshop on Autism and the Theory of Mind, Lyon, 18 May.*

Gallese, V. 2006 Embodied simulation: from mirror neuron systems to interpersonal relations. In *Empathy and fairness* (eds G. Bock & J. Goode), pp. 3–19. Chichester, UK: Wiley.

Gallese, V. & Lakoff, G. 2005 The brain's concepts: the role of the sensory–motor system in conceptual knowledge. *Cogn. Neuropsychol.* **21**, 455–479. (doi:10.1080/026432 90442000310)

Gallese, V., Keysers, C. & Rizzolatti, G. 2004 A unifying view of the basis of social cognition. *Trends Cogn. Sci.* **8**, 396–403. (doi:10.1016/j.tics.2004.07.002)

Gallese, V., Eagle, M. N. & Migone, P. 2007 Intentional attunement: mirror neurons and the neural underpinnings of interpersonal relations. *J. Am. Psychoanal. Assoc.* **55**, 131–176. (doi:10.1016/j.brainres.2006.01.054)

Gamble, C. 1993 *Timewalkers: the prehistory of global colonization*. London, UK: Penguin Books.

Gamble, C. 1996 Making tracks: hominid networks and the evolution of the social landscape. In *The archaeology of human ancestry: power, sex and tradition* (eds J. Steele & S. Shennan), pp. 253–277. London, UK: Routledge.

Gamble, C. 1998 Palaeolithic society and the release from proximity: a network approach to intimate relations. *World Archaeol.* **29**, 426–449.

Gamble, C. 1999 *The Palaeolithic societies of Europe*. Cambridge, UK: Cambridge University Press.

Gamble, C. 2007 *Origins and revolutions: human identity in earliest prehistory*. Cambridge, UK: Cambridge University Press.

Gamble, C. In press. Kinship and material culture: archaeological implications of the human global diaspora. In *Kinship and evolution* (eds W. James & H. Callan). Oxford, UK: Blackwell.

Gamble, C. S. & Porr, M. (eds) 2005 *The individual hominid in context: archaeological investigations of Lower and Middle Palaeolithic landscapes, locales and artefacts*, London, UK: Routledge.

Gell, A. 1998 *Art and agency: an anthropological theory*. Oxford, UK: Clarendon Press.

Gibson, J. J. 1979 *The ecological approach to visual perception*. Boston, MA: Houghton Mifflin.

Gosden, C. 2001 Making sense: archaeology and aesthetics. *World Archaeol.* **32**, 163–167. (doi:10.1080/0043824012 0079226)

Gosden, C. 2008 Social ontologies. *Phil. Trans. R. Soc. B* **363**, 2003–2010. (doi:10.1098/rstb.2008.0013)

Gosden, C. & Marshall, Y. 1999 The cultural biography of objects. *World Archaeol.* **31**, 169–178.

Granovetter, M. S. 1973 The strength of weak ties. *Am. J. Sociol.* **78**, 1360–1380. (doi:10.1086/225469)

Granovetter, M. S. 1983 The strength of weak ties: a network theory revisited. *Sociol. theory* **1**, 201–233. (doi:10.2307/202051)

Grèzes, J. & Decety, J. 2002 Does visual perception of object afford action? Evidence from a neuroimaging study. *Neuropsychologia* **40**, 212–222. (doi:10.1016/S00283932(01)00089-6)

Grèzes, J., Armony, J. L., Rowe, J. & Passingham, R. E. 2003 Activations related to "mirror" and "canonical" neurons in the human brain: an fMRI study. *Neuroimage* **18**, 928–937. (doi:10.1016/S1053-8119(03)00042-9)

Grove, M. & Coward, F. 2008 From individual neurons to social brains. *Cambridge Archaeological Journal*, **18**, 387–400. (doi: 10.1017/S0959774308000437)

Groves, C. P. & Pi, J. S. 1985 From ape's nest to human fix-point. *Man (n.s.)* **20**, 22–47.

Hallendy, N. 2000 *Inuksuit: silent messengers of the Arctic*. Washington, DC: University of Washington Press.

Hamilakis, Y., Pluciennik, M. & Tarlow, S. 2002 *Thinking through the body: archaeologies of corporeality*. London, UK: Kluwer Academic/Plenum Publishers.

Hawkes, K., O'Connell, J. F., Jones, N. G. B., Alvarez, H. & Charnov, E. L. 1998 Grandmothering, menopause, and the evolution of human life histories. *Proc. Natl Acad. Sci. USA* **95**, 1336–1339. (doi:10.1073/pnas.95.3.1336)

Henshilwood, C. S. & Marean, C. W. 2003 The origin of modern human behavior: critique of the models and their test implications. *Curr. Anthropol.* **44**, 627–651. (doi:10.1086/377665)

Hespos, S. J. & Spelke, E. S. 2004 Conceptual precursors to language. *Nature* **430**, 453–456. (doi:10.1038/nature02634)

Hillier, B. & Hanson, J. 1984 *The social logic of space*. Cambridge, UK: Cambridge University Press.

Hodder, I. 1990 *The domestication of Europe: structure and contingency in Neolithic societies.* Oxford, UK: Blackwell.

Hosfield, R. T. In press. Modes of transmission and material culture patterns in craft skills. In *Pattern and process in cultural evolution* (ed. S. Shennan), Berkeley, CA: University of California Press.

Hoskins, J. 1998 *Biographical objects: how things tell the stories of people's lives.* London, UK: Routledge.

Hutchins, E. 2008 The role of cultural practices in the emergence of modern human intelligence. *Phil. Trans. R. Soc. B* **363**, 2011–2019. (doi:10.1098/rstb.2008.0003)

Ingold, T. 2000 *The perception of the environment: essays in livelihood, dwelling and skill.* London, UK: Routledge.

Ingold, T. 2002 The agency of tools. *Paper presented at the Theoretical Archaeology Group (TAG) Conference, University of Manchester*, December 2002.

Johnson, A. W. & Earle, T. 1987 *The evolution of human societies.* Stanford, CA: Stanford University Press.

Jones, A. 2002 *Archaeological theory and scientific practice.* Cambridge, UK: Cambridge University Press.

Jordan, J. S. 2008 Wild agency: nested intentionalities in cognitive neuroscience and archaeology. *Phil. Trans. R. Soc. B* **363**, 1981–1991. (doi:10.1098/rstb.2008.0009)

Kent, S. 1990 A cross-cultural study of segmentation, architecture and the use of space. In *Domestic architecture and the use of space: an interdisciplinary cross-cultural study* (ed. S. Kent), pp. 127–152. Cambridge, UK: Cambridge University Press.

Knappett, C. 2005 *Thinking through material culture: an interdisciplinary perspective.* Philadelphia, PA: Pennsylvania University Press.

Knoblich, G. & Sebanz, N. 2008 Evolving intentions for social interaction: from entrainment to joint action. *Phil. Trans. R. Soc. B* **363**, 2021–2031. (doi:10.1098/rstb.2008.0006)

Kolen, J. 1999 Hominids without homes: on the nature of Middle Palaeolithic settlement in Europe. In *The Middle Palaeolithic occupation of Europe* (eds W. Roebroeks & C. Gamble), pp. 140–175. Leiden, The Netherlands: University of Leiden Press.

Kopytoff, I. 1986 The cultural biography of things: commoditization as process. In *The social life of things: commodities in cultural perspective* (ed. A. Appadurai), pp. 64–91. Cambridge, UK: Cambridge University Press.

Lakoff, G. & Johnson, M. 1980 *Metaphors we live by.* Chicago, IL: The University of Chicago Press.

Lakoff, G. & Johnson, M. 1999 *Philosophy in the flesh.* New York: Basic Books.

Law, J. 1999 After ANT: complexity, naming and topology. In *Actor network theory and after* (eds J. Law & J. Hassard), pp. 1–14. Oxford/Keele, UK: Blackwell Publishers/The Sociological Review.

Leach, E. 1973 Concluding address. In *The explanation of culture change: models in prehistory* (ed. C. Renfrew), pp. 761–771. London, UK: Duckworth.

LeDoux, J. 1998 *The emotional brain.* London, UK: Orion Books.

Lofland, L. H. 1973 *A world of strangers: order and action in urban public space.* New York, NY: Basic Books.

Maravita, A. & Iriki, A. 2004 Tools for the body (schema). *Trends Cogn. Sci.* **8**, 79–86. (doi:10.1016/j.tics.2003.12.008)

Mason, S., Hather, J. & Hillman, G. 1994 Preliminary investigation of the plant macro-remains from Dolni Vestonice II and its implications for the role of plant foods in Palaeolithic and Mesolithic Europe. *Antiquity* **68**, 48–57.

Matt Grove and Fiona Coward (2008). From Individual Neurons to Social Brains. *Cambridge Archaeological Journal,* **18**, pp. 387–400. (doi:10.1017/s0959774308000437)

McBrearty, S. & Brooks, A. S. 2000 The revolution that wasn't: a new interpretation of the origin of modern human behavior. *J. Hum. Evol.* **39**, 453–563. (doi:10.1006/jhev.2000.0435)

McGrew, W. C. 1992 *Chimpanzee material culture: implications for human evolution.* Cambridge, UK: Cambridge University Press.

Milgram, S. 1977 *The individual in a social world: essays and experiments*. Reading, MA: Addison-Wesley Publishing Company.

Mithen, S. 1996 *The prehistory of the mind: a search for the origins of art, religion and science*. London, UK: Thames and Hudson.

Mithen, S. 2005 *The singing Neanderthals: the origins of music, language, mind and body*. London, UK: Weidenfeld and Nicolson.

Niedenthal, P. M. 2007 Embodying emotion. *Science* **316**, 1002–1005. (doi:10.1126/science.1136930)

O'Connell, J. F., Hawkes, K. & Jones, N. G. B. 1999 Grandmothering and the evolution of Homo erectus. *J. Hum. Evol.* **36**, 461–485. (doi:10.1006/jhev.1998.0285)

Parker-Pearson, M. & Ramilisonina 1998 Stonehenge for the ancestors: the stones pass on the message. *Antiquity* **72**, 308–326.

Peccei, J. S. 1995 The origin and evolution of menopause: the altriciality-lifespan hypothesis. *Ethol. Sociobiol.* **16**, 425–449. (doi:10.1016/0162-3095(95)00069-0)

Prussin, L. 1989 The architecture of nomadism: gabra placemaking and culture. In *Housing, culture and design: a comparative perspective* (eds S. M. Low & E. Chambers), pp. 141–163. Philadelphia, PA: University of Pennsylvania Press.

Rapoport, A. 1969 *House form and culture*. Eaglewood Cliffs, NJ: Prentice-Hall.

Rapoport, A. 1981 Identity and environment: a cross-cultural perspective. In *Housing and identity: cross-cultural perspectives* (ed. J. S. Duncan), pp. 6–35. London, UK: Croom Helm.

Rapoport, A. 1990 Systems of activities and systems of settings. In *Domestic architecture and the use of space: an interdiscilplinary cross-cultural study* (ed. S. Kent), pp. 9–20. Cambridge, UK: Cambridge University Press.

Renfrew, C. 1998 Mind and matter: cognitive archaeology and external symbolic storage. In *Cognition and material culture: the archaeology of symbolic storage* (eds C. Renfrew & C. Scarre), pp. 1–6. Oxford, UK: Oxbow Books.

Renfrew, C. 2001 Symbol before concept: material engagement and the early development of society. In *Archaeological theory today* (ed. I. Hodder), pp. 122–140. London, UK: Polity Press.

Renfrew, C. 2008 Neuroscience, evolution and the sapient paradox: the factuality of value and of the sacred. *Phil. Trans. R. Soc. B* **363**, 2041–2047. (doi:10.1098/rstb.2008. 0010)

Rizzolatti, G. & Craighero, L. 2004 The mirror–neuron system. *Annu. Rev. Neurosci.* **27**, 169–192. (doi:10.1146/ annurev.neuro.27.070203.144230)

Roepstorff, A. 2008 Things to think with: words and objects as material symbols. *Phil. Trans. R. Soc. B* **363**, 2049–2054. (doi:10.1098/rstb.2008.0015)

Roveland, B. 2000 Footprints in the clay: Upper Palaeolithic children in ritual and secular contexts. In *Children and material culture* (ed. J. S. Derevenski), pp. 29–38. London, UK: Routledge.

Runciman, W. G. 2005 Stone Age sociology. *J. R. Anthropol. Inst.* **11**, 129–142. (doi:10.1111/ j.1467-9655.2005.00229.x)

Sanders, D. 1990 Behavioral conventions and archaeology: methods for the analysis of ancient architecture. In *Domestic architecture and the use of space: an interdisciplinary cross-cultural study* (ed. S. Kent), pp. 43–72. Cambridge, UK: Cambridge University Press.

Semaw, S., Renne, P., Harris, J. W. K., Feibel, C. S., Bernor, R. L., Fesseha, N. & Mowbray, K. 1997 2.5 Million-yearold stone tools from Gona, Ethiopia. *Nature* **385**, 333–336. (doi:10.1038/ 385333a0)

Shennan, S. 2002 *Genes, memes and human History: Darwinian archaeology and cultural evolution*. London, UK: Thames and Hudson.

Shennan, S. & Steele, J. 1999 Cultural learning in hominids: a behavioural ecological approach. In *Mammalian social learning: comparative and ecological perspectives* (eds H. O. Box & K. R. Gibson), pp. 367–388. Cambridge, UK: Cambridge University Press.

Smith, B. H. & Tompkins, R. L. 1995 Towards a life history of the hominidae. *Annu. Rev. Anthropol.* **24**, 257–279. (doi:10.1146/annurev.an.24.100195.001353)

Sofaer, J. 2006 *The body as material culture*. Cambridge, UK: Cambridge University Press.

Stout, D., Toth, N., Schick, K. & Chaminade, T. 2008 Neural correlates of Early Stone Age toolmaking: technology, language and cognition in human evolution. *Phil. Trans. R. Soc. B* **363**, 1939–1949. (doi:10.1098/rstb.2008.0001)

Strathern, M. 1988 *The gender of the gift: problems with women and problems with society in Melanesia*. Berkeley, MA: University of California Press.

Strathern, M. 1998 Social relations and the idea of externality. In *Cognitive storage and material culture: the archaeology of symbolic storage* (eds C. Renfrew & C. Scarre), pp. 135–147. Cambridge, UK: McDonald Institute.

Terrell, J. E. 2007 The rudiments of agriculture and domestication: response to Peter Bellwood's first farmers: the origins of agricultural societies. *Camb. Archaeol. J.* **17**, 100–102. (doi:10.1017/S0959774307000078)

Tilley, C. (ed.) 1993 *Interpretative archaeology*, London, UK: Berg.

Tilley, C. 1996 *An ethnography of the Neolithic*. Cambridge, UK: Cambridge University Press.

Tilley, C. 1999 *Metaphor and material culture*. Oxford, UK: Blackwell.

Tilley, C. 2004 *The materiality of stone: explorations in landscape phenomenology*. London, UK: Berg.

Turnbull, D. 1991 *Mapping the world in the mind: an investigation of the unwritten knowledge of Micronesian navigators*. Geelong, Australia: Deakin University Press.

Turner, J. H. 2000 *On the origins of human emotions: a sociological inquiry into the evolution of human affect*. Stanford, CA: Stanford University Press.

Vanhaeren, M. & d'Errico, F. 2005 Grave goods from the Saint-Germain-la-Riviére burial: evidence for social inequality in the Upper Palaeolithic. *J. Anthropol. Archaeol.* **24**, 117–134. (doi:10.1016/j.jaa.2005.01.001)

Varney Burch, J. 2007 Arctic inuit art. See http://www. arcticinuitart.com/culture/inuk.html.

Watkins, T. 2004*a* Architecture and 'theatres of memory' in the Neolithic of Southwest Asia. In *Rethinking materiality: the engagement of mind with the material world* (eds E. DeMarrais, C. Gosden & C. Renfrew), pp. 97–106. Cambridge, UK: McDonald Institute of Archaeological Research.

Watkins, T. 2004*b* Building houses, framing concepts, constructing worlds. *Paléorient* **30**, 5–24.

Watts, D. J. 2003 *Six degrees: the science of a connected age*. London, UK: Vintage.

Whitelaw, T. 1991 Some dimensions of variability in the social organisation of community space among foragers. In *Ethnoarchaeological approaches to mobile campsites: hunter-gatherer and pastoralist case studies* (eds C. S. Gamble & W. A. Boismier), pp. 139–188. Ann Arbor, MI: International Monographs in Prehistory 1.

Whitelaw, T. M. 1994 Order without architecture: functional, social and symbolic dimensions in hunter-gatherer settlement organization. In *Architecture and order: approaches to social space* (eds M. Parker-Pearson & C. Richards), pp. 217–243. London, UK: Routledge.

Wilson, P. 1988 *The domestication of the human species*. New Haven, CT: Yale University Press.

Wobst, H. M. 2000 Agency in (spite of) material culture. In *Agency in archaeology* (eds M.-A. Dobres & J. Robb), pp. 40–50. London, UK: Routledge.

Zilhao, J. 2007 The emergence of ornaments and art: an archaeological perspective on the origins of behavioural "modernity". *J. Archaeol. Res.* **15**, 1–54. (doi:10.1007/ s10814-006-9008-1)

5

Wild agency: nested intentionalities in cognitive neuroscience and archaeology

J. Scott Jordan

The present paper addresses the tensions between internalist and radical-interactionist approaches to cognitive neuroscience, and the conflicting conclusions these positions lead to as regards the issue of whether archaeological artefacts constitute 'results' or 'components' of cognition. Wild systems theory (WST) and the notion of wild agency are presented as a potential resolution. Specifically, WST conceptualizes organisms (i.e. wild agents) as open, multi-scale self-sustaining systems. It is thus able to address the causal properties of wild systems in a manner that is consistent with radical-interactionist concerns regarding multi-scale contingent interactions. Furthermore, by conceptualizing wild agents as self-sustaining embodiments of the persistent, multi-scale contexts that afforded their emergence and in which they sustain themselves, WST is able to address the semantic properties of wild agents in a way that acknowledges the internalist concerns regarding meaningful (i.e. semantic) internal states (i.e. *causal content*). In conclusion, WST agrees with radical interactionism and asserts that archaeological artefacts constitute components of cognition. In addition, given its ability to resolve tensions between the internalist and the radical interactionist approaches to cognition, WST is presented as potentially integrative for cognitive science in general.

Keywords: cognition; interactionism; internalism; self-sustaining systems; developmental systems

Removing the arrows of modernity from the archaeological perceptual field is not an easy task; it will involve a great deal of cognitive dissonance (Malafouris, 2003). Yet to tackle the complex intentionalities enacted through the materiality of the archaeological record, we need to move on and where necessary transgress the ontological tidiness of our modern taxonomies . . .

(Malafouris 2004, p. 54)

5.1. Introduction

What Malafouris seems to be after in this quotation is a rethinking of the relationship between cognitive science and archaeology, specifically as regards the manner in which we conceptualize cognition and the impact that conceptualization has on our interpretation of archaeological data. In modern taxonomies, cognition is conceptualized as an internal, centralized decision-making function that uses perceptual input in order to generate the appropriate behavioural output (Clark 1997, 2001; Jordan 2003a, 2004). Within the framework of such *internalism*, the archaeological record is conceptualized as constituting a 'result' of cognition.

Despite our long-standing commitment to internalism and the clear boundaries it implies between mind and world, many researchers in cognitive psychology (Glenberg 1997; Barsalou 1999; Zwaan 1999; Jordan 2000a,b; Wilson 2002), robotics (Brooks 1999; Anderson 2003; Steels in press), philosophy (Clark 1997, 2000; van Gelder 1998; Juarrero 1999; O'Regan & Nöe 2001; Myin & O'Regan 2002; Van Orden & Holden 2002) and archaeology (Malafouris 2004) are working to develop approaches to cognition that are much more interactionist in nature. That is, they place greater emphasis on the fact that the brain is housed in a body that is embedded in a world, and then examine the extent to which the phenomenon of cognition can be 'spread-out' as it were, across these multiple scales of interaction. Clark (2001) for example, describes research in which it was found that expert bartenders remember drink orders better than novices because they *externally* code each order by selecting a particular type of glass for that order. According to Clark, the use of such *external codes*, what he refers to as *cognitive technology*, begs the issue of whether these material artefacts are constituents or products of cognition. The distinction is important. If they are products, internalism prevails, but if they are constituents, the ontological tidiness of internalism begins to clutter as the borders between mind and world become increasingly vague, and artefacts in the archaeological record find themselves potentially conceptualized as components of mental work.

Oyama (1985) offers a potential resolution of the tension between internalism and inter-actionism. Specifically, she argues that the mind-world dichotomy inherent in internalist approaches to cognition constitutes but a special case of a more general tendency in the natural sciences to explain large-scale phenomena such as phenotypes and behaviour in terms of smaller scale 'agent-like' structures such as genes and brains, respectively. What Oyama means by this is not that researchers believe genes have minds. Rather, what she is after is our tendency to conceptualize smaller scale structure as entailing 'information', 'instructions', 'codes' or 'plans' for larger scale phenomena.

Oyama rejects this view, what she refers to as the *cognitive-causal gene*, and proposes a radically interactionist alternative, what she refers to as developmental systems theory (DST), because she believes that structures at all levels of scale are ultimately constituted of multi-scale, interaction-driven dynamics. *All* aspects of development are therefore inherently context dependent, and the science of any developmental process, from the development of a phenotype to the development of a group or a society, must account for these multi-scale contingent contexts instead of glossing over them via phrases such as *ceteris paribus*, or the use of agent-like entities that are assumed to 'pre-specify' or 'code for' larger scale order. According to this view, organisms inherit, in addition to genes, the multi-scale contexts necessary for the emergence of a phenotype—what Oyama collectively refers to as a *developmental system* (e.g. the persistence of contexts entailing available food, clothing, shelter and other organisms).

At first glance, DST seems to resolve the tension between internalist and interactionist approaches to cognition because it provides an overarching interactionist framework that successfully deconstructs the supposed agent-like properties of smaller scale entities such as genes and brains into complexes of multi-scale interactive dynamics. According to this view, the interactionists win out, cognition spreads out across the body-world boundary, and archaeological artefacts constitute the components of cognition.

Upon further reflection, however, it appears that something is missing. For while DST's untidy ontological framework seems to successfully address causality, it actually does not address the very properties of cognition and agency that have compelled scholars to use concepts such as information, code and plan. Clark (2001) expresses this concern in the following way:

> The image of brain, body, and world as a single, densely coupled system threatens to eliminate the idea of purposive agency unless it is combined with some recognition of the special way goals and

knowledge figure in the origination of some of our bodily motions. The computational/information-processing approach provides such recognition by embracing a kind of dual-aspect account in which certain inner states and processes act as the vehicles of knowledge and information.

(Clark 2001, p. 135)

What Clark seems to be getting at via the use of concepts such as 'goals', 'knowledge' and 'vehicles of knowledge and information' is the idea that there is something about brain dynamics that distinguishes them from other types of physical dynamics. Specifically, Clark wants to model brain dynamics as entailing both *causal* properties (i.e. a brain state can influence another physical state) and *semantic* properties (i.e. brain states entail content—they have meaning), what one might refer to as *causal content*. According to radical interactionism, however, concepts such as goals and knowledge should ultimately be recast in terms of multi-scale, interaction-driven dynamics. The problem with this manoeuvre, however, as eluded to by Clark, is that it only addresses the causal properties of such a dynamics. It, in no way, addresses their semantic properties.

To be sure, radical interactionists such as Oyama (1985) and van Gelder (1998) do have a point, and they are not alone, for the notion of internal causal content has been under attack for some time (e.g. Searle 1980; Chalmers 1996). However, herein lies the rub. For while radical interactionism successfully dismantles agent-based accounts of larger scale order, it does so by ignoring the semantic properties that seem to actually define cognition agency (Pacherie 2007). While the internalists, who rightly reject radical interactionism due to its failure to address cognition's semantic properties, see no way of conceptualizing agency and its associated content without positing internalized, content-bearing vehicles that, in the end, do not stand up to the scrutiny of radical interactionism.

In light of this apparent stalemate, the purpose of the present paper is to describe an approach to agency, what I refer to as wild systems theory (WST; Jordan 2003a, 2008a, in press; Jordan & Ghin 2006, 2007) that posits an account of the semantic properties of agentic states, how they emerged and how they were extended, while simultaneously doing justice to radically interactionist concerns about conceptualizing such states within a mind-world dichotomy that ultimately isolates them internally and, as a result, renders them conceptually lacking.

5.2. What is a wild system?

WST begins its approach to agency by conceptualizing organisms, not as computational systems or physical–mental systems, but as open systems (i.e. far-from-equilibrium, energy-transformation systems) that must intake, transform and dissipate energy in order to sustain themselves (Boltzmann 1905; Lotka 1945; Schroedinger 1945; Odum 1988; Vandervert 1995; Boden 1999). In addition, the context in which organisms are embedded (what is traditionally referred to as an 'environment'), is conceptualized as a self-organizing, energy-transformation hierarchy (Odum 1988; Vandervert 1995). What this means is that the natural world is conceptualized in terms of energy-transformation, such that plants are described as systems that sustain themselves via the intake and transformation of electromagnetic radiation into chemical energy, while herbivores constitute systems that sustain themselves on the chemical energy encapsulated in plants. Such an energy-transformation hierarchy is self-organizing because the structures within it emerge out of the dynamic interactions of properties within the system itself, and it is hierarchical because the availability of particular types of energy (e.g. availability of chemical energy in plants) affords the emergence of systems capable of sustaining themselves on such energy.

Within an energy-transformation hierarchy, survival (i.e. sustainment) requires that energy-transformers be capable of generating outcomes such as capturing fuel sources and avoiding predators. To do so, they must be further capable of generating coordination among the multi-scale systems of which they are constituted (e.g. neurons, neural networks, brains and bodies). Each of these different levels of scale (i.e. neurons, neural networks, brains and the body as a whole) has its own intrinsic dynamics. The spatio–temporal scale of neuronal dynamics, for example, and the factors that influence such dynamics (e.g. neuro-transmitter gradients, synapse densities and the rate of orthograde and retrograde axoplasmic transport) are nested within, yet different from the dynamics of factors critical to the genera-tion and sustainment of neural networks (e.g. neurogenesis (Edelman 1989) and cell assembly formation (Hebb 1949)). Likewise, the dynamics of both of these scales are nested within, yet nonetheless different from sustainment dynamics at the behavioural scale (e.g. behavioural selection and sustainment via reinforcement and punishment, respectively).

Achieving coordination among these multi-scale systems is continuously challenged by the fact that the dynamics at each level fluctuate continuously because (i) they are open to the flow of energy and matter, (ii) the matter–energy context in which they are embedded constantly fluctuates, and (iii) the system's dynamics influence themselves recursively. That is, each level of scale embodies its own history.

To meet the challenge of continuous, recursive multi-scale fluctuations, each level must be capable of addressing the perturbations to sustainment at its own unique level. This is what is meant by referring to such systems as *wild* systems. They must be able to address multiple scales of fluctuation *continuously* while simultaneously achieving coordination as a collective whole. Only then will they be able to produce sustainment-appropriate outcomes. In short, their moment to moment collective dynamics must be a reflection of the open (i.e. wild) multi-scale field of perturbations in which they are embedded.

5.3. Acquiring wild agency: Causality and semantics

WST's conceptualization of wild systems as multi-scale open systems is consistent with Oyama's (1985) radical interactionism. Causality at every level of scale is synergistically coupled both internally and externally (including the environmental context in which the system is embedded). But while this focus on multi-scale causality ultimately leads radical interactionism to avoid the semantic properties of certain types of wild systems (i.e. brains), WST's emphasis on sustainment within an energy-transformation hierarchy provides insight into certain unique causal properties of wild systems that, in the end, provide a means of addressing their semantic properties.

(a) Wild agents as hierarchies of self-sustaining work

A unique causal property of wild systems is that they are able to sustain themselves in an energy-transformation hierarchy because their multi-scale dynamics are *self-sustaining*. That is, their dynamics produce products that sustain the dynamics that produced the products. At the chemical level, this recursive process is known as *autocatalysis* (Kauffman 1995).

When a catalyst is produced by the very reaction it catalyses, the reaction, in essence *catalyses itself* (i.e. it sustains itself). At the level of the single cell, self-sustainment has been referred to both as autocatalysis and autopoiesis (Varela *et al.* 1991; Ruiz-Mirazo & Moreno 2004).

According to Jordan & Ghin (2006), single cells are self-sustaining in that there is an autocatalytic micro–macro synergy between the internal dynamics of the cell and the cell–environment dynamics of the cell as a whole (see Jordan & Ghin (2006), for an explanation of why they focus on autocatalysis versus autopoiesis). That is, the system is able to affect sustainment-producing changes to its relationship with the environment (i.e. attain sustenance) because the internal dynamics are coupled in such a way that fluctuations in the cell's fuel supply give rise to phase transitions in the macro-level whole (e.g. swimming and tumbling) that potentially increase the system's fuel supply (e.g. the cell ends up at a new location in a concentration gradient of nutrients). As a result, the work of the micro–macro synergy produces products (i.e. sustenance) that sustain the work of the micro–macro synergy.

At the level of the neural network, Hebb (1949) and Edelman (1989) recognized that neurons *sustain themselves* by forming connections with other neurons and becoming embedded within a neural network. Neurons that do not embed within a network die off. In short, the *work* of being a neuron (e.g. forming synapses, generating action potentials and engaging in axiomatic transport) is self-sustaining.

At the behavioural level-of-scale (i.e. the organism–environment level), Skinner (1976) recognized that *behavioural work* is self-sustaining. That is, behaviours are maintained within an organism's repertoire as a function of the products (i.e. outcomes) they produce, with reinforcing and punishing outcomes being sustained and deselected, respectively.

In a nutshell, wild agents are multi-scale open systems which are able to maintain their structural integrity because their multi-scale dynamics are self-sustaining. In addition, the work taking place among these multi-scale nested systems is recursively self-sustaining, what Bickhard (2001) refers to as recursively self-maintaining. For example, when one engages in the behavioural work of consuming an apple (i.e. finding it, picking it and eating it) the behavioural work (i.e. finding, picking and eating) produces a product (i.e. the release of chemical energy in the apple) that sustains the systems (e.g. neurons, neural networks and muscles) that made the behavioural work possible in the first place.

Jordan & Ghin (2006) assert that the emergence of such systems constituted the emergence of *natural intentionality*, in that, the micro–macro synergies of such systems are *inherently* end-directed towards self-sustainment. That is, they are capable of offsetting perturbations to the sustainment of the macro–micro synergy. Given that each level of self-sustaining work in a multi-scale self-sustaining system (e.g. neurons, brains and behaviours) must be able to offset perturbations to the work at that level of scale, each level is inherently end-directed and, therefore, *naturally intentional*. This leads to the assertion that wild agents constitute hierarchies of nested intentionalities.

It is in this sense that WST conceptualizes organisms as natural, wild agents. Not in the sense that smaller scale internal dynamics code for larger scale dynamics, as is the case in internalist approaches to agency. But rather, in the sense such systems constitute a nesting of multi-scale self-sustaining dynamics. It is the inherent end-directedness of these self-sustaining systems that, according to WST, qualifies such systems as agents.

WST's approach to agency addresses DST's concerns about conceptualizing agency in terms of small-scale 'pre-specifying' structures, for WST posits no such entities. Rather, by focusing on the unique self-sustaining causal properties of wild systems, WST provides an approach to agency that conceptualizes it in terms of multi-scale dynamic interactions. The key insight is that in wild systems, such dynamic interactions are self-sustaining and, as a result, inherently intentional (i.e. end-directed). That is, the intentionality does not reside in smaller scale, pre-specifying codes. Rather, it resides in the self-sustaining, causal properties of such systems.

(b) Wild agents and their semantic properties

Jordan & Ghin (2006) propose that the unique, self-sustaining causal properties of wild agents can be used to explain their semantic properties. Specifically, they argue that wild agents constitute *embodiments* of the multi-scale open contexts (i.e. the energy-transformation contexts) that afford their emergence and sustainment. What this means basically, is that wild agents are *naturally* and *necessarily* 'about' the multi-scale energy-transformation contexts in which they sustain themselves. They are naturally and necessarily about such contexts because their multi-scale dynamics are a reflection of the contexts that have persisted (i.e. in which they have been embedded) over the course of both their species' emergence (e.g. the persistent presence of contexts such as fuel sources, oxygen and predators) and their own individual emergence (i.e. the persistent contexts in which the individual wild system has had to sustain itself), what are typically referred to as the phylogenetic and ontogenetic time scales, respectively.

This notion of *embodied context* should not be confused with internalism. Rather, it is more consistent with Oyama's (1985) notion of a developmental system, the idea being that organisms inherit not only their genes but also the multi-scale contexts in which the interactions necessary to the emergence of a phenotype are possible (e.g. the persistence of contexts entailing available food, clothing, shelter and other organisms). Claiming that wild agents constitute self-sustaining embodiments of their developmental contexts and are therefore naturally and necessarily about these contexts is not the same as claiming their internal dynamics code for or 'represent' external dynamics. 'Aboutness' only translates to 'code' when we make internalist assumptions like 'vehicles of content'. All aspects of a wild agent are necessarily about the nesting of contexts that constitute both the agent and the context in which it is embedded (i.e. the developmental system). It just so happens, however, that different internal contexts (e.g. stomachs versus brains) are coupled with embedding contexts in different ways, and it is the nature of these couplings that gives rise to the different types of aboutness entailed by such systems.

5.4. Extending wild agency

Given that wild agents constitute embodiments of context, they can be conceptualized as *world-in-world*. That is, the natural homology of organisms and the contexts they embody indicates that wild agents do not need to be 'informed' about the context in which they are embedded (i.e. their environment) in order to be about it. They are naturally and necessarily about it. This means that by being world-in-world, no epistemic gap exists between an organism's embodied contexts and the contexts in which it is embedded. As a result, there is no need to posit 'content vehicles' that serve the dual purpose of being both causal and semantic. In addition, there is no longer any need for the input–computation–output approach to cognition that was part and parcel to internalism and its assertion of causal content. Instead of the concepts perception, action and cognition, WST conceptualizes psychological functionality in terms of *scales of sustainment*.

The concept scales of sustainment provides a gradient-oriented approach to psychological functionality, versus the trichotomy-driven approach (i.e. perception, action and cognition) of internalism. In this gradient-oriented framework, the distinguishing feature of an architecture is the distality of the time scales in which a wild agent can sustain coordinations (see figure 5.1). Whereas a single-cell organism is only capable of sustaining coordinations at the proximal scale (i.e. at its membrane interface with the context in which it is embedded), humans are further capable of simultaneously sustaining coordinations with events at the distal scale (i.e. the immediate environmental context). For example, to dance, one must continuously offset perturbations to balance. This constitutes *proximal* sustainment: the system as a whole is capable of offsetting perturbations to relationships among its nested systems, as well as the immediate context in which it is embedded. To dance in a larger distal context (e.g. dance across a crowded floor towards a friend) one must engage in proximal sustainment while simultaneously doing so in a way that avoids other dancers (i.e. offsets perturbations to one's planned distal outcome). This constitutes *distal* sustainment: the system is able to constrain its proximal sustainment in ways that offset perturbations to distal events the system is working to produce.

In addition to proximal and distal sustainment, humans are further able to engage in *virtual* sustainment. For example, in order to switch from dancing a tango to a samba, one must constrain one's distal sustainment towards producing a samba-like distal pattern versus a tango-like pattern. The switch from one *possible* distal pattern to another

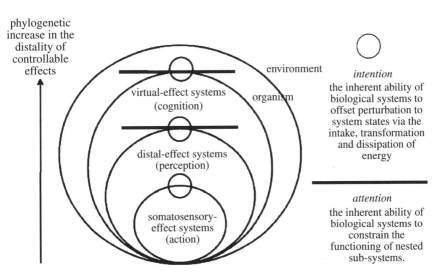

Figure 5.1. According to WST, psychological functionality is described not in terms of action, perception and cognition, but in terms of synergistically coupled scales of self-sustaining effect-control. Such multi-scale effect-control systems are able to sustain relationships with events taking place at increasingly larger spatio-temporal scales ranging from the proximal, to the distal, to the virtual. Given each level of scale is capable of offsetting perturbations, each level is inherently end-directed and therefore, naturally intentional.

constitutes virtual sustainment: the system is able to reconfigure and constrain the possible distal patterns it works to sustain.

To claim such sustainment is virtual is to say it is based on *simulation* (Metzinger 2003; Grush 2004) particularly as regards what cognitive scientists traditionally refer to as *off-line cognition* (Wilson 2002) because it is about contexts (i.e. events) that are not in the organism's immediate organism–environment context (e.g. memories and thoughts).

To review, WST conceptualizes psychological functionality in terms of synergistically yoked scales of contextual sustainment, and it does so in order to address psychological functionality in a way that is consistent with Oyama's notion of multi-scale interaction, and WST's notion of open, multi-scale systems working to sustain functional coherence (i.e. offset perturbation) at multiple scales simultaneously, both within the system's internal dynamics and within its relation to the multiple scales of context in which it is embedded. Given such sustainment necessitates perturbation offset, proximal, distal and virtual sustainment have also been referred to as proximal, distal and virtual *event-control* (Jordan 2003*b*). Within WST, sustainment and control are interchangeable, because both are used to denote perturbation offset.

Given this notion of describing the functionality of wild agents in terms of event control, the following will describe the contextual constraints that fostered the emergence of increasingly distal scales of sustainment. While doing so I attempt to describe how, within the framework of WST, external aspects of the sustainment process (i.e. aspects of the developmental system) became constitutive of what internalism would conceptualize as mental work.

(a) Extending wild agency from proximal to virtual sustainment

The key factor that seems to have propelled the extension of wild agency from proximal to virtual sustainment was the status of wild agents as energy-transformation systems. This is consistent with modelling wild agents as being nested within a self-organizing, energy-transformation hierarchy (Odum 1988; Vandervert 1995). Specifically, the energy entailed in wild agents was available for 'capture' by another system capable of using that energy to sustain itself. Doing so, however, required the latter to be capable of overcoming all the contextual factors that needed to be addressed in order to capture the fuel source. Thus, once plant energy was widely available, it provided a context that afforded the emergence of a system capable of sustaining itself on plant energy. From this perspective, herbivores can be seen as embodiments of the constraints that need to be addressed in order for a system to sustain itself on the energy encapsulated in plants, and carnivores, the constraints to be addressed to sustain a system on the energy encapsulated in herbivores. This leads to a continuing recursion on a simple theme; specifically, *the fuel source dictates the consumer*.

According to the principle that the fuel source dictates the consumer, WST asserts (Jordan & Ghin 2006, 2007) that virtual sustainment (i.e. cognition) emerged when wild agents emerged that were able to sustain coordination with events that were not present in their immediate context. Take, for example, a lion chasing a gazelle. Lotka (1945) recognized that in order to capture the energy entailed in the gazelle, the lion must propel itself as a whole on an *anticipatory* pursuit curve. What makes the pursuit curve anticipatory is the fact that the lion runs towards a location the gazelle does not yet occupy. In short, it propels itself towards the gazelle's *future*.

The reason that a lion can chase and capture a gazelle is because it has embodied the constraint of having to capture a moving energy source. Specifically, certain structures in the lion's cerebellum have access to both the movement commands leaving motor cortex and the immediate sensory consequences of the resultant movements (Kawato *et al.* 1987; Wolpert *et al.* 1998; Desmurget & Grafton 2003; Grush 2004; Newport & Jackson 2006). These cerebellar structures project back up to motor cortex and influence its activity. This is important, for it affords the lion the ability to embody, in the weights of its cerebral–cerebellar circuitry, patterns between motor commands and their resultant sensory effects. Thus, as the lion garners experience controlling its body in relation to moving prey, successful command–feedback patterns become embodied in the cerebral–cerebellar circuits, what are known as forward and inverse models (Wolpert & Kawato 1998; Blakemore *et al.* 2000; Wolpert & Ghahramani 2000; Blakemore & Decety 2001; Knoblich & Jordan 2003; Iacoboni 2005; Jordan & Hunsinger 2008b). And given these cerebral–cerebellar loops influence motor cortex and function at a time scale of 10–20 ms, versus the 120 ms time scale between motor commands and sensory feedback, the system can basically control its propulsion via virtual feedback (Clark 1997; Grush 2004), what Paulin (1993) refers to as dynamic state *estimation*, and Kawato *et al.* (1987) refer to as anticipatory motor error. What is common to the notions virtual, estimation and anticipatory is the fact that they are about the future. And even if it is only a 200 ms pending future, it is nonetheless virtual.

Such aboutness is virtual in the sense it is about future body–prey states. To be sure, it is actually about the entire developmental system in which it is embedded. But given the unique way in which brains are coupled with the developmental systems in which they are embedded, they are able to embed (i.e. embody) regularities of the developmental system and become about those regularities more so than internal contexts that are not coupled with the developmental system in a similar way (e.g. stomachs). In addition, it is possible for the lion to embody such regularities within its brain because neural networks themselves function according to the principle of self-sustaining work (Hebb 1949; Edelman 1989). Thus, since patterns of neural activity sustain themselves, factors that cause neural patterns to repeat (i.e. command–feedback patterns in cerebral–cerebellar loops and their relationship to prey patterns) become embedded (i.e. embodied) within these self-sustaining neural patterns. In addition, all of this embodied work is naturally and necessarily about the entire developmental system that has to be addressed in order for the work to sustain itself; from the single neuron, to the neural circuit, to the neuromuscular system, to the organism as a whole. Thus, as stated above, there is no epistemic divide between internal and external contexts (including virtual states)—organisms are reciprocally nested ecosystems of self-sustaining work.

(b) Virtual scale-up requires the sustainment of developmental contexts

From the perspective that the fuel source dictates the consumer, it may seem as though the evolutionary process was one of 'packing' more and more external constraints 'into' the multi-scale self-sustaining dynamics of wild agents. When used as an account of cognition, this packing perspective might leave one prone to assuming that evolution 'packed' cognition into the brain and, as a result, lead one towards internalism. But an examination of the smaller time scales at which wild agents actually sustain coordinations with their context, reveals that much of the work entailed in sustaining coordinations resides in the ability of wild agents to capitalize on the effects they have on the context in which they are embedded. Colonies of ants, for example, are able to sustain large-scale coordinations because the individual ants both excrete and detect pheromone (Dussutour et al. 2004). Thus, by altering their external context (i.e. releasing pheromone) they help generate and sustain the external conditions necessary to both individual and group sustainment.

Consistent with Oyama (1985), these sustained external contexts would constitute aspects of the ants' developmental system. Also consistent with Oyama, these contexts can function at different time scales. For example, via the release and uptake of pheromones, a colony of termites can give rise to the production of a termite hill (Sulis 1997). Here we have two time scales of *context-generation and sustainment*; specifically, pheromone release and uptake gives rise to stable termite couplings, while collections of coupled termites give rise to the termite hill. Both contexts constitute aspects of the termites' developmental system because each gives rise to external conditions (i.e. contexts) that afford both individual and group sustainment.

As another example of sustained external context, many species produce auditory alterations of their external context (i.e. generate auditory signals), which have an impact on social organization (i.e. the sustainment of social context). In certain types of insects, for example, generating synchronous or asynchronous sounds is a way for males to compete for females (Greenfield et al. 1997; Gerhardt & Huber 2002). In banded wrens (*Thryothorus pleurostictus*), overlapping another male's call is a way for males to establish dominance and maintain territorial boundaries (Hall et al. 2006). And female songbirds which hear their partner lose a vocal interaction are more likely to seek extra-pair copulations (Mennill et al. 2003).

The point here is that the scaling up of wild agents seems to have necessitated and entailed the synergistic emergence and sustainment of *coupled internal–external contexts*. In short, wild agents generate and sustain important aspects of their own developmental system. Thus, not only are wild agents naturally and necessarily about the multi-scale contexts they embody, certain of those embodied contexts are about changes in external context brought about by wild agents themselves.

This notion of coupled internal–external contexts is important to understanding the scale-up of virtual sustainment from the 200 ms zebra-future available to the lion, to the infinite possible time scales available to human imagination, for it turns out that in certain primate brains, the cerebellar–cortical circuits underlying virtual sustainment are actually open to direct external coupling with conspecifics. Specifically, cognitive neuroscientists have recently discovered neurons in area F5 of the macaque monkey (*Macaca fascicularis*) that are active both when the monkey performs a goal related action and when it observes another execute such an action (Rizzolatti et al. 2002). Using functional magnetic resonance imaging with human participants, Calvo-Merino et al. (2005) found a pre-motor activation in the human homologue of the macaque F5 when observers watched video clips of either ballet or capoeira dancers. The degree of activation, however, varied directly with the observer's level of motor expertise in a given dance form, in that ballet and capoeira experts revealed more activation in response to the dance form in which they were experts, while non-expert dancers revealed less activation, and the level did not vary with the dance type.

Collectively, these data reveal a direct, goal-related internal/external coupling between individuals. That is, when one individual produces a distal event (e.g. cracks a peanut, uses a tool or dances a ballet) the generation of that distal event produces the planning states for generating that the same distal event in the event-control systems of an observer. Elsewhere (Jordan 2007), I have referred to this phenomenon as the coupling of *intentional contexts*.

And in addition to the coupling of distal, goal-related intentional contexts, there is evidence of direct coupling of proximal, movement-related control systems (i.e. action systems). Grezes *et al.* (1998), for example, found that if participants are asked to observe meaningless and meaningful gestures (e.g. slicing bread motions with or without the presence of bread), both types of movements activate a common network involved in the analysis of hand movements (i.e. bilaterally, the occipitotemporal junction and superior occipital gyrus, and in the left hemisphere, the middle temporal gyrus and the inferior parietal lobe). Differentially, however, meaningful movements further activated inferior frontal gyrus and the fusiform gyrus, predominately in the left hemisphere (i.e. areas involved in motor planning and object identification, respectively), while meaningless actions resulted in bilateral activations of the inferior parietal lobe and the superior parietal lobule, as well as the right cerebellum (i.e. areas involved in action planning and generation, what were referred to above as forward and inverse models). Collectively, these findings indicate that the observation of another's movements, even if they are meaningless (i.e. have no obvious distal goal), results in the activation of brain processes one would use to generate those same actions oneself.

This notion of a multi-scaled coupling of intentional contexts is consistent with Iacoboni's (2005) model of imitation. According to Iacoboni, direct-coupling systems, what are referred to in the literature as 'mirroring' systems, constitute an important aspect of one's event-control systems. Specifically, he describes how the two mirroring systems, one located in pars opercularis of the inferior frontal gyrus (i.e. Brodmann area 44, the human homologue of the macaque area F5) and the other in the posterior parietal cortex (i.e. a human homologue of mirroring systems found in the inferior parietal lobe of the macaque), project onto superior temporal sulcus (STS) which, in turn, projects back onto the mirroring systems. Iacoboni asserts that the frontal mirroring system is about the distal goal, and the parietal system, that actions generated to attain the goal. He collectively refers to this neural pattern as an *efference-copy*. He does so because (i) in addition to projecting to STS, the mirroring systems also project onto the motor centres involved in bringing about the actions that will ultimately bring about the distal goal and (ii) it constitutes the plan the observer will eventually use to generate the same proximal and distal effect him/her self.

Iacoboni's referral to this neural activity as an efference-copy is revealing because it actually comprises anticipated proximal *effects* and intended distal effects, both of which are virtual and available *in the environment*. That is, producing these effects (i.e. making them occur in the environment) makes one's *anticipated* sensory effects and *intended* distal effect *public*. Thus, one's multi-scale intentional (i.e. planning) states are made public via the multi-scale pattern of effects one consistently generates. As a result, as one consistently produces a pattern of effects, this pattern can be tapped into via the mirroring systems of observers.

According to this notion of coupled, multi-scale, internal/external intentional contexts, it seems to be the case that certain primates constrain and contextualize one another's multi-scale *planning* (i.e. multi-scale virtual) states. Kinsbourne (2002) refers to such coupling as 'resonance' and argues that it constitutes the default value in human interaction. Specifically, Kinsbourne proposes that infant imitation is actually uninhibited perception 'on the fly'. That is, as a carer generates action-effect contingencies in an infant's presence, the natural, multi-scale coupling of intentional contexts results in the infant generating the same action-effect contingencies, of course to the extent the infant possesses those action-effect contingences in his/her repertoire. Only as the cortex develops inhibitory circuits, Kinsbourne argues, are we able to 'not' resonate to the action-effect contingencies of others. He cites echopraxia as further evidence of this claim.

Rizzolatti *et al.* agree with this notion of resonance, and distinguish between low- and high-level resonances. While the former refers to the ability of an organism's body movements to entrain similar movements in conspecifics (e.g. a school of fishes moving together or a flock of birds flying together), the latter refers to resonance at the level of goal related actions (e.g. a chimpanzee watching another eat a peanut, or a person watching another dance).

Collectively, the positions of Kinsbourne (2002), Rizzolatti *et al.* (2002) and Iacoboni (2005) are consistent with WST's assertion that human functionality entails the synergistic emergence and sustainment of *coupled, multi-scale, internal/external intentional contexts.* Given that these contexts are virtual (i.e. they are about *pending* actions and pending distal goals), humans can be said to be directly coupled at multiple levels of sustainment (i.e. proximal and distal) simultaneously. This natural multi-scale coupling afforded the scale-up of virtual sustainment because it was recursively self-sustaining. Again, this means that the work of engaging in multi-scale intentional coupling produced products that sustained such coupling. This requires explanation at both internal and external time scales.

As regards the internal scale, as has already been mentioned, neural networks emerge and function according to the principle of self-sustaining work (Hebb 1949; Edelman 1989). Thus, regularities embodied in self-sustaining neural dynamics are available for capture by newly emerging neural networks (Grush 2004). The aboutness of these new circuits will necessarily constitute an abstraction from the aboutness embedded and sustained in the network it is tapping into. As regards the external scale, the human ability to couple multi-scale intentional contexts further afforded, when coupled with the plasticity of neural networks, the ability to embody regularities generated in these intentional contexts. Example of such regularities would be gestures and/or vocalizations that repeatedly occurred during the sustainment of multi-scale intentional contexts (e.g. moving things together). As these regularities came to be associated (via neural embodiment) with the intentional contexts in which they occurred, they could then be generated intentionally as a means of more efficiently altering or varying the type of intentional contexts being sustained. These externalized regularities would be more virtual than the intentional contexts from which they had been abstracted, because they would be about *possibilities* for such intentional contexts. And they were (and still are) self-sustaining because by having a means of anticipatorily organizing intentional contexts, groups are able to get more energy per unit work (e.g. capture more prey during the hunt).

As an empirical example of this ability to abstract from sustained intentional contexts, Galantucci (2005) placed pairs of participants in a virtual game environment and required them to find one another. The participants were isolated from each other, and the only way they could communicate was to generate patterns of stimuli via stencil marks on a digital sketch pad. The actions required to make a mark on the stencil, however, were decoupled such that holding the stencil in a fixed position on the pad eventually resulted in a vertical line on the pad because the y-axis values of the stencil position were continuously decreased. Once the y-value equalled the lowest y-coordinate on the sketchpad, the point in the trace vanished. Thus, three quick taps on the same pad location resulted in three vertically aligned dots, while marking a horizontal line from left to right with the stencil resulted in a line that sloped upward from left to right across the pad, yet gradually disappeared (as the Y-coordinate values continued to decrease).

Galantucci created this paradigm as a way to investigate participants' ability to generate a sign system within the constraints entailed in the dynamics of the sketch pad. Decoupling the actions from the effects they produced in the communication medium (i.e. the sketch pad) prevented pairs from using previously known signs, while the relatively quick disappearance of the trace mimicked the relatively rapid decay of spoken signs.

Pairs that solved the problem (i.e. continuously found one another) were able to do so because they learned to generate a sign system that allowed them to indicate their pending moves to one another. According to WST, the participants were able to generate sign systems because the signs were constituted of *intended distal effects* (i.e. patterns on the sketch pad) which, by virtue of being consistently paired with other distal effects (i.e. members of the pair found each other or not), came to represent the participants' *planned* move on a pending turn. (Of course, this is just one of many possible meanings a sign could have.) Given these distal events (i.e. signs) referred to states that were *not in the immediate context* (i.e. planned moves and pending turns) they constitute virtual content. In short, members of the pair were generating distal effects (i.e. signs) that afforded each with the opportunity to contextualize and constrain the other's virtual event-control (i.e. thoughts or simulations).

The ability to engage in *joint virtual-event control* was meted out over time, via the pair's convergence onto a pattern of distal-effect control i.e. an agreed upon pattern of distal effects that gradually became an agreed-upon *external efference-copy* (i.e. a copy of a plan) of the members' virtual event control. Thus, just as the public display of action-effect regularities affords intentional coupling at the distal scale (i.e. in the immediate environment), continuous pairing of particular distal effects (e.g. a series of marks on a pad) with other distal events (e.g. successful distal outcomes such as finding each other in a virtual game) leads to the former 'representing' possible states of the latter which, in turn, makes possible the public display of *group* intentional states.

These external representations of intentional states constitute a necessary condition for the emergence and sustainment of joint virtual-event control. Thus, just as ant coordination and chickadee coordination necessitate the generation of external pheromone and auditory contexts, respectively, joint virtual-event control in humans necessitates the generation of external intentional contexts. In addition, Galantucci's (2005) data are consistent with WST's assertion that humans were able to generate increasingly virtual intentional contexts because the recursively self-sustaining dynamics of internal neural structure and externally sustained, multi-scale intentional contexts, allowed members to abstract and embody, in neural structure, regularities that emerged across different episodes of intentional coupling. These neural embodiments synergistically afforded additional means of intentionally altering external contexts and giving rise to externalizations that afforded joint virtual sustainment at increasingly distal time scales (e.g. calendars, written languages and mathematics). And again, this scale-up was possible because the work was self-sustaining; that is, the joint virtual-sustainment that gave rise to calendars, written languages and mathematics paid for itself because it allowed groups to acquire more energy per unit work (Odum 1988; Vandervert 1995).

As the scale-up of virtual content continued, the development system in which humans found themselves embedded became increasingly virtual (e.g. the advent of formal education contexts), and sustaining oneself within such increasingly virtual contexts required the ability to distinguish one's own, internally generated virtual contexts (i.e. thoughts) from those in which one was embedded. These are the constraints that I believe forced the emergence of the 'self' (Metzinger 2003; Ghin 2005), as well as the self-other distinction (Jordan 2003b; Knoblich & Jordan 2003; Jordan & Knoblich 2004). In short, the self emerged as foreground amidst a background of virtual others, and it did so in order to sustain itself with those others in virtual contexts (i.e. within a world of ideas). The phenomenal self then garners its semantic properties (i.e. its phenomenal properties) as do all self-sustaining systems; from the fact it is naturally and necessarily about the contexts (i.e. the externalized virtual contexts of others) it must embody in order to sustain itself.

5.5. Conclusions

The purpose of the present paper was to address the tensions that exist between internalist and radical–interactionist approaches to cognitive neuroscience, and the implications these different positions hold for our interpretation of the archaeological record. Again, if the clean borders between mind and world implied by internalism prove to be the case, archaeological artefacts constitute products of cognition. If the borders between mind and world are fuzzy and unclear however, as is claimed by radical interactionism, the mind spreads out across the body–world barrier, and archaeological artefacts come to be conceptualized as constituting components of cognition.

WST and the notion of wild agency were presented as a potential solution to this issue. By conceptualizing organisms (i.e. wild agents) as open, multi-scale self-sustaining systems, WST is able to address the causal properties of wild systems in a manner that is consistent with radical-interactionist concerns regarding multi-scale contingent interactions. And by conceptualizing wild agents as self-sustaining embodiments of the persistent, multi-scale contexts that afforded their emergence and in which they sustain themselves, WST is able to address the semantic properties of wild agents in a way that does justice to internalist concerns regarding meaningful (i.e. semantic) internal states (i.e. causal content).

In addition to simultaneously addressing the concerns of radical interactionists and internalists, WST also avoids conceptual dichotomies such as mind–body and mental–physical, as well as the increasingly problematic trichotomy of perception–action–cognition. It does so by conceptualizing psychology functionality in terms of gradients of sustainment (i.e. nested scales of event control). This, in turn, allows WST to see organisms as world-in-world, which, in turn, removes the epistemic gap between organism and environment inherent in physical–mental dichotomies. Given WST's further assertion that the sustainment of world-in-world involves the generation and sustainment of internal–external context couplings, these generated and sustained external contexts (e.g. pheromone contexts, auditory contexts and intentional contexts in ants, birds and humans, respectively) become constitutive of multi-scale sustainment. As a result, the 'anatomy' of multi-scale sustainment spreads out across these internal–external contexts. The anatomy of human intelligence therefore, conceptualized as a virtual sustainment, likewise spreads out across the other relative, intentional contexts groups are able to sustain and generate.

To be sure, one can and should investigate the multi-scale, nested intentionalities of individual wild agents (i.e. neurons, brains, behaviours and thoughts). But when this is done within the framework of WST, one is less likely to miss the multi-scale coupling of internal–external intentional contexts (i.e. what Oyama 1985, refers to as a developmental system) that allowed such individual abilities to phylogenetically and ontogenetically emerge. This, in turn, leaves one less susceptible to the mind–body, mind–brain conceptual dichotomies that can lead one to isolate mental work within the brain.

Finally, by approaching psychological functionality in terms of the homology of self-sustaining work that extends across the levels of scale investigated by chemists, biologists, psychologists, anthropologists and archaeologists, WST might be particularly well situated to serve as an integrative, interdisciplinary framework for cognitive science. Instead of constituting a science of the mind, however, it would constitute the science of multi-scale open systems. In short, a science of wild agents.

I wish to thank Colin Renfrew, Chris Frith and Lambros Malafouris for organizing the conference that inspired this work. In addition, I would like to thank the two anonymous reviewers for their very thought-provoking critiques of an earlier version of this manuscript.

References

Anderson, M. L. 2003 Embodied cognition: a field guide. *Artif. Intell.* **1491**, 91–103. (doi:10.1016/S0004-3702(03)00054-7)

Barsalou, L. 1999 Perceptual symbol systems. *Behav. Brain Sci.* **22**, 577–660. (doi:10.1017/S0140525X99002149)

Bickhard, M. H. 2001 The emergence of contentful experience. In *What should be computed to understand and model brain function?* (ed. T. Kitamura), pp. 217–237. Singapore: World Scientific.

Blakemore, S.-J. & Decety, J. 2001 From the perception of action to the understanding of intention. *Nat. Rev. Neurosci.* **2**, 561–567.

Blakemore, S.-J., Wolpert, D. M. & Frith, C. D. 2000 Why can't you tickle yourself? *Neuroreport* **11**, 11–16. (doi:10.1097/00001756-200008030-00002)

Boden, M. A. 1999 Is metabolism necessary? *Br. J. Philos. Sci.* **50**, 231–238. (doi: 10.1093/bjps/50.2.231)

Boltzmann, L. 1905 *The second law of thermodynamics.* Dordrecht, The Netherlands: Reidel.

Brooks, R. A. 1999 *Cambrian intelligence.* Cambridge, MA: MIT Press.

Calvo-Merino, B., Glaser, D. E., Grèzes, J., Passingham, R. E. & Haggard, P. 2005 Action observation and acquired motor skills: an fMRI study with expert dancers. *Cereb. Cortex* **158**, 1243–1249.

Chalmers, D. J. 1996 *The conscious mind: in search of a fundamental theory.* New York, NY: Oxford University Press.

Clark, A. 1997 *Being there: putting brain, body, and world together again.* London, UK: MIT Press.

Clark, A. 2000 Phenomenal immediacy and the doors of sensation. *J. Conscious. Stud.* **74**, 21–24.

Clark, A. 2001 *Mindware: an introduction to the philosophy of cognitive science.* Oxford, UK: Oxford University Press.

Desmurget, M. & Grafton, S. 2003 Feedback or feedforward control: end of a dichotomy. In *Taking action: cognitive neuroscience perspectives on intentional acts* (ed. S. H. Johnson-Frey), pp. 291–338. Cambridge, MA: MIT Press.

Dussutour, A., Fourcassie, V., Helbing, D. & Deneubourg, J. L. 2004 Optimal traffic organization in ants under crowded conditions. *Nature* **428**, 70–73. (doi:10.1038/nature02345)

Edelman, G. M. 1989 *Neural Darwinism: the theory of group neuronal selection.* Oxford, UK: Oxford University Press.

Galantucci, B. 2005 An experimental study of the emergence of human communication systems. *Cogn. Sci.* **29**, 737–767.

Gerhardt, H. C. & Huber, F. 2002 *Acoustic communication in insects and anurans*. Chicago, IL: The University of Chicago Press.

Ghin, M. 2005 What a self could be. *Psyche* **11**, 1–10.

Glenberg, A. M. 1997 What is memory for? *Behav. Brain Sci.* **20**, 1–55. (doi:10.1017/S0140525X97000010)

Greenfield, M. D., Tourtellot, M. K. & Snedden, W A. 1997 Precedence effects and the evolution of chorusing. *Proc. R. Soc. B* **264**, 1355–1361. (doi:10.1098/rspb.1997.0188)

Grezes, J., Costes, N. & Decety, J. 1998 Top-down effect of strategy on the perception of human biological motion: a PET investigation. *Cogn. Neuropsychol.* **15**, 553–582. (doi:10.1080/026432998381023)

Grush, R. 2004 The emulation theory of representation: motor control, imagery, and perception. *Behav. Brain Sci.* **27**, 377–442. (doi:10.1017/S0140525X04000093)

Hall, L., Illes, A. & Vehrencamp, S. L. 2006 Overlapping signals in banded wrens: long-term effects of prior experience on males and females. *Behav. Ecol.* **17**, 260–269. (doi:10.1093/beheco/arj022)

Hebb, D. O. 1949 *The organization of behavior: a neuropsycho-logical theory*. New York, NY: Wiley.

Iacoboni, M. 2005 Understanding others: imitation, language and empathy. In *Perspectives on imitation: from mirror neurons to memes* (eds S. Hurley & N. Chater), pp. 77–99. Cambridge, MA: MIT Press.

Jordan, J. S. 2000a The role of "control" in an embodied cognition. *Philos. Psychol.* **13**, 233–237. (doi:10.1080/09515080050075717)

Jordan, J. S. 2000b The world in the organism: living systems are knowledge. *Psycoloquy* **11**.

Jordan, J. S. 2003a The embodiment of intentionality. In *Dynamical systems approaches to embodied cognition* (eds W. Tschacher & J. Dauwalder), pp. 201–228. Berlin, Germany: Springer.

Jordan, J. S. 2003b Emergence of self and other in perception and action. *Conscious. Cogn.* **12**, 633–646. (doi:10.1016/S1053-8100(03)00075-8)

Jordan, J. S. 2004 The role of 'pre-specification' in an embodied cognition. *Behav. Brain Sci.* **27**, 408–409. (doi:10.1017/S0140525X04330098)

Jordan, J. S. 2008a Toward a theory of embodied communication: self-sustaining wild systems as embodied meaning. In *Embodied communication in humans and machines* (eds I. Wachsmuth, M. Lenzen & G. Knoblich). Oxford, UK: Oxford University Press.

Jordan, J. S. (in press). Forward-looking aspects of perception-action as a basis for embodied communication. *Discourse Processes*.

Jordan, J. S. & Ghin, M. 2006 (Proto-) consciousness as a contextually-emergent property of self-sustaining systems. *Mind Matter* **4**, 45–68.

Jordan, J. S. & Ghin, M. 2007 The role of control in a science of consciousness: causality, regulation and self-sustainment. *J. Conscious. Stud.* **14**, 177–197.

Jordan, J. S. & Hunsinger, M. 2008b Learned patterns of action-effect extrapolation contribute to the spatial displacement of continuously moving stimuli. *J. Exp. Psychol. Hum. Percept. Perform,* **34** (1), 113–124.

Jordan, J. S. & Knoblich, G. 2004 Spatial perception and control. *Psychon. Bull. Rev.* **11**, 54–59.

Juarrero, A. 1999 *Dynamics in action: intentional behavior as a complex system*. Cambridge, MA: MIT Press.

Kauffman, S. 1995 *At home in the universe*. New York, NY: Oxford University Press.

Kawato, M., Furukawa, K. & Suzuki, R. 1987 A hierarchical neural-network model for control and learning of voluntary movement. *Biol. Cybern.* **57**, 69–85. (doi: 10.1007/ BF00364149)

Kinsbourne, M. 2002 The role of imitation in body ownership and mental growth. In *The imitative mind: development, evolution, and brain bases* (eds A. Meltzoff & W. Prinz), pp. 311–330. New York, NY; Oxford, UK: Oxford University Press.

Knoblich, G. & Jordan, J. S. 2003 Action coordination in groups and individuals: learning anticipatory control. *J. Exp. Psychol. Learn. Mem. Cogn.* **29**, 1006–1016. (doi:10.1037/0278-7393.29.5.1006)

Lotka, A. J. 1945 The law of evolution as a maximal principle. *Hum. Biol.* **17**, 167–194.

Malafouris, L. 2004 The cognitive basis of material engagement: where brain, body and culture conflate. In *Rethinking materiality: the engagement of mind with the material world* (eds E. DeMarrasis, C. Gosden & D. Renfew), pp. 53–62. Cambridge, UK: McDonald Institute for Archaeological Research.

Mennill, D. J., Ratcliffe, L. M. & Boag, P. T. 2003 Female eavesdropping on male song contests in songbirds. *Science* **296**, 873. (doi:10.1126/science.296.5569.873)

Metzinger, T. 2003 *Being no one. The self-model theory of subjectivity*. Cambridge, MA: MIT Press.

Myin, E. & O'Regan, J. K. 2002 Perceptual consciousness, access to modality and skill theories: a way to naturalise phenomenology? *J. Conscious. Stud.* **9**, 27–45.

Newport, R. & Jackson, S. R. 2006 Posterior parietal cortex and the dissociable components of prism adaptation. *Neuropsychologia* **44**, 2757–2765. (doi:10.1016/j.neurop-sychologia.2006.01.007)

Odum, H. T. 1988 Self-organization, transformity, and information. *Science* **242**, 1132–1139. (doi:10.1126/ science.242.4882.1132)

O'Regan, J. K. & Nöe, A. 2001 A sensorimotor account of vision and visual consciousness. *Behav. Brain Sci.* **24**, 939–1011.

Oyama, S. 1985 *The ontogeny of information: developmental systems and evolution*. Cambridge, UK: Cambridge University Press.

Pacherie, E. 2007 The sense of control and the sense of agency. *Psyche* **13**, 1–30.

Paulin, M. G. 1993 The role of the cerebellum in motor control and perception. *Brain Behav. Evol.* **41**, 39–50. (doi:10.1159/000113822)

Rizzolatti, G., Fadiga, L., Fogassi, L. & Gallese, V. 2002 From mirror neurons to imitation: facts and speculations. In *The imitative mind: development, evolution, and brain bases* (eds A. Meltzoff & W. Prinz), pp. 247–266. New York, NY: Oxford University Press.

Ruiz-Mirazo, K. & Moreno, A. 2004 Basic autonomy as a fundamental step in the synthesis of life. *Artif. Life* **10**, 235–260. (doi:10.1162/1064546041255584)

Schroedinger, E. 1945 *What is life?* Cambridge, UK: The University Press; New York, NY: The Macmillan Company.

Searle, J. 1980 Minds, brains and programs. *Behav. Brain Sci.* **3**, 417–457.

Skinner, B. F. 1976 *About behaviorism*. New York, NY: Vintage Books.

Steels, L. In press. The symbol grounding problem is solved, so what's next? In *Symbols, embodiment and meaning* (eds De M. Vega, G. Glennberg & G. Graesser). New Haven, CT: Academic Press.

Sulis, W. 1997 Fundamental concepts of collective intelligence. *Nonlin. Dyn. Psychol. Life Sci.* **1**, 35–53. (doi:10.1023/A:1022371810032)

Vandervert, L. 1995 Chaos theory and the evolution of consciousness and mind: a thermodynamic–holographic resolution to the mind–body problem. *New Ideas Psychol.* **13**, 107–127. (doi:10.1016/0732-118X(94)00047-7)

van Gelder, T. J. 1998 The dynamical hypothesis in cognitive science. *Behav. Brain Sci.* **21**, 1–14. (doi:10.1017/S0140525X98000107)

Van Orden, G. C. & Holden, J. G. 2002 Intentional contents and self-control. *Ecol. Psychol.* **14**, 87–109. (doi:10.1207/S15326969ECO1401&2double_5)

Varela, F., Thompson, E. & Rosch, E. 1991 *The embodied mind: cognitive science and human experience*. Cambridge, MA: MIT Press.

Wilson, M. 2002 Six views on embodied cognition. *Psychon. Bull. Rev.* **9**, 625–636.

Wolpert, D. M. & Ghahramani, Z. 2000 Computational principles of movement neuroscience. *Nat. Neurosci.* **3**, 1212–1217. (doi:10.1038/81497)

Wolpert, D. M. & Kawato, M. 1998 Multiple paired forward and inverse models for motor control. *Neural Netw.* **11**, 1317–1329. (doi:10.1016/S0893-6080(98)00066-5)

Wolpert, D. M., Miall, R. C. & Kawato, M. 1998 Internal models in the cerebellum. *Trends Cogn. Sci.* **2**, 338–347. (doi:10.1016/S1364-6613(98)01221-2)

Zwaan, R. A. 1999 Embodied cognition, perceptual symbols, and situated models. *Discourse Process.* **28**, 81–88.

6

Between brains, bodies and things: *tectonoetic* awareness and the extended self

Lambros Malafouris

This paper presents the possible outline of a framework that will enable the incorporation of material culture into the study of the human self. To this end, I introduce the notions of *extended self* and *tectonoetic awareness*. Focusing on the complex interactions between brains, bodies and things and drawing a number of different and usually unconnected threads of evidence from archaeology, philosophy and neuroscience together, I present a view of selfhood as an extended and distributed phenomenon that is enacted across the skin barrier and which thus comprises both neural and extra-neural resources. Finally, I use the example of a gold Mycenaean signet ring to explore how a piece of inanimate matter can be seen (sometimes) as a constitutive and efficacious *part* of the human self-system.

Keywords: extended mind; material engagement; self; material culture; 'tectonoetic' awareness

6.1. Introduction: beyond this 'I' that I know

The emergence of human sense of self is arguably among the most fundamental issues of human becoming, yet it rarely occupies the focus of explicit archaeological treatment (e.g. Fowler 2003; Knappett 2005; Gamble 2007). Besides remaining a great philosophical puzzle (e.g. Shoemaker 1968; Dennett 1991; Neisser 1988; Metzinger 2003; Zahavi 2005; Humphrey 2007), the question of self, and its manifold developmental, neurophysiological and anthropological dimensions (Gazzaniga 1998; Gell 1998; Strathern 1988; Damasio 1999; Gallagher 2000a, 2005; Rochat 2001; Lewis 2003; Gillihan & Farah 2005), cannot be easily extrapolated from the archaeological record. On the one hand, archaeology, apparently, lacks any ready-made methodological substitute for the classical, albeit contentious, 'mirror self-recognition task' widely used since the pioneering work by Gallup (1970, 1979) in developmental and comparative studies of human cognition (see Gallup 1998; Rochat 2003; Bard *et al.* 2006). From an archaeological perspective, we have no way to know how, for instance, the inhabitants of the Blombos cave in Africa (D'Errico *et al.* 2005) would have reacted to the view of their face and body as seen on the surface of the mirror. On the other hand, the material culture and the other physical remains of the past may often speak in their own enactive semiotic idiom (Malafouris 2007), but they certainly lack any direct equivalent of the first person pronoun 'I' through which, as it is customarily assumed, sapient minds posit themselves as agents. Even the footprints from the muddy floor of the Niaux cave in France or the impressive handprints and hand stencils from the Chauvet cave do not suffice, *in themselves*, to give us access to the presence of selfhood or the absence of it—they can certainly be seen as indexes of an acting human body but provide no direct evidence of a self-aware acting body. From an archaeological perspective, there can be no 'immunity to error through misidentification' (see de Vignemont &

Fourneret 2004), there is always the possibility of being mistaken in past self-attribution. Words like 'me' and 'I' neither fossilize nor do they leave any readily identifiable and universal material trace. So how do we identify the presence or absence of self-awareness in the archaeological record? How do the available models and conceptual distinctions of self-knowledge—e.g. ecological/interpersonal/conceptual (Neisser 1988, 1991), minimal/narrative (Gallagher 2000a), noetic/autonoetic (Tulving 2001, 2002), pre-reflexive/reflective (Legrand 2006)—fit in and interact with the archaeological data and scales of time?

Obviously, the question about how and when we develop the sense of being oneself and what this sense of self might consist of cannot be weighed or measured, and thus it cannot be definitely decided, especially from the perspective of cognitive archaeology. But I hope to convince you in my following discussion that it can be somewhat illuminated. In any case, what we can be sure of is that the question of self cannot be avoided. And it cannot be avoided because it is always present, underlying every single aspect of human prehistory and cognitive evolution. Whether archaeology explicitly looks for the self or not, it certainly carries with it, and constantly projects into the past, the implicit image of such a self moulded on the prototype of the modern Western individual. The existence of a transparent phenomenal inner 'I' causing the human hand to move and alter the world in full awareness is assumed before and behind even the earliest artefacts recovered in the archaeological record. But when and how did humans develop the experience that they own their bodies (sense of ownership) and started to feel as the authors of their actions (sense of agency; Gallagher 2000a)? Our nearest primate relatives present a number of features indicative of a core self-system and an autobiographical self (Damasio 1999). But they never make the passage to the reflective, conceptual or 'autonoetic' stages of selfhood. The nut-cracking Kanzi can certainly effect a forceful stroke. Certainly, it is he who causes the act but he will never acquire a sense of agency or a true understanding of causality. Why is that? Is it simply the lack of language and representational thinking or maybe something more basic and difficult to discern? Every phrase written about human prehistory that implicates some sort of 'I' that acts and thinks invites this question in one form or another. And the constant danger is that our modernist epistemic predisposition towards questions of the 'what is this 'I' that I know?' type may blind us to any alternative possibilities. For instance, the possibility that before this 'I' can be a 'we' or a 'many', or, even more importantly, that the boundary of this 'I' may be changeable and extendable to the outside world rather than fixed at the surface of the skin. It is these possibilities that I wish to bring forth and explore in this paper through the notions of the *extended self* and *tectonoetic awareness*.

6.2. The self in Homer

As mentioned previously, our modernist epistemic predisposition towards questions of the 'what is this 'I' that I know?' type may blind us to any alternative ways of looking at the issue of human selfhood. I suggest that in attempting to get rid of some of the unnecessary modernist intellectual baggage, and to articulate some of the issues that will occupy our focus in this paper, the world of the Homeric epics might offer a useful starting point.

The following question by Gill may lead us directly to the heart of the matter: was the Homeric person aware 'of having, or being, a unitary self, an 'I', and conscious that it is this 'I' that makes the choice'? (Gill 1998, p. 31). Unexpectedly, for our 'common-sense dualism' and ideas about agency, over the last century, many researchers, following the lead of Snell (1960) and his influential treatment of the topic, have answered this question in the negative. In brief, the argument is that the Homeric epics show an absence of awareness of a unitary self and thus that no Homeric person can be seen to act as a fully integrated and autonomous agent. 'Agamemnon' and the other Homeric heroes do not act with full self-consciousness when they are making decisions, they are not self-aware of their doings: decisions are made *for* them rather than *by* them (Gaskin 1990).

From the above line of thinking emanates a second, equally perplexing question: if the notions of human agency and intentionality did not make any sense for the Homeric person who 'does not yet regard himself as the source of his own decisions' (Snell 1960, p. 8), then why assume, as archaeology so often does, that they made sense for humans in the Palaeolithic? If the attribution of agency—the 'who did it' question—can prove to be such a tricky and complex matter for a society of sapient minds that lived just a few centuries before the dawn of Greek philosophy and Plato's theory of ideas, then why assume the existence of such an inner *conscious* individual self painting the walls of the Chauvet cave approximately 30 000 years earlier, or even shaping a symmetric hand axe approximately hundreds of thousand years earlier? We should remind ourselves that archaeology may question the precise cognitive, and, in particular, symbolic or linguistic, capabilities of the Palaeolithic knapper, but it has never questioned the self behind the artefact. Maybe, as the philosopher Taylor (1989, p. 112) argues, underlying the 'baffling contrasts' of human agency, 'we can probably be confident that on one level human beings of all times and places have shared a very similar sense of 'me' and 'mine''. But, given what we discussed in the case of the Homeric self, from where this confidence emanates? What are the evidence that qualify such a certainty and warrant the universality of this unitary minimal self?

An easy way out of this dilemma might be of course to argue that the above-presented hypothesis about the nature of human agency in Homer is based on a misunderstanding or a misinterpretation of the Homeric poems from Snell and his followers. Indeed, there is no doubt that the problem of the Homeric self and agency is a matter of extensive debate and speculation. But we must admit that there is more at issue here than the precise conceptualization of the Homeric self. The real issue, I suggest, concerns the very possibility of a 'non-unitary' self. Upon that, even if we deny the later possibility from the Homeric world, we should keep in mind that the concept of the delimited biological individual and our common-sense unambiguous location and unitary experience of self is in trouble in more places than just Homer or the decentralized trends in the twentieth-century French philosophy. The idea of the isolated human agent that acts upon the inert and inanimate world can hardly be accommodated, or even make any sense, in a number of ethnographic contexts where the categories of persons and things are inseparably interlinked (Gell 1998) and where 'agency' and 'cause' are split. A good example can be found in the case of Melanesia where action and doing, although associated with a basic sense of body ownership, is rarely associated with a sense of authorship (Strathern 1988; Ramsey 2000).

Clearly then, the possibility of a Homeric non-unitary or 'distributed self' cannot be denied on *a priori* conceptual grounds. At least not as easily as our well-trained 'right-hemisphere interpreter' (Gazzaniga 1998) would have wanted. But if the Homeric problem of self cannot be dismissed, how can we account for it?

Let us try to approach the matter of the Homeric self through some of the available conceptual stratigraphies of selfhood. The differentiation between a 'minimal' and 'narrative' self, recently proposed by Gallagher (2000a), encapsulates all major developmental stages proposed by Neisser (1988, 1991) and offers a useful starting point to answer our question. There are two principal ways to proceed to look for the self: the first is to focus on the 'conceptual' or 'narrative' domain of selfhood and to situate the Homeric self at the centre of some fictional, personal or cultural narrative. This would be fine as long as we avoid a common mistake that such a conceptualization embodies. That is, the mistake of assuming that our own contemporary ideas and narratives of selfhood are somehow more objective and less fictional than those existing in the time of Homer. This is precisely the mistake Snell, and later also Adkins (Bernard 1993), made by interpreting the 'difference' which they recognized in the nature of the Homeric self as an 'absence' or 'deficit' of selfhood. Their normative developmental perspective firmly grounded on a Cartesian conception of what is like to be a person proper failed to recognize that an extended acting self is also a self proper, albeit of a different kind. Obviously, what Agamemnon lacks is not a proper self but simply the fundamental awareness of the organic unity of its soul parts characteristic of post-Platonic Western ideas about what a proper self should be. As Bernard (1993, p. 23) correctly observes, criticizing Snell's thesis, '[t]here is certainly one thing that Homer's descriptions of people did without, and that was a dualistic distinction between soul and the body'.

With this last consideration in mind let us now return to the second available approach to the Homeric self problem, focusing this time on the minimal domain of selfhood. It is this minimal self that is disrupted when, for instance, patients with schizophrenic delusion of control fail to identify the correct source of their own actions or mistake their intrusive thoughts for external voices (e.g. Daprati *et al.* 1997; Gallagher 2000b; Frith 2005). A deluded patient claims for example: 'Thoughts have been put in my head that do not belong to me. They tell me to dress. They check the bath water by doing this gesture' (Proust 2003, p. 504). And strange as it might appear, it is precisely this feeling of 'extraneity', a disturbance of the 'sense of agency', with the 'sense of ownership' remaining intact, that can be seen to characterize many aspects of the Homeric self. Agamemnon and the other Homeric heroes act as if they experience the world from the perspective of the 'anarchic hand' syndrome; that is, they act as if they own the hand but not the action. Should the above comparisons lead us to the rather extreme conclusion that people in the Homeric world suffered from some contagious 'agency delusion'?

Naturally, we do not have to suppose anything so bizarre. The Homeric self, I propose, is neither a 'figment of metaphysically fevered imaginations' to use, for example, Dennett's (1991) description of this sort of conceptualization, nor the sign of some sort of archaic 'Schneiderian syndrome' (see Frith 2005). A simpler solution may present itself if instead we simply recognize, following the suggestion of Clarke (1999, p. 118), that for Homer there is no mental part or true self that can be distinguished from the body because the 'body is indistinguishable from the human whole'. For Homer, the parts of the *soul* are not of a different kind than the parts of the body. Of course, this is not to deny that people in Homer had a brain and a body in the same manner that the later Greeks, modern Europeans or Melanesians do, but simply to say that they did not know that body *qua* body, but merely as the sum total of his limbs. This means that the Homeric self did not have a body in the sense that a modern individual understands what it is like or what it means to have a body from a Cartesian viewpoint. This is, however, far from a trivial issue because the kind of mind we have depends on the kind of body we are, and if that body is not experienced as a 'container', then most probably the mind of that body will not be experienced as 'contained' either (Lakoff 1987; Lakoff & Johnson 1999; Gallese & Lakoff 2005). This also explains Clarke's suggestion that to seek a word for 'body' is to ask Homer a wrong and unanswerable question. That a man should have a body makes sense only if he has another part to be distinguished from it: soul, mind, and the ghost in the machine (Clarke 1999, p. 118–9). Indeed, if we adopt Gill's 'objective-participant conception of the person'—which Gill opposes to the 'subjective-individualist conception' characteristic of the views of Snell and Adkins and of much modern Western ideas of selfhood—then the Homeric mind can be understood as a 'complex of functions which are unified (in so far as they are unified) by their interaction, rather than as constituting the locus of a unitary 'I'' (Gill 1998).

Thus, and concluding this section, I believe that there are two important lessons the debate over the Homeric self can teach us. First, that the problem of self is essentially a 'self-grounding' problem. That is, a problem of how to reconcile the distinctively unitary experience of the phenomenal self with the distributed fragmented character of the functional self and of how to ground self in action and the material world. Second, given that our objective is to ground self in action and the material world, then our point of initiation cannot take the form of some 'homunculus' however re-shaped and 'internally' redistributed this might be among the usual prefrontal, posterior temporal and inferior parietal right-hemisphere-based regions. It is one thing to say that the brain, or more specifically the right hemisphere, plays a special role in the creation of the self. It is indeed another, quite different thing to say that the self 'resides' in the right hemisphere (see also Feinberg & Keenan 2005, p. 675). The first seems to be at present a well-supported neuroscientific finding (Decety & Sommerville 2003; Gusnard 2005). The second is a good example of how a valuable finding can be turned into a category mistake, as it is often the case with questions of 'localization'; that is, questions about 'where in the brain is the self?'. *Self is more than a brain.*

A more concrete archaeological example might help us illustrate these theoretical points. Given our previous discussion of the Homeric self, a gold signet ring from Mycenae, the kingdom of Agamemnon, might offer an excellent point of reference.

6.3. A gold signet ring

Figure 6.1 depicts a gold signet ring, named as 'The battle of the Glen' from grave IV of the so-called Mycenaean Grave Circle A excavated by H. Schliemann (Schliemann 1880; Mylonas 1973; Karo 1930–3). The ring depicts a battle scene characteristic of the transition between the Middle and the Late Helladic period (middle second millennium BC) of the Greek Bronze Age that those graves signify. Moreover, it offers a visual testimony to the establishment of the heroic ethos of the Early Mycenaean warriors, which is to be glorified in the Homeric epics (Voutsaki 1993, p. 161). I shall be leaving aside the usual historical, stylistic, chronological and aesthetic archaeological considerations and focus on the question that occupies our main concern in this paper: what, if anything, can such a ring tell us about the Mycenaean self? At first, it might seem that this ring, as probably any other isolated artefact from this period, has very little to tell. It appears that the best we can do as archaeologists is try to identify the material, functional and symbolic properties of this

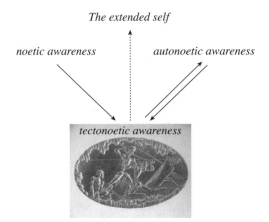

Figure 6.1. The Mycenaean gold signet ring ('The battle of the Glen') as part of the nexus of tectonoetic awareness.

object, as a representational medium, and to place them against their relevant socio-cultural context in an attempt to decipher their hidden cultural message. This might give us some useful information about the social processes to which this object was embedded in the course of its social life and thus hopefully gain some information also about the processes implicated in the construction of Mycenaean personal identity. But is this really all that the unique archaeological preoccupation with material culture can offer to the study of the self and the body? Accepting that what we call the human mind, and by extension the human self, is essentially what the brain does inevitably leaves archaeology with no other options besides the above avenue of indirect inference and symbolic interpretation. But I have argued more extensively elsewhere (Malafouris 2004, 2008*a*, 2008*c*), and I will argue again in this paper, that the above view of mind and self does not necessarily has to be the case.

But let us first start with the commonplace. As mentioned, the ring was recovered from the famous Grave Circle A at Mycenae. It was intentionally placed there most probably as part of the elaborate funerary depositional processes that we witness in the early Mycenaean funerary record. Intentional burial is, of course, one of those unique behavioural traits of the sapient mind that we can take for granted in the late European prehistory. The ring deposited beside the Mycenaean body does not mark any important Rubicon in human cognitive evolution, as it would have been the case if it was found, for instance, in a Middle Palaeolithic context (see Mellars 1989; Riel-Salvatore & Clark 2001). What it signifies in this case is the emergence of a new, i.e. Mycenaean, cultural trajectory. By the same token, the change from single contracted to collective extended inhumations that took place during that period in the Greek mainland (Dickinson 1977; Rutter 1993; Voutsaki 1997) does not tell us anything about the human symbolic capacity and self-awareness *per se* but simply signifies one of the countless possibilities about how this symbolic capacity can become actualized and transmitted in ritual, and thus cultural, time and space.

Separating biology from culture may sometimes make good analytic sense but it should not obscure the most interesting issue of how they are combined. Thus, it might be useful to remind ourselves that behind the intentional deposition of the ring as a funerary gift beside the dead Mycenaean body lays an *autonoetic* (Tulving 1983, 2001) conceptualization of human selfhood. This autonoetic self, although embodies millennia of cognitive evolution, needs to be instantiated anew, generation after generation, in cultural space and time. Through the act of burial and intentional deposition, the human sense of personal identity and continuity transcends the limits of human biology projecting into the supernatural realm of postmortem personal continuity. Whatever the period under consideration, what intentional burial first and above all signifies is a new understanding of 'body ownership' and the 'projecting self'. Placed in such an analytic context, the presence of a funerary offering, whether a Palaeolithic hand axe or a Mycenaean gold signet ring, should be seen, at least in the first instance, not as the index of the human symbolic capacity, but of the equally unique human capacities for 'prospection' (i.e. thinking about the future) and self-projection. I shall return to the issue of self-projection again in §4. For now, having made those basic points concerning the ring as a funerary offering and as a part of the burial practice, it is important to keep in mind that, most probably, this ritual or funerary dimension of the ring constitutes only a small part, probably the last part, of its cultural biography and life history. Thus, more important to consider is the possible efficacy of the ring as a component of the Mycenaean-lived body and phenomenal self.

To this end, already, simply by looking at the variety of material and personal ornaments arrayed around the Mycenaean dead body from the same context that this ring was found (Dickinson 1977), one can get a first idea about the range of biographical possibilities (Kopytoff 1986, p. 66), which, especially if compared against the limited Middle Helladic social *habitus*, are indicative of a new self-awareness. This new awareness is testified in a number of important changes, one of which is the emphasis on the depiction of the human figure, and of the Mycenaean warrior in particular, that we see emblematized and commemorated on the signet ring. Does this mean, as Crowley suggests, that 'the human is now important enough in the scheme of things to take the centre stage' (Crowley 1989, p. 211)? Or, is it simply that new techniques of the body (Mauss [1934] 1973) and of social memory become active or available during that period? Whatever the correct answer, the fact remains that, from a long-term perspective, artefacts like the ring potentially signify important changes in the Mycenaean experience and understanding of what means to be a self and having a body. Thus, the critical question we need to tackle concerns the precise nature of the relation between the Mycenaean ring and the Mycenaean self in the above process of cultural change. That is, we need to ask what the ring does and how it might have affected the Mycenaean self and body. What, in other words, is the causal efficacy of the ring in the Mycenaean cognitive and self-system? These are the sort of questions I wish to explore in the following sections by introducing the notions of extended self and tectonoetic awareness.

6.4. The extended self: From embodiment to the act of embodying

To begin with, let me clarify that the notion of extended self I propose here is not confined to the temporal autobiographic dimension of personal continuity, or else the sense of oneself as an individual existing over time, that Neisser (1988) proposed. Although the proposal sketched here incorporates the ecological and interpersonal dimensions or criteria of self-knowledge discussed also in Neisser's scheme, it is essentially a proposal grounded upon the material engagement approach and the recently developed hypotheses of extended and distributed cognition (Hutchins 1995; Clark 1997; Clark & Chalmers 1998;

Malafouris 2004, 2008*a,b*; Renfrew 2006). Also important to clarify is that the notion of the extended self should not be understood as denoting some independent layer (social, cultural, technological or other) added to the periphery of some 'internal' and thus 'real' biological proto-self (bodily or neuronal). The extended self is rooted and inextricably coupled with the supposedly 'immune' compartments of the bodily self. It should be seen neither as an external layer of materiality—what anthropologists would call, a 'second' or 'social skin' (Turner 1993 [1980])—nor as simply the emergent property of some higher narrative, conceptual or representational self-dimension.

The idea of mind and by extension of selfhood that I want to bring forth through the notion of extended self is that of a self that is located neither inside nor outside the brain/body, but is instead constantly enacted in-between brains, bodies and things and thus irreducible to any of these three elements taken in isolation. Even though the self is by nature grounded and inextricably bound up with the body, it also escapes the natural confines of any single body or brain. The extended self I am proposing here is not simply a self embodied; it is a self enacted through *the act of embodying*.

This minor shift in perspective, *from embodiment to the act of embodying*, has some important implications that should be better spelled out. No doubt, with the advent of the embodied cognition approach, a successful step has been made towards resolving the traditional mind-body dichotomy. Nonetheless, the grounding of human cognition in bodily experience, and the concomitant recognition that the body shapes rather than simply contains the mind (Goldin-Meadow 2003; Gallagher 2005; Gallese 2005; Gallese & Lakoff 2005), did not in itself succeed to dissolve the ontological bounds of the *res cogitans*. Despite stretching the mind as far as the body's surface, the conventional use and understanding of the embodied character of the human cognitive agent remains, more often than not, trapped inside the biological boundaries of the individual. Consequently, the traditional drawback of cognitive science, i.e. mistaking the properties of the system for the properties of the person (see also Hutchins 1995, p. 366), holds still. Obviously, the purpose of the above remarks is not to dispute the close interdependence of hand and brain function. What I am suggesting here is nothing more than what the classical phenomenological question of the blind man's stick pointed out some decades ago: consider a blind man with a stick. Where does the blind man's self begin? (Merleau-Ponty 1962, p. 143; Bateson 1973, p. 318) To leave material culture outside the human self-system is like leaving the stick outside the blind man's sensory system. More simply, if there is such a thing as the embodied self, then it is a self that constantly projects and extends itself beyond the skin actively engaging and incorporating its material surroundings via the interface of the body. Embodiment is not a delimiting property—far from it. It is instead the main perturbatory channel through which the world *touches us*, is *attached to us* and even *becomes part of us*.

But how does all these hold up against empirical evidence? At first sight, the above premises might seem difficult to follow from the perspective of neuroscience. For one thing, understanding the precise effects of things on the functional anatomy of the human brain is not an easy task and the evidence that bears on this question is hard to come by, especially in humans. Nonetheless, recent studies of visuotactile interactions exploring the effects of the temporary or permanent incorporation of inanimate objects (such as clothes, jewellery, tools, etc.) into the body schema (see also Iriki *et al.* 1996; Berti & Frassinetti 2000; Maravita *et al.* 2001; Holmes & Spence 2004, 2006; Holmes *et al.* 2004; Maravita & Iriki 2004) may well be seen as already articulating some very interesting possible points of intersection between archaeology and neuroscience. Thus, a more careful look at some recent findings in this domain, combined and informed with some classical phenomenological observations, might help us expose some basic aspects of the hidden bio-social anatomy of extended selfhood.

A good example can be found in the case of the distinction between *extrapersonal* space (the behavioural space that surrounds the body outside the hand-reaching distance) and *peripersonal* space (the behavioural space that immediately surrounds the body within the hand-reaching distance; Berti & Frassinetti 2000). Both animal and human neurophysiological studies show clear evidence that these two types of behavioural space are not represented homogeneously in the brain. What is more significant for our present purposes, however, is that this neural dissociation between near and far spaces can be associated with the use of tools. As Berti & Frassinetti (2000, p. 415) have shown, the use of objects and tools exert strong plastic effects in the cognitive topography of peripersonal space. More specifically, in their study, a right-hemisphere stroke patient showed a clear dissociation between near and far spaces in the manifestation of visual neglect—visual neglect is impairment in the processing and exploration of the space contralateral to the brain lesion—thus providing concrete experimental evidence that 'an artificial extension of the patient's body (the stick) caused a re-mapping of far space as near space' (Berti & Frassinetti 2000, p. 415).

But returning to our previous discussion of the Mycenaean ring, it is probably the case of the 'anosognosic' patient discussed by Berlucchi & Aglioti (1997) which offer our best evidence about how an ordinary personal possession, like a ring, can become coextensive with our body. This case study (published originally at *Neuroreport* (Aglioti *et al.* 1996)) refers to a 73-year-old woman who after a large right-hemisphere stroke exhibited a total unawareness of her severe left-arm paralysis and repeatedly affirmed that the paralysed hand belonged to someone else. The peculiarity of this case was that the patient while able to see and describe the rings she had worn for years and was currently wearing on her left, now disowned hand, she resolutely denied their ownership. What makes this case even more interesting is that the patient immediately recognized these rings as her own when they were shifted to her right hand or displayed in front of her. In fact, not only she could identify the rings as her own but also was able to produce a great deal of autobiographical information about them. We should also note that the patient could easily acknowledge ownership of other personal belongings (e.g. a keyholder or a comb), which, in her previous experience, had not been ordinarily associated with the left hand and that in this case identification was not affected when those objects where in contact with the disowned hand.

Neurological findings, such as those presented above, cannot be easily extrapolated to fit our proposed scheme of extended selfhood. Nonetheless, they offer valuable indications and often resonate with our key premise that objects and tools attached to the body can be seen or treated as parts of the body as the biological body itself. According to Berlucchi & Aglioti, the denial of ownership of the left-hand rings, observed in the above-discussed anosognosic patient, was conditional 'not only on they being seen on the disowned hand, but also on the existence of a previous systematic association between them and that hand' (Berlucchi & Aglioti 1997, p. 561). From the perspective of archaeology and the material engagement approach, the crucial question lies on how precisely do we go about to understand the nature of these systematic associations between biology and culture or brains and things. This brings us to the notion of tectonoetic awareness.

6.5. Tectonoetic awareness: Between brains, bodies and things

The term tectonoetic derives from the Greek *tecton* for carpenter or builder—signifying more generally the maker and the poetic art of construction—and the word *noûs* for mind or intellect (see also Renfrew's tectonic phase, 2007; 2008). I introduce this term for two main reasons. First, in order to signify the form of *enactive knowing through* that characterizes human self-awareness in the context of material engagement. Second, in order to overcome the unwanted connotations of conventional terminology in the cognitive sciences, which, by leaving material culture outside the human cognitive system, fail to capture the 'act of embodying' as a continuous and interactive coordination between neural and extra-neural physical resources.

A good way to illustrate the key property and distinctive feature of tectonoetic awareness relevant to our previous discussion of extended selfhood is by placing it against the background of the distinction between noetic and autonoetic consciousness initially proposed by Tulving in his *Elements of episodic memory* (1983). This will also enable us to link our discussion of self with the issue of memory, which, we should not forget, is probably the key property for the constitution of self as a historical object.

For Tulving, the key difference between noetic and autonoetic awareness lies in the following: whereas noetic consciousness refers simply to the act of knowing, autonoetic consciousness refers to the process of self-recollection which involves the mental reinstatement of past events and experiences. Thus, for Tulving, autonoetic consciousness is the defining property of episodic memory, whereas noetic awareness is identified with semantic memory.

Seen from the angle of our previous considerations, two major drawbacks can be easily identified relevant to this model. On the one hand, both types of awareness have been conceived as being strictly of a 'mental' kind. For instance, episodic memory and autonoetic consciousness are clearly subsumed under the general category of 'mental time travel', which refers both to the capacity of remembering past experiences and to the ability of prospection (also known as self-projection); that is, thinking, imagining and planning about the future. On the other hand, although according to Tulving (1983, 2001, 2002) episodic memory develops later in ontogeny compared with semantic memory, his theory offers no specific guidelines about how the two memory systems interact in the course of their developmental (ontogenetic and phylogenetic) trajectories. Thus, Tulving's interpretation of infantile amnesia, as associated with the absence of a truly developed episodic memory and self-awareness prior to the age of five, leave us with no explanation about what makes possible this transition from noetic awareness to autonoetic self-awareness.

Following that one may argue that the notions of noetic and autonoetic awareness, although successfully pointing out the significance of subjective time and remembrance in the constitution of self, lack the ecological grounding that would have enabled the material anchoring of autonoetic consciousness. This is precisely the role that *tectonoetic* awareness comes to play signifying the active mediating role of material culture in the ontogenetic and phylogenetic passage from noetic to autonoetic consciousness. The basic assumption behind tectonoetic awareness is simple: a self or a person cannot emerge (ontogenetically or phylogenetically) aside from a process of material engagement. Tectonoetic consciousness should not be understood as a distinct separate stage between the two—although this can be argued to be the case from an ontogenetic viewpoint—but as a scaffolding process of ongoing structural coupling that grounds in action and integrates the noetic and autonoetic aspects of selfhood.

But where does all this leave us? How the above theoretical premises can help us answer our previous question about the causal efficacy and relationship of the ring with the Mycenaean self-system? Elsewhere I have used the example of the blind man's stick to develop a hypothesis proposing that the functional structure and anatomy of the human brain is a dynamic construct remodelled in detail by behaviourally important experiences which are mediated, and often constituted by the use of material objects and artefacts which for that reason should be seen as continuous integral parts of the human cognitive architecture (Malafouris 2008c). I suggest that the relationship between tectonoetic awareness and the Mycenaean ring can be understood along similar lines.

In particular, the thing we should probably note first is that the ring, beyond its significance as a personal ornament, embodies strong mnemonic potential. Not only the formulaic character of the iconic scene that we see depicted on the ring's surface points to a mnemonic function not dissimilar to 'the repetitive phrases and standard epithets in oral poetry' (Crowley 1989, p. 211), but whereas the oral formula may hardly be conceived of as a separate entity—meaning divorced both from the rest of the sentence and its performance context—the ring as a material object is capable of taking on a separate life of its own. Thus, beyond its obvious inscriptive qualities, the ring, as an object, embodies a dynamic cognitive biography that conventional notions like that of 'external symbolic storage' (Donald 1991) cannot fully accommodate. As Rowlands observes:

> Objects are culturally constructed to connote and consolidate the possession of past events associated with their use or ownership. They are there to be talked about and invested with the memories and striking events associated with their use. The link between past, present and future is made through their materiality. Objects of a durable kind assert their own memories, their own forms of commentary and therefore come to possess their own personal trajectories.
>
> (Rowlands 1993, p. 144)

The complex associative enchainment between the 'internal' and 'external' elements of remembering that such objects embody has two major implications. First, the biological limits of working memory (7 plus or minus 2; Miller 1956) no longer apply. Second, the structure of the cognitive process has changed. The ring has reorganized the circuitry and thus the nature of the cognitive operations involved. The noetic, semantic knowing, grounded in the physical and thus permanent structure of the ring is transformed to an autonoetic, episodic remembering, which is now constitutively intertwined with the ring's social life (figure 6.1).

Thus, the ring as a portable and transparent bodily attachment enables the passage to explicit self-recognition through objectification. The capacity of the ring to modify and reshape the body, to which it becomes attached, suggests that the ring may cut across the conventional 'body image'/'body schema' distinctions and by extension the subject–object divide. It should be borne in mind that the importance of the physicality of the artefact derives from its ability to act as a bridge between the mental and physical worlds. In our case, the materiality of the ring offers a bridge between personal and peripersonal space and grounds in action the different aspects of Mycenaean self-consciousness. Incorporated by the Mycenaean body, the ring potentially liberates the self from the here and now of ordinary experience; that is, from the temporal simultaneity and spatial coincidence of the subjective body so it can now be enchained into its social surrounding. In this connection, a possible synergy between object ownership and body ownership might offer an interesting link between the way humans come to feel that they own their body in comparison with other aspects of their material surrounding.

Of course, it needs to be underlined that Mycenaean self-objectification manifests in many different forms and is realized through a variety of material media. Yet, the main effect is the same, the Wittgensteinian immune 'I-as-subject' engaging the artefact is turned into a non-immune 'I-as-object'.

Another salient example of this process can be found in the case of the Mycenaean sword. As I argue in more detail elsewhere, for the Mycenaean warrior, like the one we see in the scene depicted on the ring, the centre of consciousness and bodily awareness is not some internal Cartesian 'I' but the tip of the sword (Malafouris 2008b). The act of grasping the Mycenaean sword involves much more than a purely mechanical process of visuo-proprioceptive realignment of the Mycenaean body; it is also an act of incorporation which provides a new basis for self-recognition and self-awareness. The grasping of the sword as an act of embodying brings forth a new manifestation of tectonoetic awareness, the phylogenetic roots of which can already be traced in the 'temporal binding effects' (Haggard et al. 2002) of the earliest acts of tool knapping. The intentional stance of the Mycenaean person is partially determined by the skilled embodied engagements made possible by the use of the sword. Representational 'content' and 'aboutness' are not to be found inside the cabinet of the Mycenaean head, they are instead negotiated between the hand and the sword.

Similar to what we discussed in the case of the ring, the Mycenaean sword becomes a means of self-objectification and offers a portable material anchor for the blending of time, memory and consciousness (see Hutchins 2005). The sword should not be seen as an isolated detached object, because, once in the hand of the warrior, it is already an inseparable organic part of the warrior's body; an artificial, yet fully incorporated, body part in itself. This process of material engagement, which initiates as a distributed action assembly of brains, bodies and things and through time results in a new kind of 'we' intentionality (Tomasello et al. 2005)—not between humans, but between humans and things—constitutes the crux of *human tectonoetic consciousness*. Maybe it is the lack of a true *tectonoetic consciousness* that deprives the nut-cracking Kanzi from becoming a fully conscious agent.

6.6. Final discussion

We naturally come to think that we have a self, as the philosopher Taylor (1989, p. 112) remarks, in the same way that we have legs, arms or livers. What is more important, however, is that 'distinctions of locale, like inside and outside, seem to be discovered like facts about ourselves, and not relative to the particular way, among other possible ways, we construe ourselves'. For indeed, 'who among us can understand our thought being anywhere else but inside, 'in the mind'?'

In this paper, I argued that the situated character of the human condition demands that human selfhood cannot be characterized and understood simply according to some internal, fixed and biologically predetermined taxonomy of bodily properties. A great deal of cultural parameters that operate beyond the skin needs to be taken under consideration. Unfortunately, the complex and dynamic nature of these extra-organismic causal factors means that they cannot be easily accommodated by conventional experimental (imaging or behavioural) protocols. Rings, like the one we discussed here, are not allowed in the fMRI scanner. Nonetheless, they do leave their trace in our cerebral architecture and in some cases can be seen as parts of our self. This type of, what we may call, 'epistemic extrasomatic neglect' has some drastic implications on our understanding of the human self and the sapient mind, which can only be counterbalanced by a new integrative and cross-disciplinary articulation of the problem of self that will incorporate all the relevant parameters to it. An important methodological implication of that, and this is what constitutes the crux of my argument in this paper, is that the common distinction between a physical and a social body—the first being the domain of life sciences and the second of anthropology/archaeology—can no longer be sustained. The two-body idea, one physical and another social or symbolic, as originally posed by Douglas (1970, p. 93), needs to be replaced with a more interactive framework. The aim of this framework should not be to translate a biological story into a cultural story and vice versa, but instead to discover possible links and construct conceptual bridges between the two.

It is only through the understanding of what being a self involves for an organism embedded in the world and thinking through things and its body that one will be able to search efficiently for the signatures of self-consciousness (neuronal, bodily, cultural or other). 'Mind', as the philosopher Clark (1997, p. 53) points out, 'is a leaky organ, forever escaping its 'natural' confines and mingling shamelessly with body and with the world'. And it is precisely this powerful metaphor that I applied here in the study of self. An epistemic unification of self cannot be achieved either by adding isolated neural, bodily and material correlates of self or by reducing the one to the other. It can be achieved by attempting to discern the connections and possible causal links between these different aspects of selfhood as they interact across the skin barrier and the scales of time.

The research presented here was funded by the Balzan Foundation.

References

Aglioti, S. A., Smania, N., Manfredi, M. & Berlucchi, G. 1996 Disownership of left hand and objects related to it in a patient with right brain damage. *Neuroreport* **8**, 293–296. (doi:10.1097/00001756-199612200-00058)

Bard, K., Todd, B. K., Bernier, C., Love, J. & Leavens, D. A. 2006 Self-awareness in human and chimpanzee infants: what is measured and what is meant by the mark and mirror test. *Infancy* **9**, 191–219. (doi:10.1207/s15327078 in0902_6)

Bateson, G. 1973 *Steps to an ecology of mind*. London, UK: Granada.

Berlucchi, G. & Aglioti, S. A. 1997 The body in the brain: neural bases of corporeal awareness. *Trends Cogn. Sci.* **20**, 560–564.

Bernard, W. 1993 *Shame and necessity*. Loss Angeles, CA; London, UK: University of California Press.

Berti, A. & Frassinetti, F. 2000 When far becomes near: remapping of space by tool-use. *J. Cogn. Neurosci.* **12**, 415–420. (doi:10.1162/089892900562237)

Clark, A. 1997 *Being there: putting brain, body and world together again*. Cambridge, MA: MIT Press.

Clark, A. & Chalmers, D. 1998 The extended mind. *Analysis* **58**, 10–23. (doi:10.1111/1467-8284.00096)

Clarke, M. 1999 *Flesh and spirit in the songs of Homer*. Oxford, UK: Clarendon press.

Crowley, J. L. 1989 Subject matter in Aegean art: the crucial changes. In *Transition. Le Monde Egeen du BronzeMoyen au Bronze Récent* (ed. R. Laffineur), pp. 203–214. Liège, Belgium: Universitè de l'Etat à Liège. Aegaeum 3.

Damasio, A. R. 1999 *The feeling of what happens: body and emotion in the making of consciousness.* New York, NY: Harcourt.

Daprati, E., Franck, N., Georgie, N., Proust, J., Pacherie, E. & Dalery, J. 1997 Looking for the agent: an investigation into consciousness of action and self consciousness in schizophrenic patients. *Cognition* **65**, 71–86. (doi:10.1016/S0010-0277(97)00039-5)

D'Errico, F., Henshilwood, C., Vanhaeren, M. & van Niekerk, K 2005 Nassarius kraussianus shell beads from Blombos Cave: evidence for symbolic behaviour in the Middle Stone Age. *J. Hum. Evol.* **48**, 3–24. (doi:10.1016/j.jhevol.2004.09.002)

Decety, J. & Sommerville, J. A. 2003 Shared representations between self and other: a social cognitive neuroscience view. *Trends Cogn. Sci.* **7**, 527–533. (doi:10.1016/j.tics.2003.10.004)

Dennett, D. C. 1991 *Consciousness explained.* Boston, MA: Little, Brown & Co.

de Vignemont, F. & Fourneret, P. 2004 The sense of agency. *Conscious. Cogn.* **13**, 1–19. (doi:10.1016/S1053-8100(03) 00022-9)

Dickinson, O. T. P. K. 1977 *The origins of Mycenean civilisation. Studies in Mediterranean archaeology*, vol. 49. Göteburg, Sweden: Paul Åströms Förlag.

Donald, M. 1991 *Origins of the modern mind.* Cambridge, MA: Harvard University Press.

Douglas, M. 1970 *Natural symbols: explorations in cosmology.* London, UK: Barrie & Jenkins.

Feinberg, T. E. & Keenan, J. P. 2005 Where in the brain is the self? *Conscious. Cogn.* **14**, 661–678. (doi:10.1016/j.concog.2005.01.002)

Frith, C. D. 2005 The self in action: lessons from delusions of control. *Conscious. Cogn.* **14**, 752–770. (doi:10.1016/j.concog.2005.04.002)

Fowler, C. 2003 *The archaeology of personhood: an anthropological approach.* London, UK: Routledge.

Gallagher, S. 2000a Philosophical conceptions of the self: implications for cognitive science. *Trends Cogn. Sci.* **4**, 14–21. (doi:10.1016/S1364-6613(99)01417-5)

Gallagher, S. 2000b Self-reference and schizophrenia: a cognitive model of immunity to error through misidentification. In *Exploring the self: philosophical and psycho-pathological perspectives on self-experience* (ed. D. Zahavi), pp. 203–239. Amsterdam, The Netherlands; Philadelphia, PA: John Benjamins.

Gallagher, S. 2005 *How the body shapes the mind.* Oxford, UK: Oxford University Press.

Gallese, V. 2005 Embodied simulation: from neurons to phenomenal experience. *Phenomenol. Cogn. Sci.* **4**, 23–48. (doi:10.1007/s11097-005-4737-z)

Gallese, V. & Lakoff, G. 2005 The brain's concepts: the role of the sensory-motor system in reason and language. *Cogn. Neuropsychol.* **22**, 455–479. (doi:10.1080/026432904 42000310)

Gallup, G. G. 1970 Chimpanzees: self-recognition. *Science* **167**, 86–87. (doi:10.1126/science.167.3914.86)

Gallup, G. G. 1979 Self-awareness in primates. *Am. Sci.* **67**, 417–21.

Gallup, G. G. 1998 Self-awareness and the evolution of social intelligence. *Behav. Process.* **42**, 239–247. (doi:10.1016/S0376-6357(97)00079-X)

Gamble, C. 2007 *Origins and revolutions, human identity in earliest prehistory.* Cambridge, UK: Cambridge University Press.

Gaskin, R. 1990 Do Homeric heroes make real decisions? *Class. Q.* **40**, 1–15.

Gazzaniga, M. S. 1998 *The mind's past.* Berkeley, CA: University of California Press.

Gell, A. 1998 *Art and agency: an anthropological theory.* Oxford, UK: Oxford University Press.

Gill, C. 1998 *Personality in greek epic, tragedy, and philosophy.* Oxford, UK: Clarendon Press.

Gillihan, S. J. & Farah, M. J. 2005 Is self special? A critical review of evidence from experimental psychology and cognitive neuroscience. *Psychol. Bull.* **131**, 76–97. (doi:10.1037/0033-2909.131.1.76)

Goldin-Meadow, S. 2003 *Hearing gesture: how our hands help us think.* Cambridge, MA: Harvard University Press.

Gusnard, D. A. 2005 Being a self: considerations from functional imaging. *Conscious. Cogn.* **14**, 679–697. (doi:10.1016/j.concog.2005.04.004)

Haggard, P., Clark, S. & Kalogeras, J. 2002 Voluntary action and conscious awareness. *Nat. Neurosci.* **5**, 382–385. (doi:10.1038/nn827)

Holmes, N. P. & Spence, C. 2004 The body schema and the multisensory representation(s) of peripersonal space. *Cogn. Process.* **5**, 94–105. (doi:10.1007/s10339-004-0013-3)

Holmes, N. P. & Spence, C. 2006 Beyond the body schema: visual, prosthetic, and technological contributions to bodily perception and awareness. In *Human body perception from the inside out* (eds G. Knoblich, I. M. Thornton, M. Grosjean & M. Shiffrar), pp. 15–64. Oxford, UK: Oxford University Press.

Holmes, N. P., Calvert, G. A. & Spence, C. 2004 Extending or projecting peripersonal space with tools: multisensory interactions highlight only the distal and proximal ends of tools. *Neurosci. Lett.* **372**, 62–67. (doi:10.1016/j.neulet.2004.09.024)

Humphrey, N. K. 2007 The society of selves. *Phil. Trans. R. Soc. B* **362**, 745–754. (doi:10.1098/rstb.2006.2007)

Hutchins, E. 1995 *Cognition in the wild*. Cambridge, MA: MIT Press.

Hutchins, E. 2005 Material anchors for conceptual blends. *J. Pragm.* **37**, 1555–1577. (doi:10.1016/j.pragma.2004.06.008)

Iriki, A., Tanaka, M. & Iwamura, Y. 1996 Coding of modified body schema during tool use by macaque postcentral neurones. *Neuroreport* **7**, 2325–2330.

Karo, G. 1930–3 *Die Schachtgraber von Mykenai*. Munich, Germany: Bruckmann.

Knappett, C. 2005 *Thinking through material culture: an interdisciplinary perspective*. Philadelphia, PA: University of Pennsylvania Press.

Kopytoff, I. 1986 The cultural biography of things: commoditization as process. In *The social life of things* (ed. A. Appadurai), pp. 64–91. Cambridge, UK: Cambridge University Press.

Lakoff, G. 1987 *Women, fire, and dangerous things: what categories reveal about the mind*. Chicago, IL; London, UK: University of Chicago Press.

Lakoff, G. & Johnson, M. 1999 *Philosophy in the flesh: the embodied mind and its challenge to western thought*. New York, NY: Basic Books.

Legrand, D. 2006 The bodily self: the sensori-motor roots of pre-reflexive self-consciousness. *Phenomenol. Cogn. Sci.* **5**, 89–118. (doi:10.1007/s11097-005-9015-6)

Lewis, M. 2003 The development of self-consciousness. In *Agency and self-awareness* (eds J. Roessler & N. Eilan), pp. 275–295. Oxford, UK: Oxford University Press.

Malafouris, L. 2004 The cognitive basis of material engagement: where brain, body and culture conflate. In *Rethinking materiality: the engagement of mind with the material world* (eds. E. DeMarrais, C. Gosden & C. Renfrew), pp. 53–62. Cambridge, UK: The McDonald Institute for Archaeological Research.

Malafouris, L. 2007 Before and beyond representation: towards an enactive conception of the palaeolithic image. In *Image and imagination: a global history of figurative representation* (eds C. Renfrew & I. Morley), pp. 289–302. Cambridge, UK: The McDonald Institute for Archaeological Research.

Malafouris, L. 2008*a*. At the Potter's wheel: an argument for material agency. In *Material agency: towards a non-anthropocentric perspective* (eds C. Knappett & L. Malafouris), pp. 19–36. New York, NY: Springer.

Malafouris, L. 2008*b*. Is it 'me' or is it 'mine'? The Mycenaean sword as a body-part. In *Past bodies* (eds J. Robb & D. Boric), pp. 115–23. London, UK: Berghahn.

Malafouris, L. 2008*c*. Beads for a Plastic Mind: the 'Blind Man's Stick' (BMS). Hypothesis and the Active Nature of Material Culture. *Camb. Archaeo. J.* **18**(3), 401–414. (doi:10.1017/S0959774308000449)

Maravita, A. & Iriki, A. 2004 Tools for the body (schema). *Trends Cogn. Sci.* **8**, 79–86. (doi:10.1016/j.tics.2003.12.008)

Maravita, A., Husain, M., Clarke, K. & Driver, J. 2001 Reaching with a tool extends visual-tactile interactions into far space: evidence from crossmodal extinction. *Neuropsychologia* **39**, 580–585. (doi:10.1016/S0028-3932 (00)00150-0)

Mauss, M. [1934] 1973 Techniques of the body. *Econ. Soc.* **2**, 70–88. (doi:10.1080/03085147300000003)

Mellars, P. 1989 Major issues in the emergence of modern humans. *Curr. Anthropol.* **30**, 349–385. (doi:10.1086/203755)

Merleau-Ponty, M. 1962 *Phenomenology of perception.* London, UK: Routledge.

Metzinger, T. 2003 *Being no one.* Cambridge, MA: MIT Press.

Miller, G. A. 1956 The magical number seven, plus or minus two. *Psychol. Rev.* **63**, 81–97. (doi:10.1037/h0043158)

Mylonas, G. E. 1973 *O Taphikos Kyklos B ton Mykenon.* Athens, Greece: Archaeological Society.

Neisser, U. 1988 Five kinds of self-knowledge. *Philos. Psychol.* **1**, 35–59.

Neisser, U. 1991 Two perceptually given aspects of the self and their development. *Dev. Rev.* **11**, 197–209. (doi:10.1016/0273-2297(91)90009-D)

Proust, J. 2003 Thinking of oneself as the same. *Conscious. Cogn.* **12**, 495–509. (doi:10.1016/S1053-8100(03) 00077-1)

Ramsey, A. 2000 Agency, personhood and the 'I' of discourse in the Pacific and beyond. *J. R. Anthropol. Inst.* **7**, 101–115.

Renfrew, C. 2006 Becoming human: the archaeological challenge. *Proc. Br. Acad.* **139**, 217–238.

Renfrew, C. 2007 *Prehistory, the making of the human mind.* London, UK: Weidenfeld & Nicolson.

Renfrew, C. 2008 Neuroscience, evolution and the sapient paradox: the factuality of value and of the sacred. *Phil. Trans. R. Soc. B* **363**, 2041–2047. (doi:10.1098/rstb.2008.0010)

Rochat, P. 2001 *The infant's world.* Cambridge, MA: Harvard University Press.

Rochat, P. 2003 Five levels of self-awareness as they unfold early in life. *Conscious. Cogn.* **12**, 717–731. (doi:10.1016/S1053-8100(03)00081-3)

Rowlands, M. 1993 The role of memory in the transmission of culture. *World Archaeol.* **25**, 141–151.

Riel-Salvatore, J. & Clark, G. A. 2001 Grave markers. *Curr. Anthropol.* **42**, 450–478. (doi:10.1086/321801)

Rutter, J. B. 1993 The prepalatial Bronze age of the southern and central Greek Mainland. *Am. J. Archaeol.* **97**, 745–797. (doi:10.2307/506720)

Schliemann, H. 1880 *Mycenae. A narrative of researches and discoveries at Mycenae and Tiryns.* New York, NY: Charles Scribner's Sons, Bell & Howell Co.

Shoemaker, S. 1968 Self-reference and self-awareness. *J. Philos.* **65**, 555–567. (doi:10.2307/2024121)

Snell, B. 1960 *The discovery of the mind.* New York, NY: Harper & Row.

Strathern, M. 1988 *The gender of the gift.* Berkeley, CA: University of California Press.

Taylor, C. 1989 *Sources of the self.* Cambridge, UK: Cambridge University Press.

Tomasello, M., Carpenter, M., Call, J., Behne, T. & Moll, H. 2005 Understanding and sharing intentions: the origins of cultural cognition. *Behav. Brain Sci.* **28**, 675–735. (doi:10.1017/S0140525X05000129)

Tulving, E. 1983 *Elements of episodic memory.* Oxford, UK: Clarendon Press.

Tulving, E. 2001 Episodic memory and common sense: how far apart? *Phil. Trans. R. Soc. B* **29**, 1505–1515. (doi:10.1098/rstb.2001.0937)

Tulving, E. 2002 Episodic memory: from mind to brain. *Annu. Rev. Psychol.* **53**, 1–25. (doi:10.1146/annurev.psych.53.100901.135114)

Turner, T. 1993 [1980] The social skin. In *Reading the social body* (eds C. B. Burroughs & J. Ehrenreich), pp. 15–39. Iowa City, IA: University Iowa Press.

Voutsaki, S. 1993 Society and culture in the Mycenaean World: an analysis of mortuary practices in the Argolid, Thessaly and the Dodecanese. PhD thesis, University of Cambridge, Cambridge.

Voutsaki, S. 1997 The creation of value and prestige in the Aegean Late Bronze Age. *J. European Archaeol.* **5**, 34–52.

Zahavi, D. 2005 *Subjectivity and selfhood: investigating the first-person perspective.* Cambridge, MA: Bradford Books; The MIT Press.

7

Social ontologies

Chris Gosden

There is room for considerable cooperation between archaeology and neuroscience, but in order for this to happen we need to think about the interactions among brain–body–world, in which each of these three terms acts as cause and effect, without attributing a causally determinant position to any one. Consequently, I develop the term social ontology to look at how human capabilities of mind and body are brought about through an interaction with the material world. I look also at the key notion of plasticity to think about not only the malable nature of human brains, but also the artefactual world. Using an example from the British Iron Age (approx. 750 BC–AD 43), I consider how new materials would put novel demands on the bodies and brains of people making, using and appreciating objects, focusing on an especially beautiful sword. In conclusion, I outline some possible areas of enquiry in which neuroscientists and archaeologists might collaborate.

Keywords: ontology; plasticity; brain–body–world; materials

7.1. Introduction

Neuroscientists study the brain to throw light on human capabilities, sometimes glossed as mind. Archaeologists study objects to understand past human collectivities, sometimes glossed as society. Both mind and society are abstract entities, somewhat hard to bring into contact due to their ghostliness. Rather than now concentrating on these two ghosts, mind and society, both neuroscientists and archaeologists are emphasizing material aspects of the brain in its body on the one hand and the physical properties of objects as they affect the body on the other. The triangle of brain–body–world is the point at which neuroscience and archaeology meet. What is needed to make this meeting most productive is a series of ideas that allow us to think about brains, bodies and material things in combination. In the first part of this article, I set out what I hope will be some bridging concepts between the two disciplines, before sketching out how these might be worked through in an empirical case.

I shall develop a notion of a social ontology, which holds that human life unfolds through an equal input from materials and from people, as a key bridging concept. People and materials bring out the characteristics of each other in particular cultural contexts, so that we need to think both about the manifold characteristics of people, and of things, as well as the manners in which they might relate through webs of connection. It follows that human social life cannot be understood apart from its material entailments, so that our lives arise from a combination of human skills in dealing with materials, the varying qualities and quantities of those materials and the social impacts of both skills and materials. In what follows, I shall outline some of the implications of the view that skilled bodies and socializing materials help constitute the nature of human life, looking first at some theoretical concerns, before moving on to more concrete implications.

Ontology is a word with varied meanings, but one key element is that it designates a theory of reality. Such a view implies a thinking being who constructs a theory about how the world is and works, which can be tested or put at risk against physical reality. Physical reality, at least as conceived of in a western modern view, is seen crucially in terms of cause and effect as constructed by the physical science disciplines of physics, chemistry and biochemistry. Such views are obviously historically contingent and culturally constructed, so that many in the world have developed very different images of reality, and now new pictures of ontology are emerging in western academia. Interestingly, there is some considerable synergy between new western views and those found elsewhere. Key to western rethinking is that ontology is an achievement of people and things together, rather than an appreciation of the giveness of the world. If we follow this line of thought, the world we come to know and understand is the world we work and engage with. Our picture of that world derives from our modes of activity within the world and activity is a joint product of people and the material world. This is definitely not a socially constructivist view of the world in which we create an image of reality deriving from our social and cultural conditions of life and also not an objectivist view in which the nature and structure of reality will impose itself upon, or reveal itself to, any suitably trained and disinterested observer. Ontology is an active matter arising from modes of interested activity as people go about the process of daily life with substances such as earth, wood, skins or clay, which, as the focuses of activity, all have in their role to play in shaping, channelling or constraining that activity. In this creation of a mode of reality, a form of active understanding, people bring the capabilities of human beings to play, which derive from the nature of hearing, taste, sight, sound, muscular activity or the processes of digestion, whereas materials are material each in their own way. This means that there are not two modes of being, where the physical world of cause and effect meets the more interesting, but less tangible, realm of social relations. Just as there is no objective reality to be more or less encompassed in a theory of how reality works, so there are no pure social relations. All relations between people are also material in their form and content. Such a mixing of people and of things brings into question the academic division between the physical sciences on the one hand and the human or social sciences on the other. The massive nature of this edifice makes us realize how much entrenched thought needs to be overcome to start thinking in a maner which mixes people and things. A first step in this overcoming is to look at how people objectify themselves in objects and how objects subjectify themselves in people (to paraphrase Marx in the *Grundrisse*).

Nowadays, many in the social sciences are starting to think about the combined capacities of people and things. To some degree, this represents a harking back to older issues in anthropology and archaeology. I shall look first at nineteenth century interests in concepts such as animism, before briefly looking at more contemporary thought.

7.2. Modes of achieving an ontology

In his synthetic book *Primitive culture*, Tylor (1871) put forward an evolutionary progression in the history of human thought and understanding, which saw a movement from magic to religion to science. The first of these terms designated a mode of operation and understanding in which people attempted to intercede with and manipulate the spiritual powers of the world through spells and acts. His notion of magic was linked to the idea of animism in which it was thought that the world contains a large number of powers and spirits inhabiting various plants, animals and objects, which might then be animated and able to intervene in human lives. Magic and animistic beliefs differed from religions in which powers were concentrated in a more or less singular god who needed to be supplicated through prayer. Both of these were essentially false understandings of the way in which the world works, according to Tylor, with a truer understanding only coming about with the rise of modern science over the last few centuries. However, it is often said that Tylor did not make clear the distinctions among his three key terms of magic, religion and science, so that in many ways magic and science were linked as modes of affecting the world, the first spurious and naive, the second rigorous and based on a real understanding of the modes of operation of matter. Both were opposed to religion. In a much more recent book, Tambiah (1990) has surveyed modes of magical, scientific and religious thought, looking at Malinowski's counterview to that of Tylor, in which magic was seen as a performative act, which galvanized the community into various ways of confronting a problem—it was not the claims to truth that were the defining feature of magic for Malinowski, but its rhetorical power and social effectiveness. Tambiah is ultimately convinced by neither of these thinkers but takes his lead from Lévy-Bruhl (1926) who sums up so-called 'primitive' thought as one of participation, which posits the consubstantiality of people and things, whereby the same set of processes are seen to animate the world as a whole, whether the human or the non-human element. Tambiah refines this view to say that there are two basic human orientations to reality, one which stresses causality and the other participation. Both modes of understanding are found in all human cultural forms, but in a different balance, with more romantic modes of understanding still alive and well in the rationalistic, scientific West.

Lévy-Bruhl's views find echoes in those being developed by Latour and others nowadays (Stengers 2000; Latour 1993, 2005). The difference between these twenty-first century views and those of a century earlier is that the nature of the material and human material engagements are the key starting point rather than modes of thought about reality. There are a number of key thinkers who are covering similar intellectual ground emphasizing the entangled nature of people and of things. Latour has developed what he calls 'symmetrical anthropology' in which he says that in any analysis both things and people must be included and that we should not prejudge the capacities of either, especially as we in the west tend to think of people as active and objects as passive. More animistic notion of things should be encouraged so that we can look at what sorts of circumstances things will have a determinant effect on people. One of the key issues that Latour has focused on is scientific decision making in which he wants to get away from either a social constructivist view of science, in which it is seen that it is the social and cultural preconceptions of scientists that determine their results, or a purely empiricist mode, whereby the nature of material realities being studied leads inevitably to conclusions about how the world works. Rather, a more entangled view is the only realistic possibility, Latour feels that the cultural preconceptions of scientists are always put at risk and challenged by the nature of the phenomena they are investigating. The analytical point of science and technology studies is to work out how decisions about complex questions, such as global warming or bovine spongiform encephalopathy, are reached looking at the relative weights of the evidence and cultural or political considerations in reaching conclusions. A second current thinker who draws inspiration from animistic forms of thought in looking at the relations between people and things is Ingold (2000). Ingold wants to shift our basic set of images about the world and people, together with the language used to describe it. He uses metaphors of growth and development to look at the manner in which people grow into sets of relationships with plants, animals and materials in manners which change all within that relationship. People's capabilities come about in the context of particular sets of ecological relationships (where ecology is used broadly to include human products) through play, performance and labour in a manner which is profoundly interactive and doing away with any fixed divisions between culture and nature. Intelligence is enacted, coming into being through work in the world, so that thought and reflection are dependent upon people's action rather than the actions directed by mental structures. Another anthropological thinker, Alfred Gell, has been very influential of late (Gell 1998). Gell has looked at objects commonly considered to be art (a problematical category in any case) and said that our primary question of such objects (and maybe, by extension, of all objects) should not be what do they mean, but what do they do? Gell attends to how people affect people and the relations between people. Key examples for him are objects which enchant through the complexity of their making, the high degree of skill needed to produce them and the materials used in them. Objects which enchant can overawe and influence people, so that they find it hard to resist the blandishments of their makers in other spheres, such as those of exchange. Enchanting objects are active presences in our lives, influencing a whole range of social relations between people. Each of these thinkers have significant differences in their approach, but they all are more or less united in their attempts to understand human life as developing in a partnership with the world.

This is my point of emphasis too and it is an important opening position in thinking about brains, bodies and worlds. We need to join two areas of thought, concerning identity on the one hand and the nature of our relationship with the world on the other. The mode of our presentation of ourselves as members of groups and as individuals is intimately tied up with our understanding of the other and of how the world works more generally. Modes of presentation of self take at least two forms: Mauss (1935) noted that the techniques of the body used for performing our most frequent acts of daily life are open to approval, recognition and evaluation by the social group as a whole, so that when they work they are efficacious both practically and socially; the presentation of self also takes more staged and performative forms, through housing, clothing, ornament and burial to name only a few, and these forms are at once material and social. Thus, in order to present a human individual or a group, the world needs to be mobilized in particular ways that depend partly on the material nature of the world and partly on the methods of mobilization. As groups and individuals are brought into being, subverted or reinforced, so is the world given particular forms to be understood in a determinate range of ways. At its heart, the joint process of becoming and knowing is a process of transubstantiation whereby the values attaching to the forms that objects take help attach values to people, with the reverse also being true— the forms that people take help attach values to objects. The notion of the formal qualities of things is key—it is the forms that things and people take which gives them impact, an impact which is felt in human terms as emotions and feelings. The crucial nexus is between aesthetics, deriving from an appreciation of form, and emotion which is a means of describing the human impacts of form. The senses are the key link here, educated in different ways by material things in various parts of the world, so that sensing is not the simple apprehension of material things and their positions in space or changes through time. Perception is what Noe has called 'enactive' (Noë 2005)—it helps explore the world and to form categories as things are sensed from within the context of action on the world. Action is directed by the forms of things, but also creates or changes those forms.

One thing uniting most of these views is their stress on dynamic relations between people and things. Into this broader discussion of dynamism, neuroscience brings a key concept—that of plasticity. My crude understanding of this notion as applied to the brain is that the activities of the body help to differentially develop areas of the brain, so that relative size and shape of different areas depend on the most common actions of the brain's owner. A famous example of this is the right hippocampus of the London cab driver which is more developed than in most people, due to the acquisition of The Knowledge, encompassing all the complex mass of routes through London (Maguire *et al.* 1997). Archaeologists are very aware of the plasticity of the object world (although they would seldom use that term). The manner in which space is constructed as new settlements are laid out, landscapes develop and routeways come and go is complemented by changes in the artefactual world, so that when new materials are brought in their novel properties create unprecedented possibilities and constraints. The brain has its part to play in these changes, helping develop new modes of engagement. A key element of the recursive relationship between people and the world is the plasticity of both brains and objects: brains help make new objects, which in turn help create new brains.

Let us consider these issues from an archaeological and therefore object-centred perspective, before returning to the possible links between neuroscience and archaeology.

7.3. Iron Age ontologies

I am going to look at a single artefact from the later Iron Age period in Britain. The Iron Age in Britain ran from approximately 750 BC until the Roman invasion of AD 43 and for most of this time, people lived in a series of small settlements surrounded by arable fields and keeping animals such as sheep, cows and pigs. As might be expected, they had a varied set of crafts ranging among textile making, pottery, carpentry and metal working. They were also skilled at shaping their landscapes, digging long ditches, sometimes many miles long presumably as land boundaries and creating large centres of activity with impressive banks, ditches and gateways known as hill forts. We can guess that most people in the population shared many skills in common needed for growing food, processing and cooking it, as well as the skills to build houses, rear animals, make pots and work wood. Some skills were obviously much more restricted, including those of metalworking and weaving. The name of the period derives from one of the materials found commonly at this time—iron being one stage in the so-called Three Age System developed generally for Europe in the earlier nineteenth century and still in use with many qualifications today. The naming of the Stone, Bronze and Iron Ages represents the centrality of material culture to archaeological thought from its earliest beginnings. New approaches can potentially make use of an enormous amount of analysis and thick description contained in 150 years of archaeological accounts in Europe and on other continents. I shall attempt to give a hint of how this might be done, to flesh out the notion of a social ontology.

I shall start with one complex item, which, as it happens, is made partly of iron: the so-called Kirkburn sword. This is one of 274 swords, sword fragments and scabbards found in the British Isles during the later Iron Age (see Stead (2006) for details of all the material). There are differences of style and life histories between the south of England and the north at this time, so that in the south swords were predominantly thrown into rivers and in the north the ones we have were mainly placed in graves. In either case, there were probably many which did not make it into the archaeological record. The Kirkburn sword, which comes from East Yorkshire in the northeast of England, was found with the inhumation of a man who was lying on his back with his head orientated to the north. The sword was underneath him and placed upside down.

The Kirkburn sword was a complex construction which it is worth looking at in some detail (figure 7.1 gives some impression of the handle of the sword and the upper part of the scabbard). The sword has an iron blade of some 697 mm long (obscured by the scabbard from which it cannot be removed due to corrosion). The sword has a handle made of multiple components, which protrudes from the scabbard that is made of a front plate of bronze, which is decorated and a rear plate of iron, with a suspension loop to attach it to a belt probably made of animal skin (see figure 7.2 for an exploded reconstruction of the scabbard as understood from X-ray analysis and visual inspection). The lower part of the scabbard is covered in a chape that has enamelled glass decoration. The handle of the sword is especially complicated. In its upper part (or pommel), it is composed of an iron frame containing a piece of carved horn through which iron roundels have been fastened, separated from the horn by bronze washers. These roundels were covered with sheet iron coated with red glass, applied in a liquid state to a roughened (or keyed) surface. The handle itself is a cylinder of horn also covered in sheet iron with cells excised, which was then filled with red glass, so that the contrast between the iron and the glass forms a complicated pattern, which is different on the forward facing side of the handle from that nearer the human body. The bottom of the hilt and the top of the scabbard also have roundels covered in red glass.

Figure 7.1. The handle and top of the scabbard of the Kirkburn sword.

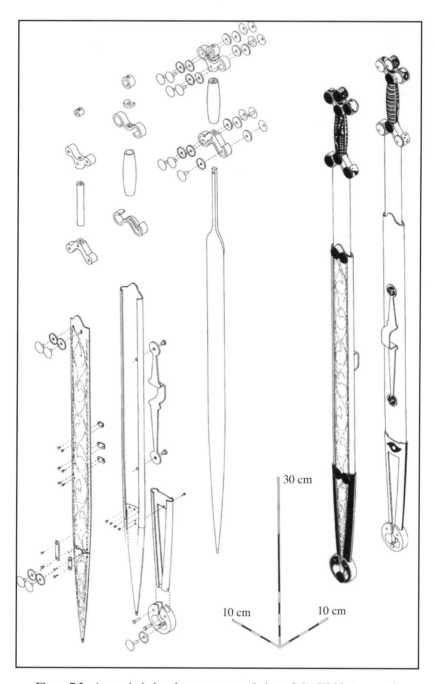

Figure 7.2. An exploded and a reconstructed view of the Kirkburn sword.

Below these, the outer face of the scabbard, made of bronze, is covered with so-called tendril and leaf decoration engraved onto the surface of the plate, terminating in curved triangular decorations on one side, but forming a continuous curved tendril on the other linking the design along the whole length of the scabbard. The bottom of the scabbard, known as the chape, is rather corroded now but has a circular shape, which was once covered in red glass.

The sword and scabbard condense many histories, some local to them and others from long ago and far away. The sword was made in approximately 250 BC, but may have been deposited in the grave some 150 years later. It had a complex history as can be seen from a number of repairs. At some stage, the front and back scabbard plates were split longitudinally and then rejoined; on the back, iron plate riveting was used, which was much cruder than the original work. To split a scabbard without destroying it would have required much skill as well as being a violent act. It is worth noting in passing that many swords and other objects were 'killed' before deposition by bending or breaking, acts which often required metalworking skills possessed only by a few. In the case of the Kirkburn sword, violence was acted on it at some point during its life cycle rather than at its end. There were other forms of damage to the scabbard deriving from more general use which had also been repaired. The chape has also had a half plate added to it as a repair, with a slightly different decoration from the original piece. These repairs and the time gap between production and burial indicate a long and complex biography linking a number of human generations, with the sword and scabbard being a possibly important link in generating human genealogies. The splitting of the scabbard and other aspects of its story might well have acted as a mnemonic for stories to be maintained and told, a key material prompt to an oral culture.

The Kirkburn sword is one of the three, which are so similar in the details of the roundels on the handle, enamelling, length of blade and decoration that they were almost certainly produced in the same workshop and probably by one person. The other two swords were from the burial site of Wetwang Slack, a few miles from Kirkburn, in burials of men with carts or chariots (Stead 2006, swords with Stead's catalogue numbers 173 and 174—the Kirkburn sword is 172). Unlike the Kirkburn, these swords have little evidence of repair and may have been placed in graves much closer to their production date of 250 BC. Although the Kirkburn burial did not contain a cart (which often had fine metal adornments for the cart and the horses that pulled it), there were similarities in the burial rite. Both the body at Kirkburn and that at Wetwang with sword 173 had been speared after death with three iron spears in the former case and seven in the latter. What this might indicate shall be considered below. We can also not be sure why there were such differences in the life cycles of the three swords, but it must have been something to do with particular conjunctions between objects and people.

The Kirkburn sword also contains much longer histories that we can peek into now, with at least one history for every material used to make the sword. The horn of the handle represents the oldest element of the technology by far. Fine working of bone and horn occurred from approximately 40 000 years ago in the Upper Palaeolithic of Europe from when we have the first good evidence, but bone working for tools and ornaments goes back much longer, probably at least to the point at which the first stone tools were used some 2.4 Myr ago. Bronze working in Britain has a much lesser antiquity, but still predates the Kirkburn sword by some 1500 years. Bronze is an alloy of copper with tin or lead. Copper was first worked in the eighth millennium BC by Neolithic communities in the Middle East where it took its place as beads and small ornaments alongside other brightly coloured stones and shells. Around the sixth millennium in either northern Mesopotamia or Anatolia, the first metals were smelted, a process whereby copper ores were heated in a reducing atmosphere low in oxygen, with charcoal, to produce molten metal. Copper smelting moved across Europe, from a possible point of independent invention in the Balkans, to reach Britain in approximately 2500 BC. It is probable that the control of firing for pottery, a rather older technology, provided the know-how for the earliest smelters. Copper is difficult to cast and is a very soft metal. However, when it is combined with between 5 and 10% tin (lead alloys came later), it is much more ductile and forms a harder finished product known as bronze. Bronze first occurred in Anatolia and Mesopotamia in approximately 3000 BC and spurred the need for considerable trade, as tin is a rare metal and is almost never found in conjunction with copper. Bronze working started in Britain in approximately 2200 BC after a brief period of copper working. A few centuries later, bronze working started in northern China and southeast Asia.

Copper and bronze metallurgy are technologies like no other which preceded them (except possibly for cookery) in that they are radically transformative, starting with the stone of the ore body which is transformed into a liquid but then re-crystallized as a solid. Once this point is reached, the object can be melted down and reformed, a common aspect of the life cycle of metal artefacts. The working of metals requires a large amount of embodied knowledge. Ancient metallurgists were able to control firing temperatures in the smelt or forge, as well as the atmospheres around the objects, add quantities of metals together very precisely or arrive at a desired surface finish for an object, all without the thermometer or means of measuring gases or precise means of estimating weight. Some of this knowledge would have been transmitted orally, but books, plans or chemical formulae were all absent, so that much would have come from learning the heft of the tools, the colour of flames or metal and the right amount of air to pump in with the bellows. Bodily intelligence, rather than mental construction, was the key to skilled productive activity. Intensely skilled activity was needed at the point of production, which would also have encompassed many other materials and forms of work in the world to supply wood or charcoal for the furnaces, wax to fill moulds in the so-called lost wax process, and other metal and stone tools which would have been needed for working. Once bronze became common, trade was needed to bring together the various components of the alloy, so that modes of travel, skills of rhetoric and persuasion, and the creation of other items to be traded were all necessary to cement deals in ways that made material sense but also helped oil the sets of relations between people. Bronze technology created a great range of new objects—axes and ornaments, chisels and tools, and later swords and daggers, objects developed for the first time in the Bronze Age with profound implications for human relations. New skills were needed to make bronze artefacts, but once these spread through the population re-skilling was needed on a large scale, not only in terms of using functional items, but also skills of perception and discrimination as people became adept at recognizing and understanding the new sets of styles and varieties of bronze form brought about. People were re-skilled and re-socialized, being brought into new relations with materials and with each other, arriving at novel understandings of both.

Bronze spread fairly fast once invented, but iron was a much more reluctant technology. The first iron was worked in Anatolia in approximately 2200 BC (when bronze working initially arrived in Britain), but remained a very minor component of metallurgy for many centuries. Iron working probably started in Britain in approximately 1000 BC

(Collard *et al.* 2006), but it did not become common for another 300 years. Such a time lag gives the lie to the old Three Age System in which it was thought that a new superior technology would quickly displace the old. This successive and progressive view of technology is profoundly misleading for Europe at least, where technologies are often accumulative with a new one being added to the older forms, rather than replacing them. Bronze was repositioned by iron working, not eradicated, with many ornamental and other items being produced in bronze through the Roman period and beyond. It is worth bearing in mind that prehistoric European iron working was quite a different mode of production than bronze and, although they are both joined in the modern mind through a general equivalence between metal working techniques, this might not have been the case in the Iron Age. It is only possible to melt iron, and thus to cast it, once a temperature of 1530°C is reached and while the capacity to do this developed in China from the ninth century BC, this did not occur until well into the historical period in Europe. Iron objects, like swords, were formed not in moulds, but by hammering when hot. Also, there are formidable problems in removing the metal from the slag in the smelting process, it then needs to be combined with charcoal and other materials to gain the right degree of hardness and finally quenched, a process by which the temperature of the hot-worked object is rapidly reduced, usually achieved through immersion in a liquid such as water or oil. Bronze transforms from rock to liquid to solid but iron is changed within a solid state and through considerable difficulty, manual labour and danger. There are indications that bronze and iron were treated differently in Iron Age Britain. Bronze was often deposited in watery places of rivers or bogs, whereas iron is more commonly found in the ditches around settlements or pits within them. Hingley (2006) has recently studied the deposition of iron objects generally in Iron Age and Roman Britain, working on the general premise widespread in British archaeology that varying modes of deposition of objects in rivers, ditches, isolated hoards or in graves often represent purposive acts rather than casual loss, telling us a lot about people's attitudes to objects and the world more generally. There is a shift from deposition of iron objects, such as the so-called currency bars, in the ditches enclosing settlements in the Iron Age to deep burial in wells or deep pits within settlements in the Romano–British period. Iron may have held a number of associations, partly concerning danger, so that its presence at boundaries might have protective effect and these might be derived from the difficulties of production, but also regeneration due to the fact that iron rusts and decays easily in comparison with bronze, gold or silver. Iron can be taken out of the ground as ore, formed but then put back into the ground as artefact, possibly to help maintain general forms of fertility. The possible association between iron and danger on the other hand might be reinforced by the fact that the bodies in the graves at Kirkburn and Wetwang were pierced with iron spears, in some sort of apotropaic act in which iron was more efficacious than bronze. Whatever the accuracy of these observations, they alert us to the fact that we need to attend to the whole life cycle of objects from production, use and final discard as each element in this process has important things to say about the ontologies involved.

The final material involved in the Kirkburn sword is red enamel or glass. This is probably a by-product of copper working. From approximately 750 BC in Britain and Europe, there was a desire for red materials on metal objects, so that early pieces were inlaid with coral from the Red Sea or amber from the Baltic. Starting in approximately 400 BC, red glass (and later yellow and turquoise) was added to artefacts of iron and bronze. The glass may have been originally imported from the eastern Mediterranean. The history of glass working is still being investigated, but production probably goes back to Mesopotamia in approximately 2500 BC where glass is linked to the development of glazes, first as a covering for quartz crystals and later for pottery. Glass was also made in Britain, with the Kirkburn sword being a striking, but in many ways typical, example of enamelling using red as the sole or dominant colour. We seem to be dealing with definite aesthetics here in which red, with its possible associations with blood and danger, played a key role.

A further example of aesthetics, as well as an important part of the broader histories in which the Kirkburn sword played a role, are the modes of decoration known as 'Celtic art'. The enamelling that we have just mentioned is found throughout Europe, but is an especially marked element of British Iron Age decoration. The wave and tendril decoration on the scabbard is found on many thousands of items in Britain and across western and central Europe. These engraved decorations, together with three-dimensional decorative forms, such as neck torcs, linked a large number of communities through common styles. Many of the vegetal motifs may have an ultimate origin in Greek art, which itself was influenced by the Middle East, but these undergo a series of transformations as they cross Europe. Objects in these styles are first found in Britain probably from approximately 300 BC onwards, but by the time the Kirkburn sword was made in approximately 250 BC, a series of insular styles had developed with their own forms of artefacts, an emphasis on red enamel and special modes of engraved ornament.

In stylistic terms, the Kirkburn sword can be seen to condense a number of spatial scales. The smallest scale is the local workshop which produced it and at least two other recognizably similar swords with their own particularities; but this object also belongs to a class of northern British swords which show links with those from Ireland. At the most expansive scale, the sword is part of a conjunction of form and decoration found over large areas of Europe and which lasted for many hundreds of years in a changing manner. Each of these material histories, local and short-term or widespread and ancient, would have had significance for any single object. Things were positioned within a dense skein of relations stretching back to many millennia, not known in detail but giving general qualities to materials and the people involved with them, as well as leading to more particular local engagements.

7.4. Plastic ontologies

A sword, like the one found at Kirkburn, required many skills. The many materials that went into the sword's making were probably beyond the compass of a single individual, so that a number of skilled bodies collaborated in its production. There was also the training of the arm, hand, eye and whole body needed to wield the sword in a skilled manner, which must also be linked to the skills of appreciating the forms, colours and surfaces of the sword, in movement or at rest. A sword like this could combine a scintillating moment of movement with a long-term biography of the sword itself and the lineages of the materials from which it was made. Objects extend and change the body schemas of those using them and their interactions with others. Our peripersonal space is that within the reach of limbs and this can be extended through objects, both in terms of our reach and effective action, and also through extending the image our brains have of our bodies (Holmes & Spence 2004). Peripersonal space also reaches out in interpersonal space within which much face-to-face social life is enacted. The creation of a sword has considerable implications for all these forms of space and the links between people through objects. We can consequently argue that a world of metals helped to create quite different sets of social ontologies to those found in the Neolithic when metals did not exist. We could put forward as a point to be argued that a world of metals engaged the whole body more than many previous materials. To be skilled with a sword involves all parts of the human anatomy from feet to forehead, albeit with a concentration of attention on that composite region from the shoulder to the tip of the sword. It also requires a skilled and changing perception of any others with swords in the vicinity. Even another skilled sword wielder can quickly create an interpersonal space that will absorb all one's attention! The axe, a key instrument in the Neolithic, was probably not really a weapon in any case and would have required quite different skills of use, focusing on repetitive chopping actions in contrast to the varied chops, parries and thrusts of a sword. Peripersonal space and social interaction were constructed differently in the two periods.

Things can be seen to animate in the sense that they bring different muscular and sensory modalities into play, creating in the process different senses of the body and relations with other bodies. The conjoined nature of people and things, bringing each other into being, has at least three implications for brain research. The first concerns the long-term history of the structure of the brain. Human ancestors have used tools for at least 2.6 Myr, over which period brains have changed hugely in size and structure. Can we discern long-term effects of making the world on the nature of the brain, which has in the short-term been continually reshaped by bodies and their objects? Secondly, are different types of action and use of objects differentially effective in shaping brains and bodies? Can we make a distinction between sedentary activities, like flint knapping, in which hands, eyes and arms are heavily engaged, but the rest of the body more passive, and whole-body activities, such as dancing or sword use, in which the organism as a totality is involved? Lastly is an area of considerable technical difficulty as far as brain scanning is concerned—what are the linked effects of objects and bodies within social settings? Joint attention and joint intention studies show how people are joined and directed towards certain features of the world in their interactions with objects. Can we start to look at the forms of brain activity brought about by people and things in combination, as the characteristics of people are highlighted by things and the capacities of things are highlighted by skilled human users?

The world of the Iron Age in Britain brought into use more varied sets of materials than those of the preceding Neolithic and Bronze Ages. More materials in play would have the effect (one would guess) of engaging more aspects of bodies and brains. The Iron Age was about to be succeeded by Britain's incorporation into the Roman Empire, which brought about a further explosion of new things and in much greater quantities than ever before, often deployed in a world suddenly more rectilinear in its forms. Here, too, is cause for thought. As far as we can tell, the people of the Iron Age created few straight lines. The carpentered interior environments of the Romans created straight walls in contrast to earlier circular huts, with domestic spaces joined by the legendary straightness of the Roman roads. Human sensibilities were re-tuned bringing about unprecedented forms of social ontology, which might also have involved different (more linear?) conceptions of cause and effect (Gosden 2005a,b). In the world of the present, interesting cross-cultural work could be carried out on the brains and bodies of people brought up with different geometries of domestic spaces and of landscape organization.

Archaeology, commonly seen as the study of the old, and neuroscience, with its reputation for being at the cutting edge of twenty-first century technologies and debates, might seem poles apart. If it is true, however, that action through objects reshape the brain, then archaeologists know a lot about objects and would like to know much more about the brain and its histories. There are many benefits of collaborative work, especially if we avoid sliding into either neural determinism, in which the brain is seen as the centre of the human world or as an object fetishism, which holds that objects make people. The complex actions and interactions of brains, bodies and worlds are what make us human and historical. I hope to have shown that an idea like social ontology can help us track the complicated interactions of the neural and the artefactual, which will only really be possible through programmes of inter-disciplinary work.

I would like to thank Chris Frith, Lambros Malafouris and Colin Renfrew for inviting me the Sapient Mind Symposium and for the stimulation it provided. Duncan Garrow and two anonymous referees provided excellent comments on this manuscript.

References

Collard, M., Darvill, T. & Watts, M. 2006 Ironworking in the Bronze Age? Evidence from a 10th century BC settlement at Hartshill Copse, Upper Bucklebury, West Berkshire. *Proc. Prehist. Soc.* **72**, 367–436.

Gell, A. 1998 *Art and agency: an anthropological theory*. Oxford, UK: Clarendon Press.

Gosden, C. 2005a Material culture and long-term change. In *The sage handbook of material culture* (eds C. Tilley, W Keane, S. Kuechler, M. Rowlands & P. Spyer), pp. 425–442. London, UK: Sage Publications.

Gosden, C. 2005b What do objects want? *J. Archaeol. Method Theory* **12**, 193–211. (doi:10.1007/s10816-005-6928-x)

Hingley, R. 2006 The deposition of iron objects in Britain during the Later Prehistoric and Roman periods: contextual analysis and the significance of iron. *Britannia* **37**, 213–257.

Holmes, N. & Spence, C. 2004 The body schema and multi-sensory representation(s) of peripersonal space. *Cogn. Process.* **5**, 94–105. (doi:10.1007/s10339-004-0013-3)

Ingold, T. 2000 *The perception of the environment*. London, UK: Routledge.

Latour, B. 1993 *We have never been modern*. New York, NY; London, UK: Harvester Wheatsheaf.

Latour, B. 2005 *Reassembling the social: an introduction to actor-network theory*. Oxford, UK: Oxford University Press.

Lévy-Bruhl, L. 1926 *How natives think*. London, UK: George Allen and Unwin.

Maguire, E. A., Frackowiak, R. S. J. & Frith, C. D. 1997 Recalling routes around London: activation of the right hippocampus in taxi drivers. *J. Neurosci.* **17**, 7103–7110.

Mauss, M. 1935 Les techniques du corps. *J. Psychol.* **32**, 271–293.

Noë, A. 2005 *Action in perception*. Cambridge, MA: MIT Press.

Stead, I. 2006 *British Iron Age swords and scabbards*. London, UK: The British Museum Press.

Stengers, I. 2000 *The invention of modern science*. Minneapolis, MN: The University of Minnesota Press.

Tambiah, S. J. 1990 *Magic, science, religion and the scope of rationality*. Cambridge, UK: Cambridge University Press.

Tylor, E. B. 1871. *Primitive culture: researches into the development of mythology, philosophy, religion, language, art, and custom*, vols. 2. London, UK: John Murray.

8

The role of cultural practices in the emergence of modern human intelligence

Edwin Hutchins

Innate cognitive capacities are orchestrated by cultural practices to produce high-level cognitive processes. In human activities, examples of this phenomenon range from everyday inferences about space and time to the most sophisticated reasoning in scientific laboratories. A case is examined in which chimpanzees enter into cultural practices with humans (in experiments) in ways that appear to enable them to engage in symbol-mediated thought. Combining the cultural practices perspective with the theories of embodied cognition and enactment suggests that the chimpanzees' behaviour is actually mediated by non-symbolic representations. The possibility that non-human primates can engage in cultural practices that give them the appearance of symbol-mediated thought opens new avenues for thinking about the coevolution of human culture and human brains.

Keywords: cultural practices; evolution of cognitive processes; chimpanzee cognition; symbol-mediated thought; enacted representations

8.1. Seeking the sources of modern human cognition: Culture and brain

Many accounts of how humans became the creatures they are rely on speculations about changes in the neural architecture of the human brain. For example, Clark (2001, ch. 8) says, 'The idea is that some relatively *small* neural (or neural/bodily) difference was the spark that lit a kind of intellectual forest fire. The brain is, let us assume, wholly responsible (courtesy, perhaps of some quite small tweak of the engineering) for the fulfillment of some precondition of cultural and technological evolution'. It is certainly the case that anatomically modern human brains are different in important ways from the brains of any other present or past primates. Let us call these underlying preconditions cognitive capacities. In this paper, I will argue that the human cognitive system is best conceived as a distributed system that transcends the boundaries of the brain and body. This system includes objects, patterns, events and other living beings in the setting in which human (and non-human) cognition takes place. This is the so-called 'distributed cognition' premise. While it is certainly possible and productive to study processes that are internal to individuals, cognitive outcomes, including category assignments, inferences, decisions, judgements and so on, are often better understood as properties of the distributed cognitive system than as properties of any of the individuals participating in the distributed system. When cognition is understood this way, then it also becomes clear that cultural practices provide transformative elements of the human cognitive system. High-level cognitive outcomes emerge from the orchestration of the elements of distributed cognitive systems by cultural practices. This fact also implies that we must be careful when attributing cognitive processes to individuals who are engaged in cultural practices. There is a danger of attributing to the individual cognitive properties that belong to the larger distributed system.

The idea here is that a good deal of contemporary thinking, and probably an even greater proportion of ancient thinking, happens in *interaction* of brain and body with the world. This seems innocent enough and many people take it to mean simply that thinking is something that happens in the brain as a consequence of interaction with the world. That is not the claim being made here. The claim here is that, first and foremost, thinking *is* interactions of brain and body with the world. Those interactions are not evidence of, or reflections of, underlying thought processes. They are instead the thinking processes themselves.

If true, this approach to cultural practices has many implications. An obvious implication is that if two cognitive systems include different cultural practices, they can have dramatically different functional properties even when the brains and other physical resources in the system are identical. We are all familiar with this fact, and it is a primary motivation for educational activities.[1]

With respect to the emergence of modern human intelligence, this approach to cultural practices has some less obvious implications. First, because outcomes typically arise from the orchestration of capacities by practices, cognitive capacities cannot be inferred directly from outcomes. The mediation of the relation between capacities and outcomes by cultural practices also means that the evolutionary value of cognitive capacities cannot be inferred directly from the supposed use of cognitive outcomes. The material and social world are structured by cultural historical processes in a cognitive ecology. Outcomes are often the product of interactions between persons (capacities orchestrated by cultural practices) with the material and social world. The interpretation of cognitive capacities, as revealed by experimental methods, must be informed by an analysis of the cultural practices of experimentation. That is, because every experiment proceeds by the deployment of cultural practices in a richly structured material and social context, attributing the observed cognitive outcomes directly to the participants (subjects) may be problematic.

If cultural practices can transform cognitive systems, it means that the commonly assumed ordering of evolution and history can be rearranged (Ingold 2000, p. 392). Rather than assuming that biological evolution must have acted first to make our ancestors' brains capable of language and cultural processes, after which cultural history took over to produce the presently observed diversity of languages and cultures, it seems equally probable that the innovations that make modern thought possible were innovations in cultural practices. Once having arisen in the social world, of course, such changes would create new selective pressures to which biological evolution could respond (Strum *et al.* 1997; Hutchins 2006).

Undoubtedly, anatomically modern human intelligence emerges (in real time, not historically speaking for the moment) from the operation in the here and now of a system that includes a brain that is anatomically different from the brains that are involved in the emergence of animal intelligences. But how shall we sort out the relative contributions of cultural practices from those of brain anatomy?

8.2. How cultural practices produce cognitive outcomes

Cultural practices are the things people do and their learned ways of being in the world. For my purposes, a practice will be labelled cultural if it exists in a cognitive ecology such that it is constrained by or coordinated with the practices of other persons. Virtually all external representations are produced by cultural practices. All forms of language are produced by and in cultural practices. Speaking is accomplished via discursive cultural practices. The specifics of each language require its speakers to attend to some distinctions and permit them to ignore others. This 'thinking for speaking' (Slobin 1987, 1996) implies that even low-level perceptual processes are often organized by cultural practices. Cultural practices include particular ways of seeing (or hearing, or feeling, or smelling) the world. Cultural practices are not cultural models traditionally construed as disembodied structural representations of knowledge. Rather they are fully embodied skills. Cultural practices organize the action in situated action.

Humans inhabit the worlds that are full of cultural meaning. The enaction approach (Havelange *et al.* 2003; Thompson 2007) reminds us that every meaning that is apprehended is made, not received. Noë's (2004) contention that perception is something we do, not something that happens to us, is especially true for the perception or apprehension of cultural meaning.

(a) Two systems of preliterate cultural practices

Let us consider two cases of preliterate cultural practices that are the foundation of important adaptive cognitive accomplishments: reading the sky as a sidereal calendar and navigating Micronesian style. I choose the practices of preliterate cultures here because literacy introduces many complexities and its effects permeate the cognition of literate societies.

On Boyowa Island in the Trobriand Islands of Papua New Guinea, a small number of specialists are given the responsibility of setting the agricultural calendar for all of the island's villages. Early in 1976, as part of a 2-year ethnographic study on Boyowa, I inter-viewed a magician cum astronomer named Dauya. Dauya lived in Wawela village, which is one of the only villages on the island with an unobstructed view of the eastern horizon. The weather patterns in the Solomon Sea vary from year to year, so that yearly changes in the weather, the onset of dry weather for example, are only approximate indicators of the season. Linking the timing of the preparations of the gardens to changes in the weather may leave the crops subject to unfavourable conditions months later. The problem is to fix the agricultural calendar to a seasonal calendar that is not subject to year-to-year variability in the timing of weather changes. Dauya does this by examining the sky. His general observation of the movement of a large number of named constellations tells him when he should begin making careful observations of the dawn sky. He searches for Kibi (what we call the Pleiades) among the stars that are visible just before dawn. When Kibi is visible in the predawn glow, then it is time to begin preparing the gardens. This happens at the time of each year known on our calendars as early June. The search for Kibi in the dawn sky is a non-trivial activity. It depends on where and when Dauya locates his body on the beach at Wawela. It depends on the orientation of his body to the pre-dawn sky. His looking often involves first finding other, more prominent, stars and then using his embodied knowledge of their spatial relations to determine where to focus his attention in the search for Kibi. Dauya's incremental construction of the star patterns that may be partly occluded by cloud is a complex form of active interaction with the sky. The success of the process depends on Dauya's brain, of course, but also on his body and his eyes, and on a set of traditional cultural practices that orchestrate the interactions among a complex collection of elements. The physical properties of the night sky play a role too. For example, the stars are not evenly spaced in the sky. Their clumpy distribution makes the construction of constellations (groups of stars that can be conceived as being more related to one another than to other stars) possible.[2]

Dauya can do this job because he has been enculturated into the practices of Trobriand astronomy. The knowledge base (both procedural and declarative) that he commands is the product of millennia of incremental development. Dauya's cognitive accomplishment depends on this tradition and on the institutionalization of his role and the implied social relations of the astronomer to the other villagers. So, while it is certainly true that changes have taken place in Dauya's brain as a consequence of acquiring the skills of a Trobriand astronomer, it is not correct to say that the cognitive capacity to fix the agricultural calendar resides in Dauya's brain. That capacity is a property of the complex cognitive ecology that includes Dauya's brain, his body, his eye, the sky and the cultural practices that put all of the other parts into coordination in a productive way. Sidereal calendars are widespread in preliterate societies. The cognitive accomplishment of determining the seasons with great precision—regardless of the weather that is occurring—is orchestrated by a set of ways of seeing the sky and a way of being in the social and material world.

Setting a sidereal calendar is a relatively simple cultural practice. Let us now consider a more complex activity (perhaps one of the most complex activities) practiced in preliterate societies. Micronesian navigators routinely cross long stretches of open ocean without reference to any tools or material representations. They reliably make landfall on tiny specks of coral (Gladwin 1970; Lewis 1972; Hutchins 1983, 1995). Micronesian navigation is a form of embodied cultural practice. The navigators direct their attention to the night sky in ways similar to those used by Dauya to construct a sidereal calendar. The Micronesians see not only a calendar, but also a compass in the sky. They also master a set of cultural practices for attending to the sensations of their own bodies while sailing to judge the angle of the path of the canoe to the prevailing swell in darkness. One of their cultural practices seemed especially puzzling to Western researchers. When out of sight of land, Micronesian navigators imagine that their canoe is stationary under the dome of the sky and that the islands move past them.[3] These and many other cultural practices of seeing, imagining and remembering are orchestrated into a complex system that produces the powerful cognitive outcome of being able to guide a canoe over long distances without charts or other tangible navigation tools. Like the Trobriand sidereal calendar, this system is a cultural accomplishment, not the achievement of any individual. And like the Trobriand case, even in the moment of individual practice, the system that accomplishes the navigation feat includes the navigator, his environment for action and the learned cultural practices that establish and maintain the required relations among the elements of the distributed system.

These two examples illustrate how cultural practices build upon the human biological endowment to produce cognitive accomplishments. In fact, all high-level cognition is a product of a system that includes cultural practices, habits of attending, ways of using the body in interaction with one's material and social surrounds.

(b) A simple capacity and a family of practices

Key elements of the two palaeoastronomy systems described above are that a pattern in the world is simultaneously seen and 'seen as' something else entirely. Individual stars are seen, but groups of stars are seen as a related collection, a constellation. Seeing a constellation is an act of imagination, not a simple perception. A constellation may be seen as having a shape, a name and even a persona. This phenomenon of 'seeing as' is both very old and absolutely fundamental to cognition. While seeing stars as a constellation produces a static structure, the process of seeing the constellation is often dynamic. Trajectories are applied across some stars to create a path that leads to other stars in the constellation. The super-position of an imaginary trajectory onto visible structure is a powerful cognitive strategy for transforming spatial relations into temporal relations. We must assume that humans have an innate capacity to perform this superposition. But cultural practices organize this capacity into a surprising range of cognitive outcomes. A very early instance of this strat-egy appears in the construction of stone tools approximately 300 000 years ago (Wynn 1989). By that time, our ancestors were apparently imagining trajectories along the edge of stone tool cores. By striking the core in the order implied by the trajectory, a controlled sequence of impacts could be produced. In non-literate societies, counting tasks are often shaped by placing the objects to be counted in space such that the superposition of a simple trajectory across the objects ensures that each object is counted once and only once. The 'method of loci' is a more complex practice by which ideas are associated with spatial locations. A simple trajectory superimposed on the locations produces a sequence of ideas. In a theatre, an actor can remember his lines by associating them with elements of the architecture. A more complex version of the method relies on assigning the ideas to a remembered or imagined space rather than onto elements of the actual space occu-pied by the user of the method. While this strategy is known to us as a strategy developed by Greek orators, it also appears to structure many narratives in non-literate societies. For example, Trobriand Island myths often unfold across an imagined geographical space onto which a simple trajectory is superimposed, thus producing a sequence of events (Harwood 1976; Hutchins 1986). In contemporary settings, assembly and inspection sequences are often controlled by arraying objects in space such that a sequence can be created by superimposing a simple trajectory on the spatial array (Kirsh 1995). The widespread (but by no means universal) practice of standing in a queue involves *seeing* spatial order *as* a proxy for temporal order (Hutchins 2005). Finally, reading is a cultural practice par excel-lence, and it depends on the superimposition of trajectories of attention over spatial arrays of words or symbols, thus producing a temporal sequence of attending.

Imagining a trajectory across perceptible space is the basis for the more complex practice of superimposing an imagined trajectory on imagined space. This latter practice appears in cognitive linguistics as the 'trajectory image schema' and has been shown to underlie a wide range of conceptual structures (Lakoff 1987, p. 443; Gibbs 2006, pp. 95–96).

(c) Enacting high-level cognition in the cultural practices environmentally coupled gesture: science and technology

The practices of imagination via environmentally coupled gesture (Goodwin 1994) permit people to add motion to otherwise static external structures. A child imagines the arrival of her doll in the toy kitchen by animating the doll and moving her into the doll house. A pilot moves his hands across a control panel in an aeroplane while imagining the invisible flow of fuel in a pipe (Hutchins & Palen 1997). A biochemist imagines the dynamics of a molecule by aligning her hands with a graphical display and then moving her hands (Becvar *et al.* 2005). A brain scientist imagines a fictional deformation of a section of brain by touching a diagram and then moving her hands (Alač & Hutchins 2004). A ship navigator imagines non-existent lines of position by moving his fingers over a chart (Hutchins 2006). An architect moves his fingers on a building diagram and imagines the movements of an occupant of a building that has not yet been constructed (Murphy 2004). In each of these cases, two kinds of seeing as are combined. Each makes use of a rich, culturally elaborated static medium (doll house, control panel, molecular diagram, brain image, navigation chart and architect's rendering). The static medium is both seen as a thing in itself and seen as the thing it represents. One's own body is simultaneously seen and seen as something quite different from a body. The dynamic relation of the body to culturally meaningful objects allows the body to be seen as some dynamic aspect of the domain that is represented by the objects. The body provides animation to an otherwise static cognitive lifeworld.

Cultural practices that orchestrate this seeing as phenomenon produce a huge range of cognitive effects in modern human intelligence. When humans engage in symbolic processes, they are engaging in cultural practices for seeing as. Since symbolic representation is a culturally orchestrated activity, one wonders how such a state of affairs might have arisen. What role did cultural practices play in the cognitive lives of our distant ancestors? What role do they play in the cognitive lives of non-humans? Unfortunately, cultural practices leave only indirect evidence in the archaeological record, so reconstructions of the practices of our ancestors are necessarily speculative.[4] Things are a little clearer with contemporary non-humans because in some cases, the transformative effects of cultural practices are directly observable. For example, it is widely accepted that with extensive language training some human-enculturated chimpanzees are capable of symbol-mediated behaviour. This is a nice demonstration of the idea that the acquisition of cultural practices can transform the cognitive abilities of non-humans.

8.3. Cultural practices upgrade the mind of the chimpanzee

Thompson *et al.* (1997) caused some excitement recently by arguing that chimpanzees can do symbol-mediated reasoning (as indicated by the performance on a conceptual match-to-sample task) without prior language training. They claim to show that the chimpanzee mind can be 'upgraded' to a mind that can represent and reason about abstract relationships. According to Thompson *et al.*, this upgrade is achieved because the chimpanzees learn to treat physical tokens as symbols for abstract relationships and then can covertly manipulate (in this case, match) imagined symbols. Treating tokens as symbols is an instance of a cultural practice of seeing as discussed above. The chimpanzees appear to learn how to do this as they engage in social interactions with their keepers. This is relevant to the current argument because it shows that *a qualitative change of just the sort that is presumed to underlie the shift from pre-symbolic to symbolic reasoning could occur in a non-human primate as a consequence of a change in a cultural practice without any change in the nature of the animal's brain.* In this section, I will argue that while participating in cultural practices with humans in the experimental context does produce new cognitive outcomes for the chimpanzees, the reasoning they perform is probably not based on symbolic representations.

The key phenomena of the Thompson, Oden & Boysen study are these. It is known that infant chimpanzees who can match objects on the basis of physical appearance cannot match conceptual relations among objects even when given extensive training. However, infant chimpanzees do perceive 'similarities and differences between exemplars of identity and non-identity relationships despite their inability to judge the equivalence of such relationships in a conceptual matching task' (Thompson *et al.* 1997, p. 32). Thus, sensitivity to abstract relations exists before any training, but the animals cannot use that perceptual ability to judge relations among relations among objects.

Three activities are involved in the experimental procedure. There is a conditional discrimination task in which the chimpanzee learns to match tokens to the abstract property of same or different in the relation between pairs of objects. There is a physical match-to-sample task in which the chimpanzee faced with two alternative pairs chooses the alternative pair that is a match to a sample pair. Finally, there is the conceptual match-to-sample task in which a chimpanzee faced with two alternative pairs (neither of which is a physical match to the sample pair) chooses the alternative pair that exemplifies the within-pair relation, same or different, exemplified by the sample pair. The five animals in the study were all traditionally reared captive chimpanzees (*Pan troglodytes*). Four of the five were adults and one was a juvenile. One of the adults had received language training. The other three adults had a history of conditional discrimination training, as well as a 'history of counting in which they had been trained to associate Arabic numerals with numeric arrays' (Thompson *et al.* 1997, p. 32). The juvenile had neither language training nor training on conditional discrimination.

(a) Conditional discrimination task

The animals used in the experiment lived in a group housing complex in which they had access to indoor and outdoor areas. They 'had been taught to 'take turns' at entering an adjacent test room for experimental sessions'. We do not know the details of their day-to-day interactions with their keepers but we must presume that they know many ways to coordinate their behaviour with their human handlers. One of these is to participate in experiments. Critically, four of these animals also had the experience of *conditional discrimination training* using tokens and multiple pairs of objects.

A Lexan window extends along one side of the experiment room separating a chimpanzee indoor area from an experimenter area. There is a narrow shelf on the experimenter's side of the Lexan window. Stimuli can be presented by the experimenter on the shelf, and the chimpanzee can respond by touching images that appear on a touch-sensitive video monitor that is located in the chimpanzee side of the test room at right angles to the window. Rewards can be dispensed via a plastic tube that projects through the window. The experimenter presents a pair of objects on the shelf. The chimpanzee then chooses a token, from the two presented on the video monitor screen, to go with the pair of objects that has been presented. If the objects in the pair were physically identical, the animal was rewarded for choosing a particular token, in this case a heart shape. When presented with a pair of non-identical objects, the animal was rewarded for choosing a different token, in this case a diagonally shaped token. In this activity, Thompson *et al.* say that the tokens may be said to serve as a code for abstract relations among pairs of objects.

Thompson *et al.* then make a surprising prediction concerning chimpanzee performance on the conceptual match-to-sample task. They predict that chimpanzees who have had conditional discrimination training 'should match conceptually on their first encounter with the problem' (Thompson *et al.* 1997, p. 33). And the prediction is borne out by the experiments. The three chimpanzees who had no prior language training and no prior experience with conceptual matching tasks, but who had learned to code relations using physical tokens, did reliably succeed on the very first trials of the conceptual match-to-sample tasks. The language-trained chimpanzee that also had conditional discrimination training was successful. The juvenile that had neither conditional discrimination training nor language training, and that the authors say was not really enculturated into the experimental activities did not succeed at conceptual match-to-sample.

(b) Conceptual match-to-sample task

Blocks of physical match-to-sample trials were alternated with blocks of conceptual match-to-sample trials. In both physical and conceptual match-to-sample trials, an experimenter places a sample object pair on a shelf in the experimenter's side of the window. The choice alternatives then appear on the video screen. Two choice alternatives appear. In the physical match-to-sample task, one of the alternative pairs is a physical match to the sample pair. Choosing the physical match pair is considered to be the correct response. In the conceptual match-to-sample task, one is a pair of identical objects (but not identical to the sample pair) and the other is a pair of non-identical objects (neither identical to the elements of the sample pair). The chimpanzee indicates its choice by touching an alternative pair on the video screen. In the conceptual match-to-sample trials, choosing the identical pair alternative in response to an identical sample pair and choosing the non-identical alternative pair in response to the non-identical sample pair are considered correct responses. Since the alternative pairs never share objects with the sample pairs, correct performance requires the animal to match the relation between the objects in the sample object pair with the relation between the objects in the alternative object pair. Thus, it is conceptual relations rather than objects that must be matched. All responses, whether correct or not, were rewarded in the conceptual matching trials.

Thompson *et al.* argue that the experience of the conditional discrimination task provides the chimpanzee with the means to perform conceptual match-to-sample: the ability to represent the concepts of identity and non-identity and to code those representations with specific tokens. Thompson *et al.* say that the 'function of the token (learned in the conditional discrimination training) is to provide an animal with a concrete icon for encoding an otherwise abstract propositional representation' (Thompson *et al.* 1997, p. 41). Chimpanzees with these skills encounter the conceptual matching task. They encounter the sample pair, and they can partially deploy their skill with these objects by classifying the relation between the sample pair of objects. According to Thompson *et al.*, the chimpanzee can imagine choosing the token that would be chosen with this sample pair. But when they turn to the computer touch screen to choose a token, the tokens that were learned in the conditional discrimination task are not present. The chimpanzee encounters instead two alternative pairs of objects on the screen. The chimpanzee can then imagine choosing the token that would be chosen with each of the alternative pairs. Finally, the chimpanzee can choose the alternative pair that is associated with the symbol that matches the symbol associated with the sample pair. They describe the choice process as follows: 'The chimpanzee can now covertly match these representational icons (e.g. heart and diagonal) against the symbolic representation of heart or diagonal evoked by the sample' (Thompson *et al.* 1997, p. 42). Thompson *et al.* refer to this process as *covert symbol matching*.

The 'covert symbol matching' interpretation of the chimpanzees' behaviour assumes that the tokens play a role in the performance of the task. However, the experiment provides no direct evidence that this is the case. The covert process that is offered as an explanation is not observable. The involvement of the tokens is inferred from the lack of a competing explanation for the animals' behaviour.

(c) A reinterpretation of chimpanzee match-to-sample behaviour

I would like to attempt an alternative interpretation, one that is based on a combination of the cultural practices perspective with the theory of embodied cognition and enaction. This reinterpretation reinforces the point about the role of practices, but also provides a cautionary lesson about the attribution of the presumed abilities. Let us look more closely at the experiments.

It is important to note that the animals that participated in these experiments are enculturated. The distinction between 'human-enculturated' and 'traditionally reared captive' animals is not that the animals are enculturated in one case and not enculturated in the other. Of course, animals in both the human-enculturated and the traditionally reared captive conditions are enculturated into human practices. The difference has to do with the relation of the practices into which the animals are enculturated to the activities that humans normally engage in. If the practices are those of everyday human life, then the animal is said to be human enculturated. However, if the practices are those of the special form of human life that is animal experimentation, then the animal is enculturated, but is said to be not 'human enculturated'. If the practices are those of everyday life of the species as it lives in the wild, the animals are said to be not enculturated. The key observation here is that all animals in this study were enculturated to the settings of psychological experimentation. In a recent survey of experimental methods in research on social attention in non-human primates, Johnson & Karin-D'Arcy (2006) point out, 'Ecological validity also demands recognizing that the laboratory setting, itself, constitutes an ecology—that is, a complex set of relationships between the subject and its social and physical environment. This entails, in part, acknowledging that every trial is a social interaction.'

First, consider the conditional discrimination task. According to Thompson *et al.*, prior training on the conditional discrimination task is the key experience. As explained above, the chimpanzee will be rewarded for choosing a heart-shaped token in response to a pair of identical objects or choosing a diagonal-shaped token in response to a pair of non-identical objects. This interaction between experimenter and chimpanzee has the structure of a game. It is a repeated interaction with a reliable script-like structure. A particular abstract property of the experience of the interaction with the pair of objects must be 'noted'. The socially situated object-mediation activity is what brings the process of noticing this socially foregrounded property into coordination with the action of choosing a token to go with it. Learning to participate in a practice such that the choosing activity is made contingent on the noticing activity makes the relational property of the pair (identical or non-identical) part of what the interaction is about.

The animals' performance on the conditional discrimination task, thus, has two parts: discriminating identity pairs from non-identity pairs and learning to associate the appropriate token with each kind of pair. Thompson *et al.* focus on the tokens and give insufficient attention to the process of making the discrimination. We know that chimpanzees have the perceptual capacities needed to distinguish identical pairs from non-identical pairs. But this relation among the pair of objects is 'seen' much as a constellation is seen by humans.

Seeing a within-pair relation is an act of imagination, not a simple perception. No one knows precisely what this seeing consists of for the chimpanzees. Thompson *et al.* refer to this as the 'relational dimension within pairs' the chimpanzees were using to 'denote sameness between pairs'. They say, 'Regardless of the functional within-pair relational dimension, the resulting matching judgement of relational equivalence between relations (AA = BB; CD = EF) could not be based on physical dimensions of colour shape or size'. This is probably true, but what of the process of seeing the relational dimension within pairs? Whatever this process is, the experience of finding the relation that humans denote as 'same' will be different in character from the experience of finding the relation that humans denote as 'different'. According to enactment theory (Havelange *et al.* 2003; Thompson 2007), the process or practice of seeing the within-pair relations is an enacted representation of the relation. The pair relation is 'brought forth' or 'rendered present' by this practice. While this representation is not symbolic, it may still be sufficient to enable some subsequent cognitive processes. For example, these enacted representations may be sufficient for judging relations among enacted representations. If that is true, then there is no need for token-as-symbol mediation in order to do conceptual match-to-sample tasks.

The success of chimpanzees at physical match-to-sample is not surprising. Physical matching is a common component of the practices that captive chimpanzees engage in. Note that with the enacted representation (a practice learned in the context of conditional discrimination task) it is not necessary to use the tokens to 'code' the relation. The chimpanzee can use the newly acquired practice to enact the relation between the sample pair.[5] It can use the same practice to enact the relations among the alternative pairs. It can then match the enacted representations to do either physical or conceptual match-to-sample. The physical match-to-sample trials have two additional helpful structural elements. First, the correct pair not only matches the relation, as seen via the practice of enacting the representation of the relation, but matches the physical properties as well. Second, the correct responses—those achieved redundantly by the physical matching procedure and by the use of the new cultural practice—are rewarded. In the experiment, physical match-to-sample can scaffold conceptual match-to-sample performance because the chimpanzee can employ the same cultural practices in both types of trial blocks.

The sufficiency of the enacted representation as a mediator of subsequent relational matching is especially probable when the enacted representation developed by a given animal is used by that same animal later to do conceptual match-to-sample. The enacted representation developed by one animal would be of no use to another animal because, given the rich and personal experiential nature of the representation, it would be difficult or impossible to communicate it to another animal. Symbolic representations would not be needed to support memory of a rich experience, but they are a way to solve the problem of dealing with the restricted bandwidth of inter-animal (inter-personal) communication (Minsky & Papert 1988; Hutchins & Hazlehurst 2002).

Vygotsky (1978) said that all higher level cognitive processes appear twice. They appear first as inter-psychological processes and only later appear as intra-psychological processes. The practice of discriminating between identity pairs and difference pairs arises in the conditional discrimination activity. Because this discrimination is always socially scaffolded in the conditional discrimination activity, we cannot know whether or not it is available as an intra-psychological process. The fact that it appears to mediate conceptual match-to-sample is an indication that the practice of discriminating identity from non-identity has been internalized. This practice is a resource that can be used later in both the physical match-to-sample task (where it works redundantly with physical matching practices to guide choices under conditions of differential reinforcement) and in the conceptual match-to-sample task where it is the principal mediator of task performance.

Thompson *et al.*'s inference that the chimpanzee must entertain a 'notion' that the token is a label may be illusory. The chimpanzee may be able to participate in this cultural practice without entertaining any such notion. From a phenomenological perspective, the desire to attribute a notion like this to the chimpanzee is a symptom of an analyst's point of view on a cognitive system, and is driven by an unarticulated assumption that reasoning about abstract properties requires symbolic representations. The enaction framework provides an alternative explanation.

The process of mediation by enacted representation described here is just as covert as the symbol matching process suggested by Thompson *et al.* Why should we prefer this explanation to theirs? First, it is simpler. The enacted representation is a precondition for the symbol mediation as described by Thompson *et al.* The enacted representation is the experienced activity to which the labels can be attached. And the enacted representation is sufficient for the observed behaviour. Second, approaching this phenomenon from the embodiment perspective highlights the animal's engagement with the task world. The data are not reported in sufficient detail to support an analysis of the development of the practice. All we know is that the frequency of correct responses increases during the conditional discrimination task. However, the embodiment perspective predicts that it should be possible to track the development of the practice through changes in the patterns of the animal's allocation of attention and in patterns of eye gaze or body motion.

Thompson *et al.* consider it unproblematic to say that the tokens are codes for the relations in the world. But this is a sort of short hand that obscures important phenomena. The within-pair relation does not have an existence in the world independent of the activity of seeing it there. The token can be associated with this activity of seeing the within-pair relations. That is, the cultural practice of using symbols consists of associating the cultural practice of apprehending the physical form of a symbol with other cultural practices that enact symbolic or non-symbolic representations. The chimpanzees are doing something important and cognitively powerful here. But what they are doing still probably falls short of full blown symbol-mediated cognition.

Given the right sort of scaffolding—mixing physical match-to-sample with conceptual match-to-sample in a carefully organized ecology of cultural practices—the chimpanzees do seem to judge relations among relations. This is a cognitive accomplishment that is orchestrated by cultural practices in a particular carefully arranged social and material context. Even if it is not full blown symbolic processing, it is accomplishing the same thing that symbol processing was assumed to be accomplishing in this activity. The experimental activity elicits a set of practices that orchestrate the capacities of the chimpanzee in interaction with the material and social world in a way that produces the matching of the within-pair relations of the alternative to the within-pair relation of the sample. The cognitive outcome, performing conceptual match-to-sample, is still not a capacity that belongs to the chimpanzee. If conceptual match-to-sample exists in this case, it belongs to the experiment as a complex system of cultural practices.

The same must be true of many human cognitive abilities as well. Many cognitive outcomes produced by human activity systems are properties of our interactions with material and social settings, but we routinely mistake them for properties of ourselves (Hutchins 1995, ch. 9). Our cultural practices guide us to direct our attention to aspects of our material and social surroundings in ways that produce powerful cognitive outcomes. Many of our practices depend on our being able to imagine aspects of the material and social worlds and then being able to direct our attention to those imagined worlds. How many human performances that are assumed to be mediated by symbolic processes are actually orchestrated in other ways? No one knows. In order to answer these questions, we will need more systematic observations of naturally occurring cognitive activities.

8.4. The costs of ignoring cultural practices

Even some of the best theorizing about the origins of modern human intelligence is fundamentally disembodied. For example, Donald (1991) develops the notion of Exogram as 'a memory record outside the brain'. This seems friendly enough to the distributed cognitive view, but it has the unintended side effect of rendering cultural practices invisible. Memory is a process, and theorizing an object in the world as a memory record hides the process that is necessary to engage a material pattern *as* a memory record. This engagement process, what the phenomenologists would call seeing as or 'rendering present' should be the focus of cognitive analysis. Yet it lies outside the field of view of an approach that speaks of 'memory records outside the brain'.

According to contemporary neurophilosophy, brains have evolved to anticipate the dynamics of adaptive courses of action (Churchland *et al.* 1994). In a seminal paper, Rumelhart *et al.* (1986) said that humans are good at three things: finding patterns in experience, interacting with the world and imagining simple dynamics.

As useful as these specifications of what the human cognitive system is good at seem, they say nothing about the organization of thinking processes. What determines which patterns are found in experience? The nature of sensory apparatus and gestalt principles provide biases that make some possible patterns more salient than others. Beyond that, however, we are in the realm of cultural practices. Both the techniques of perceiving patterns and the organization of the system of patterns that are perceived are matters of cultural practice. A huge literature in cognitive anthropology and linguistics documents the variability in systems of categorization. What organizes human interactions with the world? The answer to this question is: cultural practices—twice. Cultural practices organize interactions with the world first by furnishing the world with the cultural artefacts that comprise most of the structure with which we interact. Second, cultural practices orchestrate our interactions with natural phenomena and cultural artefacts that produce cognitive outcomes. What determines how the dynamics of the world are imagined? The answer again is at least partly cultural practices. The engagement of the brain and body with the social and material world through the performance of cultural practices accomplishes several important functions at once. It is the principal, and perhaps the only, means of producing high-level cognitive processes. The enactment of embodied, non-symbolic representations, through which phenomena are seen as instances of culturally meaningful events and objects, is a cultural practice, not a passive innate process. And this is essential, because the existence of symbolic processes requires both a special set of practices for seeing symbols as symbols and a set of practices for enacting the representations with which symbols can be associated. Imagining interactions with the world takes place both online, while the interactions are taking place in the present world, and offline in memory and anticipation when the world is imagined. The offline imagination of enacted representations is a very powerful cultural practice. This includes the practice of imagining the dynamics of an imagined world of symbols.

By failing to see the role of cultural practices in the operation of the human cognitive system, we risk distorting our accounts of human intelligence. The appeal of ignoring cultural practices is understandable because if evolving cultural practices are excluded from the discussion, then the problem of explaining cognition can be reduced to two principal elements: the cognitive/functional capacities and the neuro/brain processes that produce the capacities.

I have tried to show the role of cultural practices in the orchestration of the elements of a distributed cognitive system which includes the brain, the body and the material and social worlds. I claim that higher level human cognition is produced by these distributed systems. But this complicates things significantly. When we understand cognition to be fundamentally embodied, distributed and constituted in part by cultural practices, then there are few kinds of human cognitive development that can be fully understood without reference to cultural practices.

The temptation to ask what the brain is doing is motivated by the dominant explanatory logic in cognitive science. Under that scientific cultural practice, one imagines an abstract, generally disembodied, cognitive process or ability and then tries to imagine how the brain could do it. But this is a mistake, because the answer sought depends on how the question was framed. For example, building on tacit assumptions about symbolic representations, Thompson *et al.* concluded that chimpanzees covertly match internal representations of shape tokens which serve as labels for abstract relations. But searching the chimpanzee brain for the neural structures that could support the use of internal representations of tokens as components of propositional representations of abstract relations is probably misguided. In the case of chimpanzee match-to-sample, we saw that the mediation of the task is in the cultural practices that enact non-symbolic representations. There is no need of an internal symbolic mediator. The assumption that there must be an internal symbolic mediator is driven by a set of unexamined assumptions and practices that constitute the culture of contemporary cognitive science. As long as the phenomena to be explained are constructed in the scenarios in which the brain is functionally isolated from the body and the cultural world, then our explanations will posit processes in the brain that do not belong there.

Cultural practices organize the interactions of persons with their social and material surroundings. These interactions are the locus of inter-psychological processes. Culturally constituted inter-psychological processes change through historical time. They are also targets for internalization as intra-psychological processes. Intra-psychological processes set the selective pressures for the evolution of biological cognitive systems. Therefore, rather than imagining that 'some relatively *small* neural (or neural/bodily) difference was the spark that lit a kind of intellectual forest fire' (Clark 2001), it is equally probable that a series of small changes in cultural practices gave rise to new high-level inter-psychological processes, which in turn shaped certain intra-psychological processes, and these in turn favoured certain small neural or neural/bodily differences over other neural or neural/bodily differences. Adaptation to these selective pressures could lead to population-wide changes in neural or neural/bodily systems, which would in turn make possible new cultural practices. In this account, there is no reason to favour changes in the brain over innovations in cultural practices as drivers of primate cognitive development.

I thank Colin Renfrew, Chris Frith and Lambros Malaforis, conveners of the symposium titled, 'The sapient mind: archaeology meets neuroscience' at the McDonald Institute, Cambridge, 14–16 September 2007. I am also grateful to two anonymous reviewers for identifying problems with an earlier draft. The problems that remain are my own. My research in the Trobriand Islands of Papua New Guinea (1975–1976) was supported by a predoctoral grant from the Social Science Research Council. The work on Micronesian navigation was supported by a postdoctoral fellowship from the Alfred P. Sloan Foundation.

Endnotes

1 This is also probably the best explanation of the Flynn effect—the observation that measured IQ seems to be rising in developed countries over the past century. Changing cultural practices better prepare children to produce the cognitive outcomes that are called for by traditional measures of IQ (Flynn 2007).
2 Interestingly, some of the constellations recognized in the Trobriand system roughly match constellations identified in our own tradition. Some of these similarities suggest the operation of the gestalt laws of continuity and proximity. However, cross-cultural variability in the composition of constellations shows that gestalt laws are not sufficient to account for the observed culturally specific groupings.
3 This conceptual transformation produces important cognitive economies (See Hutchins & Hinton 1984).
4 Some aspects of practices can sometimes be inferred from their material residues, as is the case for stone tools, but even with contemporary explicitly symbolic practices such as literacy, what can be inferred about cultural practices from material residues is limited.
5 Unfortunately, Thompson et al. do not say how much time elapsed between the conditional discrimination training and the conceptual match-to-sample trials.

References

Alač, M. & Hutchins, E. 2004 I see what you are saying: action as cognition in fMRI brain mapping practice. *J. Cogn. Cult.* **4**, 629–661. (doi:10.1163/1568537042484977)
Becvar, L., Hollan, J. & Hutchins, E. 2005 Hands as molecules: representational gestures as cognitive artifacts for developing theory in a scientific laboratory. *Semiotica* **156**, 89–112. (doi:10.1515/semi.2005.2005.156.89)
Churchland, P., Ramachandran, V. & Sejnowski, T. 1994 A critique of pure vision. In *Large-scale neuronal theories of the brain* (eds C. Koch & J. Davis), pp. 23–65. Cambridge, MA: MIT Press.
Clark, A. 2001 *Mindware: an introduction to the philosophy of cognitive science.* New York, NY: Oxford University Press.
Donald, M. 1991 *Origins of the modern mind: three stages in the evolution of culture and cognition.* Cambridge, MA: Harvard University Press.
Flynn, J. R. 2007 *What is intelligence?* New York, NY: Cambridge University Press.
Gibbs, R. 2006 *Embodiment and cognitive science.* New York, NY: Cambridge University Press.
Gladwin, T. 1970 *East is a big bird.* Cambridge, MA: Harvard University Press.
Goodwin, C. 1994 Professional vision. *Am. Anthropol.* **96**, 606–633. (doi:10.1525/aa.1994.96.3.02a00100)
Harwood, F. 1976 Myth, memory, and the oral tradition: cicero in the Trobriands. *Am. Anthropol.* **78**, 783–796. (doi:10.1525/aa.1976.78.4.02a00040)
Havelange, V., Lenay, C. & Stewart, J. 2003 Les representations: mémoire extern et objets techniques. *Intellectica* **35**, 115–131.

Hutchins, E. 1983 Understanding micronesian navigation. In *Mental models* (eds D. Gentner & A. Stevens), pp. 191–225. Hillsdale, NJ: Lawrence Erlbaum Associates.

Hutchins, E. 1986 Myth and experience in the Trobriand Islands. In *Cultural models in language and thought* (eds D. Holland & N Quinn), pp. 269–289. New York, NY: Cambridge University Press.

Hutchins, E. 1995 *Cognition in the wild*. Cambridge, MA: MIT Press.

Hutchins, E. 2005 Material anchors for conceptual blends. *J. Pragmatics* **37**, 1555–1577. (doi:10.1016/j.pragma.2004.06.008)

Hutchins, E. 2006 The distributed cognition perspective on human interaction. In *Roots of human sociality: culture, cognition and interaction* (eds N. Enfield & S. Levinson), pp. 375–398. Oxford, UK: Berg Publishers.

Hutchins, E. & Hazlehurst, B. 2002 Auto-organization and emergence of shared language structure. In *Simulating the evolution of language* (eds A. Cangelosi & D. Parisi), pp. 279–305. London, UK: Springer.

Hutchins, E. & Hinton, G. 1984 Why the islands move. *Perception* **13**, 629–632. (doi:10.1068/p130629)

Hutchins, E. & Palen, L. 1997 Constructing meaning from space, gesture, and speech. In *Discourse, tools, and reasoning: situated cognition and technologically supported environments* (eds L. Resnick, R. Säljö, C. Pontecorvo & B. Burge), pp. 23–40. London, UK: Springer.

Ingold, T. 2000 *The perception of the environment: essays on livelihood, dwelling and skill*. New York, NY: Routledge.

Johnson, C. & Karin-D'Arcy, M. R. 2006 Social attention in nonhuman primates: a behavioral review. *Aquat. Mamm.* **32**, 423–442. (doi: 10.1578/AM.32.4.2006.423)

Kirsh, D. 1995 The intelligent use of space. *Artif. Intell.* **73**, 31–68. (doi:10.1016/0004-3702(94)00017-U)

Lakoff, G. 1987 *Women, fire and dangerous things*. Chicago, IL: University of Chicago Press.

Lewis, D. 1972 *We the navigators*. Honolulu, HI: University of Hawaii Press.

Minsky, M. & Papert, S. 1988 *Perceptrons: expanded edition*. Cambridge, MA: MIT Press.

Murphy, K. 2004 Imagination as joint activity: the case of architectural interaction. *Mind Cult. Act.* **11**, 270–281.

Noë, A. 2004 *Action in perception*. Cambridge, MA: MIT Press.

Rumelhart, D., Smolensky, P., McClelland, J. & Hinton, G. 1986 Schemata and sequential thought processes in PDP models. In *Parallel distributed processing: explorations in the microstructure of cognition*, vol. 2 (eds J. McClelland, D. Rumelhart, & the PDP research group), pp. 7–57. Cambridge, MA: MIT Press.

Slobin, D. 1987 Thinking for speaking. *Proc. Berkeley Linguist. Soc.* **13**, 435–445.

Slobin, D. 1996 From "thought and language" to "thinking for speaking.". In *Rethinking linguistic relativity* (eds J. Gumperz & S. Levinson), pp. 70–96. Cambridge, MA: Cambridge University Press.

Strum, S. C., Forster, D. & Hutchins, E. 1997 Why machiavellian intelligence may not be machiavellian. In *Machiavellian intelligence II: extensions and evaluations* (eds A. Whiten & R. Byrne), pp. 50–85. Cambridge, UK: Cambridge University Press.

Thompson, E. 2007 *Mind in life*. Cambridge, MA: Harvard University Press.

Thompson, R., Oden, D. & Boysen, S. 1997 Language-naive chimpanzees *(Pan troglodytes)* judge relations between relations in conceptual matching-to-sample task. *J. Exp. Psychol. Anim. Behav. Process.* **23**, 31–43. (doi:10.1037/0097-7403.23.1.31)

Vygotsky, L. 1978 In *Mind in society: the development of higher psychological processes* (ed. M. Cole), Cambridge, MA: Harvard University Press.

Wynn, T. 1989 *The evolution of spatial competence*. Urbana, IL: University of Illinois Press.

9

Evolving intentions for social interaction: from entrainment to joint action

Günther Knoblich and Natalie Sebanz

This article discusses four different scenarios to specify increasingly complex mechanisms that enable increasingly flexible social interactions. The key dimension on which these mechanisms differ is the extent to which organisms are able to process other organisms' intentions and to keep them apart from their own. Drawing on findings from ecological psychology, scenario 1 focuses on entrainment and simultaneous affordance in 'intentionally blind' individuals. Scenario 2 discusses how an interface between perception and action allows observers to simulate intentional action in others. Scenario 3 is concerned with shared perceptions, arising through joint attention and the ability to distinguish between self and other. Scenario 4 illustrates how people could form intentions to act together while simultaneously distinguishing between their own and the other's part of a joint action. The final part focuses on how combining the functionality of the four mechanisms can explain different forms of social interactions. It is proposed that basic interpersonal processes are put to service by more advanced functions that support the type of intentionality required to engage in joint action, cultural learning, and communication.

Keywords: joint action; intention; evolution of social interaction; tool use; communication; social cognitive neuroscience

9.1. Introduction

Humans have an amazing ability to cooperate with one another to achieve things they cannot achieve alone. Almost every single action we perform is embedded in a long chain of events that involves hundreds, if not thousands, of interacting people. Think of the simple act of making coffee. The coffee maker had been designed by a team of engineers, assembled by a team of workers and delivered to a store through the workings of a logistics company before you went to buy it. A similar complex chain of social interactions brought coffee beans, milk and sugar, as well as mug and spoon into your kitchen. Whereas some forms of human social interaction appear to be unique in their complexity, there are also many basic forms of human social interaction, some of which seem to be shared with other animals (cf. Barresi & Moore 1996; Tomasello & Call 1997), be it bees communicating the location of food sources (e.g. Riley *et al.* 2005), a school of fish moving in synchrony (e.g. Stone *et al.* 2003), lions hunting together (Stander 1991) or apes grooming one another (de Waal 1989). How can we distinguish between different forms of social interaction, and what are the mechanisms underlying them?

We will discuss four different scenarios to specify increasingly complex mechanisms that enable increasingly flexible social interactions. The key dimension on which these mechanisms differ is the extent to which organisms are able to process other organisms' intentions and keep them apart from their own. Of particular interest to us is the ability to engage in joint action, defined as any form of social interaction where two or more individuals coordinate their actions in space and time to bring about a change in the environment (Sebanz *et al.* 2006a). We will start with a brief review of previous thinking about the role of intentions in social interaction. In four scenarios, we will then move from the interaction of 'intentionally blind' organisms to that of organisms that can simultaneously keep their own and others' intentions in mind, discussing different notions of intention used in current research as we go along. Finally, we will consider how combining the functionality of the four mechanisms can explain different forms of social interactions. Our guiding hypothesis is that basic interpersonal processes are put to service by more advanced functions that support the type of intentionality required to engage in joint action.

9.2. The role of intention in previous thinking

The distinction between controlled and automatic processing (Schneider & Shiffrin 1977) has dominated psychological research on social cognition for the last three decades (Bargh 1984; Wegner & Bargh 1997; Greenwald *et al.* 2002) and continues to be strong (e.g. Dijksterhuis & Nordgren 2006). In this distinction, consciousness and intentionality are equated (controlled = conscious, automatic = unconscious), leading to a categorical distinction between intentional and non-intentional processes within individual cognitive systems. Accordingly, there has been a strong focus on individual processing of social information, which is alive and well in current research in social cognitive neuroscience (Lieberman 2007; Ochsner 2007). Social psychologists have been keen to demonstrate how social stimuli affect social behaviours outside of awareness (e.g. Banaji & Hardin 1996; Dijksterhuis & van Knippenberg 1998; Dasgupta & Greenwald 2001; Bargh & Williams 2006). Research on shared intentions and reciprocity in social interactions has tended to be restricted to the conscious, controlled level (see Smith & Semin (2004) for an alternative approach).

Individual higher-level cognition has also been the focus of the philosophical main stream within cognitive science, addressing the representation of mental states like desires and beliefs (e.g. Fodor 1975) rather than intentions. Most relevant for the present purpose is the work on Theory of Mind, our ability to attribute mental states to others (see Flavell 2004 for a review). This work has guided research on social cognitive development towards the study of explicit knowledge about others and has influenced research on the neural underpinnings of mind reading (e.g. Vogeley *et al.* 2001; Frith & Frith 2006; Saxe 2006; Apperly 2008). One central question of Theory of Mind research has been how individuals reason about one another (e.g. Wimmer & Perner 1983; Repacholi & Gopnik 1997). Some theories suggest that knowing and reasoning about the social world are not much different from knowing and reasoning about other domains such as physics (Gopnik & Wellman 1992; Saxe 2005). Only recently, there has been increasing interest in how the development of intentional action affects social understanding and social interaction (Gergeley *et al.* 2002; Elsner & Aschersleben 2003; Sommerville & Woodward 2005; Tomasello *et al.* 2005; Falck-Ytter *et al.* 2006).

In another philosophical approach, philosophy of action (e.g. Searle 1983; Bratman 1987; Mele 1992; Pacherie 2005), intention is a central construct. Philosophers of action have explicitly addressed intentions arising in reciprocal social interaction where people work together (Bratman 1992; Tuomela 1993; Gilbert 2003). One main issue of this debate is whether individuals' intentions mainly refer to their part in a social interaction or whether they refer to what the group as a whole wants to achieve ('we-intentions', see Pettit & Schweikard 2006). Philosophical approaches to joint action have influenced empirical work on collaborative activities with a focus on language use (Clark 1996; Brennan 2005), but otherwise have rarely been subject to empirical testing. At the same time, the contribution of lower-level processes to social interaction has hardly been considered. This has led philosophers to postulate complex intentional structures that often seem to be beyond human cognitive ability in real-time social interactions—leading to a sort of 'intention inflation'.

In contrast to the approaches described above, several schools of thought, broadly pertaining to embodied cognition (cf. Clark 1997; Barsalou 2008), have stressed that higher-level cognition is grounded in basic perception and action processes or emerges out of the interaction of the organism with its environment (Gibson 1979; Smith & Thelen 1994; Port & van Gelder 1995; Van Orden et al. 2003). Only recently, it has been recognized that these assumptions may have fundamental implications for social interaction (Rizzolatti & Arbib 1998; Barsalou et al. 2003; Gallese et al. 2004; Arbib 2005; Knoblich & Sebanz 2006; Marsh et al. 2006; Sebanz et al. 2006a; Sommerville & Decety 2006; Spivey 2007). The core idea is that basic perceptual and motor processes are sufficient to enable many basic forms of social interaction and are still part of the machinery that makes more complex social interactions possible.

If one assumes that these basic forms of social interactions are not void of intentions (Shaw 2001; Jordan & Ghin 2007), it seems possible that the evolution of intentional mechanisms could be the key dimension that has enabled increasingly sophisticated social interactions (Barresi & Moore 1996; Tollefsen 2005; Tomasello et al. 2005; Pacherie & Dokic 2006). In the following we will spell out this idea based on recent empirical findings, thereby attempting to bridge the gap between embodiment accounts and purely cognitive accounts of social interaction (cf. Barresi & Moore 1996). We start with a scenario where organisms lack any functionality that would allow them to share or recognize intentions.

9.3. Scenario 1: Social couplings between 'socially blind' individuals

Scenario 1 illustrates social interactions as envisaged by ecological psychology (Marsh et al. 2006). In this scenario, the behaviour of two moving actors A1 and A2 can become coupled either because they mutually affect each other's behaviour (entrainment; figure 9.1a) or because an object (O) in the environment provides the same individual action opportunity for both actors (simultaneous affordance; figure 9.1b). To illustrate entrainment, two people sitting next to each other in rocking chairs tend to synchronize their individual rocking frequencies. To illustrate simultaneous affordance, buffets invite hungry people to pile food onto their plates, resulting in converging movement towards the buffet and a high density of people moving around it.

In order to properly interpret concepts such as affordance and entrainment, it is important to keep in mind that ecological psychology is probably the most radical version of embodiment, rejecting any notion of representation that is internal to the actor. In this

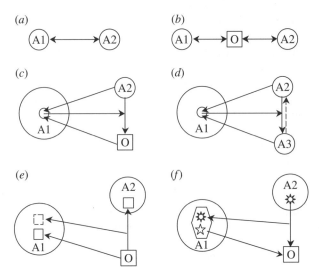

Figure 9.1. In scenario 1 (*a, b*) actor A1 and actor A2 become entrained either through (*a*) reciprocal interaction or (*b*) through objects (O) that have the same affordance for both of them. In scenario 2 (*c, d*) an actor (A1) perceives a second actor (A2) interacting with an object (O), or with another individual (A3). A1 uses his/her own action repertoire to simulate observed actions identifying (*c*) the actor-object relation or (*d*) the actor–actor relation. In scenario 3, (*e*) an actor (A1) perceives a second actor (A2) looking at an object (O). A1 simulates A2's perception of O. A1 is able to keep apart the simulated percept from his/her own perception. In scenario 4, (*f*) an actor (A1) perceives a second actor (A2) acting upon an object (O). A1 simulates A2's intention regarding (O) based on the perceived actor–object relation. A1 is able to keep apart the simulated intention from his/her own intention.

emphatically interactionist view of how actors and environment relate (Gibson 1979; Turvey 1990; Shaw 2001), it is assumed that information arises as an invariant relation between actors' dynamically changing movements and their dynamically changing perception. As a consequence, perception and movement reciprocally (co-)specify each other. In contrast to most cognitive science notions, intentions are not considered as a mental or psychological state within a person. Instead they are considered to be a property of the ecosystem (Shaw 2001) arising in the interaction between organisms and their environment. Accordingly, intentions are considered to be an aspect of the physical world rather than the mental world. A key concept that illustrates this notion is 'affordance', which refers to 'action possibilities', that a particular environment provides for an organism given the organism's particular action repertoire. A further implication of the ecological approach is that actor–object relations and actor–actor relations are considered as being governed by the same dynamical principles.

The central role of dynamical relationships in the ecological framework has led researchers in this field to primarily explore temporal synchronization during social interaction. The first studies tested the assumption that the same dynamical principles hold when a single person coordinates the movement of two limbs (Kugler & Turvey 1987; Kelso 1995) and when two people coordinate the movement of one limb each (Schmidt *et al*. 1990; Mottet *et al*. 2001). This is expected because in both cases two moving entities become entrained, regardless of whether they belong to one or two people (Spivey 2007).

It was found that participants swinging one leg each from left to right in a coordinated fashion showed a dynamical relation between their legs, which is typically observed in single participants moving two limbs in a coordinated fashion. In particular, as they sped up together, they switched from a less stable parallel mode where they both synchronously swung their legs in the same direction ($\gg$, $\ll$) to a more stable symmetric mode where they both synchronously swung their legs in opposite directions ($<$ $>$, $>$ $<$). The same pattern was observed when single participants moved two limbs synchronously. Similar results have been obtained for pendulum swinging (Schmidt et al. 1998).

Later studies showed that similar temporal entrainment effects occur even when people are not instructed to synchronize their movements (Schmidt & O'Brien 1997; Richardson et al. 2005). A suitable example for this comes from a study where two participants sat side by side in rocking chairs that had more or less similar natural rocking frequencies (Richardson et al. 2007, 2008). This was manipulated by positioning weights on a platform attached at the base of the chair (the higher the weight, the slower the natural rocking frequency). Participants either looked at each other's chairs or looked away from one another. In the condition where they looked at one another, they tended to rock together in synchrony even when the natural frequencies of the rocking chairs differed. In a sense, participants rocked against natural frequencies in order to rock in synchrony.

Whereas entrainment arises in a direct interaction between two (or more) organisms perceiving each other, the ecological framework seems to leave room for another mechanism of coordinated behaviour that is mediated by object affordances (cf. 'funktionale Toenung', von Uexkull 1920; Gibson 1977). When two organisms have a similar action repertoire and perceive the same object, they are likely to exhibit similar behaviours because the object 'affords' (invites) the same actions for them. Although object affordances have been studied extensively in research on individual perception (Jones 2003), we are not aware of any psychological research looking at the role of affordances in coordinating behaviour between different individuals.

Note that some researchers have started to explore how the presence of another person provides affordances for acting together (Richardson et al. 2007, 2008). This is different from the mechanism we consider here, because in our scenario actors do not perceive actor–object relations. We mean the simple fact that if somebody spreads bread crumbs on a Venetian Piazza he/she will probably be surrounded by dozens of pigeons that, presumably, are not looking for company. Such simultaneous affordances can probably act as a magnet for 'social encounters' which increase the likelihood of direct interactions between individuals, such as entrainment.

9.4. Scenario 2: Relating to others through action simulation

Scenario 2 depicts social interaction as envisaged by extensions of James's ideomotor theory (James 1890; extensions: Prinz 1997, Jeannerod 1999, Hommel et al. 2001) and supported by findings on mirroring (Decety & Grezes 1999, 2006; Rizzolatti & Craighero 2004). The ideomotor approach maintains that individuals perceive others' actions in the light of their own action repertoire (see figure 9.1c, d). Perceiving an actor manipulating an object activates a corresponding representation of the perceived action in the observer. Through this match, the observer simulates performing the perceived action. The same applies to perceiving how one actor directs his/her actions at another. To illustrate, when one sees someone grasping a glass of beer, one's own motor programmes of grasping a glass get partially activated leading to a simulation of the observed action. Similarly, when one sees someone patting a third person on the shoulder, the motor programmes for patting will be partially activated in the observer.

In contrast to the ecological approach, the ideomotor approach puts intentional representations into the organism and postulates an interface between perception and action that allows observers to simulate intentional action in others. Two central components of this interface can be distinguished. The first component is a representational level of common codes (Prinz 1997) capturing aspects of a situation that remain invariant across situations where one acts upon objects or individuals oneself and situations where one perceives another person acting upon objects or individuals. These invariants can lie in the effect the action has on the object (action effect, Hommel et al. 2001) or in the movement with which the action is implemented. The second component consists of simulation mechanisms tapping into the observer's motor system (Blakemore & Decety 2001; Grush 2004; Wilson & Knoblich 2005). These mechanisms can be used not only to derive action goals during or after observing actions (Bekkering et al. 2000; Rizzolatti & Craighero 2004; Hamilton & Grafton 2006), but can also be used to predict the outcomes of actions as they unfold (Knoblich & Flach 2001; Umiltá et al. 2001; Schubotz & von Cramon 2004; Wilson & Knoblich 2005). In a nutshell, the assumption is that when one observes others' actions, one can project intentional relations guiding one's own object- or person-directed actions onto observed actions.

There is rich empirical evidence to support the mechanisms outlined above (for a recent review see Keysers & Gazzola 2006), ranging from single cell studies in monkeys to behavioural and brain imaging studies in humans. The ideomotor approach received broad attention following the discovery of mirror neurons in the ventral premotor (Gallese et al. 1996) and inferior parietal (cf. Fogassi et al. 2005) cortex of macaque monkeys (hence the term 'mirroring'). These neurons fire not only when the monkey performs an object-directed action, such as grasping a grape, but also when the monkey observes another individual perform the same action. Thus, mirror neurons provide a neural substrate for the direct perception-action match described above. In humans, brain activity is observed in analogue areas not only when they observe object-directed actions but also when they observe pure bodily movements (Decety et al. 1997; Buccino et al. 2001, 2004; Grezes et al. 2003), such as dancing (Calvo-Merino et al. 2005; Cross et al. 2006). Behaviourally, the close link between perception and action manifests itself in facilitation and interference effects, where it is easier to perform the same actions one is concurrently observing (Stürmer et al. 2000; Brass et al. 2001) and more difficult to perform actions opposite to those concurrently observed (Kilner et al. 2003).

So far, our discussion has focused on how the ideomotor machinery allows an observer to identify actor–object relations. Hardly explored so far is the question of how actor–actor relationships are perceived (but see Prinz in press). Does action simulation also occur when one perceives an organism acting upon another, such as when a monkey perceives one monkey grooming another? It would be surprising if this were not the case—otherwise one would need to assume that monkeys are able to distinguish between actor and object relations and actor–actor relations and that a perception–action match occurs only for the former. Another question that arises in this context is how the action simulation mechanism deals with situations where two organisms interact. Whereas actor–object relations are asymmetrical by definition (actor acts upon object), actor–actor relations are frequently symmetric with two organisms acting upon each other. This raises the question of whose actions get simulated, those of one actor, the other or both? We will come back to this issue in our discussion of the next scenario.

9.5. Scenario 3: Sharing perceptions with others

Scenario 3 (see figure 9.1e) depicts social interaction as envisaged by developmental psychologists studying joint attention (Moore & D'Entremont 2001; Tomasello & Carpenter 2007). Research on joint attention addresses the question of how people manage to attend to the same objects or actors in the world together (Eilan *et al.* 2004). Two different components of joint attention can be distinguished. One is the ability to derive the location an observed actor is attending to, using cues such as eye gaze (Flom *et al.* 2006) or body orientation (Jellema *et al.* 2000) to simulate what the other perceives or does not perceive. A further critical component is to relate one's own and the observed actor's perceptual experiences, and in particular, to determine whether these experiences are shared (Tomasello & Carpenter 2007). Thus, the focus is on shared perceptions rather than shared intentions. However, we believe that the self-other distinction arising in the attention domain may pave the way for keeping one's own and others' intentions apart.

Empirical studies on joint attention have focused more on developmental trajectories than on specific mechanisms. One central finding is that the ability to derive the location to which an observed actor is attending (e.g. gaze following) develops earlier than the ability to relate one's own and others' perceptions, both phylogenetically (Kaminski *et al.* 2005) and ontogenetically (Tomasello *et al.* 2005). Gaze following has been shown in behavioural studies on goats (Kaminski *et al.* 2005), dogs (Hare & Tomasello 2005) and chimpanzees (Hare *et al.* 2000). Single cell studies in monkeys have revealed that neurons in the anterior part of the superior temporal sulcus may crucially contribute to the ability to follow others' gaze and to determine what they are seeing (e.g. Jellema *et al.* 2000). In contrast, the ability to relate one's own and others' perceptions seems to be present only in humans (Tomasello & Carpenter 2007) emerging from 12 months of age onwards (Moore & D'Entremont 2001; Liszkowski *et al.* 2004).

The mechanisms behind the ability to relate one's own and others' perceptions are still somewhat under-specified. Tomasello *et al.* (2005, p. 682) refer to a 'special motivation to [...] perceive together with others'. However, the functional mechanisms that need to be in place to achieve this ability are not spelt out. Clearly, in order to determine to what extent perceptions are shared with others, one needs to be able to keep the perceptions of self and other apart. This is a crucial difference to the previous two scenarios. In the present scenario, an observed actor–object or actor–actor relationship leads to a perceptual simulation of what the actor perceives (cf. current imagined schema, Barresi & Moore 1996), which is separable from one's own perception. In addition to this separation, one needs to postulate mechanisms that compare the two perceptions. Such mechanisms may drive the development of new actions to guide others' attention, e.g. pointing somewhere the other should look (Kita 2003).

It is somewhat unsatisfying that one needs to suddenly resort to a mechanism that keeps self and other apart without being able to explain how it came into existence. One possible solution is to look for aspects of the previous two (simpler) scenarios that can support a developing self–other differentiation (cf. Rochat 2003). In the ecological scenario 1, there is an asymmetry in respect to how one interacts with actors (entrainment) or with objects (affordances). Whereas objects tend to remain stationary, other actors tend to move. This could lead to particular invariances that only exist in the interaction with other actors and would thus provide dynamical cues to distinguish between actors and objects. Such an animate–inanimate distinction (e.g. Wheatley *et al.* 2007) could be a first step towards distinguishing between self and other, because it paves the way for 'conceiving' of oneself as an actor and not an object.

Within the ideomotor scenario 2, a further avenue towards distinguishing self and other arises through the asymmetry between actor–object relations and actor–actor relations. The latter are special in that one can not only simulate carrying out an observed action but that one may also develop the ability to simulate what it feels like being the recipient of the observed action. Evidence for this type of simulation comes from brain imaging studies demonstrating that the brain areas involved in feeling touch are also activated when one sees someone else being touched (e.g. Keysers *et al.* 2004). Similarly, observing someone receiving a painful stimulation leads to activation in brain areas involved in feeling pain (e.g. Singer *et al.* 2004). The two different types of simulation, in turn, could give rise to a basic distinction between actor and recipient (agents and patients), which could be a further building block the self–other distinction rests on. Simulating the two roles of the actor–actor relationship could pave the way for conceiving of oneself as actor and recipient and to attribute the complementary role to an entity like oneself, which becomes the 'other'. These and further developments could become channelled into a coherent representation of self and other and thus provide the functionality needed for scenario 3.

9.6. Scenario 4: Intending with others

Scenario 4 (see figure 9.1*f*) illustrates the intentional machinery that completes the minimal functionality that is needed to engage in joint action. Unlike the previous three scenarios, we cannot link this scheme directly to a particular theoretical approach. It shares some similarities with the Theory of Mind approach because a central component is to distinguish between one's own and others' mental states. However, we focus on the representation of intentions rather than beliefs or desires (cf. Pacherie 2005). Furthermore, our actors share the same physical environment enabling them to derive intentions from perceived actor–object and actor–actor relations. In contrast, Theory of Mind research typically uses more abstract tasks where participants are not directly involved in a social interaction.

We propose that three critical components are needed to explain how people can form intentions to act together while simultaneously distinguishing between their own and the other's parts of a joint action. First, actors need to be able to derive the intentions behind object-directed actions (Runeson & Frykholm 1983; Grezes *et al.* 2004) and actor-directed actions (Heider & Simmel 1944; Schultz *et al.* 2005). This is different from the action simulation described in scenario 2, because it implies that the other is perceived as an intentional agent (Dennett 1987).

Second, the actors in scenario 4 need to be able to keep derived intentions separate from their own intentions. This could be achieved through a similar mechanism of self–other distinction as the one needed to keep one's own and others' perceptions apart in scenario 3. Whereas these assumptions are straightforward, the third assumption is critical and miraculous at the same time. There needs to be an intentional structure that allows an actor to relate his/her own intention and the other's intention to an intention that drives the joint activity (Roepstorff & Frith 2004). In other words, two actors need to share an intention, but they also need to plan their respective parts in order to achieve the intended outcome. This creates a link to philosophical accounts of joint action as described in the introduction, but we will argue below that people only resort to this high level if the simpler functionality described in the previous scenario is inefficacious.

Even though the third assumption sounds quite intricate, there is some empirical evidence providing at least partial support for it. When distributing two parts of a task between two actors, we found that each actor represented not only his or her own part of the task but also the other's part of the task (Sebanz et al. 2003, 2005). Compared with performing the same part of the task alone, acting together led to increased demands on executive control, as actors needed to decide whether it was their turn or the other's turn to act (Sebanz et al. 2006b). Finally, using fMRI (Sebanz et al. 2007), we found evidence that acting together led to increased brain activity in areas involved in self–other distinction (ventral medi-ofrontal cortex, cf. Brass et al. 2005; Mitchell et al. 2005; Amodio & Frith 2006). Thus, these findings suggest that humans have a strong tendency to take others' tasks (and the related intentions) into account, while at the same time possessing mechanisms to keep them apart. An open question is how joint intentions are formed, and how individual intentions are related to them when two people perform a joint action.

9.7. Linking the scenarios

So far, we have described different social functions in isolation. However, we believe that their full power only reveals itself once they work in concert. Thus, we do not think of these functions as being contained in relatively isolated modules but as organized in a highly interactive hierarchical network with the simple sensor–imotor mechanisms described in scenario 1 on the bottom and the joint intentionality described in scenario 4 on top. This is similar to the assumptions made by hierarchical models of individual action control (Koechlin et al. 2003; Pacherie 2005; Jordan & Ghin 2007). Of course, this implies that the functionality of lower levels is retained when more complex functions arise and that the functionality of the latter depends on the former. At the same time we assume that simpler mechanisms tend to be controlled by more complex ones. As a consequence, the functionality of lower levels is embedded in new control structures and can be used in a more flexible way. In the following, we will illustrate how embedding the functionality of scenarios 1–3 within the intentional machinery postulated in scenario 4 can support different forms of joint action.

Embedding mechanisms for entrainment and simultaneous affordance within joint intentionality allows one to understand a variety of joint actions that require synchronous actions. Examples where joint action depends on entrainment are easily found in domains like music, art and sport. Think of two drummers creating a particular rhythm together or show dancers like Radio City Music Hall's Rockettes moving in synchrony. Some of the studies on interpersonal synchronization described earlier actually presuppose this kind of interaction between joint intentionality and entrainment. Instructing participants to synchronize their actions (e.g. Schmidt et al. 1990) implies that each of them will have the intention of performing the same action as the other participant at the same time. This is usually not discussed in the ecological accounts of social interaction because it would require assuming some form of internal representation of intention, which is square to the fundamental ecological credo (Marsh *et al.* 2006).

Combining simultaneous affordance with joint intentionality allows one to address the issue of how different actors perform non-identical actions upon the same object to achieve a joint goal. For example, the way people lift a two-handled basket depends on whether they lift it alone or together. When alone, a person would normally grasp each handle with one hand. When together, one person would normally grasp the left handle with his/her right hand and the other person would grasp the right handle with his/her left hand. Thus, embedded in joint intentionality, simultaneous affordance changes into a joint affordance, inviting two different actions from two co-actors. In other situations, joint affordance can help co-actors to determine when one needs the help of the other. This was demonstrated in a recent experiment (Richardson *et al.* 2007, 2008; experiment 4) where participants lifted planks of ascending or descending length from a conveyor belt by touching them at their ends. Of interest was at which length participants would switch from solo lifting to joint lifting and vice versa. The result of interest here was that the switch occurred as a function of the participants' combined arm span. Thus, the plank's affordance depended on the team's joint action capabilities.

What can we gain from embedding action simulation (scenario 2) in joint intentionality (scenario 4)? The main gain is that it becomes possible to keep apart action simulations that pertain to one's own actions from action simulations that pertain to others' actions (cf. Knoblich & Jordan 2002; Decety & Grezes 2006). The idea is that common codes and the ensuing simulation mechanisms can be used to plan one's own actions as well as to predict others' actions and their outcomes, in parallel and in relation to a jointly intended outcome.

Examples where such parallel simulations would come in handy abound in music, art and sports. Consider two jazz musicians improvising together. Each of them needs to predict what the other will be doing next in order to keep dissonances within the range allowed by a particular style. Likewise, aerial acrobats need not only have exquisite timing, but they also need to predict how their partner's movements unfold. Finally, the happiest moments in watching football arise when the midfielder of the team one supports passes the ball to a spot that the striker will reach before the defenders of the opposing team can catch up with him.

Using a simple tracking task that can be performed alone or together, Knoblich & Jordan (2003) investigated whether teams are able to coordinate their actions with respect to future outcomes of their joint activity as successfully as a single actor performing the whole task alone. The results showed that co-actors took their respective actions into account and learned to reciprocally adjust their actions so that their coordination was almost indistinguishable from the coordination individuals could achieve with their two hands. In this task, good coordination could only be achieved through integrating the effects of one's own and the other's actions into a prediction of the joint outcome. Thus, the findings provide behavioural evidence for the parallel simulation assumption.

A recent brain imaging study where people performed actions identical or complementary to those they had observed provides further support for this assumption (Newman-Norlund *et al.* 2007). Activation in areas pertaining to the mirror system (premotor and parietal cortex) was stronger when the participants performed complementary actions than when they performed the same action as the one observed. This suggests that the perceived action and one's own action were simulated in parallel. Finally, in behavioural studies using the same experimental paradigm, it was found that participants were as fast at responding to pictures of actions by performing complementary actions as by performing identical actions (Van Schie *et al.* submitted). This is surprising given that perceiving an action should activate the corresponding motor programme, facilitating performance of the same action. However, the finding can be explained if one assumes that a higher-level intentional structure controlled action simulation.

Finally, what can we gain from embedding joint attention mechanisms (scenario 3) within joint intentionality? Tomasello *et al.* (2005) provide a detailed discussion of this question, which will not be copied here. In a nutshell, being able to represent one's own and others' intentions allows one to determine whether one's partner has sufficient and adequate perceptual information to perform his/her part of the task. If this is not the case then one can employ attention-guiding gestures such as pointing in order to actively direct the other's attention to locations providing this perceptual information (cf. Liszkowski *et al.* 2004). For instance, when repairing a bike together, one may point out the location of the screwdriver to one's partner when one sees the other looking around while holding a screw in his/her hand.

9.8. Beyond immediate social interaction: Culture

In the previous sections we have seen how basic social interactions differ in respect to the extent to which others are perceived as acting intentionally. Embedding basic processes of social interaction and action understanding within joint intentionality has allowed us to address a broad variety of joint activities. However, so far we have ignored two main players that have probably revolutionized the ways in which organisms can interact, tool use and symbolic communication. Of course, we are not able to do justice to these players in this final section (nor will we be able to explain how coffee makers get into kitchens). Instead, we will provide two interfaces for our toolless, non-verbal organism, which may help to get it admitted into a larger society.

Let us start with tools. First traces of tool use are likely to be found in our actors in scenario 2. At this level, individuals may be able to discover that they can use one object to manipulate another. This would lead to an extension of their action repertoire that includes not only pure actor–object relations but also actor–object relations that are mediated by what we would consider a simple tool such as a stick. In fact, there is evidence that macaque monkeys are well able to learn to use tools in order to obtain desirable objects (Iriki *et al.* 1996; Imamizu *et al.* 2000) and that apes make use of tools in the wild (Breuer *et al.* 2005). In accordance with the action simulation account, this extension of one's own action repertoire would probably lead to a corresponding understanding of other actors performing similar tool-mediated actions.

However, scenario 2 does not entail any means for learning tool use through imitation. We suggest that the full machinery for joint intentionality described in scenario 4 needs to be in place before the know-how about tools can be passed on between individuals or generations. In other words, whereas each actor in scenario 2 needs to discover a tool anew, actors in scenario 4 have the 'intentional equipment' to find ways of sharing tool-related discoveries. The via regia to achieve this is, of course, imitation. Thus we concur with Tomasello *et al.*'s (2005) view that imitation of tool use became only possible once joint intentionality was in place and that it went hand in hand with tool-making abilities that created the first artefacts.

Once these two abilities were in place, cultural evolution could thrive. However, it is very important to remember that even the low-level mechanisms described in scenario 1 gain new relevance once cultural transmission starts. The creation of enduring artefacts opened up a whole new world of affordances and ways of interacting with the world in a direct manner. The resulting fact that artefacts embody socially transmitted knowledge about ways of interacting with objects is hardly ever acknowledged in the research on object perception.

Turning to symbolic communication, the potential interface with our non-verbal system is straightforward. We concur with Clark (1996) that language can be regarded as an extremely powerful coordination device for joint action, cementing the self–other distinction, defining different potential roles for actors and extending the temporal horizon of joint activities. Accordingly, joint intentionality would be a prerequisite for symbolic communication. Discussing the many different accounts of language evolution is way beyond the scope of this article. However, we do believe that even symbolic communication remains grounded to some extent in the basic interpersonal functions described in our scenarios.

A study by Shockley *et al.* (2003) clearly demonstrates how the entrainment mechanism of scenario 1 reappears in conversation. They showed that people talking to each other synchronized their postural sways (micromovements of the body that are needed to maintain an upright body position) even when they could not see one another. This demonstrates that the rhythm of language (prosody) remains coupled to the rhythm of the body.

Studies on mimicry during conversation (Chartrand & Bargh 1999) suggest a link to the action simulation mechanisms of scenario 2. People talking to each other have a tendency to mimic each other's mannerisms such as wiggling one's foot or touching one's face. This can be interpreted as an overt behaviour reflecting a spillover of non-inhibited action tendencies arising through simulation that takes on the function of keeping up the bond between speakers (Lakin & Chartrand 2003).

Finally, the work of Richardson & Dale (2005) provides evidence for the contribution of the joint attention mechanisms of scenario 3 to conversation. They recorded eye movements of speakers talking about the happenings between different characters from a famous TV series while the speakers were looking at their pictures. The eye movements of listeners who could remember well what the speaker had said coincided more closely in space and time with the speaker's eye movements than those of listeners who remembered less. This shows that joint attention can play a crucial role in successful conversation. A similar conclusion can be drawn from Clark & Krych's (2004) finding that people who were attending to the same workspace while performing a joint action communicated less and more efficiently than people who did not share the same workspace. This suggests that joint attention can reduce the need for language use in joint action.

We would like to conclude with an observation that seems almost paradoxical in the context of the present discussion. Social psychologists and sociologists increasingly use dynamical principles very similar to those described in scenario 1 for modelling large-scale interactions that occur on a cultural level. Examples are the spreading of certain opinions and attitudes (Vallacher *et al.* 2002) or the development of cooperation strategies in a society (Axelrod *et al.* 2002). Thus, once one proceeds from an individual level of analysis to a societal level of analysis, things seem to start all over again at the most basic, socially blind level.

References

Amodio, D. M. & Frith, C. D. 2006 Meeting of minds: the medial frontal cortex and social cognition. *Nat. Rev. Neurosci.* **7**, 268–277. (doi:10.1038/nrn1884)

Apperly, I. A. 2008 Beyond simulation–theory and theory–theory: why social cognitive neuroscience should use its own concepts to study "Theory of Mind". *Cognition* **107**, 266–283. (doi:10.1016/j. cognition.2007.07.019)

Arbib, M. A. 2005 From monkey-like action recognition to human language: an evolutionary framework for neuro-linguistics. *Behav. Brain Sci.* **28**, 105–124. (doi:10.1017/ S0140525X05000038)

Axelrod, R., Riolo, R. L. & Cohen, M. D. 2002 Beyond geography: cooperation with persistent links in the absence of clustered neighborhoods. *Pers. Soc. Psychol. Rev.* **6**, 341–346. (doi:10.1207/ S15327957PSPR0604_08)

Banaji, M. R. & Hardin, C. 1996 Automatic stereotyping. *Psychol. Sci.* **7**, 136–141. (doi:10.1111/ j.1467-9280.1996. tb00346.x)

Bargh, J. A. 1984 Automatic and conscious processing of social information. In *Handbook of social cognition* (eds R. S. Wyer & T K. Srull), pp. 1–44. Hillsdale, NJ: Lawrence Erlbaum Associates.

Bargh, J. A. & Williams, E. L. 2006 The automaticity of social life. *Curr. Dir. Psychol. Sci.* **15**, 1–4. (doi:10.1111/j.0963-7214.2006.00395.x)

Barresi, J. & Moore, C. 1996 Intentional relations and social understanding. *Behav. Brain Sci.* **19**, 107–154.

Barsalou, L. W. 2008 Grounded cognition. *Annu. Rev. Psychol.* **59**, 617–645. (doi:10.1146/annurev. psych.59. 103006.093639)

Barsalou, L. W., Niedenthal, P. M., Barbey, A. & Ruppert, J. 2003 Social embodiment. In *The psychology of learning and motivation*, vol. 43 (ed. B. Ross), pp. 43–92. San Diego, CA: Academic Press.

Bekkering, H., Wohlschläger, A. & Gattis, M. 2000 Imitation of gestures in children is goal-directed. *Q. J. Exp. Psychol. A* **53**, 153–164. (doi:10.1080/027249800390718)

Blakemore, S.-J. & Decety, J. 2001 From the perception of action to the understanding of intention. *Nat. Rev. Neurosci.* **2**, 561–567.

Brass, M., Bekkering, H. & Prinz, W. 2001 Movement observation affects movement execution in a simple response task. *Acta Psychol. (Amst.)* **106**, 3–22. (doi:10.1016/S0001-6918(00)00024-X)

Brass, M., Derfuss, J. & von Cramon, D. Y. 2005 The inhibition of imitative and overlearned responses: a functional double dissociation. *Neuropsychologia* **43**, 89–98. (doi:10.1016/j. neuropsychologia.2004.06.018)

Bratman, M. E. 1987 *Intention, plans, and practical reason*. Cambridge, UK: Cambridge University Press.

Bratman, M. E. 1992 Shared cooperative activity. *Philos. Rev.* **101**, 327–341. (doi:10.2307/2185537)

Brennan, S. E. 2005 How conversation is shaped by visual and spoken evidence. In *Approaches to studying world-situated language use: bridging the language-as-product and language—action traditions* (eds J. Trueswell & M. Tanenhaus), pp. 95-129. Cambridge, MA: MIT Press.

Breuer, T., Ndoundou-Hockemba, M. & Fishlock, V. 2005 First observation of tool use in wild gorillas. *PLoS Biol.* **3**, 2041–2043. (doi:10.1371/journal.pbio.0030380)

Buccino, G., Binkofski, F., Fink, G. R., Fadiga, L., Fogassi, L. & Gallese, V. 2001 Action observation activates premotor and parietal areas in a somatotopic manner: an fMRI study. *Eur. J. Neurosci.* **13**, 400–404. (doi:10.1046/j.1460-9568.2001.01385.x)

Buccino, G., Vogt, S., Ritzl, A., Fink, G. R., Zilles, K., Freund, H.-J. & Rizzolatti, G. 2004 Neural circuits underlying imitation learning of hand actions: an event-related fMRI study. *Neuron* **42**, 323–334. (doi:10.1016/S0896-6273(04)00181-3)

Calvo-Merino, B., Glaser, D. E., Grezes, J., Passingham, R. E. & Haggard, P. 2005 Action observation and acquired motor skills: an fMRI study with expert dancers. *Cereb. Cortex* **15**, 1243–1249. (doi:10.1093/cercor/bhi007)

Chartrand, T & Bargh, J. 1999 The chameleon effect: the perception-behavior link and social interaction. *J. Pers. Soc. Psychol.* **76**, 893–910. (doi:10.1037/0022-3514.76.6.893)

Clark, H. H. 1996 *Using language*. Cambridge, UK: Cambridge University Press.

Clark, A. 1997 *Being there: putting brain body and world together again*. Cambridge, MA: MIT Press.

Clark, H. H. & Krych, M. A. 2004 Speaking while monitoring addressees for understanding. *J. Mem. Lang.* **50**, 62–81. (doi:10.1016/j.jml.2003.08.004)

Cross, E. S., Hamilton, A. F. & Grafton, S. T 2006 Building a motor simulation de novo: observation of dance by dancers. *Neuroimage* **31**, 1257–1267. (doi:10.1016/j.neu-roimage.2006.01.033)

Dasgupta, A. G. & Greenwald, A. G. 2001 Exposure to admired group members reduces automatic intergroup bias. *J. Pers. Soc. Psychol.* **81**, 800–814. (doi:10.1037/0022-3514.81.5.800)

Decety, J. & Grezes, J. 1999 Neural mechanisms subserving the perception of human actions. *Trends Cogn. Sci.* **3**, 172–178. (doi:10.1016/S1364-6613(99)01312-1)

Decety, J. & Grezes, J. 2006 The power of simulation: imagining one's own and other's behavior. *Brain Res.* **1079**, 4–14. (doi:10.1016/j.brainres.2005.12.115)

Decety, J., Grezes, J., Costes, N., Perani, D., Jeannerod, M., Procyk, E., Grassi, F. & Fazio, F. 1997 Brain activity during observation of actions. Influence of action content and subject's strategy. *Brain* **120**, 1763–1777. (doi:10.1093/brain/120.10.1763)

Dennett, D. C. 1987 *The intentional stance.* Cambridge, MA: MIT Press,

de Waal, F. 1989 *Peacemaking among primates.* Cambridge, MA: Harvard University Press.

Dijksterhuis, A. & Nordgren, L. F. 2006 A theory of unconscious thought. *Perspect. Psychol. Sci.* **1**, 95–109. (doi:10.1111/j.1745-6916.2006.00007.x)

Dijksterhuis, A. & van Knippenberg, A. 1998 The relation between perception and behavior or how to win a game of trivial pursuit. *J. Pers. Soc. Psychol.* **74**, 865–877. (doi:10.1037/0022-3514.74.4.865)

Eilan, N., Hoerl, C., McCormack, T & Roessler, J. 2004 *Joint attention: communication and other minds.* Oxford, UK: Oxford University Press.

Elsner, B. & Aschersleben, G. 2003 Do I get what you get? Learning about the effects of self-performed and observed actions in infancy. *Conscious. Cogn.* **12**, 732–751. (doi: 10.1016/S1053-8100(03)00073-4)

Falck-Ytter, T., Gredeback, G. & von Hofsten, C. 2006 Infants predict other people's action goals. *Nat. Neurosci.* **9**, 878–879. (doi:10.1038/nn1729)

Flavell, J. 2004 Theory-of-Mind development: retrospect and prospect. *Merrill-Palmer Q.* **50**, 274–290. (doi:10.1353/mpq.2004.0018)

Flom, R., Lee, K. & Muir, D. (eds) 2006 *Gaze-following: its development and significance.* Hillsdale, NJ: Lawrence Erlbaum Associates.

Fodor, J. A. 1975 *The language of thought.* New York, NY: Crowell.

Fogassi, L., Ferrari, P. F., Gesierich, B., Rozzi, S., Chersi, F. & Rizzolatti, G. 2005 Parietal lobe: from action organization to intention understanding. *Science* **308**, 662–667. (doi:10.1126/science.1106138)

Frith, C. D. & Frith, U. 2006 The neural basis of mentalizing. *Neuron* **50**, 531–534. (doi:10.1016/j.neuron.2006.05.001)

Gallese, V., Fadiga, L., Fogassi, L. & Rizzolatti, G. 1996 Action recognition in the premotor cortex. *Brain* **119**, 593–609. (doi:10.1093/brain/1 19.2.593)

Gallese, V., Keysers, C. & Rizzolatti, G. 2004 A unifying view of the basis of social cognition. *Trends Cogn. Sci.* **8**, 396–403. (doi:10.1016/j.tics.2004.07.002)

Gergeley, G., Bekkering, H. & Kiraly, I. 2002 Developmental psychology: rational imitation in preverbal infants. *Nature* **415**, 755.

Gibson, J. J. 1977 The theory of affordances. In *Perceiving, acting, and knowing: toward an ecological psychology* (eds R. Shaw & J. Bransford), pp. 67–82. Hillsdale, NJ: Lawrence Erlbaum Associates.

Gibson, J. J. 1979 *The ecological approach to visual perception.* Boston, MA: Houghton Mifflin.

Gilbert, M. 2003 The structure of the social atom: joint commitment as the foundation of human social behavior. In *Socializing metaphysics* (ed. F. Schmitt), pp. 39–64. Lanham, MD: Rowman & Littlefield.

Gopnik, A. & Wellman, H. 1992 Why the child's theory of mind really is a theory. *Mind Lang.* **7**, 145–171.

Greenwald, A. G., Banaji, M. R., Rudman, L. A., Farnham, S. D., Nosek, B. A. & Mellott, D. S. 2002 A unified theory of implicit attitudes, stereotypes, self-esteem, and self-concept. *Psychol. Rev.* **109**, 3–25. (doi:10.1037/0033-295X.109.1.3)

Grezes, J., Armony, J. L., Rowe, J. & Passingham, R. E. 2003 Activations related to "mirror" and "canonical" neurones in the human brain: a fMRI study. *Neuroimage* **18**, 928–937. (doi:10.1016/S1053-8119(03)00042-9)

Grezes, J. C., Frith, C. D. & Passingham, D. E. 2004 Inferring false beliefs from the actions of oneself and others: an fMRI study. *Neuroimage* **21**, 744–750. (doi:10.1016/S1053-8119(03)00665-7)

Grush, R. 2004 The emulation theory of representation: motor control, imagery, and perception. *Behav. Brain Sci.* **27**, 377–442. (doi:10.1017/S0140525X04000093)

Hamilton, A. F. & Grafton, S. T 2006 Goal representation in human anterior intraparietal sulcus. *J. Neurosci.* **26**, 1133–1137. (doi:10.1523/JNEUROSCI.4551-05.2006)

Hare, B. & Tomasello, M. 2005 Human-like social skills in dogs? *Trends Cogn. Sci.* **9**, 439–444. (doi:10.1016/j.tics. 2005.08.010)

Hare, B., Call, J., Agnetta, B. & Tomasello, M. 2000 Chimpanzees know what conspecifics do and do not see. *Anim. Behav.* **59**, 771–786. (doi:10.1006/anbe.1999.1377)

Heider, F. & Simmel, M. 1944 An experimental study of apparent behavior. *Am. J. Psychol.* **57**, 243–249. (doi:10.2307/1416950)

Hommel, B., Müsseler, J., Aschersleben, G. & Prinz, W. 2001 The theory of event coding (TEC): a framework for perception and action. *Behav. Brain Sci.* **24**, 849–937.

Imamizu, H., Miyauchi, S., Tamada, T., Sasaki, Y., Takino, R., Pütz, B., Yoshioka, T. & Kawato, M. 2000 Human cerebellar activity reflecting an acquired internal model of a new tool. *Nature* **403**, 192–195. (doi:10.1038/350 03194)

Iriki, A., Tanaka, M. & Iwamura, Y. 1996 Coding of modified body schema during tool use by macaque postcentral neurones. *Neuroreport* **7**, 2325–2330.

James, W. 1890 *The principles of psychology*. New York, NY: Holt.

Jeannerod, M. 1999 The 25th Bartlett lecture. To act or not to act: perspectives on the representation of actions. *Q. J. Exp. Psychol. A* **52**, 1–29. (doi:10.1080/027249899391205)

Jellema, T., Baker, C. I., Wicker, B. & Perrett, D. I. 2000 Neural representation for the perception of the intentionality of actions. *Brain Cogn.* **44**, 280–302. (doi:10.1006/brcg.2000.1231)

Jones, K. S. 2003 What is an affordance? *Ecol. Psychol.* **15**, 107–114. (doi:10.1207/S15326969 ECO1502_1)

Jordan, J. S. & Ghin, M. 2007 The role of control in a science of consciousness: causality, regulation and self-sustainment. *J. Conscious. Stud.* **14**, 177–197.

Kaminski, J., Riedel, J., Call, J. & Tomasello, M. 2005 Domestic goats, *Capra hircus*, follow gaze direction and use social cues in an object choice task. *Anim. Behav.* **69**, 11–18. (doi:10.1016/j.anbehav.2004.05.008)

Kelso, J. A. S. 1995 *Dynamic patterns*. Cambridge, MA: MIT Press.

Keysers, C. & Gazzola, V. 2006 Towards a unifying neural theory of social cognition. *Prog. Brain Res.* **156**, 383–406.

Keysers, C., Wicker, B., Gazzola, V., Anton, J., Fogassi, L. & Gallese, V. 2004 A touching sight: SII/PV activation during the observation and experience of touch. *Neuron* **42**, 335–346. (doi:10.1016/S0896-6273(04)00156-4)

Kilner, J. M., Paulignan, Y & Blakemore, S. J. 2003 An interference effect of observed biological movement on action. *Curr. Biol.* **13**, 522–525. (doi:10.1016/S0960-9822(03)00165-9)

Kita, S. (ed.) 2003 *Pointing: where language, culture, and cognition meet*. Mahwah, NJ: Lawrence Erlbaum Associates.

Knoblich, G. & Flach, R. 2001 Predicting action effects: interactions between perception and action. *Psychol. Sci.* **12**, 467–472. (doi:10.1111/1467-9280.00387)

Knoblich, G. & Jordan, S. 2002 The mirror system and joint action. In *Mirror neurons and the evolution of brain and language* (eds M. I. Stamenov & V. Gallese), pp. 115–124. Amsterdam, The Netherlands: John Benjamins.

Knoblich, G. & Jordan, S. 2003 Action coordination in individuals and groups: learning anticipatory control. *J. Exp. Psychol. Learn.* **29**, 1006-1016. (doi:10.1037/0278-7393.29.5.1006)

Knoblich, G. & Sebanz, N. 2006 The social nature of perception and action. *Curr. Dir. Psychol. Sci.* **15**, 99–104. (doi:10.1111/j.0963-7214.2006.00415.x)

Koechlin, E., Ody, C. & Kouneiher, F. 2003 The architecture of cognitive control in the human prefrontal cortex. *Science* **302**, 1181–1185. (doi:10.1126/science.1088545)

Kugler, P. N. & Turvey, M. T.1987 *Information, natural law, and the self-assembly of rhythmic movement.* Hillsdale, NJ: Lawrence Erlbaum Associates.

Lakin, J. & Chartrand, T. L. 2003 Using nonconscious behavioral mimicry to create affiliation and rapport. *Psychol. Sci.* **14**, 334–339. (doi:10.1111/1467-9280.14481)

Lieberman, M. D. 2007 Social cognitive neuroscience: a review of core processes. *Annu. Rev. Psychol.* **58**, 259–289. (doi:10.1146/annurev.psych.58.110405.085654)

Liszkowski, U., Carpenter, M., Henning, A., Striano, T & Tomasello, M. 2004 Twelve-month-olds point to share attention and interest. *Dev. Sci.* **7**, 297–307. (doi:10.1111/j.1467-7687. 2004.00349.x)

Marsh, K. L., Richardson, M. J., Baron, R. M. & Schmidt, R. C. 2006 Contrasting approaches to perceiving and acting with others. *Ecol. Psychol.* **18**, 1–38. (doi:10.1207/s15326969eco 1801_1)

Mele, A. R. 1992 *Springs of action.* Oxford, UK: Oxford University Press.

Mitchell, J. P., Banaji, M. R. & Macrae, C. N. 2005 The link between social cognition and self-referential thought in the medial prefrontal cortex. *J. Cogn. Neurosci.* **17**, 1306–1315. (doi:10.1162/0898929055002418)

Moore, C. & D'Entremont, B. 2001 Developmental changes in pointing as a function of attentional focus. *J. Cogn. Dev.* **2**, 109–129. (doi:10.1207/S15327647JCD0202_1)

Mottet, D., Guiard, Y., Ferrand, T. & Bootsma, R. J. 2001 Two-handed performance of rhythmical Fitts' task by individuals and dyads. *J. Exp. Psychol. Hum.* **27**, 1275–1286.

Newman-Norlund, R. D., van Schie, H. T, van Zuijlen, A. M. J. & Bekkering, H. 2007 The mirror neuron system is more active during complementary compared with imitative action. *Nat. Neurosci.* **10**, 817–818. (doi:10. 1038/nn1911)

Ochsner, K. N. 2007 Social cognitive neuroscience: historical development, core principles, and future promise. In *Social psychology: a handbook of basic principles* (eds A. Kruglanksi & E. T. Higgins), pp. 39–66. New York, NY: Guilford Press.

Pacherie, E. 2005 Towards a dynamic theory of intentions. In *Does consciousness cause behavior? An investigation of the nature of volition* (eds W. P. Banks & S. Gallagher), pp. 145–167. Cambridge, MA: MIT Press.

Pacherie, E. & Dokic, J. 2006 From mirror neurons to joint actions. *Cogn. Syst. Res.* **7**, 101–112. (doi:10.1016/j. cogsys.2005.11.012)

Pettit, P. & Schweikard, D. 2006 Joint actions and group agents. *Philos. Soc. Sci.* **36**, 18–39. (doi:10.1177/00483 93105284169)

Port, R. F. & van Gelder, T. 1995 *Mind as motion.* Cambridge, MA: MIT Press.

Prinz, W. 1997 Perception and action planning. *Eur. J. Cogn. Psychol.* **9**, 129–154. (doi:10.1080/ 713752551)

Prinz, W. In press. Mirrors for embodied communication. In *Embodied communication* (eds I. Wachsmuth, M. Lenzen & G. Knoblich). Oxford, UK: Oxford University Press.

Repacholi, B. M. & Gopnik, A. 1997 Early reasoning about desires: evidence from 14- and 18-month olds. *Dev. Psychol.* **33**, 12–21. (doi:10.1037/0012-1649.33.1.12)

Richardson, D. C. & Dale, R. 2005 Looking to understand: the coupling between speakers' and listeners' eye movements and its relationship to discourse comprehension. *Cogn. Sci.* **29**, 1045–1060.

Richardson, M. J., Marsh, K. L. & Schmidt, R. C. 2005 Effects of visual and verbal couplings on unintentional interpersonal coordination. *J. Exp. Psychol. Hum.* **31**, 62–79.

Richardson, M. J., Marsh, K. L. & Baron, R. M. 2007 Judging and actualizing intrapersonal and interpersonal affordances. *J. Exp. Psychol. Hum.* **33**, 845–859.

Richardson, M. J., Marsh, K. L., Isenhower, R., Goodman, J. & Schmidt, R. C. 2008 Rocking together: dynamics of intentional and unintentional interpersonal coordination. *Hum. Mov. Sci.* **26**, 867–891. (doi:10.1016/j.humov.2007. 07.002)

Riley, J. R., Greggers, U., Smith, A. D., Reynolds, D. R. & Menzel, R. 2005 The flight paths of honeybees recruited by the waggle dance. *Nature* **435**, 205–207. (doi:10.1038/nature03526)

Rizzolatti, G. & Arbib, M. A. 1998 Language within our grasp. *Trends Neurosci.* **21**, 188–194. (doi:10.1016/S0166-2236(98)01260-0)

Rizzolatti, G. & Craighero, L. 2004 The mirror-neuron system. *Annu. Rev. Neurosci.* **27**, 169–192. (doi:10.1146/annurev.neuro.27.070203.144230)

Rochat, P. 2003 Five levels of self-awareness as they unfold early in life. *Conscious. Cogn.* **12**, 717–731. (doi:10.1016/ S1053-8100(03)00081-3)

Roepstorff, A. & Frith, C. 2004 What's at the top in the top-down control of action? Script-sharing and 'top–top' control of action in cognitive experiments. *Psychol. Res. Psych. Fors.* **68**, 189–198.

Runeson, S. & Frykholm, G. 1983 Kinematic specification of dynamics as an informational basis for person-and-action perception: expectation, gender recognition, and deceptive intention. *J. Exp. Psychol. Gen.* **112**, 585–615. (doi:10.1037/0096-3445.112.4.585)

Saxe, R. 2005 Against simulation: the argument from error. *Trends Cogn. Sci.* **9**, 174–179. (doi:10.1016/j.tics.2005.01.012)

Saxe, R. 2006 How and why to study theory of mind with fMRI. *Brain Res.* **1079**, 57–65. (doi:10.1016/j.brainres.2006.01.001)

Schmidt, R. C. & O'Brien, B. 1997 Evaluating the dynamics of unintended interpersonal coordination. *Ecol. Psychol.* **9**, 189–206. (doi:10.1207/s15326969eco0903_2)

Schmidt, R. C., Carello, C. & Turvey, M. T 1990 Phase transitions and critical fluctuations in the visual coordination of rhythmic movements between people. *J. Exp. Psychol. Hum.* **16**, 227–247.

Schmidt, R. C., Bienvenu, M., Fitzpatrick, P. A. & Amazeen, P. G. 1998 A comparison of intra- and interpersonal interlimb coordination: coordination breakdowns and coupling strength. *J. Exp. Psychol. Hum.* **24**, 884–900.

Schneider, W. & Shiffrin, R. M. 1977 Controlled and automatic human information processing: 1. Detection, search, and attention. *Psychol. Rev.* **84**, 1–66. (doi:10.1037/0033-295X.84.1.1)

Schubotz, R. I. & von Cramon, D. Y 2004 Sequences of abstract nonbiological stimuli share ventral premotor cortex with action observation and imagery. *J. Neurosci.* **24**, 5467–5474. (doi:10.1523/JNEUROSCI.1169-04.2004)

Schultz, J., Friston, K. J., O'Doherty, J., Wolpert, D. M. & Frith, C. D. 2005 Activation in posterior superior temporal sulcus parallels parameter inducing the percept of animacy. *Neuron* **45**, 625–635. (doi:10.1016/j.neuron.2004.12.052)

Searle, J. 1983 *Intentionality*. Cambridge, UK: Cambridge University Press.

Sebanz, N., Knoblich, G. & Prinz, W. 2003 Representing others' actions: just like one's own? *Cognition* **88**, B11–B21. (doi:10.1016/S0010-0277(03)00043-X)

Sebanz, N., Knoblich, G. & Prinz, W. 2005 How two share a task. *J. Exp. Psychol. Hum.* **31**, 1234–1246.

Sebanz, N., Bekkering, H. & Knoblich, G. 2006a Joint action: bodies and minds moving together. *Trends Cogn. Sci.* **10**, 70–76. (doi:10.1016/j.tics.2005.12.009)

Sebanz, N., Knoblich, G., Prinz, W. & Wascher, E. 2006b Twin peaks: an ERP study of action planning and control in co-acting individuals. *J. Cogn. Neurosci.* **18**, 859–870. (doi:10.1162/ jocn.2006.18.5.859)

Sebanz, N., Rebbechi, D., Knoblich, G., Prinz, W. & Frith, C. 2007 Is it really my turn? An event-related fMRI study of task sharing. *Soc. Neurosci.* **2**, 81–95. (doi:10.1080/17470910701 237989)

Shaw, R. E. 2001 Processes, acts, and experiences: three stances on the problem of intentionality. *Ecol. Psychol.* **13**, 275–314. (doi:10.1207/S15326969ECO1304_02)

Shockley, K., Santana, M. V. & Fowler, C. A. 2003 Mutual interpersonal postural constraints are involved in cooperative conversation. *J. Exp. Psychol. Hum.* **29**, 326–332.

Singer, T., Seymour, B., O'Doherty, J., Kaube, H., Dolan, R. J. & Frith, C. D. 2004 Empathy for pain involves the affective but not sensory components of pain. *Science* **303**, 1157–1162. (doi:10.1126/science.1093535)

Smith, E. R. & Semin, G. R. 2004 Socially situated cognition: cognition in its social context. *Adv. Exp. Soc. Psychol.* **36**, 53–117.

Smith, L. B. & Thelen, E. (eds) 1994 *A dynamic systems approach to development*. Cambridge, MA: MIT Press.

Sommerville, J. A. & Decety, J. 2006 Weaving the fabric of social interaction: articulating developmental psychology and cognitive neuroscience in the domain of motor cognition. *Psychon. Bull. Rev.* **13**, 179–200.

Sommerville, J. A. & Woodward, A. L. 2005 Pulling out the intentional structure of human action: the relation between action production and processing in infancy. *Cognition* **95**, 1–30. (doi:10.1016/j.cognition.2003.12.004)

Spivey, J. M. 2007 *The continuity of mind*. New York, NY: Oxford University Press.

Stander, P. E. 1991 Cooperative hunting in lions: the role of the individual. *Behav. Ecol. Sociobiol.* **29**, 445–454.

Stone, L., He, D., Becker, K. & Fishelson, L. 2003 Unusual synchronization of red sea fish energy expenditures. *Ecol. Lett.* **6**, 83–86. (doi:10.1046/j.1461-0248.2003.00401.x)

Stürmer, B., Aschersleben, G. & Prinz, W 2000 Correspondence effects with manual gestures and postures: a study of imitation. *J. Exp. Psychol. Hum.* **26**, 1746–1759.

Tollefsen, D. 2005 Let's pretend! Children and joint action. *Philos. Soc. Sci.* **35**, 75–97. (doi:10.1177/0048393104 271925)

Tomasello, M. & Call, J. 1997 *Primate cognition*. New York, NY: Oxford University Press.

Tomasello, M. & Carpenter, M. 2007 Shared intentionality. *Dev. Sci.* **10**, 121–125. (doi:10.1111/j.1467-7687.2007.00573.x)

Tomasello, M., Carpenter, M., Call, J., Behne, T & Moll, H. 2005 Understanding and sharing intentions: the origins of cultural cognition. *Behav. Brain Sci.* **28**, 675–735. (doi:10.1017/S0140525X05000129)

Tuomela, R. 1993 *The importance of us: a philosophical study of basic social notions*. Palo Alto, CA: Stanford University Press.

Turvey, M. T 1990 Coordination. *Am. Psychol.* **45**, 938–953. (doi:10.1037/0003-066X.45.8.938)

Umiltá, M. A., Kohler, E., Gallese, V., Fogassi, L., Fadiga, L., Keysers, C. & Rizzolatti, G. 2001 I know what you are doing: a neurophysiological study. *Neuron*. **31**, 155–165. (doi:10.1016/S0896-6273(01)00337-3)

Vallacher, R. R., Read, S. J. & Nowak, A. 2002 The dynamical perspective in personality and social psychology. *Pers. Soc. Psychol. Rev.* **6**, 264–273. (doi:10.1207/S15327957PSPR 0604_01)

Van Orden, G. C., Holden, J. G. & Turvey, M. T 2003 Self-organization of cognitive performance. *J. Exp. Psychol. Gen.* **132**, 331–350. (doi:10.1037/0096-3445.132.3.331)

Van Schie, H., Van Waterschoot, B. & Bekkering, H. Submitted. Understanding action beyond imitation: reversed compatibility effects of action observation in imitation and joint action.

Vogeley, K. *et al.* 2001 Mind reading: neural mechanisms of theory of mind and self-perspective. *Neuroimage* **14**, 170–181. (doi:10.1006/nimg.2001.0789)

von Uexküll, J. 1920 *Theoretische biologie*. Berlin, Germany: Springer.

Wegner, D. M., & Bargh, J. 1997 Automaticity and mental control. In *The handbook of social psychology* (eds S. T Gilbert, S. T Fiske, & G. Lindzey), pp. 446–449, 4th edn. New York, NY: McGraw Hill.

Wheatley, T., Milleville, S. C. & Martin, A. 2007 Understanding animate agents. *Psychol. Sci.* **18**, 469–474. (doi:10.1111/j.1467-9280.2007.01923.x)

Wilson, M. & Knoblich, G. 2005 The case for motor involvement in perceiving conspecifics. *Psychol. Bull.* **131**, 460–473. (doi:10.1037/0033-2909.131.3.460)

Wimmer, H. & Perner, J. 1983 Beliefs about beliefs: representation and constraining function of wrong beliefs in young children's understanding of deception. *Cognition* **13**, 103–128. (doi:10.1016/0010-0277(83)90004-5)

10

Social cognition

Chris D. Frith

Social cognition concerns the various psychological processes that enable individuals to take advantage of being part of a social group. Of major importance to social cognition are the various social signals that enable us to learn about the world. Such signals include facial expressions, such as fear and disgust, which warn us of danger, and eye gaze direction, which indicate where interesting things can be found. Such signals are particularly important in infant development. Social referencing, for example, refers to the phenomenon in which infants refer to their mothers' facial expressions to determine whether or not to approach a novel object. We can learn a great deal simply by observing others. Much of this signalling seems to happen automatically and unconsciously on the part of both the sender and the receiver. We can learn to fear a stimulus by observing the response of another, in the absence of awareness of that stimulus. By contrast, learning by instruction, rather than observation, does seem to depend upon awareness of the stimulus, since such learning does not generalize to situations where the stimulus is presented subliminally. Learning by instruction depends upon a meta-cognitive process through which both the sender and the receiver recognize that signals are intended to be signals. An example would be the 'ostensive' signals that indicate that what follows are intentional communications. Infants learn more from signals that they recognize to be instructive. I speculate that it is this ability to recognize and learn from instructions rather than mere observation which permitted that advanced ability to benefit from cultural learning that seems to be unique to the human race.

Keywords: social; cognition; signals; meta-cognition; culture; observation

10.1. What is social cognition?

As currently used, the term 'cognition' refers to the many different processes by which creatures understand and make sense of the world. The term does much the same work as was previously done by the term 'information processing' and is strongly influenced by developments in computing beginning in the 1940s. Perception, attention, memory and action planning would all be examples of cognitive processes. All these processes are important in social interactions and the study of information processing in a social setting is referred to as social cognition. 'The goal of social cognition is to provide mechanistic, process-oriented explanations of complex social phenomena' (Winkielman & Schooler in press). In this paper, I want to consider whether there are aspects of cognition that are specifically social and specifically human.

When we interact with the environment, psychologists have traditionally started from the input. Signals arising from the environment impinge upon us. Sensations are detected by our sense organs such as the eyes. The sensations (e.g. light of a certain wavelength) are turned into perceptions (e.g. the colour of the fruit) on the basis of prior knowledge and current context. Then, decisions are made about what should best be done in response to these perceptions (e.g. Is the fruit ripe? Should I eat it?). Actions are planned and finally output is initiated in the form of motor movements (e.g. grasping the fruit). Within this general framework of stimulus and response, we can have a subset of processes concerned with social stimuli (e.g. reading facial expressions), social decisions (Should I trust this person?) and social responses (making facial expressions).

(a) Mirror systems and social stimuli

There is currently much interest in mirror systems in the brain. A mirror system is defined as a collection of brain regions that are active when we do or experience something ourselves, and also when we observe someone else doing the same thing or having the same experience. The concept originated from the observation of neurons in the frontal cortex of the monkey, which respond when the monkey performs a specific action (e.g. picking up a peanut) and also when the monkey observes someone else performing the same action (Rizzolatti & Craighero 2004). These neurons are now known as mirror neurons. In humans, mirror systems have been identified for emotion (Singer *et al.* 2004; Botvinick *et al.* 2005) and touch (Blakemore *et al.* 2005) as well as action (Rizzolatti & Craighero 2004). It seems plausible that systems that link actions and experiences in the self with actions and experiences in others are likely to have an important role in social cognition. We might even define one class of social stimuli as those stimuli that activate mirror systems. However, we also need to consider what value such stimuli might have in helping us to navigate successfully through the social world.

10.2. Social stimuli that tell us about the world

(a) Avoiding danger

Physical disgust is an instinctive emotional reaction to sights and smells which helps us to avoid food poisoning or infection. The sight of someone with an expression of disgust is a signal that they are in contact with something that we should avoid. There is a mirror system for disgust (Wicker *et al.* 2003). When we see a disgusted face, we feel disgusted ourselves and may automatically take avoiding action before we consciously recognize the expression or discover the cause of the disgust.

We can tell a similar story for fear for which there is also evidence of a mirror system (Morris *et al.* 1996). The sight of a fearful face is a signal that there is something for us to be afraid of, and, as with disgust, elicits fear in the observer. In the case of fearful expressions, there are several experiments demonstrating that the presentation of a fearful face elicits physiological signs of fear in observers, even when they are not aware of seeing the face (e.g. Whalen *et al.* 1998). Elizabeth Phelps and her colleagues (Olsson & Phelps 2004) have shown that people can learn to fear an object (such as a blue square) simply by watching someone else being conditioned to fear that object, because each time the blue square is presented the person observed receives a painful shock. This learning by observation occurs even when the conditioned stimulus (the blue square) is masked and the observer is unable to report when this stimulus occurs. The most probable mechanism underlying this subliminal learning by observation is classical Pavlovian conditioning. We know (Ohman & Mineka 2001) that someone can be conditioned when the conditioned stimulus (CS, e.g. a blue square) is presented subliminally and followed by a shock (the unconditioned stimulus, US). In the case of subliminal learning by observation, the unconditioned stimulus is the sight of the face of the person in pain, since this stimulus elicits 'pain' in the observer.

Disgust and fear are signals emanating from other peoples' faces that indicate that there is something in their immediate environment to be avoided. However, a face can also supply a signal that the person should be avoided. When confronted with unknown people, there is a high level of inter-subject agreement that certain faces look trustworthy, while others look untrustworthy. The presentation of untrustworthy faces elicits activity in the amygdala, a physiological sign that avoiding action should be taken. This seems to be an automatic response, since it occurs whether subjects are explicitly asked to rate faces for trustworthiness or are attending to an irrelevant aspect of the faces such as sex (Winston *et al.* 2002). Unlike readings of the facial expression of fear, our reading of the facial expression of untrustworthiness seems to be an example of prejudice. While there is considerable agreement between people as to what an untrustworthy face looks like, there is no evidence for any validity for this reading. Presumably our idea about what an untrustworthy face looks like has been acquired through culture. Yet, this cue is still processed automatically, like signals of fear.

(b) Learning which things are nice and which are nasty: social referencing

Closely related mechanisms can explain the phenomenon of social referencing (Feinman *et al.* 1992). Learning about the world from other people is particularly important during infancy when so much is novel. Confronted with a novel object or situation, the infant will look at his or her mother. A smile will cause the infant to approach while a frown will elicit avoidance. In this way, the infant can learn about a basic property of things in the world: whether they are nice or nasty. However, the infant does not learn about anything or from anyone. Through evolutionary history, the brain is pre-prepared to learn more rapidly about threatening stimuli, such as snakes (Mineka & Ohman 2002). Infant monkeys rapidly learn to fear snakes by observing fear in a model, but do not learn to be afraid of a flower by such observation (Cook & Mineka 1989). Initially, human infants learn about the world from observing their mothers, rather than strangers (Zarbatany & Lamb 1985). However, at 14 months, they will learn from a familiarized stranger (Klinnert *et al.* 1986) and by 24 months strangers are used as a source for learning (Walden & Kim 2005).

Like all signals, those used in social referencing are inherently ambiguous. The default assumption is that signs of fear tell us that an object is nasty and should be avoided. But, instead of telling us about the object, the signal could be telling us about the person showing fear. Perhaps this person has an abnormal attitude to this object, such as a phobia. Fourteen-month-old infants do not seem to make this distinction. They behave as if signals only tell us about the object, not about the person signalling (Gergely *et al.* 2007). However, by the age of 18 months, infants are able to make this distinction. I shall come back to this problem of the signal and the signaller in §6.

(c) Finding locations of interest

In order to learn, from his or her mother's expression, whether an object is nice or nasty, the infant must know which object his or her mother is looking at. The infant can do this by taking into account the eye gaze direction of his or her mother. We are very accurate at gauging eye gaze direction (Anstis *et al.* 1969). Furthermore, when we see a person with averted gaze, we tend, automatically, to look at the place at which they are looking. We expect there to be something of interest at this location. Bayliss & Tipper (2006) used eye gaze direction in various faces as cues in a spatial attention task. Some faces gave valid cues, some neutral and some invalid cues. There is known to be a strong validity effect of eye gaze cues (Driver *et al.* 1999). Subjects are much slower to identify objects that appear in the opposite location to that indicated by the eye gaze direction (invalid cue). Bayliss & Tipper found that this effect occurred even for faces that consistently looked in the wrong direction. Subjects seemed to be unaware of these contingencies. However, after testing, the subjects rated the faces giving invalid spatial cues as appearing less trustworthy. We see two social processes here that seem to be largely automatic and unconscious. First, the shift of attention that is caused by observing someone's eye gaze direction and, second, the learning about how helpful people are from their behaviour.

10.3. Social responses mirror social stimuli

From a stimulus-response perspective, social cognition is very symmetrical. One person's stimulus is another person's response. This symmetry is most obvious in the various examples of the mirror system. I observe your fearful expression (a social stimulus), which causes me to make a fearful expression (a social response). Social interactions typically involve chains of such stimuli and responses. For example, Keltner & Buswell (1997) consider the case of the expression of embarrassment. Our protagonist has committed a social *faux pas* and his companions express anger. He responds by expressing embarrassment. His companions express sorrow as an empathic response to his discomfort. His appeasement has worked and every one expresses happiness.

In this example, the facial movements made by the participants not only express emotions, but they also have a communicative role. For our protagonist's appeasement to work, it is enough that he expresses the emotion of embarrassment. He does not have to feel it. Evidence that the expression of emotions has a strong communicative role comes from the observation that the presence of others markedly influences the magnitude of facial responses (Parkinson 2005). For example, Bavelas *et al.* (1986) demonstrated that an observer shows much greater signs of sympathy (via motor mimicry) when the person they are watching is in eye contact with them. The cynic might conclude that these facial movements do not reflect sympathy, but rather reputation management. The sender wishes to persuade the observer that he, the sender, is a sympathetic person. However, this interpretation requires that the expression of sympathy should be deliberate and consciously controlled. It is my feeling, and this opinion must be tested experimentally, that most of these facial movements are automatic and occur without conscious control. In §6*b*, I will consider those special signals that are deliberately communicative.

(a) Mirroring responses

When we interact with someone we often mirror each other's movements and mannerisms, leading to synchronized leg-crossing, nodding and so on. This is known as the chameleon effect (Chartrand & Bargh 1999). We are unaware of this mirroring, but, when it occurs, it creates the feeling that we have good rapport with each other. This good feeling is not just directed at our companion, but to the world in general (van Baaren *et al.* 2004). We seem to be learning, not so much that this is a good person, but that the world is a good place. This unconscious mirroring can be seen as a consequence of activity in the brain's mirror system. Simply observing someone else move activates the same movements in the observer. Indeed, it is difficult to make a movement different from the one you are observing (Kilner *et al.* 2003). All these effects that we have mentioned so far are automatic and unconscious. Neither the sender nor the receiver need be aware that they are exchanging signals. Indeed, the rapport associated with the chameleon effect may be destroyed if we become aware that we are being imitated (Lakin & Chartrand 2003). Instead, we may feel we are being mocked.

10.4. Social signals that convey information

We can use social signals to help us attain our goals. If I am looking for a drink at a reception I can use the density of people in different parts of the room or the direction of their movements as signals indicating the probable location of the drinks table. Most of the time we use such social signals emitted by people (our conspecifics). But we can also use such signals from species other than our own. We train dogs to point at quarry such as hares and game birds and the Romans famously used geese to warn them of danger. And it is not just us. Many species use signals from other species to help them achieve their goals (Danchin *et al.* 2004). The important aspect of these signals is that they are emitted by agents, rather than objects. It is therefore important to be able to detect agents.

(a) Detecting agents

We use very simple cues for detecting agents. A basic distinction is between self-propelled objects and non-self-propelled objects. An infant perceives causality when the motion of a non-self-propelled object is changed by another object. He or she perceives intention when a self-propelled object changes motion (Premack 1990). Infants treat self-propelled objects as agents with goals (Luo & Baillargeon 2005). Another important sign of agency is contingent behaviour. Infants will treat an inanimate object as an agent having communicative abilities and goal-directed behaviour, if the object interacts contingently with them or another person (Johnson 2003). Adults also, even though they know they are observing inanimate objects, such as triangles moving on a screen, are irresistibly driven to interpret the movements of these objects in terms of goals and intentions (Heider & Simmel 1944). This detection and interpretation of agents from movements seems to depend upon an automatic and highly stimulus-driven perceptual system (Scholl & Tremoulet 2000).

10.5. Beyond stimulus-response psychology: goals and actions

More recently, psychologists have started to think that the interaction between the person and the environment should be described the other way round. Rather than starting from a stimulus in the environment, the starting point is inside me and concerns my goals. What is currently my most pressing goal? How can this goal be best achieved given my prior knowledge and the current context? On the basis of the answers to these questions, I perform an act upon the world (engineers call this the input). This act will cause new signals to strike my senses (engineers call this the output) and I will learn whether or not the act has brought me nearer to my goal. The difference between what I expected and what actually occurred is the error signal that drives the system and enables me to approach my goals (Sutton & Barto 1998). Within this framework also we can define subsets of processes with specifically social functions. In particular, we can define social goals. Social goals are shared goals and therefore involve at least two people. Shared goals are most obviously involved in joint action, when at least two people are required to perform a task or when a task can be performed better by two people than by one person on his own. Successful joint action benefits from communication and also from trust. A shared goal is also implied when one person works for the benefit of others. However, social goals can also be competitive, as when one person tries to deceive another.

(a) Alignment in joint action

Various kinds of alignment between the two participants are essential for the prosecution of shared actions. We need a shared vocabulary so that we can communicate and shared goals so that we can engage in joint activities. Clark (1996) has called this common ground. This sharing must occur at many levels of representation. For example, we should share each other's perception of the world. The starting point for sharing the world that we perceive is to align the focus of our attention. This process is called joint attention and is typically achieved by pointing at an object. This leads to the triadic relationship in which two people focus their attention on the same object. Background and foreground in their two perceptual worlds are now aligned. The wish to share attention in this way can be observed in infants as young as 12 months (Tomasello *et al.* 2005). Many aspects of alignment are achieved by deliberate communication. The infant points at the object he or she wants. Adults verbally agree on the joint goal towards which their action is aimed. However, there are many aspects of alignment that occur automatically.

(b) Automatic alignment of goals

When we perform a task with someone we develop a shared representation of the whole task even though we are only performing part of it. In one paradigm (Sebanz *et al.* 2003), a pair of participants performed a 'go-nogo' task, sitting along side each other. Even though no interpersonal coordination was required, each actor integrated the co-actor's alternative action into their own action planning. This resulted in an action selection conflict when a stimulus required a different action from each actor (e.g. a 'nogo' response from one actor and a 'go' response from the other; Tsai *et al.* 2006). This effect seems to be automatic.

For this sort of alignment, simple imitation of action enabled by the mirror system is not sufficient. Having shared goals does not always mean that we should mirror each other's actions (Sebanz *et al.* 2006). For example, when two people are carrying a heavy object, one may walk backwards, while the other walks forwards. This complementary form of control often enables a joint action to be more efficient than the same action performed by a single person (Reed *et al.* 2006).

Automatic processes during joint action have been studied most extensively in relation to spoken dialogue (e.g. Pickering & Garrod 2004). For example, speakers give largely unconscious eye gaze signals to control turn-taking in discourse (Hedge *et al.* 1978). Likewise, they use interjections like 'ah' and 'um' to signal, respectively, forthcoming smaller or larger delays in speaking so as to avoid premature interruption (Clark & Fox Tree 2002). Two speakers also become more similar in their use of syntax. Branigan *et al.* (2000) asked pairs of speakers to take turns in describing pictures to each other. One speaker was a confederate of the experimenter and produced descriptions that systematically varied in syntactic structure. This primed a similar syntactic structure in the other speaker's subsequent description.

All these signals, which so strongly affect our verbal interactions, are largely unconscious and their role often comes as a surprise when revealed by clever experiments. In the next section, I shall consider the deliberate use and interpretation of signals.

10.6. The interpretation of signals

(a) Learning by observation and learning by instruction

Most of the cognitive processes I have discussed so far function without awareness. People show emotional responses to fearful faces even though they are not aware of having seen the face (Morris *et al.* 1999). People also show emotional responses to untrustworthy faces even when they are attending to some other aspect of the face such as sex (Winston *et al.* 2002). We have also seen that the automatic imitation that comprises the chameleon effect only works when the participants are unaware that they are being imitated (Lakin & Chartrand 2003). In all these examples, the participants are unaware that they are sending or receiving signals. Thus, many social processes can occur without conscious awareness. There is much less evidence, however, as to whether certain social processes cannot occur in the absence of awareness.

The one exception is the study by Olsson & Phelps (2004) on the learning of fear through instruction. We have already seen that people can learn associate fear with an unseen stimulus during classical Pavlovian conditioning and also by the observation of someone else being conditioned. People can also learn by instruction (Phelps *et al.* 2001), that is, by being told that the stimulus (e.g. a blue square) will be followed by a painful shock. However, this learning by instruction does not generate a response when the stimulus is unseen. My interpretation of this result is that, when learning by instruction, we learn that the blue square is a signal that means that a shock will soon be coming. We cannot extract the meaning of this signal when it is processed below the level of consciousness. Response to the subliminal signal of fear can only be learned through a more primitive process of long-term association.

(b) Deliberate signalling and knowledge transfer

The same important distinction applies when we consider the sender of the signals. This is the contrast between signals that result from involuntary responses to the object and signals sent with deliberate communicative intent. For example, a mother might deliberately simulate fear she did not feel in order to keep the infant away from a dangerous object. However, in most cases, deliberate signals are not deceptive. When directed at infants, deliberate signals are usually intended to teach (Csibra & Gergely 2006). Teaching is a particular kind of knowledge transfer, i.e. transfer by instruction. It is distinctly different from knowledge transfer by observation. A mother can display her knowledge simply by engaging in some skilled activity. The infant can learn by observing this activity. Indeed, this may be the only way in which infant apes acquire knowledge from their mothers (e.g. Maestripieri *et al.* 2002). In teaching knowledge transfer by instruction, the mother explicitly demonstrates her knowledge and ensures that the infant is in a receptive state for acquiring this knowledge.

(c) Ostention

A typical teaching scenario is as follows. The mother first establishes eye contact with the infant, the mother then looks at and points to an object and the mother names the object. The first signal in the process, the mother looking at the infant, is not just a means of attracting the infant's attention, but it is also an *ostensive* gesture (Sperber & Wilson 1995). An ostensive gesture indicates that the signal that follows will be a deliberate communication about something of relevance to the receiver, 'I am about to tell you something useful'.

Infants show special sensitivity to the 'ostensive' cues that signal the teacher's communicative intention to manifest new and relevant knowledge about a referent object. This kind of signalling is what occurs when learning by instruction is intended. For example, the rapid learning of the names for things that occurs during infancy seems to depend upon the infant recognizing the referential intentions of other people (Bloom 2002). In other words, an infant remembers a name when he or she recognizes that the adult is deliberately naming the object for his or her benefit. An example of the role of ostensive gestures in teaching comes from a study where infants learned a novel action on an object. Infants rapidly learned to turn on a light by touching a box with their head (Meltzoff 1988) when demonstration of this action was preceded by eye contact. But hardly any infants learned to imitate this action if it was not preceded by eye contact (Király *et al.* 2004).

Apart from eye contact, having one's name called is a very common ostensive signal. Infants are very sensitive to their name being called from the age of 4.5 months (Mandel *et al.* 1995). Another ostensive signal is the use of 'motherese' when talking to infants. Infants pay more attention to motherese than to normal adult speech (Fernald 1985) because they know that motherese is directed at them.

There is some evidence that this special kind of learning through instruction may be uniquely human (Maestripieri *et al.* 2002). While apes can learn by observation, there is little evidence for deliberate instruction of the use and recognition of ostensive signals that instruction will be forthcoming. Learning through observation can certainly lead to the spread of knowledge through a group creating a form of culture, but this mechanism will be far less efficient than the one based on deliberate instruction.

(d) What do we learn about the world from instructions?

An ostensive signal indicates that the signals that follow are instructions that will reveal something relevant to us about the world. But how do we know whether these signals are valid? It seems that our default assumption is that these signals will be valid. We know, however, that signallers may sometimes be mistaken or deliberately deceptive. Csibra & Gergely (2006) suggest that, at 14 months, infants assume that signals following an ostensive gesture (i.e. instructions) are always valid. As a result, they combine the information from different sources to get a best estimate of what the referent object is really like. They do not recognize that different signallers may have different attitudes to the same object. By 18 months, infants recognize that different people have different attitudes to the same object. This is the same age at which infants begin to show an understanding of pretence (Friedman & Leslie 2007), recognizing that their mother has a special attitude to a banana, by pretending it is a telephone.

But once we realize that different signallers have different attitudes to objects, how do we decide which is the 'correct' attitude? However we make this decision, the mere fact that we have made it brings in all sorts of interesting social processes. Does the correct attitude depend upon the context? Are some people privileged signallers whose instructions are always treated as valid? In the early stages of infancy, the mother usually has this privileged status. Is there a standard or normal attitude to objects from which a few people deviate? This is why we can refer to some people as phobics because their attitude to objects (e.g. birds) is non-standard. Do we define out-groups as people with systematically different attitudes to objects from us?

The point I am making here is that, when we acquire knowledge from signals deliberately intended to instruct, we are entering the world of a much richer culture than can be obtained by learning through observation. It is this ability to deliberately share knowledge that makes the human mind unique. The cognitive essence of this ability is to recognize that certain signals are deliberately emitted and intended to instruct. This kind of cognition is sometimes called meta-cognition. It requires that we reflect on our own cognition, in this case the process of expressing and receiving signals. Meta-cognition is intimately associated with self-consciousness.

These signals upon which we can reflect are not restricted to vocalizations or gestures. Marks and arrangements of inanimate objects can also be used as deliberate signals. In this way, material becomes part of culture. Perhaps it is this ability to reflect upon our own signals that provided the basis for the extraordinary achievements of the human race during the last few thousand years. This development did not depend upon changes in the basic cognitive apparatus present in the human brain, but on the knowledge acquired by others and passed onto us by deliberate instruction.

C.F. is supported by the Wellcome Trust and the Danish National Research Foundation.

References

Anstis, S. M., Mayhew, J. W. & Morley, T. 1969 The perception of where a face or television "portrait" is looking. *Am. J. Psychol.* **82**, 474–489. (doi:10.2307/1420441)

Bavelas, J. B., Black, A., Lemery, C. R. & Mullett, J. 1986 I show how you feel—motor mimicry as a communicative act. *J. Pers. Soc. Psychol.* **50**, 322–329. (doi:10.1037/0022-3514.50.2.322)

Bayliss, A. P. & Tipper, S. P. 2006 Predictive gaze cues and personality judgments: should eye trust you? *Psychol. Sci.* **17**, 514–520. (doi:10.1111/j.1467-9280.2006.01737.x)

Blakemore, S. J., Bristow, D., Bird, G., Frith, C. & Ward, J. 2005 Somatosensory activations during the observation of touch and a case of vision-touch synaesthesia. *Brain* **128**, 1571–1583. (doi:10.1093/brain/awh500)

Bloom, P. 2002 Mindreading, communication and the learning of names for things. *Mind Lang.* **17**, 37–54.

Botvinick, M., Jha, A. P., Bylsma, L. M., Fabian, S. A., Solomon, P. E. & Prkachin, K. M. 2005 Viewing facial expressions of pain engages cortical areas involved in the direct experience of pain. *Neuroimage* **25**, 312–319. (doi:10.1016/j.neuroimage.2004.11.043)

Branigan, H. P., Pickering, M. J. & Cleland, A. A. 2000 Syntactic co-ordination in dialogue. *Cognition* **75**, B13–B25. (doi:10.1016/S0010-0277(99)00081-5)

Chartrand, T. L. & Bargh, J. A. 1999 The chameleon effect: the perception-behavior link and social interaction. *J. Pers. Soc. Psychol.* **76**, 893–910. (doi:10.1037/0022-3514.76.6.893)

Clark, H. H. 1996 *Using language*. Cambridge, UK: Cambridge University Press.

Clark, H. H. & Fox Tree, J. E. 2002 Using uh and um in spontaneous speaking. *Cognition* **84**, 73–111. (doi:10.1016/S0010-0277(02)00017-3)

Cook, M. & Mineka, S. 1989 Observational conditioning of fear to fear-relevant versus fear-irrelevant stimuli in rhesus monkeys. *J. Abnorm. Psychol.* **98**, 448–459. (doi:10.1037/0021-843X.98.4.448)

Csibra, G. & Gergely, G. 2006 Social learning and social cognition: the case for pedagogy. In *Processes of change in brain and cognitive development: attention & performance XXI* (eds Y. Munakata & M. H. Johnson), pp. 249–274. Oxford, UK: Oxford University Press.

Danchin, E., Giraldeau, L. A., Valone, T. J. & Wagner, R. H. 2004 Public information: from nosy neighbors to cultural evolution. *Science* **305**, 487–491. (doi:10.1126/science.1098254)

Driver, J., Davis, G., Ricciardelli, P., Kidd, P., Maxwell, E. & Baron-Cohen, S. 1999 Gaze perception triggers reflexive visuospatial orienting. *Vis. Cogn.* **6**, 509–540. (doi:10.1080/135062899394920)

Feinman, S., Roberts, D., Hsieh, K. F., Sawyer, D. & Swanson, K. 1992 A critical review of social referencing in infancy. In *Social referencing and the social construction of reality in infancy* (ed. S. Feinman), pp. 15–54. New York, NY: Plenum Press.

Fernald, A. 1985 4-month-old infants prefer to listen to motherese. *Infant Behav. Dev.* **8**, 181–195. (doi:10.1016/S0163-6383(85)80005-9)

Friedman, O. & Leslie, A. M. 2007 The conceptual underpinnings of pretense: pretending is not 'behaving-as-if'. *Cognition* **105**, 103–124. (doi:10.1016/j.cognition.2006.09.007)

Gergely, G., Egyed, K. & Kiraly, I. 2007 On pedagogy. *Dev. Sci.* **10**, 139–146. (doi:10.1111/j.1467-7687.2007.00576.x)

Hedge, B. J., Everitt, B. S. & Frith, C. D. 1978 The role of gaze in dialogue. *Acta Psychol. (Amst.)* **42**, 453–475. (doi:10.1016/0001-6918(78)90033-1)

Heider, F. & Simmel, M. 1944 An experimental study of apparent behavior. *Am. J. Psychol.* **57**, 243–249. (doi:10.2307/1416950)

Johnson, S. C. 2003 Detecting agents. *Phil. Trans. R. Soc. B* **358**, 549–559. (doi:10.1098/rstb.2002.1237)

Keltner, D. & Buswell, B. N. 1997 Embarrassment: its distinct form and appeasement functions. *Psychol. Bull* **122**, 250–270. (doi:10.1037/0033-2909.122.3.250)

Kilner, J. M., Paulignan, Y. & Blakemore, S. J. 2003 An interference effect of observed biological movement on action. *Curr. Biol.* **13**, 522–525. (doi:10.1016/S0960-9822(03)00165-9)

Király, I., Csibra, G. & Gergely, G. 2004 The role of communicative-referential cues in observational learning during the second year. *Paper presented at 14th Biennial Int. Conf. on Infant Studies, Chicago, IL, USA.*

Klinnert, M. D., Emde, R. N., Butterfield, P. & Campos, J. J. 1986 Social referencing—the infants use of emotional signals from a friendly adult with mother present. *Dev. Psychol.* **22**, 427–432. (doi:10.1037/0012-1649.22.4.427)

Lakin, J. L. & Chartrand, T. L. 2003 Using nonconscious behavioral mimicry to create affiliation and rapport. *Psychol. Sci.* **14**, 334–339. (doi:10.1111/1467-9280.14481)

Luo, Y. & Baillargeon, R. 2005 Can a self-propelled box have a goal? Psychological reasoning in 5-month-old infants. *Psychol. Sci.* **16**, 601–608. (doi:10.1111/j.1467-9280.2005.01582.x)

Maestripieri, D., Ross, S. K. & Megna, N. L. 2002 Mother–infant interactions in western lowland gorillas *(Gorilla gorilla gorilla):* spatial relationships, communication, and opportunities for social learning. *J. Comp. Psychol.* **116**, 219–227. (doi:10.1037/0735-7036.116.3.219)

Mandel, D. R., Jusczyk, P. W. & Pisoni, D. B. 1995 Infants' recognition of the sound patterns of their own names. *Psychol. Sci.* **6**, 314–317. (doi:10.1111/j.1467-9280.1995.tb00517.x)

Meltzoff, A. N. 1988 Infant imitation after a 1-week delay—long-term-memory for novel acts and multiple stimuli. *Dev. Psychol.* **24**, 470–476. (doi:10.1037/0012-1649.24.4.470)

Mineka, S. & Ohman, A. 2002 Phobias and preparedness: the selective, automatic, and encapsulated nature of fear. *Biol. Psychiatry* **52**, 927–937. (doi:10.1016/S0006-3223(02) 01669-4)

Morris, J. S., Frith, C. D., Perrett, D. I., Rowland, D., Young, A. W., Calder, A. J. & Dolan, R. J. 1996 A differential neural response in the human amygdala to fearful and happy facial expressions. *Nature* **383**, 812–815. (doi:10.1038/383812a0)

Morris, J. S., Ohman, A. & Dolan, R. J. 1999 A subcortical pathway to the right amygdala mediating "unseen" fear. *Proc. Natl Acad. Sci. USA* **96**, 1680–1685. (doi:10.1073/pnas. 96.4.1680)

Ohman, A. & Mineka, S. 2001 Fears, phobias, and preparedness: toward an evolved module of fear and fear learning. *Psychol. Rev.* **108**, 483–522. (doi:10.1037/0033-295X.108.3.483)

Olsson, A. & Phelps, E. A. 2004 Learned fear of "unseen" faces after Pavlovian, observational, and instructed fear. *Psychol. Sci.* **15**, 822–828. (doi:10.1111/j.0956-7976.2004.00762.x)

Parkinson, B. 2005 Do facial movements express emotions or communicate motives? *Pers Soc. Psychol. Rev.* **9**, 278–311. (doi:10.1207/s15327957pspr0904_1)

Phelps, E. A., O'Connor, K. J., Gatenby, J. C., Gore, J. C., Grillon, C. & Davis, M. 2001 Activation of the left amygdala to a cognitive representation of fear. *Nat. Neurosci.* **4**, 437–441. (doi:10. 1038/86110)

Pickering, M. J. & Garrod, S. 2004 Toward a mechanistic psychology of dialogue. *Behav. Brain Sci.* **27**, 169–190.

Premack, D. 1990 The infant's theory of self-propelled objects. *Cognition* **36**, 1–16. (doi:10.1016/ 0010-0277(90) 90051-K)

Reed, K., Peshkin, M., Hartmann, M. J., Grabowecky, M., Patton, J. & Vishton, P. M. 2006 Haptically linked dyads: are two motor-control systems better than one? *Psychol. Sci.* **17**, 365–366. (doi:10.1111/j.1467-9280.2006.01712.x)

Rizzolatti, G. & Craighero, L. 2004 The mirror-neuron system. *Annu. Rev. Neurosci.* **27**, 169–192. (doi:10.1146/annurev.neuro.27.070203.144230)

Scholl, B. J. & Tremoulet, P. D. 2000 Perceptual causality and animacy. *Trends Cogn. Sci.* **4**, 299–309. (doi:10.1016/S1364-6613(00)01506-0)

Sebanz, N., Knoblich, G. & Prinz, W. 2003 Representing others' actions: just like one's own? *Cognition* **88**, B11–B21. (doi:10.1016/S0010-0277(03)00043-X)

Sebanz, N., Bekkering, H. & Knoblich, G. 2006 Joint action: bodies and minds moving together. *Trends Cogn. Sci.* **10**, 70–76. (doi:10.1016/j.tics.2005.12.009)

Singer, T., Seymour, B., O'Doherty, J., Kaube, H., Dolan, R. J. & Frith, C. D. 2004 Empathy for pain involves the affective but not sensory components of pain. *Science* **303**, 1157–1162. (doi:10.1126/science.1093535)

Sperber, D. & Wilson, D. 1995 *Relevance: communication and cognition,* 2 edn. Oxford, UK: Blackwell.

Sutton, R. S. & Barto, A. G. 1998 *Reinforcement learning: an introduction.* Cambridge, MA: MIT Press.

Tomasello, M., Carpenter, M., Call, J., Behne, T. & Moll, H. 2005 Understanding and sharing intentions: the origins of cultural cognition. *Behav. Brain Sci.* **28**, 675–691. (doi:10.1017/ S0140525X05000129)

Tsai, C. C., Kuo, W. J., Jing, J. T., Hung, D. L. & Tzeng, O. J. 2006 A common coding framework in self-other interaction: evidence from joint action task. *Exp. Brain Res.* **175**, 353–362. (doi:10.1007/s00221-006-0557-9)

van Baaren, R. B., Holland, R. W., Kawakami, K. & van Knippenberg, A. 2004 Mimicry and prosocial behavior. *Psychol. Sci.* **15**, 71–74. (doi:10.1111/j.0963-7214.2004.01501012.x)

Walden, T. A. & Kim, G. 2005 Infants' social looking toward mothers and strangers. *Int. J. Behav. Dev.* **29**, 356–360.

Whalen, P. J., Rauch, S. L., Etcoff, N. L., McInerney, S. C., Lee, M. B. & Jenike, M. A. 1998 Masked presentations of emotional facial expressions modulate amygdala activity without explicit knowledge. *J. Neurosci.* **18**, 411–418.

Wicker, B., Keysers, C., Plailly, J., Royet, J. P., Gallese, V. & Rizzolatti, G. 2003 Both of us disgusted in My insula: the common neural basis of seeing and feeling disgust. *Neuron* **40**, 655–664. (doi:10.1016/S0896-6273(03)00679-2)

Winkielman, P. & Schooler, J. In press. Unconscious, conscious, and meta-conscious in social cognition. In *Social cognition: the basis of human interaction* (eds F. Strack & J. Forster). Philadelphia, PA: Psychology Press.

Winston, J. S., Strange, B. A., O'Doherty, J. & Dolan, R. J. 2002 Automatic and intentional brain responses during evaluation of trustworthiness of faces. *Nat. Neurosci.* **5**, 277–283. (doi:10.1038/nn816)

Zarbatany, L. & Lamb, M. E. 1985 Social referencing as a function of information source—mothers versus strangers. *Infant Behav. Dev.* **8**, 25–33. (doi:10.1016/S0163-6383 (85)80014-X)

11

Neuroscience, evolution and the sapient paradox: the factuality of value and of the sacred

Colin Renfrew

The human genome, and hence the human brain at birth, may not have changed greatly over the past 60 000 years. Yet many of the major behavioural changes that we associate with most human societies are very much more recent, some appearing with the sedentary revolution of some 10 000 years ago. Among these are activities implying the emergence of powerful concepts of value and of the sacred. What then are the neuronal mechanisms that may underlie these consistent, significant (and emergent) patterns of behaviour?

Keywords: evolution of mind; speciation and tectonic phases; sedentary revolution; value; the sacred

11.1. Introduction

The human mind over the past 10 000 years, in most areas of the world, has developed symbolic concepts of such evident factuality that it is difficult for us now to imagine life without them. These include notions of value (including money), of number and measure, of individual people of high status and power, and of material things that embody the sacred and the forbidden. These are often considered givens of the human condition. Yet these features are not 'givens' at all—they are emergent features of the past 10 000 years. How are such fundamental changes in the human condition supported in the brain? The problem for the neuroscientist and the evolutionary archaeologist is to understand how this has come about on so short a time frame, when the human genome has been established for much longer, certainly since the out-of-Africa dispersals of some 60 000 years ago (Forster 2004; Mellars 2006a,b). This problem indeed relates to the sapient paradox (Renfrew 1996): that the biological basis of our species has been established for at least that time (and perhaps for as much as 200 000 years), while the novel behavioural aspects of our 'sapient' status have taken so long to emerge or to construct themselves, or rather that they have done so very recently. This must lay emphasis upon the plasticity of the human brain (its capacity to adapt within a single lifespan to new conditions) and on the aspects of the socialization process of shared experience.

Both this plasticity and the socialization process imply the significance of the development of neuronal networks in early childhood. As will be argued below, the mechanisms in question must form part of the learning process of the individual, a process shared with and participated in by other individuals in the society in question. These processes must favour the development and fixing of symbolic relationships and representations. In many cases, these are not simply verbal or conceptual relationships. Instead they involve contact with and understanding of the material world.

For the archaeologist, the challenge is to understand how human societies, through their interactions with the material world, came to bring about the transformations in life and culture over the millennia drawing upon a hardware (the human genome) that may not have changed significantly in the space of 10 000 years. This invites a cognitive archaeology: the archaeology of mind (Renfrew 1982; Renfrew & Zubrow 1994; Mithen 1996). For the neuroscientist, the equivalent challenge may be to show how the potential capacities of the human mind, presumably present 60 000 years and more ago, were brought into play, through the activities of successive generations of individuals, within specific trajectories of cultural development, so that human performance (and with it human existence) was profoundly transformed. The perspective has, in one sense, to be long term (phylogenetic), but if the genetic basis for the neonate in each generation is the same, the differences between succeeding generations must be explained within the learning processes of the individual in each generation (i.e. ontogenetically).

To approach these problems effectively may require a partnership between neuroscientists and archaeologists working on different aspects of the human condition. To do so will require a perspective that recognizes that 'mind' is the result of embodied experience and of material engagement with the world (Clark 1997; Malafouris 2004), so that the neuroscience of embodied experience and of social engagement will be crucially relevant. One crucial component of that experience and engagement is located within the individual human brain (inside the individual cranium), which seems to be the special preserve of the neuroscientist. But the only conceivable solution to the sapient paradox requires that the performance of this brain should be seen within a short-term evolutionary context where genomic change is probably not significant.

In what follows the evolutionary context, on the basis of recent archaeological understanding, will first be outlined in part I (§2). In part II (§3) an attempt will be made to consider and define more closely some of the emerging properties of the human mind for which some understanding of the neurological basis might be sought. For it is presumably on the basis of the neurological endowment of our species, present, even if still latent, within the human genome more than 60 000 years ago, that these emergent properties have been constructed.

11.2. Part I. The evolutionary context: The speciation and tectonic phases

(a) The speciation phase

Recent DNA studies (e.g. Forster 2004) appear to have resolved many of the controversies about the evolutionary ancestry of *Homo sapiens*. The multi-regional hypothesis, according to which hominin ancestors (such as *Homo erectus* or *Homo ergaster*) in various continents made their contributions, has given way to the out-of-Africa hypothesis, which states that the ancestors of all living humans were present in Africa prior to the dispersals *ca* 60 000 years ago (Foley & Lahr 2003; Mellars 2006*b*; Mellars *et al.* 2007). The departure from Africa of mtDNA haplogroups M and N provided the ancestry for all living humans elsewhere, while closely related humans remaining in Africa were ancestral to most subsequent Africa populations (other than M and N descendents subsequently back migrating).

The behavioural attributes associated with the new species are not so easy to define. Until a couple of decades ago (before the impact of that clear DNA picture), it was possible to speak of a 'human revolution' (Mellars & Stringer 1989). This was most clearly seen in southwest Europe where the transition from *Homo neandertalensis* to *H. sapiens* by *ca* 40 000 BP was accompanied by a range of new behaviours. It was suggested by some that this was the time when a capacity for complex speech first developed, and perhaps for self-conscious reflection also. These archaeologically attested behaviours (Mellars 1991) included: a shift in the production of stone tools from a 'flake' technology to a 'blade' technology, and an increase in the complexity of the stone tools produced; the appearance of artefacts made of bone, antler and ivory; increased tempo of change with regional diversification; the appearance for the first time of a wide range of beads and personal adornments; significant change in both the economic and social organization of human groups; and the development (although restricted mainly to France and Spain) of 'naturalistic' art.

More recently, work on the Middle Stone Age of southern Africa (McBrearty & Brooks 2000) has led scholars to situate the emergence of most of these features (although emphatically not the Franco-Cantabrian cave art) to a period prior to 70 000 years BP, where many of them are seen at sites including the Blombos Cave (Henshilwood & Marean 2003; Henshilwood *et al.* 2004). They are therefore plainly documented there prior to the out-of-Africa dispersals of *ca* 60 000 BP. Moreover fossil remains of what seem to be anatomically modern humans are found at sites such as Herto in Ethiopia as far back as 200 000 years ago. The appearance of the behavioural traits in question may have been more gradual and more piecemeal than has formerly been thought, so that the term 'revolution' has to be used with caution (Gamble 2007). There is no agreement at present as to whether speech capacity emerged by *ca* 200 000 BP with *H. sapiens*, or earlier and gradually over a much longer period. The discovery of clearly intentional patterning on fragments of red ochre from the Blombos Cave (at *ca* 70 000 BP) is interesting when discussing the origins of symbolic expression. But it is entirely different in character, and very much simpler than the cave paintings and the small carved sculptures which accompany the Upper Palaeolithic of France and Spain (and further east in Europe) after 40 000 BP.

For the purposes of the present paper, I would like to emphasize the (slightly over-simplified) point that in biological, i.e. genetic, terms the evolution of our species must have been effectively accomplished by the time of the out-of-Africa dispersals. Molecular genetics does of course indicate diversity among living humans, but on a relatively minor scale. All human societies share the same capacity for complex speech. Moreover, although we do not yet have ancient DNA from human fossils dating to the millennia following those dispersals, there is no reason to suggest that the human genome 60 000 years ago differs significantly and systematically from that of today. What we may term the 'speciation phase' of human evolution (Renfrew 2006, p. 224, 2007a, p. 94), the period when biological and cultural coevolution worked together to develop the human genome and the human species, as we know it, was fulfilled already 60 000 years ago. This implies that the basic hardware—the human brain at the time of birth—has not changed radically since that time.

That brings us to the sapient paradox.

(b) The tectonic phase

The life of the hunter-gatherers who left Africa some 60 000 years ago does not appear to have differed very significantly from those remaining in Africa, and indeed from their predecessors. These were relatively small bands of gatherers and hunters, leading a mobile existence, with no permanent places of residence. Their tool kits were often restricted to the artefacts that they could carry with them. In some respects they had highly sophisticated social relationships and technologies. Their ancestors had long known the use of fire. They were adept at using stone-tipped projectiles and at hunting in groups. As they peopled the continents of the earth, the different groups and lineages developed their own adaptations to the environment and their own trajectories of development. Interactions between neighbouring groups were very localized, so that in most respects the subsequent cultural evolution of the different territorial groups was an independent process, although always on the basis of the shared genetic and cultural heritage which they had brought with them from Africa.

It is important to remember that what is often termed cave art—the painted caves, the beautifully carved 'Venus' figurines—was during the Palaeolithic (i.e. the Pleistocene climatic period) effectively restricted to one developmental trajectory, localized in western Europe. It is true that there are just a few depictions of animals in Africa from that time, and in Australia also. But Pleistocene art was effectively restricted to Franco-Cantabria and its outliers.

It was not until towards the end of the Pleistocene period that, in several parts of the world, major changes are seen (but see Gamble (2007) for a more nuanced view, placing more emphasis upon developments in the Late Palaeolithic). They are associated with the development of sedentism and then of agriculture and sometimes stock rearing. At the risk of falling into the familiar 'revolutionary' cliché, it may be appropriate to speak of the Sedentary Revolution (Wilson 1988; Renfrew 2007a, ch. 7). Along with village life, implying much larger permanent communities, there came in the Near East a whole range of new artefacts, including querns, grindstones, and polished stone tools, along with pottery and other products implying the controlled use of fire. New ritual practices appeared involving the use of shrines and sometimes of human representations. Long-distance trade developed, as did local stylistic zones. More importantly, new concepts arose—the institutional facts discussed by the philosopher Searle (1995). It is at this time that the notions of personal and heritable property must have become significant (Renfrew 2001). The pace of change became much more rapid.

Although the details are different in each area, we see a kind of sedentary revolution taking place in western Asia, in southern China, in the Yellow River area of northern China, in Mesoamerica, and coastal Peru, in New Guinea, and in a different way in Japan (Scarre 2005). In most of these places pottery soon came into use, and there were other features resembling the early developments in western Asia, including new ritual and cult practices, although each area had its own characteristic innovations. In each case they were soon sustained by the domestication of local plants, and in some cases animals. And often these were expansive economies. The increase in population density permitted by agricultural production and by sedentary life was accompanied by population expansions and agricultural dispersals, in some cases also generating the spread of specific languages and language families.

From a distance and to the non-specialist anthropologist, this Sedentary Revolution looks like the true Human Revolution. It was then that patterns of living changed directly and trajectories of development were initiated which in some areas soon led to the rise of urban life and of state societies and indeed to the rise of literacy.

Why did it all take so long? If the sapient phase of human evolution was accomplished some 60 000 years ago, why did it take a further 50 000 years for these sapient humans to get their act together and transform the world? That is the sapient paradox.

I believe that it presents a significant challenge to the neuroscientist. The hardware was there 60 000 years ago (in the sense of the genetically inherited component represented by the human genome). Why did it take the software—the (phylogenetically) accumulating skills along each trajectory of growth, transmitted to each new generation through the ontogenetic learning process—so long to develop?

This phase of human development, succeeding the speciation phase, may be termed the *tectonic phase* (from the Greek τεκτων, carpenter, builder; Renfrew 2006, p. 224, 2007*a*, p. 97). The construction of culture and society then developed rapidly on the basis of new forms of material engagement with the world by human individuals, leading to new and transformed relationships.

(c) Childhood learning and neuronal pathways

Culture is transmitted through learning (from parents as well as neighbours) and can thus be inherited as well as accumulated through association (Shennan 2002). Language itself is a very good example. For while the capacity to learn a language is part of the hardware—it is passed on genetically—the specific language that one first speaks comes about through early learning. The skills of the hunter-gatherer, such as the making of flint or wooden tools, or the making of fire, were accumulated in this way, just as are those much more recent skills of reading and writing.

Crucial among these skills for humans, as White (1949) so effectively emphasized, is the capacity to use symbols. Language, with its sophisticated use of symbols, was clearly a feature of the human condition well before 60 000 years ago. It was, however, during the tectonic phase that material things, artefacts, came to have great importance for their symbolic significance. Indeed the use of material symbols may be claimed as one of the most striking features of the tectonic phase until the development of writing, and with it of new forms of external symbolic storage (Donald 1991).

In §3, I want to focus upon two kinds of material symbol which came to play a very central role in human life and experience, and the neurological implications of which would merit investigation.

They are crucial to the understanding of the neurological basis of human behaviour. The chronology outlined above indicates that the analysis of the hardware of the human brain itself, established for more than 60 000 years, is not sufficient to generate an understanding of some of the principal aspects of human behaviour. The changes since that time, including the development of those special symbolling capacities outlined below, must form part of any coherent analysis. This paper strives to define this problem more closely, and invites the reframing of the problem in more specifically neuroscientific terms.

11.3. Part II. Factual realities of the tectonic phase: Value and belief

I would like to turn now to some of the enduring features of human existence as experienced at the present time, and indeed for many centuries or millennia. So pervasive are they that one would imagine them to have been 'hard-wired' into our brains, a 'given' of the human condition, established for us along with many other capacities through the human genome.

The interesting observation that archaeology allows us to make, however, is that some of these enduring features are nonetheless emergent features that occur, at least along some developmental trajectories, at a certain point in the archaeological record, prior to which they are simply not seen. So pervasive and influential are they that they must, one feels, have a neurological basis. But it is a basis that comes into play only at a specific and quite recent point in the evolutionary trajectory of human (phylogenetic) development.

(a) Intrinsic value

Let us start with gold. A bar of gold has an allure that is almost physical. The image of the miser taking pleasure in counting the coins of gold that constitute his wealth is a familiar one. For most of us, in the tradition of western capitalism, founded upon the monetary economy of the classical world, itself based upon the early mercantile economy of the first urbanism in western Asia, gold is a familiar valuable. Even if, since the early twentieth century, it has no longer been the basic standard of value, reserves of gold still underlie many currencies. Early colonists from Europe found similar circumstances in India and the Far East, where gold was highly prized. The situation was rather different in the Americas, but there too, before the arrival of the *conquistadores*, gold was highly valued.

When we look at the golden treasures of the classical world (like the Treasure of Panagyurishte, or the burial casket from the alleged tomb of Phillip of Macedon) or the golden coffin and face mask of the pharaoh Tutankhamun, it is easy to accept that gold is a substance of intrinsic value, and that this is one of enduring realities of human existence. However if we go back a few 1000 years, before the bronze age of Europe and before the early dynasties of Egypt and of Sumer, we find a very different situation. Before that time gold was accorded no significance whatever.

The earliest significant finds of golden artefacts come from the copper age cemetery of Varna in Bulgaria, by *ca* 4500 BC, and from others of the same area and period. The context of deposition in the graves allows one to infer that at Varna, gold was in fact highly valued (Renfrew 1986), which indeed needs to be demonstrated rather than assumed, if circular arguments are to be avoided. There are various opportunities in the archaeological record for recognizing specific contexts indicating that a particular material was considered valuable. Materials chosen for personal adornment, for example, for necklaces, or bracelets, head decoration, earrings, labrets, etc., when consistently so used, may give such an indication. Those used for other decorative purposes, such as inlay work offer similar indication, as well as materials used for artefacts likely to be involved in bodily contact, such as drinking cups. The hoarding of quantities of material can also be indicative, for instance as observed in shipwrecks. In Varna there is another significant indication, where gold leaf was used to give the impression that a stone shaft-hole axe was in fact made of gold.

The important point, however, is that before that time, gold was not collected or accorded any significance as a material of value. Native gold was undoubtedly available in some areas in metallic form but it was not exploited, so that this is not simply a question of the technology of extraction. We can safely conclude that in Europe and western Asia gold became a commodity of high value at a fairly well-defined time in each region. One can indeed show that the interest in gold, and the ascription of high value to it, came about at about the same time that another metal, copper, was becoming interesting as a material that could be worked, first through cold working and annealing and later by casting. Alloying of copper with tin to make bronze was a subsequent development. From that time on it seems that gold indeed became a commodity of 'intrinsic' value, but not before that time.

The intrinsic value of gold is, of course, culturally ascribed. It is what the philosopher Searle (1995) would call an 'institutional fact'. It attains its factuality within a given context in much the same sense that we can say that A and B are 'man and wife' if they have been properly married in an officially recognized ceremony. It is not what Searle would call a 'brute fact' of nature (as might be the fact that A and B were the biological parents of child C).

Of course there are other materials generally regarded as of intrinsic value (Clark 1986). Diamonds are forever and jade has been specially valued from early times in many cultures—in Neolithic Europe and especially in Neolithic China, but not earlier, not during the Palaeolithic of either region. Interestingly, marine shells and sometimes animal teeth were indeed used as adornments during the Palaeolithic and their use has recently been suggested as one of the behaviours by which our species *H. sapiens* may be recognized (Vanhaeren *et al.* 2006), but such early exploitation of minerals is rare, and metals make their appearance only later. Objects of gold or jade are not found accompanying burials in the Early Neolithic period, or earlier. Nor are hoards (buried accumulations of such materials) found at such early times, although they do occur later, testifying to the newly acquired importance of these materials. Of course most of the materials regarded as of intrinsic value do have physical properties to recommend them. The 'noble' metals do not oxidize easily. Many precious stones are very hard as well as brightly coloured. But these properties have not been enough, in themselves, to make these materials generally and universally valued. Their high value in each case is culture and context specific: an institutional fact.

What interests us here, however, is not whether this or that material is the more highly valued, but the very notion of value itself. Elsewhere I have sought to analyse some of the relationships involved (Renfrew 2001, 2007*a*, ch. 8).

In an exchange system (see figure 11.1) the notion of commodity implies both the measurement of quantity of the commodity and the possibility of exchange, where a quantum of one commodity may be regarded as equivalent to a defined quantity of another. It is of course the fungibility of gold—its use as the basis for coinage, and then as

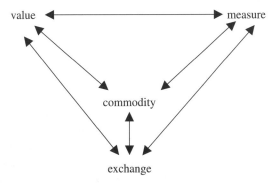

Figure 11.1 The place of a concept of value within a commodity-based exchange system.

the underwriting material for a monetary currency in general—that gives it its particular significance in the modern world. But underlying that is its basic allure—that to the informed eye it incorporates and represents high value. It offers also the possibility of the accumulation of aggregate value, i.e. wealth, in a way previously only accessible through the accumulation of livestock.

Gold is a powerful motivating force. Explorers have devoted their lives in searching for it. Bankers have spent their lives hoarding it. Adventurers and criminals have endangered their lives and those of others in misappropriating it.

To recapitulate, during the Palaeolithic period gold was nowhere valued, nor were there other commodities that we can recognize as highly valued—unless marine shells that were already used for personal decoration and jewellery. The notion of high value came to be established in those regions where it did emerge only after what may be termed the sedentary revolution, and not generally at an early date among agrarian societies. But when it did come to be valued, its impact was considerable, and has since been taken up by money (Renfrew 2003, pp. 182–184). Most of us work for money, are paid in money and measure success by money.

I would like to see what light could be shed upon the powerful motivating force that materials or sums of high value, exemplified by gold, can generate. It relates to the material itself—the process is one of material engagement (Malafouris 2004; Renfrew 2004). This seems to be an important point. From the inception of the sedentary revolution, material things came to take a more important role in human affairs. Property, ownership and the accumulation of wealth became possible. They were accompanied by new power relationships, in which positions of personal high status became hereditary. The material engagement process led also to technological advances, for instance in the field of pyrotechnology. Yet the process is mediated also by cognitive aspects. Gold as a material is known to be of value and that sense of value is shared by the community.

The question is obviously of interest since most societies today are structured on the basis of value and finance. What is the neurological basis for these strong and enduring motivating forces? They have an effectiveness that often seems to be intuitive. The respect accorded to valuables such as gold is not always based upon verbal formulations. It depends often upon contexts of use, in some cases of ritual use. The 'factuality' of value is often not based upon verbal propositions but upon the reality that artefacts of this material are valued, and that they are used in contexts where high value is implicit.

(b) The power of the sacred

The archaeology of religion has become a well-defined area of research (Renfrew 1985; Boyer 1994; Mithen 1998; Insoll 2004). To explore the neurological basis of religious experience would be an interesting undertaking, but one difficult to extend to earlier time periods unless there are rich material indications in the archaeological record. However, as with the foregoing case of the construction of value and the identification of valuables, religious practice, as documented by material things, can indeed be observed archaeologically. It may be recognized through the identification of sanctuaries and shrines, through the depiction in two or three dimensions of deities, priests and worshippers, in the iconography of religious belief, and in evidence for the conduct of ritual where an orientation towards the supernatural or transcendental may be inferred. The specific indications that allow the practice of ritual to be inferred have recently been the subject of much discussion (e.g. Renfrew 1994; Insoll 2004; Barrowclough & Malone 2007). Nor should the possible distinctions between ritual and cult be ignored (Kyriakidis 2006; Renfrew 2007b)—the practice of ritual does not necessarily imply the transcendental focus generally implied by the term cult.

Once again, such evidence for religious practices is first seen, along various trajectories of development in different regions, at about the time of the sedentary revolution. (The specially early case of the European Upper Palaeolithic should again be recognized, with its cave art and its figurines, and might indeed be interpreted as a an exceptionally early case of incipient sedentism.)

It can be suggested, however, that religious faith, implying a coherent system of religious beliefs and practices, is an emergent feature of human experience, just as are the concepts of wealth and of value, discussed above.

What then are the neurological mechanisms that operate when the strong emotions evoked by faith and by the sacred come into play? As an example, I should like to highlight the special significance accorded to religious relics. This can involve a veneration which again entails a factuality accorded to such material things as a tooth of the Buddha or a fragment of the True Cross. To the non-believer these things have no intrinsic worth, and the discussion may be related to that for gold, as outlined above. Within a context of belief, however, such relics are the source of miracles. Their sacred quality is again such that powerful human motivations are generated, on a large scale, in relation to them.

These sacred materials are sometimes of great antiquity, in Muslim as well as Christian tradition, and sacred things have a powerful role in the early religions of Mesoamerica. I would like to obtain a clearer understanding of the neurological mechanisms that allow specific sacred objects to have such a potent effect upon the individual believer. And once again it seems particularly interesting that the emotions of intensity of faith involved would seem not to be a direct and integral part of the phenotype and genotype of *H. sapiens* at the time of the out-of-Africa dispersals—or at any rate we have no evidence for them at so early a date.

11.4. Conclusion

Such powerful passions and beliefs as those involved in the recognition of high value and the veneration of the sacred must presumably have secure neurological foundations. But I have sought to show that these are nonetheless emergent properties, developing in human societies over the past 10 000 years or so, in many cases from the time of the sedentary revolution. Since the human genome has been established for at least the past 60 000 years, these features cannot be regarded as a direct and immediate consequence of the aspects of the genome which emerged during the speciation phase. Special mechanisms must therefore have come into play. Their potential must be inherent in the genome, as it has been for at least 60 000 years. But the material and social contexts of human societies, first effective around the time of the sedentary revolution, made possible their emergence and expression.

The mechanism, as suggested earlier, can only lie in the learning capacities of each child. For each child, coming to participate in the phylogenetic acquisition of culture, as the trajectory of cultural development unfolds, can only do so through the personal (ontogenetic) acquisition of skills and experience. This he or she may accomplish through the development of new neuronal networks in early childhood (Changeux 1985). But although these must be situated within the brains of individuals, the social, interpersonal relationships involved also imply different kinds of engagement with the material world. It is there that we must situate the development of mind, in the sense indicated above, rather than simply that of the 'brain'. The development of these significant factors governing behaviour must have a basis in the neuroscience of the brain.

References

Barrowclough, D. A. & Malone, C. (eds) 2007 *Cult in context, reconsidering ritual in archaeology*. Oxford, UK: Oxbow Books.

Boyer, P. 1994 *The naturalness of religious ideas: a cognitive theory of religion*. Berkeley, CA: University of California Press.

Changeux, J. P. 1985 *Neuronal man, the biology of mind*. New York, NY: Oxford University Press.

Clark, G. 1986 *Symbols of excellence, precious materials as expressions of status*. Cambridge, UK: Cambridge University Press.

Clark, A. 1997 *Being there: putting brain, body and world together again*. Cambridge, MA: MIT Press.

Donald, M. 1991 *Origins of the modern mind: three stages in the evolution of culture and cognition*. Cambridge, MA: Harvard University Press.

Foley, R. A. & Lahr, M. M. 2003 On stony ground: lithic technology, human evolution and the emergence of culture. *Evol. Anthropol.* **12**, 109–122. (doi:10.1002/evan.10108)

Forster, P. 2004 Ice ages and the mitochondrial DNA chronology of human dispersals: a review. *Phil. Trans. R. Soc.* **B 359**, 255–264. (doi:10.1098/rstb.2003.1394)

Gamble, C. 2007 *Origins and revolutions, human identity in earliest prehistory*. Cambridge, UK: Cambridge University Press.

Henshilwood, C. S. & Marean, C. W. 2003 The origin of modern human behaviour—critique of the models and their test implications. *Curr. Anthropol.* **44**, 627–651. (doi:10.1086/377665)

Henshilwood, C. S., d'Errico, F., Vanhaeren, M., Van Niekerk, K. & Jacobs, Z. 2004 Middle Stone Age shell beads from South Africa. *Science* **304**, 404. (doi:10.1126/science.1095905)

Insoll, T. 2004 *Archaeology, ritual, religion*. London, UK: Routledge.

Kyriakidis, E. 2006 *Ritual in the Bronze Age Aegean: the Minoan peak sanctuaries*. London, UK: Duckworth.

Malafouris, L. 2004 The cognitive basis of material engagement: where brain, body and culture conflate. In *Rethinking materiality: the engagement of mind with the material world* (eds E. DeMarrais, C. Gosden & C. Renfrew), pp. 53–62. Cambridge, UK: McDonald Institute.

McBrearty, S. & Brooks, A. S. 2000 The revolution that wasn't: a new interpretation of the origins of modern human behaviour. *J. Hum. Evol.* **39**, 453–563. (doi:10.1006/jhev.2000.0435)

Mellars, P. M. 1991 Cognitive changes and the emergence of modern humans in Europe. *Camb. Archaeol. J.* **1**, 63–76.

Mellars, P. 2006a Why did modern human populations disperse from Africa *ca.* 60,00 years ago? A new model. *Proc. Natl Acad. Sci. USA* **103**, 9381–9386. (doi:10.1073/pnas.0510792103)

Mellars, P. 2006b Going east: new genetic and archaeological perspectives on the modern human colonization of Eurasia. *Science* **313**, 796–800. (doi:10.1126/science.1128402)

Mellars, P. & Stringer, C. (eds) 1989 *The human revolution, behavioural and biological perspectives on the origins of modern humans*. Edinburgh, UK: Edinburgh University Press.

Mellars, P., Boyle, K., Bar-Yosef, O. & Stringer, C. (eds) 2007 *Rethinking the human revolution*. London, UK: McDonald Institute.

Mithen, S. 1996 *The prehistory of the mind*. London, UK: Thames & Hudson.

Mithen, S. 1998 The supernatural beings of prehistory and the external storage of religious ideas. In *Cognition and material culture: the archaeology of symbolic storage* (eds C. Renfrew & C. Scarre), pp. 97–106. Cambridge, UK: McDonald Institute.

Renfrew, C. 1982 *Towards an archaeology of mind (inaugural lecture)*. Cambridge, UK: Cambridge University Press.

Renfrew, C. 1985 Towards a framework for the archaeology of cult practice. In *The archaeology of cult: the sanctuary at Phylakopi* (ed. C. Renfrew), pp. 11–26. London, UK: British School at Athens.

Renfrew, C. 1986 Varna and the emergence of wealth in prehistoric Europe. In *The social life of things* (ed. A. Appadurai),pp. 141–146. Cambridge, UK: Cambridge University Press.

Renfrew, C. 1994 The archaeology of religion. In *The ancient mind* (eds C. Renfrew & E. Zubrow), pp. 47–54. Cambridge, UK: Cambridge University Press.

Renfrew, C. 1996 The sapient behaviour paradox: how to test for potential? In *Modelling the early human mind* (eds P. Mellars & K. Gibson), pp. 11–15. Cambridge, UK: McDonald Institute.

Renfrew, C. 2001 Symbol before concept: material engagement and the early development of society. In *Archaeological theory today* (ed. I. Hodder), pp. 122–140. Cambridge, UK: Polity Press.

Renfrew, C. 2003 *Figuring it out*. London, UK: Thames & Hudson.

Renfrew, C. 2004 Towards a theory of material engagement. In *Rethinking materiality: the engagement of mind with the material world* (eds E. DeMarrais, C. Gosden & C. Renfrew), pp. 23–32. Cambridge, UK: McDonald Institute.

Renfrew, C. 2006 Becoming human: the archaeological challenge. *Proc. Br. Acad.* **139**, 217–238.

Renfrew, C. 2007a *Prehistory, the making of the human mind*. London, UK: Weidenfeld & Nicolson.

Renfrew, C. 2007b The archaeology of ritual, cult and of religion. In *The archaeology of ritual* (ed. E. Kyriakidis), pp. 101–122. Los Angeles, CA: Cotsen Institute, University of California.

Renfrew, C. & Zubrow, E. (eds) 1994 *The ancient mind*. Cambridge, UK: Cambridge University Press.

Scarre, C. (ed.) 2005 *The human past*. London, UK: Thames & Hudson.

Searle, J. 1995 *The construction of social reality*. Harmondsworth, UK: Penguin Press.

Shennan, S. 2002 *Genes, memes and human history*. London, UK: Thames & Hudson.

Vanhaeren, M., d'Errico, F., Stringer, C., James, S. L., Todd, J. A. & Mienis, H. K. 2006 Middle Paleolithic shell beads in Israel and Algeria. *Science* **312**, 1785–1788. (doi:10.1126/science. 1128139)

White, L. A. 1949 *The science of culture: a study of man and civilization*. New York, NY: Grove.

Wilson, P. 1988 *The domestication of the human species*. New Haven, CT: Yale University Press.

12

Things to think with: words and objects as material symbols

Andreas Roepstorff

This paper integrates archaeology, anthropology and functional brain imaging in an examination of the cognition of words and objects. Based on a review of recent brain imaging experiments, it is argued that in cognition and action, material symbols may be the link between internal representations and objects and words in the world. This principle is applied to the sapient paradox, the slow development of material innovation at the advent of the anatomically modern human. This translates the paradox into a long-term build-up of extended and distributed cognition supported by development in the complexity of material symbols.

Keywords: archaeology; symbols; extended mind; anthropology; brain imaging; meaning

12.1. Introduction

The intersection between archaeology and neuroscience examined in this special issue presents a somewhat personal challenge. Trained mainly in social anthropology, I am affiliated with an institute that also includes three departments of archaeology, and it is here I find some of my closest collaborators. I spend much of my research time in an interdisciplinary brain imaging unit, where we place most of our discussions, experiments and analyses in a neurocognitive framework. This publication therefore presents me with an opportunity to reflect on the different styles of thinking (Fleck 1979; Hacking 1992; Crombie 1994; Roepstorff 2001) inherent in those disciplines and in the social anthropology I feel most at home in. I shall argue, in parallel with many other contributors to this special issue, that some version of an 'extended mind' hypothesis is a good candidate for a conceptual meeting point between the disciplines of archaeology, neuroscience and anthropology. However, crucial to this is a notion of 'symbols'—or more generally 'signs' to those semiotically inclined. For some, notion of signs or symbols appear to be central in linking up the work that objects do with the type of processes that goes on in brains.

This will set the scene for explorations

 (i) of some brain imaging studies of how symbols work in brains,
 (ii) of a particular study, conducted in our group, of what happens when objects become signs of 'something', and
 (iii) of Colin Renfrew's *sapient paradox*.

12.2. Neuroscience and archaeology: An anthropological perspective

It has been forcefully argued by Chris Gosden that archaeologists generally show a preoccupation with 'things', in all their specific materiality. To outsiders, this fascination with
the particularities of objects, their style, manufacture, use, history, migration, etc. may, at
times, appear almost idiosyncratic. However, it rests on a fundamental insight, namely
that the apparent thingness of things, the fact that they appear just to be there as given in
some way, is an end product of a long chain of transformations, which changes the material into concrete objects. The underlying argument appears to be that mapping this chain
of transformation in all its cumbersome details is key to understanding the type of society in which the object was produced, and—at least since the turn towards a cognitive
archaeology (Renfrew & Zubrow 1994)—also the mindset of the people who made it.
There is in this insistence on the importance of things a very important lesson to be
learned for the rest of the humanities and social sciences: things are not only representatives of some broad understanding of 'material culture' which again is part of a larger
notion of 'culture'. Rather, objects in themselves do work in very particular ways. They
are not only additions to the social or emergent properties of the social, but they are
indeed the very stuff from which human society is built. In archaeology, this understanding parallels and indeed pre-dates the recent discovery of the importance of things in
versions of social theory such as actor-network theory (Latour 1996, 2005) and postmod-
ern ethnography (Henare et al. 2006). This very brief and cursory analysis of the thought
style of archaeology just says that if anything, archaeology is about things.

But what about neuroscience, then? It is almost trivial to say that neuroscientists have a
certain preoccupation with brains in all their complexities. Whether it is through the study
of anatomical structure, haemodynamic couplings between blood flow, metabolism and
activity, patterns in neuronal firing or release of transmitter substances into tiny clefts and
crevices, the 'brain', both as a concrete entity and as a metaphysical framing, forms the
reference point for neuroscience. This latent brain-centrism has obvious consequences the
moment tools from neuroscience are used to address issues that used to be almost exclusively in the domain of psychology, economics, philosophy and other disciplines of the
social sciences and humanities. What the new neurosciences, i.e. social (Cacioppo 2002),
cognitive (Gazzaniga 2000), affective (Panksepp 1998), etc., bring to the fields of intellectual discourse is to relate these processes, the social, the cognitive, the affective, etc., to
the brain. This is a laudable, promising and highly interesting approach. However, there
is an accompanying risk that, partly lured by the style of argumentation and reasoning,
the phenomena studied may become trapped in the brain. It is as if 'brains' do all the
work, and the person, the surroundings, the others, the experience, mind, etc. are at best
scaffoldings for the workings of the brain. And this is, of course, a very different story.

If archaeology is preoccupied with things, and neuroscience with brains, what, then, is
anthropology preoccupied with, what can it bring to an interdisciplinary smorgasbord?
Arguably, one of the most important developments in anthropological theory in the last
decades has been the reflexive turn, first, perhaps, brought out in the seminal realization
that the prime activity of anthropologists is to write (Clifford & Marcus 1986; see also
Sangren 2007). One reading of this development is that a prime concern of anthropologists is anthropology. The slightly more friendly version is a preoccupation with how
stories and facts come about and an attempt at using one's own trajectory and tradition

as an exemplary case for understanding this. This can be seen in the recent drive towards ethnographies and anthropologies of knowledge (Agrawal 1995; Roepstorff 2001; Barth 2002). Obviously, this paper is written very much within such a perspective, although implications of the inherent social reflexivity for what brains do are hardly touched upon here (see Petersen *et al.* in press). However, for the present discussion, two other things stand out as a prime concern for anthropologists: symbols (Turner 1967) and exchange (Mauss 1954). The notion that the social is inherently about reciprocity and exchange and that 'the cultural', a loaded term these days, involves particular ways of establishing symbols and significations appears to be something that most anthropologists would agree on, in spite of any other theoretical disagreement they may have.

12.3. The challenge

This very cursory description of the three perspectives on 'the human' leaves us with an epistemological question and a very concrete challenge. First, the question: should one treat the different approaches as inherently arbitrary and conventional, and hence able to be replaced with other styles of thinking, or is there something in the topic studied that appears to afford a particular style of thinking? To cut a long story short, I will argue for a realist position: there is something at stake in each perspective. The challenge, then, becomes to relate and superimpose the preoccupations of the archaeologist, the anthropologist and the neuroscientist into one framework, which is if not entirely coherent then at least productive. This would, very concretely, translate into something like: say something sensible about how things in the outer world come to do something to brains by way of symbols and 'exchange'. A critical issue here is how to mediate between inside and outside, between things in a pure form, and 'mind' as it emerges out of and constrains processes in the brain. This story, if we take the symbolic notion seriously, becomes a story not only of physical objects and physical neurons, but also about other thing-like entities, about words, symbols, meanings and those chains of transformations they undergo.

There are multiple strains of thinking that explore such models. Today, they are usually found in and around the hypotheses of distributed cognition (Hutchins 1995) and extended mind (Clark & Chalmers 1998). But it is worth noting that there is a very long and twisted story of such theorizing, which involves important foci outside of the Anglo-American world, e.g. in post-revolutionary Russia (Voloshinov 1986; Vygotsky 1986) and structuralist Paris (Lévi-Strauss 1988). I will in this paper only examine a version of this, found in a recent paper by Andy Clark on 'Material symbols' (Clark 2006*b*). It almost seems to fit hand-in-glove the type of framework I called for above, as it attempts to link processes in the mind, and I think ultimately in the brain, with the environment through material symbols, which at the same time are very concrete and tangible.

12.4. Material symbols

Clark (2006*a*) develops his idea of material symbols through an examination of language. He has previously argued that language is the ultimate artefact (Clark 1997), like other objects it is part of an extended and augmented repertoire for cognition and action. In his recent work, he does not discuss exhaustively other forms of material symbols such as images, representations and things in general, but there is little in the analysis to suggest that words are unique in this respect. Rather, they appear as a special case of a much more general understanding of how the material also becomes symbolic. Let us see what is at stake in his own words:

> The idea on offer, then, is that the symbolic environment (very broadly construed) can sometimes impact thought and learning *not* by some process of full-translation, in which the meanings of symbolic objects are exhaustively translated into an inner code, a mentalese, or even a Churchland-style neuralese, but by something closer to coordination. On the coordination model, the symbolic environment impacts thought by activating such other resources (the usual suspects [e.g. attention, memory AR]) *and* by using either the objects themselves (or inner image-like internal representations of the objects) as additional fulcrums of attention, memory and control. In the maximum strength version, these symbolic objects quite literally appear as elements in representationally hybrid thoughts.
>
> (Clark 2006*b*, p. 300)

This 'hybrid' model of language caches in on a *complementary* action of 'actual material symbols (and image like encodings of such symbols) and more biologically basic models of internal representation' (op. cit. 304). In other words, people do not think in a generalized, abstract internal language of representation, instead they think through concrete things, with words being a special case. The strength of this approach, Clark argues (Clark 2006*b*), is that it concurs several possibilities on cognition.

(i) Otherwise inaccessible contents can be learnt and grasped by agents skilled in the use of perceptually simple tokens that reify complex ideas.
(ii) The presence of material symbols (or images thereof) can productively alter the fulcrums of attention, perception and action.
(iii) Material symbols (or their shallow imagistic encodings) can coordinate the fulcrums of attention, perception a nd action.

This leads Clark to conclude that 'minds like ours are indeed transformed by the web of material symbols and epistemic artefacts' (op. cit.).

12.5. The functional neuroimaging of symbols

Andy Clark's notion of material symbols appears to sketch a model where the beloved things of the archaeologist through symbolic processes, which the anthropologist cherishes, may impact on the mind by creating coordinated reverberations in the neuronal networks of the neuroscientist. This may appear to deliver the kind of framework asked for. But how does it hold up against empirical evidence? There is surprisingly little work done in brain imaging on the cognitive effects of symbols and objects *per se*, but a number of studies, particularly of language, throw some light on how words, as a particular class of symbols, work on the brain.

12.6. Words and sentences in the brain

Inspired by lesion findings, a long range of studies have examined whether different forms of words carry different localizations in the brain. Starting out from highly imprecise categories, these studies have become increasingly sophisticated, and there is now strong converging evidence that the semantics of particular a word category is accompanied by a particular neuronal signature, such that words, depending on their meaning, tie in with brain regions that are not dedicated to language. In recent experiments, it has, for example, been demonstrated that colour words and form words activate specific, relevant networks (Pulvermuller & Hauk 2006) while action verbs related to different body parts (e.g. lick, kick, pick) appear to be able to link in with the neuronal representation of these body parts (Pulvermuller 2005).

The story becomes more complicated once words are embedded in sentences rather than when presented as free-standing units. The problem is that the meaning of any particular word is highly confined and constrained by the context of the other words (Gennari et al. 2007).

A recent highly elegant experiment took the elements of narratives and presented them as either isolated words, single sentences or small narratives. They could demonstrate that as words became embedded in an increasingly complex context, there was a recruitment of an increasingly extended network of brain regions. For single words, this included Wernicke's area (a classic low-level 'language area'), sentences further evoked Broca's area in the inferior frontal gyrus (another classic language area), while narratives also evoked the medial prefrontal cortex and the temporoparietal cortex, areas not typically associated with linguistic processing (Xu et al. 2005). We have shown (Wallentin et al. 2005a) that motion verbs increase activity in typical 'motion' areas of the brain (in the left posterior middle temporal cortex), even in sentences with static semantics (e.g. 'the road goes into the forest') when compared with sentences with static verbs (e.g. 'the road is in the forest'). In other sentences with motion verbs, changing the target of the sentence from concrete (e.g. 'the man goes into the house') to abstract (e.g. 'the man goes into politics') radically shifts the contrastive brain activation from a typical bilateral posterior temporoparietal 'spatial navigation' pattern to a typical 'language-like' left-lateralized inferior-frontal pattern (Wallentin et al. 2005b).

All these experiments suggest, not surprisingly, that the specific activity evoked by words is strongly constrained by the context they occur in, and that the overall neuronal resonance created by words interacts with non-linguistic brain areas involved in representing processes that the words represent. This hypothesis is supported by a set of experiments where we studied the difference between accessing a scenario that had been presented visually and linguistically. Depending on the type of information accessed, there were consistent overlaps in the activity of relevant regions, such as precuneus and hippocampus, irrespective of whether the stimuli had been presented as visual displays or as sentences describing the scenario (Wallentin et al. 2006, 2007). How do these findings play themselves out against the material symbol hypothesis outlined above? There appears to be some evidence that once a set of words, as a special case of symbols, is perceived and understood, it comes to stand for that which it represents. That is, it may activate, draw on, coordinate and resonate with, depending on the choice of metaphors, brain areas associated with that which the symbol stands for. This is apparently a circular argument but in the process it ties the fluffy symbolic in with the material, in the sense that once words are understood by a person, they become material instantiations in some form in the brain of that person. It is not because words inherently code for what they stand for—Ferdinand Saussure got rid of that idea long ago when he pronounced the arbitrariness of the signifier in relation to the signified (Saussure *et al.* 1931). Instead, a word through prior use in context becomes material in linking up between the present and the past, as exemplified in what it previously has stood for. This is the famous Saussurean conventions, and it may activate the reverberations that surround the word to use a Bakhtinian/Voloshinovian term (Voloshinov 1986; Wallentin *et al.* 2007), the coordination of memory and attention, to use Clark's phrase, or perhaps resonance in a neuronal network.

12.7. Symbols allow for anticipation and condensation

However, the sceptical reader may argue, this may work well for words but how does it translate into other forms of symbols? Very little is known about that, it has hardly been on the cognitive neuroscience agenda. However, a recent EEG experiment may be interpreted along those lines. Widmann and colleagues in Helsinki examined what would happen when the convention for a symbolic representation was broken. They exposed subjects to two different pitches, a high pitch and a low pitch. Immediately prior to each sound, a bar on a screen would indicate which sound to expect, a low bar suggested a low pitch while a high bar suggested a high pitch.

Every now and then, there would be a mismatch between the symbol and the subsequent sound. An analysis of these deviants, which broke with the anticipation established by the prior symbolic representation, demonstrated that 100 ms after the sound that had been misrepresented, a particular neuronal signature, arguably arising from the primary auditory cortex, had already been generated. To quote the authors: 'These results suggest that the auditory system can establish a representation of an expected stimulus on the basis of visual symbolic information' (Widmann *et al.* 2004). The experiment is a nice example of cross-modal interaction, of how a stimulus in one sensory domain may set up an expectation in another sensory domain. Increasingly, symbols have become useful structures in neuronal network models, also within modalities. A recent paper (Konig & Kruger 2006) argues that symbols, understood as 'condensed and discrete semantic representatives for certain pieces of knowledge....on which operations can be performed and which correspond to relevant functional relations in this framework', may emerge in neuronal networks. Konig & Kruger claim that these 'up-stream' entities represent condensed pieces of knowledge that are no longer analogue. Instead, they function as arguments in a framework of transformations that realize predictions (p. 325). Applied to Widmann *et al.*'s experiment, these symbols appear, then, to be able to resonate across specific sensory modalities.

This suggests that something which has the properties of symbols clearly exist as material entities in world space, e.g. in the form of words and images. According to Konig & Kruger, it may also emerge as material entities in brain space, defined as complexes of condensed knowledge and predictions that allow for anticipation across brain regions. But it does not tell us much about how the particular materiality of concrete things can come to do any kind of brain work.

12.8. Puzzling objects

One of our postgraduates recently set out to examine how object configurations could be imbued with meaning (Tylén *et al.* 2007). With a background in cognitive semiotics, Kristian Tylén was very interested in how well-known objects in unusual configurations can almost call out for an interpretation. To investigate the brain activations associated with this, he constructed a set of test images of everyday objects, which he presented to volunteers in a passive viewing task in an fMRI scanner. In half of the images, the configurations of the objects were highly unusual, such as a hand axe inserted into a printer or a gold fish swimming in a blender. The other pictures showed similar objects in 'ordinary' situations. Subsequently, subjects' experiences were probed in a post-scan interview to rate whether they thought that a particular constellation had been set up with a communicative purpose. These subjective data were then used for a *post hoc* analysis of the imaging data (Jack & Roepstorff 2002).

Based on our hypothesis, apparently confirmed by the post-scan interviews, we had expected to find activation to the intentional configurations in the now semi-classical 'theory-of-mind' areas in the medial prefrontal cortex (Amodio & Frith 2006) when people read a communicative intent in the image. However, even when applying very liberal statistical thresholds, this particular region was completely empty. Instead, striking bilateral activities were found in the ventral stream of the visual system and in the pars triangularis of the inferior frontal gyrus, a part of Broca's area. The latter region is particularly interesting because it has been implicated in language production, comprehension and retrieval.

To our knowledge, this is the first study of how passive viewing of material objects, given a proper contrastive context, comes to tap into what has traditionally been considered classical language areas. What is at stake here is, perhaps, another instance of material symbolism. It can be phrased as puzzling superimpositions of well-known objects, but equally it is a production of new meanings, new coordinations in brains, new reverberations in networks, based on the very material symbolicity of the particular objects established by prior use, conventions and expectations. It offers a thinking through things, not because the objects have to be translated into a new mentalese language, but because the clash between the objects, which appear as material symbols both in world space and in brain space, calls out for new configurations. Whereas the previous studies showed how words, in brain space, can come to act as that which they represent, this study suggests that objects, given the right configurations, can come to look almost like words.

Thereby, to paraphrase Clark, the presence of material symbols (or images thereof) productively plays with the fulcrums of attention, perception and action through an interplay with more biologically basic models of internal representation. It is highly tempting to do the neurophrenological trick, and place the productive play in the bilateral pars triangularis activation, and the internal representations somewhere along the ventral stream of object processing.

12.9. Thinking with words and objects

Based on an analysis of recent brain imaging experiments, framed within Clark's notion of material symbols, I have attempted to show how the material world, including words, objects and representations, may come to a productive interplay with previous experiences, as they are represented as particular configurations in brains: resonances; coordinations; or whatever else we should call them. It appears to allow for 'the world' to be a major driving force in providing objects that are at the same time material and symbolic, just as the representations in the brain are. I have elsewhere argued that it may be through such high-level resonances, tongue-in-cheek called top-top interactions (Roepstorff & Frith 2004), that human communication can occur (Roepstorff 2004). Translated into the framework developed here, this implies that words and other material symbols in the world may in the brain function as symbols in Konig & Kruger's sense, as condensations in frameworks of predictions and past experiences (see also Jordan 2008). This does not entail a translation into a generalized, abstract new mentalese, rather it may be the symbols themselves, which are material both 'on the outside' and 'on the inside', although not in the same material, that do the work, usually in a shared social world of experiential condensations already established around particular symbols. Such analysis has long been laid out for old-style symbols of classical anthropological analysis that were mainly characterized by their immaterial meaning (Turner 1967). However, what Clark's perspective seems to offer is, on the one hand, an anchoring in material, in world and in brains, and, on the other hand, a set of mechanisms that may apply both to objects and words, and to other forms of representations. It is still a somewhat open idea and to advance it further will require investigations and conceptual developments of material symbols, in the form they take both in brains and in the world.

Clark and other distributed cognition researchers seem to suggest that structures in the environment are crucial for allowing cognition, action and other processes that are traditionally conceived of as mental. They may be so by providing elements for scaffolding, both externally and internally. Renfrew (1996) has cogently coined *the sapient paradox* to describe the apparently puzzling finding that in the first 60 000 years from the putative emergence of anatomically modern humans, approximately 100 000 years ago, nothing much happened when seen through the archaeological record of material findings. However, if cognition and other mental processes do not occur in brains in isolation but are embedded in material and social relations and objects, it may take a lot of bootstrapping—at the same time mental and the material (Johannsen forthcoming; Read 2008)—to create the possibilities for that unprecedented process of innovation, which began approximately 10 000–15 000 years ago (op. cit.). If one accepts the idea of the 'anatomical modern human', Renfrew's sapient paradox can hence be translated into a statement that 'anatomy' does not do it alone. Instead, constructions and exchanges of both words and objects—material symbols in other words—may have been absolutely crucial in setting up an environment within which innovation and development could take place. Understanding such interactions appears to require sensitivity to the materiality of objects and to the processes of symbolicity and exchange, and it may indicate a field where archaeology and anthropology can provide highly pertinent contributions to contemporary discussions in cognitive research and neuroscience.

Comments from the editors and from two anonymous reviewers greatly improved this paper, their inputs are much appreciated! A.R. was supported in this research by grants from the National Danish Research Foundation and the Danish Research Council for Communication and Culture.

References

Agrawal, A. 1995 Dismantling the divide between indigenous and scientific knowledge. *Dev. Change* **26**, 413–439.

Amodio, D. M. & Frith, C. D. 2006 Meeting of minds: the medial frontal cortex and social cognition. *Nat. Rev. Neurosci.* **7**, 268–277. (doi:10.1038/nrn1884)

Barth, F. 2002 An anthropology of knowledge. *Curr. Anthropol.* **43**, 1–18. (doi:10.1086/324131)

Cacioppo, J. T. 2002 *Foundations in social neuroscience. Social neuroscience series*. Cambridge, MA: MIT Press.

Clark, A. 1997 *Being there: putting brain, body and world together again*. Cambridge, MA: MIT Press.

Clark, A. 2006*a* Language, embodiment and the cognitive niche. *Trends Cogn. Sci.* **10**, 370–374. (doi:10.1016/j.tics.2006.06.012)

Clark, A. 2006*b* Material symbols. *Philos. Psychol.* **19**, 291–307. (doi:10.1080/0951508060 0689872)

Clark, A. & Chalmers, D. J. 1998 The extended mind. *Analysis* **58**, 10–23. (doi:10.1111/1467-8284.00096)

Clifford, J. & Marcus, G. E. (eds) 1986 *Writing culture*. Berkeley, CA: University of California Press.

Crombie, A. C. 1994 *Styles of scientific thinking in the European tradition: the history of argument and explanation especially in the mathematical and biomedical sciences and arts*. London, UK: Duckworth.

Fleck, L. 1979 *Genesis and development of a scientific fact*. Chicago, IL: Chicago University Press.

Gazzaniga, M. S. 2000 *The new cognitive neurosciences*. Cambridge, MA: MIT Press.

Gennari, S. P., MacDonald, M. C., Postle, B. R. & Seidenberg, M. S. 2007 Context-dependent interpretation of words: evidence for interactive neural processes. *Neuroimage* **35**, 1278–1286. (doi:10.1016/j.neuroimage.2007.01.015)

Hacking, I. 1992 'Style' for historians and philosophers. *Stud. Hist. Philos. Sci.* **23**, 1–20. (doi:10.1016/0039-3681(92)90024-Z)

Henare, A. J. M., Holbraad, M. & Wastell, S. 2006 *Thinking through things: theorising artefacts in ethnographic perspective*. Abingdon, UK: Milton Park; New York, NY: Routledge.

Hutchins, E. 1995 *Cognition in the wild*. Cambridge, MA: MIT Press.

Jack, A. I. & Roepstorff, A. 2002 Introspection and cognitive brain mapping: from stimulus-response to script-report. *Trends Cogn. Sci.* **6**, 333–339. (doi:10.1016/S1364-6613(02)01941-1)

Johannsen, N. N. Forthcoming. Technology and conceptualization: cognition on the shoulders of history. In *The cognitive life of things: recasting the boundaries of the mind* (eds L. Malafouris & C. Renfrew). Cambridge, UK: McDonald Institute for Archaeological Research.

Jordan, J. S. 2008 Wild agency: nested intentionalities in cognitive neuroscience and archaeology. *Phil. Trans. R. Soc. B* **363**, 1981–1991. (doi:10.1098/rstb.2008.0009)

Konig, P. & Kruger, N. 2006 Symbols as self-emergent entities in an optimization process of feature extraction and predictions. *Biol. Cybern.* **94**, 325–334. (doi:10.1007/s00422-006-0050-3)

Latour, B. 1996 On interobjectivity. *Mind Cult. Act.* **3**, 228–245. (doi: 10.1207/s15327884mca0304_2)

Latour, B. 2005 *Reassembling the social: an introduction to actor-network-theory*. Oxford, UK; New York, NY: Oxford University Press.

Lévi-Strauss, C. 1988 *The jealous potter*. Chicago, IL: University of Chicago Press.

Mauss, M. 1954 *The gift; forms and functions of exchange in archaic societies*. Glencoe, IL: Free Press.

Panksepp, J. 1998 *Affective neuroscience: the foundations of human and animal emotions*. New York, NY: Oxford University Press.

Petersen, M. B., Roepstorff, A. & Serritzlew, S. In press. Social capital in the Brain. In *Handbook of research on social capital* (eds G. Tinggaard & G. Svendsen). Cheltenham, UK: Edward Elgar Publishing.

Pulvermuller, F. 2005 Brain mechanisms linking language and action. *Nat. Rev. Neurosci.* **6**, 576–582. (doi:10.1038/nrn1706)

Pulvermuller, F. & Hauk, O. 2006 Category-specific conceptual processing of color and form in left fronto-temporal cortex. *Cereb. Cortex* **16**, 1193–1201. (doi:10.1093/cercor/bhj060)

Read, D. 2008 Biology is only part of the story.... *Phil. Trans. R. Soc. B* **363**, 1959–1968. (doi:10.1098/rstb.2008.0002)

Renfrew, C. 1996 The sapient behaviour paradox: how to test for potential? In *Modelling the early human mind* (eds P. Mellars & K. Gibson), pp. 11–15. Cambridge, UK: McDonald Institute.

Renfrew, C. & Zubrow, E. B. W. 1994 *The ancientmind: elements of cognitive archaeology. New directions in archaeology.* Cambridge, UK; New York, NY: Cambridge University Press.

Roepstorff, A. 2001 Facts, styles and traditions. Studies in the ethnography of knowledge. PhD dissertation, Department of Social Anthropology, Aarhus University.

Roepstorff, A. 2004 Cellular neurosemiotics: outline of an interpretive framework. In *Studien zur Theorie der Biologie*, vol. 6 (ed. J. Schult) Biosemiotik—Praktische Anwendung und Konsequenzen für die Einzeldisziplinen, pp. 133–154. Berlin, Germany: Verlag fur Wissenschaft und Bildung.

Roepstorff, A. & Frith, C. D. 2004 What's at the top in the top-down control of action? Script-sharing and 'top-top' control of action in cognitive experiments. *Psychol. Res.* **68**, 189–198. (doi:10.1007/s00426-003-0155-4)

Sangren, P. S. 2007 Anthropology of anthropology? Further reflections on reflexivity. *Anthropol. Today* **23**, 13–16. (doi:10.1111/j.1467-8322.2007.00523.x)

Saussure, F. de., Bally, C., Sechehaye, C. A. & Riedlinger, A. 1931 *Cours de linguistique generale.* Paris, France: Payot.

Turner, V. W. 1967 *The forest of symbols; aspects of Ndembu ritual.* Ithaca, NY: Cornell University Press.

Tylén, K., Wallentin, M. & Roepstorff, A. 2007 *From object to symbol: everyday objects used for communicational means elicit activity in brain areas associated with verbal language.* Poster presented at the conference Language in Cognition, Cognition in Language, University of Aarhus, Oct. 13, 2007.

Voloshinov, V. N. 1986 *Marxism and the philosophy of language.* Cambridge, MA: Harvard University Press.

Vygotsky, L. S. 1986 *Thought and language.* Cambridge, MA: MIT Press.

Wallentin, M., Lund, T. E., Ostergaard, S., Ostergaard, L. & Roepstorff, A. 2005a Motion verb sentences activate left posterior middle temporal cortex despite static context. *Neuroreport* **16**, 649–652. (doi:10.1097/00001756-20050 4250-00027)

Wallentin, M., Østergaard, S., Lund, T. E., Østergaard, L. & Roepstorff, A. 2005b Concrete spatial language: see what I mean? *Brain Lang.* **92**, 221–233. (doi:10.1016/j.bandl.2004.06.106)

Wallentin, M., Roepstorff, A., Glover, R. & Burgess, N. 2006 Parallel memory systems for talking about location and age in precuneus, caudate and Broca's region. *Neuroimage* **32**, 1850–1864. (doi:10.1016/j.neuroimage.2006.05.002)

Wallentin, M., Weed, E., Ostergaard, L., Mouridsen, K. & Roepstorff, A. 2007 Accessing the mental space-spatial working memory processes for language and vision overlap in precuneus. *Hum. Brain Mapp.* (Epub ahead of print.)

Widmann, A., Kujala, T., Tervaniemi, M., Kujala, A. & Schroger, E. 2004 From symbols to sounds: visual symbolic information activates sound representations. *Psychophysiology* **41**, 709–715. (doi:10.1111/j.1469-8986.2004.00208.x)

Xu, J., Kemeny, S., Park, G., Frattali, C. & Braun, A. 2005 Language in context: emergent features of word, sentence, and narrative comprehension. *Neuroimage* **25**, 1002–1015. (doi:10.1016/j.neuroimage.2004.12.013)

13

Why religion is nothing special but is central

Maurice Bloch

It is proposed that explaining religion in evolutionary terms is a misleading enterprise because religion is an indissoluble part of a unique aspect of human social organization. Theoretical and empirical research should focus on what differentiates human sociality from that of other primates, i.e. the fact that members of society often act towards each other in terms of essentialized roles and groups. These have a phenomenological existence that is not based on everyday empirical monitoring but on imagined statuses and communities, such as clans or nations. The neurological basis for this type of social, which includes religion, will therefore depend on the development of imagination. It is suggested that such a development of imagination occurred at about the time of the Upper Palaeolithic 'revolution'.

Keywords: religion; sociality; imagination; evolution

13.1. Introduction

This paper reconsiders how we should approach the study of the evolution of religion. The discussion leads me, however, to a more general consideration of the way social cognition has been approached in recent literature. This reconsideration bears in mind the kind of problems that Colin Renfrew has called the 'sapient paradox'. The paper proposes a cognitively and neurologically more probable scenario for the development of religion than certain recent theories that are questioned by the problems he highlights.

The problems I am referring to are particularly thrown into focus by a series of theories that originate in Sperber's suggestion that religious-like beliefs are to be accounted for by a subtle mix of intuitive human capacities based on evolved neurological modules, and certain, very limited, representations that, because they go against the core knowledge that the modules suggest, are therefore 'counter-intuitive' and 'intriguing' (Sperber 1985). The motivation for these theories is to seek an answer to a question. How could a sensible animal like modern *Homo sapiens*, equipped by natural selection with efficient core knowledge (or modular predispositions), i.e. knowledge well suited for dealing with the world as it is, hold such ridiculous ideas as: there are ghosts that go through walls; there exist omniscients; and there are deceased people active after death? The authors who hold such a theory of religion give the following answers to this question. First, our core knowledge ensures that, however bizarre such ideas might seem at first, when they are more closely examined, they, in fact, turn out to be mainly disappointingly intuitive. Second, even though beliefs in supernatural things nevertheless do involve a *few* counter-intuitive aspects, if only by definition, these are possible owing to accidental misapplications of core knowledge to domains for which it is not designed. These limited misapplications are, however, so alluring that they make these minimally counter-intuitive beliefs spread like wildfire. They thus become key elements in religions (e.g. Boyer 1994, 2001; Pyysiainen 2001).

The problems with these theories that I shall discuss here do not necessarily imply outright rejection. They are what might be called 'upstream' objections since they occur even before we consider the main proposals. The first objection echoes a similar one long ago made by Durkheim, but it has been reformulated more recently by Barrett (2004) when he points out that it is odd to account for such a central phenomenon in the history of mankind as religion in terms of minor cognitive malfunctions. My second objection is that those who propose such theories forget the fact that anthropologists have, after countless fruitless attempts, found it impossible to usefully and convincingly cross-culturally isolate or define a distinct phenomenon that can analytically be labelled 'religion'.[1] The third problem with such theories is that they explain religion as a product of core knowledge or modular capacities, such as naive physics, number, naive biology and naive psychology, all of which, with the possible exception of the last, we share with all our anthropoid relatives. Such a proposal is therefore unconvincing simply because no other animal than humans manifests any behaviour that is remotely like what is usually called religion. This lack also seems to be the case for all hominids or hominims, apart from post-Upper Palaeolithic modern Sapiens. In other words, the explanations that I am challenging account for a highly specific and general characteristic of modern Humans, what they call religion, by general factors that have existed for millions of years before the Upper Palaeolithic revolution when the phenomenon first manifested itself.

The alternative story I propose here avoids these problems. It argues that religious-like phenomena in general are an inseparable part of a key adaptation unique to modern humans. This is the capacity to imagine other worlds, an adaptation that I shall argue is the very foundation of the sociality of modern human society. This neurological adaptation occurred most probably fully developed only around the time of the Upper Palaeolithic revolution.

13.2. The transactional and the transcendental

For heuristic reasons, a consideration of chimpanzee society can serve as a starting point. I turn towards our nearest surviving relatives in order to stress, as is so often the case in the evolutionary literature, a major difference between them and us. Of course, we cannot assume that contemporary chimpanzee social organization is necessarily like that of early *Sapiens*. There is no way to know; especially since the social organizations of the two extant species of chimpanzees are radically different though both are equally closely, or equally remotely, related to us. In this case, it is not the similarity but the difference that is revealing and this difference provides us with something like a thought experiment that enables us to reflect on certain characteristics of human society.

Chimpanzees do not have anything which remotely resembles the many and varied phenomena that have been labelled religion in anthropology. Indeed, this was probably also true of early Sapiens. But, more importantly, there is also something else that chimpanzees, and probably early Sapiens, do not have. This is social roles or social groups, understood in one particular sense of the word social.

Of course, chimpanzee social organization is highly complex. For example, the dominant animal is not necessarily the biggest or the one who can hit the hardest. Dominance seems to be achieved as much by machiavellian politicking as it is by biting. Also, chimpanzees do create long-lasting coalitions, often of females, and these may well dominate the social organization of the group (De Waal 2000). Such roles and groupings are of a type that I call here the *transactional* social. This is because such roles and groups are the product of a process of continual manipulation, assertions and defeats. This type of social is also found in modern humans.

However, what chimps do not have is the kind of phenomenon that used to be referred to as 'social structure' in the heyday of British social anthropology (Radcliffe-Brown 1952). This I shall label here as the *transcendental* social. The transcendental social consists of essentialized roles and groups.

Essentialized roles exist separately from the individual who holds them. Rights and duties apply to the role and not to the individual. Thus, a person who is a professor should act 'as a professor' irrespective of the kind of person he/she is at any particular stage in the transactional social game. Similarly, in central Madagascar, as a younger brother, I should walk behind my older brother; as a woman, I should not raise my voice in a mixed gathering. All this applies, however powerful I have actually become, even if my prestige is greater than that of my older brother or of a man.

Essentialized groups exist in the sense that a descent group or a nation exists. These groups have phenomenal existence not because the members of the descent group or the nation are doing certain kinds of thing together at particular moments, or because they have been together doing certain kind of things at particular moments in the sufficiently recent past so that it is reasonable to assume that they retain the capacity to behave now in similar ways. One can be a member of an essentialized transcendental group, or a nation, even though one never comes in contact with the other members of the descent group or the nation. One can accept that others are members of such groups irrespective of the kind of relationship one has had with them or that one can suppose one is likely to have with them. Such groups are, to use Benedict Anderson's phrase, 'imagined communities' (Andersen 1983).

As noted above, in stressing the system of essentialized roles and groups, I am emphasizing what British social anthropologists, such as Radcliffe-Brown, were referring to when they spoke of social structure. However, my position is theoretically very different from theirs. For them, the human social was equated with the network of such roles and groups. For me, these phenomena are only a *part* of the social: they are the transcendental social.

The transcendental social is not all there is to human sociality. There is plenty of transactional social in human sociality that occurs side by side or in combination with the transcendental social. The transactional social exists irrespective of the role-like essentialized statuses and the essentialized groups of the transcendental social, though it may use the existence of the transcendental social as one of the many counters used in the transactional game. Human sociality is thus, as Durkheim stressed, double. It has its transactional elements *and* transcendental element. Chimpanzee sociality, by contrast, is single because the transcendental social does not exist among the chimpanzees.

The double character of the human social can be illustrated by the example of a Malagasy village elder I have known for a long time. By now, he is old, physically weak and a little bit senile. He has difficulty in recognizing people. He spends most of his days in a foetal position wrapped up in a blanket. Yet he is treated with continual deference, consideration, respect and even fear. Whenever there is a ritual to be performed, he has to be put in charge so that he can bless the participants. When he is treated with great respect he is being behaved to, and he accordingly behaves towards others as a transcendental elder. This does not mean, however, that he is not also within the transactional social system. While as a transcendental elder he is little different to what he was when he was in his prime several years ago, as a transactional player he has lost out completely in the machiavellian game of influence, and nobody takes much note of him anymore or of his opinions since in the continual power play of daily life he has become insignificant.

This kind of duality is impossible in chimpanzee society. There, once you are weak or have lost out in the continual wheeling and dealings of power, you lose previous status. In an instant, a dominant animal is replaced in his role (De Waal 2000). A chimpanzee's rank depends entirely on what those it interacts with believe it can do next. Chimpanzees do pay respect to each other in all sorts of ways... for instance, bowing to a dominant animal, but once this animal has lost out in the power game, this behaviour stops instantly. A social position in chimpanzee society never *transcends* the predictable achievements of the individual. This absence of transcendental roles is where the fundamental difference between chimpanzee and human sociability lies. The Malagasy in the village where this elder lives bow to him just as much now that he is weak as they ever did, even though he has become obviously without transactional influence. It is important to remember, however, that the respect shown to him does not mean that he is an elder all the time. The people, who interact with him, and probably himself, represent him in two ways. These two ways are not experienced as contradictory, but they are clearly distinguished and made visible by the behaviour of all concerned. Everybody knows that he is a weak old man whose hands shake and whose memory is going, and people sometimes behave towards him in terms of that representation, even with occasional cruelty. They also behave towards him in terms of the respect as described above. Thus, he belongs to two networks and, although the two are different, the transcendental network is taken into account in the transactional network while the transactional network affects the transcendental network only indirectly; for example, when another person is ultimately able to replace an elder in his transcendental role through revolutionary manipulation (for example in a traditional African society, convincing people that he is a witch; Middelton 1960).

In order to fully understand the role of an elder such as the one I have in mind, it is essential also to remember that, as a transcendental being, he is part of something that appears as a system, even though this systematicity may be something of an illusion. The transcendental elder implies the existence of transcendental juniors, of transcendental affines, transcendental grandchildren, etc. The transcendental network involves gender roles, thereby creating transcendental women and men. It is a system of interrelated roles and it is this complexity of interrelations at the transcendental level that most critically distinguishes the human social from the sociality of other species.

This transcendental network also includes what the structural functionalists called 'corporate groups', but which I have referred to above as essentialized groups. These are transcendental groups. By this, I mean that, for example, members of a clan are dual. At the transactional level, they differ from each other just as much or as little as they do from people of the next clan. But, in the transcendental social mode, all members of such a group are identical as transcendental members. They are, as is often said, 'one body'. As one body, they differ absolutely, and all in the same way, from those others in the other clan. The transcendental character of such groups is made all the more evident when we realize that the composition of such groups, whether they are clans or nations, may equally include the living and the dead. Thus, when in the transcendental one-body mode, members can make such bizarre statements as 'We came to this country two hundred years ago'. The transcendental can thus negate the empirically based transactional in which people do not live for 200 years. Thus, the transactional social can as much ignore the present physical state of an elder as it can ignore death and individuality. The transcendental network can with no problem include the dead, ancestors and gods as well as living role holders and members of essentialized groups. Ancestors and gods are compatible with living elders or members of nations because all are equally mysterious invisible, in other words transcendental.

13.3. The transcendental social and religion

This social indissoluble unity between the living and the dead and between what is often called the 'religious' and the 'social' has never been better explained than in a famous article by Igor Kopytoff 'Ancestors as elders in Africa' (Kopytoff 1971). Although the article is phrased as a criticism of earlier work by Fortes, it actually follows the latter author closely. Kopytoff points out how in many African languages the same word is used for living elders and for dead ancestors whom, it has often been said in the literature, Africans 'worship'. This is because in a sense, in the transcendental sense, they are the same kind of beings. Kopytoff stresses how both ancestors and elders have much the same powers of blessing and cursing. This leads him to assert that to talk of 'ancestor worship', and thereby to suggest something analogous to an Abrahamic notion of a distinction between material and spiritual beings, is an ethnocentric representation that imposes *our* categorical opposition between the natural and the supernatural, or between the 'real' and the religious, onto people for whom the contrast does not exist.

I accept much of Kopytoff's and Fortes' argument and want to expand it. What matters here is that if they are right, there is no reason why we cannot reverse his argument, something that Kopytoff himself suggests. If dead ancestors in an 'ancestor-worshipping society' are the same ontological phenomena as elders, then elders have the same ontological status as ancestors. If there is a type of phenomenon that merits the appellation ancestor worship, which suggests the kind of things that have often been called religion, then there is also elder worship or elder religion. And since elders are part of a system, there is in the traditional sense, junior religion, descent group religion, man religion, woman religion, etc.

Although to talk in this way may be fun, we have to use our words with the meanings that they have historically acquired. So it might be better to rephrase the point and say that what has been referred to above as the transcendental social and phenomena that we have ethnocentrically called religion are part and parcel of a single unity. This implies that the English word religion, inevitably carrying with it the history of Christianity, is misleading for understanding such phenomena as ancestor worship since, in such cases, there is not the same boundary between the 'supernatural' and the 'natural' as that perceived to occur in societies caught in the history of the Abrahamic religions. The boundary exists also in these cases, however, and it occurs between one type of social (the transcendental social including the phenomena that have been called religion) and the transactional social. This boundary is clear in the kind of society I am referring to and explains the two different ways of acting towards the Malagasy elder noted above.

The inseparability of the transcendental social and the religious is not only manifested in cases of so-called ancestor worship. Hinduism is a phenomenon that is often assumed to be comparable with the Abrahamic religions, but such an equation is misleading for the same reasons as apply to the African examples discussed previously. For example, Fuller begins his study of popular Hinduism by pointing out that a wife should, and indeed does, at some moments, treat her husband in the same way as she treats the gods. The same gestures and bodily positions are used in both cases in performing *puja* and the husband can thus be said to be a 'god' to his wife in the Hindu sense of god. The point is that here also the transcendental social husband and wife role is part of one single over-arching transcendental hierarchical social system that includes the gods (Fuller 1992).

The societies I have discussed above clearly present a challenge for the kind of theories referred to at the beginning of this article, i.e. the theories advocated by, among others, Boyer. This is because they explain a phenomenon that can only be distinguished from a greater whole: the transcendental social, by using a contrast between the religious and the secular that is borrowed from a relatively modern system of representations that simply does not apply in their cases. Consequently, I shall argue that it is the greater whole in its totality, i.e. the transcendental, that needs to be explained. However, such a redefinition of the project presents an obvious difficulty. If Boyer is wrong to take a specific type of society, those with religion, to represent the human condition in general, is it not equally wrong to take specific other societies, those discussed in this paper so far, as representing human nature?

13.4. Historical excursions

In what follows I argue that this is not so because societies with religion are the subsequent product of an inessential and superficial modification of the societies discussed above. A full demonstration of this point would require much more space than is available in this short paper. What follows is therefore nothing more than a tentative sketch of what such a proposal would look like. So, in order to explain how a certain state of affairs occurred for some, and only some, human groups, I move to a historical argument to argue that it is in certain specific historical circumstances (admittedly of great importance for the majority of mankind though not for all) that the kind of phenomena we call religious take on a separate appearance that seems to distinguish it from the more inclusive transcendental social.

The creation of an apparently separate religion is closely tied to the history of the state. It has long been noted that in early states such as Mesopotamia, Egypt, China, the early Andean states and many other places that the religious and the 'political' were insepara-ble. Frankfort long ago argued that in ancient Egypt, pharaoh was a visible god interact-ing on a compatible footing with the invisible gods. The organization of the state was part of the divine order (Frankfort 1948). The ancient Egyptian kingdom was part of an explicit cosmic ordering of space and time. The recurrence of the flooding of the Nile was represented as the consequence of the repetitive cyclic action of the gods, including the pharaoh. The world was centred on the capital with distant uncivilized, barely human, peripheral peoples far from its centre. Egypt was, to borrow the Chinese phrase, the empire of the centre. All this is the familiar attribute of what has been called divine king-ship, whether it is that of the Swazi, Indic states or the Mesopotamian city-states.

The transcendental representation of such states was not all there was to political organization. There were also other available transactional representations of the state, pharaoh, time and space. In much the same way as the Malagasy elder is dual, it was also possible to see the pharaoh in more straightforward terms, and that was in spite of the prodigious efforts that were made to transform him through his palace and his tomb into an empirical manifestation of his transcendental side.

The transcendental construction of such states is also accompanied by another corollary process. The development of the Merina state in Madagascar in the eighteenth and nineteenth century shows how the *construction* of the symbolic state is accompanied by a partial *destruction* and *reformulation* of the symbolism of the subjects. Thus, certain key attributes of elders/ancestors were forcibly transferred from local descent groups to the king and his palace (Bloch 1986). Interestingly, a similar process involving the diminution of the transcendental social of subjects for the benefit and construction of the royal transcendental has been examined for early Egypt by Wengrow (2006).

Thus, the royal centralized transcendental construction depends on the partial destruction or at least transformation of the symbolical system of subjects. In Madagascar, the focus of the symbolism of the subjects migrated, thanks to violent encouragement, from the house to the tomb, as the palace became the symbolical *house* of the kingdom with the ruler as its central 'post' (in Malagasy, *Andry* the root of the word for ruler *Andriana*: lord; Bloch 1995). Similarly, and in more detail, I described how the descent group ritual of circumcision subsequently became orchestrated by the state and how certain aspects were taken away from the elders to become constitutive elements of grand-state occasions. The descent groups *lost* key elements to the representative of the state and were punished if they attempted to perform the full ritual independently (Bloch 1986).

Since in such systems the transcendental social and the religious are identical, it is not just the religious that is being reorganized in a centralized state and sucked up to a point into a centralized, organized, organic-seeming system, it is the whole transcendental social. The creation of this transcendental holistic image of the complete kingdom, including gods and men, thus requires the creation of the incompleteness and disorganization of the subjects' transcendental social, which can only be made complete in the kingdom.

After such a process a change that is different to the symbolic centralization of the state happens. States are unstable and political systems continually collapse. That causes a new problem. When the royal state collapses at the hand of its enemies, the subjects find themselves bereft because the construction of the state had previously made them transcendentally incomplete and the state, after its collapse, is not there anymore to complete them.

The same Malagasy example can again illustrate this point. The growth of the Merina kingdom in the nineteenth century had led to the circumcision ritual being partly taken out of the transcendental construction of descent groups and being placed in the realm of the symbolical construction of the kingdom. However, in 1868, when the Merina kingdom became disorganized, in part owing to the influence of Christianity, the ruler failed to perform the royal circumcision ritual. At that point, a popular movement arose which sought to *force* him to perform it.

Why did the subjects feel bereft by the royal non-performance when originally the ritual had been their privilege? Why should they seek the state that in many ways exploited them? Because, given the previous process, when the state collapsed, they were left with nothing but their incomplete transcendental social and, for reasons that I cannot explain, it seems as if the deprivation process is irreversible. Thus, when the state, having confiscated a large part of the

transcendental social so as to create its own ordered pseudo totality of cosmic order, then collapsed, a totalizing transcendental representation without its political foundation remained,
floating in mid air, so to speak. This begins to look like what we call religion. For example, the
collapse of the political base of the transcendental social may lead to the occurrence of these
ritual, sacred, pseudo-royal systems of Africa that so fascinated Frazer, where as Evans-
Pritchard said, the king 'reigns but does not rule' (Evans-Pritchard 1948). It is what leads to
shadow 'states' that only exist in mystical form as spirits that possess mediums. Examples of
these are found among the Shona or in western Madagascar where they were caused, Feeley-
Harnik argues, by the collapse of the political as a consequence of colonial rule (Feeley-
Harnik 1991). This is also what explains the bizarre institutions of contemporary European
monarchies. These post-state states are 'religions', i.e. phenomena apparently distinct from the
rest of the transcendental social.

The Abrahamic religions offer another example of the process. The historian of
Judaism and of early Christianity, J. Z. Smith, argues that Jewish monotheism must be
understood as the product of a longing for the unified, centralized, holistic transcendental Mesopotamian city-states with Ziggurats at their centre. These were a kind of state
that the Jews, as minor peripherals to that system, hardly ever managed to achieve for
themselves, or, when they did, did so on a tiny fragile scale. Early Judaism is therefore also
a transcendental incomplete residue: religion. This residue was modelled on the
Mesopotamian prototype with, at its centre, the Ziggurat in a purely religious form,
i.e. the temple in Jerusalem (Smith 1982).

With this sort of situation, we therefore get religions that are only apparently separate
from the transcendental social state, but this separation is always uncomfortable and
unfinished and it leads to the kind of flirting processes between state and religion that has
characterized history in much of the Abrahamic world. At least in Europe and those
great sways of Asia and Africa that are still under the ghostly spell of ancient Mesopotamia
and Egypt this flirting takes various forms. One form of the process involves new states
taking on, ready made, one of these politically detached religions issued from clearly
different political entities. Rome was an example of the process. Imperial Rome became one
of these centralized systems where political conquest led to the creation of a transcendental
social representation of the state through making incomplete the transcendental social of
subjects. Yet the transcendental construction never worked very well and when Rome got
into even more trouble than usual, the system broke down. This led to the adoption of
foreign and abandoned centre religions, therefore, 'hungry' for the recovery of their lost
politico/transcendental social element, e.g. Judaism, other eastern religions and ultimately,
one of the many forms of Christianity. Rome was therefore taking on the religious side of
a centralized system from a collapsed tiny city-state as a late attempt at reorganization of
a unified transcendental (Beard *et al.* 1998).

The process repeated itself. When, in the seventh century, the Franks began to develop
centralized entities in western Europe, they picked up Christianity and, so to speak, 'put
it on' with modifications to make it fit. One of the most spectacular moments was when
Charlemagne in 800 invented a ritual that made him the Holy Roman Emperor with bits
borrowed from the old testament, from Frankish rituals and of course, above all, from
Roman rituals (Nelson 1987).

The other form of the relation between religion and the state, made necessary by their
previous separation as a result of the collapse of a centralized unit, is for the religious bit
to try to grow back its lost political undercarriage. Again and again, the popes tried.

The Ayatollah Khomeini was more successful. Most of the movements that have been called millenarians try this sort of thing. Mormon history furnishes a particularly interesting example. Joseph Smith started the Mormon religion in the eastern USA for people who were heirs to a Christian religion that at many removes was heir to a long history of trouble between the religious-like pretensions of the state and the state-like pretensions of religion. However, the Mormons were in a place where the state was weak and, unusually, where the totalizing cosmological pretensions of post-state religion were strikingly incoherent, largely because they were meant to apply to a country not included in the cosmology of the Bible. So the Mormons put that to right by finding a Gospel that did mention the New World and its inhabitants and, in their creative enthusiasm, began to rebuild the political part of the destroyed transcendental entity. Not surprisingly, this annoyed the other state in Washington and they had to try to build it up in the desert, which, amazingly, they just about succeeded in doing. At the centre of this renewed unitary entity, where the transcendental social and religious were again to be an inseparable totality as in ancient Egypt or Mesopotamia, they built their temple: a temple that looks strikingly like a Ziggurat.

13.5. Conclusion

The point of these historical excursions is to suggest that the separation of religion from the transcendental social in general is, even in the places where it appears at first to exist, superficial and transient. In any case, this superficial phenomenon has occurred in human history only relatively recently.

It is this transcendental social in its totality that should be our focus. It is what distinguishes the human social from that of other closely related animals, such as chimpanzees. It is a unique characteristic and an essential part of human sociality, which, as often suggested, is *the* fundamental difference between humans and other anthropoids. An explanation of its occurrence cannot thus be in terms of a minor evolutionary adaptation, or misadaptation, as is suggested by Boyer-type theories.

Such a conclusion is negative, but it is possible to propose a more positive and fruitful one.

What the transcendental social requires is the ability to live very largely in imagination. We often act towards elders, kings, mothers, etc., not in terms of how they appear to the senses at any particular moment but as if they were something else: essential transcendental beings. Once we realize this omnipresence of the imaginary in the everyday, nothing special is left to explain concerning religion. What needs to be explained is the much more general question, how it is that we can act so much of the time towards visible people in terms of their invisible halo. The tool for this fundamental operation is the capacity for imagination. It is while searching for neurological evidence for the development of this capacity and of its social implications that we, in passing, will account for religious-like phenomena. Trying to understand how imagination can account for the transcendental social, and incidentally religion, is a quite different enterprise to accounting for the religious for itself in terms of modules, or core knowledge, which, in any case, we share with other primates. Unlike this, imagination does seem to distinguish us from chimpanzees and perhaps also distinguishes post-Upper Palaeolithic humans from their forebears.

A number of recent writers have suggested something along the same lines. In a book by Paul Harris about imagination, the author shows how the ability to engage spontaneously in pretend play begins very young and develops in a multitude of ways such as creating 'imaginary friends' and other forms of explicit make believe. Such imagination practice seems essential for normal human development. Nothing like that occurs in other species. Clearly, this capacity is necessary for engaging in the transcendental social as defined above, inevitably including the religious like. The selective advantage this form of sociality procures explains its evolutionary potential. It is central to human life. Harris suggests this centrality in an adventurous introduction when he notes that the first evidence for such a capacity is the cave paintings of Europe dating back to *ca* 40 000 years ago (Harris 2000). He might have gone a bit further back to what has been called the Upper Palaeolithic revolution, one feature of which was the first suggestion of transcendental roles found in grand burial.

Again, in a parallel argument, also taking empirical data on ontological development as its starting point, Hannes Rakoczy connects the imagination and the transcendental social even more explicitly (Rakoczy 2007). In that work, and that of his co-workers, this is referred to as 'status functions' but it is as yet little developed. However, the argument is strikingly similar to that proposed above and totally congruent. It does not however, like Harris, touch on the topic of religion, but according to my argument, this is inevitably subsumed under this type of discussion of the social.

To explain religion is therefore a fundamentally misguided enterprise. It is rather like trying to explain the function of headlights while ignoring what motorcars are like and for. What needs to be explained is the nature of human sociability, and then religion simply appears as an aspect of this that cannot stand alone. Unfortunately, the recent general discussion on social cognition does not succeed in doing the job that is needed to understand the transcendental social either. This is because, for the most part, it has considered the human social as an elaboration and an expansion of the type of social found in other animals, especially other primates (Dunbar 2004). This is useful but it obscures a fundamental *difference* between humans and others. Such an approach only pays attention to the transactional, or the 'Machiavellian' social, since that is what is shared by, for example, baboons and humans. It ignores the uniquely human transcendental social that represents a qualitative difference with other non-human socialities. What is essential to understand is the evolution of this specificity. Concentrating on that equally unique human capacity, imagination seems the most fruitful approach in that enterprise and, in passing, we will also account for religion since it is nothing special.

Endnote

1   Boyer insists that he is not talking about religion in the usual sense, but he does not define what he is talking about and he has no problem in entitling his books: *The naturalness of religious ideas: a cognitive theory of religion* and *Religion explained*.

References

Andersen, B. 1983 *Imagined communities: reflections on the origin and the spread of nationalism.* London, UK: Verso.
Barrett, J. 2004 *Why would anyone believe in god?* Walnut Creek, CA: Alta Mira Press.

Beard, M., North, J. & Price, J. 1998 *Religions of Rome*, vol. 2. Cambridge, UK: Cambridge University Press.

Bloch, M. 1986 *From blessing to violence: history and ideology in the circumcision ritual of the Merina of Madagascar*. Cambridge, UK: Cambridge University Press.

Bloch, M. 1995 The symbolism of tombs and houses in Austronesian societies with reference to two Malagasy cases. *Austronesian Studies* **August 1995**, 1–26. (Taipei.)

Boyer, P. 1994 *The naturalness of religious ideas: a cognitive theory of religion*. Berkeley, CA: University of California Press.

Boyer, P. 2001 *Religion explained: the evolutionary origins of religious thought*. New York, NY: Basic Books.

De Waal, F. 2000 *Chimpanzee politics: power and sex among apes*. Baltimore, MD: Johns Hopkins University Press.

Dunbar, R. 2004 *The human story*. London, UK: Faber and Faber.

Evans-Pritchard, E. E. 1948 *The divne kingship of the Shilluk of the Nilotic Sudan*. Cambridge, UK: Cambridge University Press.

Feeley-Harnik, G. 1991 *The green estate: restoring independence in Madagascar*. Washington, DC: Smithsonian Institution Press.

Fuller, C. 1992 *The camphor flame: popular Hinduism and society in India*. Princeton, NJ: Princeton University Press.

Frankfort, H. 1948 *Kingship and the gods*. Chicago, IL: Chicago University Press.

Harris, P. 2000 *The work of the imagination: understanding children's world*. Oxford, UK: Blackwell.

Kopytoff, I. 1971 Ancestors as elders. *Africa* **41**, 129–142.

Middelton, J. 1960 *Lugbara religion*. London, UK: Oxford University Press.

Nelson, J. 1987 The Lord's anointed or the people's choice: Carolingian royal rituals. In *Rituals of royalty* (eds D. Cannadine & S. Price), pp. 137–180. Cambridge, UK: Cambridge University Press.

Pyysiainen, I. 2001 *How religion works*. Leiden, The Netherlands: Brill.

Radcliffe-Brown, A. R. 1952 *Structure and function in primitive society*. London, UK: Cohen and West.

Rakoczy, H. 2007 Play, games and the development of collective intentionality. In *Conventionality in cognitive development: how children acquire representations in language thought and action* (eds C. Kalish & M. Sabbagh), pp. 53–67. New directions in child and adolescent development, no. 115. San Francisco: Jossey-Bass.

Smith, J. Z. 1982 *Imagining religion: from Babylon to Jonestown*. Chicago, IL: University of Chicago Press.

Sperber, D. 1985 Anthropology and psychology: towards an epidemiology of representations. *Man* (*N.S.*) **20**, 73–89.

Wengrow, D. 2006 *The archaeology of early Egypt. Social transformations in north-east Africa, 10,000–2,650 BC*. Cambridge, UK: Cambridge University Press.

Index